Some Wild Visions

Recent titles in
RELIGION IN AMERICA SERIES
Harry S. Stout, General Editor

Some Wild Visions

*Autobiographies by Female Itinerant Evangelists
in Nineteenth-Century America*

ELIZABETH ELKIN GRAMMER

OXFORD
UNIVERSITY PRESS
2003

OXFORD

UNIVERSITY PRESS

Oxford   New York

Auckland   Bangkok   Buenos Aires   Cape Town   Chennai
Dar es Salaam   Delhi   Hong Kong   Istanbul   Karachi   Kolkata
Kuala Lumpur   Madrid   Melbourne   Mexico City   Mumbai   Nairobi
São Paolo   Shanghai   Taipei   Tokyo   Toronto

Copyright © 2003 by Elizabeth Elkin Grammer

Published by Oxford University Press, Inc.
198 Madison Avenue, New York, New York 10016

www.oup.com

Oxford is a registered trademark of Oxford University Press

Quotations from *Strangers and Pilgrims: Female Preaching in America, 1740–1845*,
by Catherine Brekus, are used by permission of the University of North Carolina Press.
An earlier version of chapter 4 appeared in the *Arizona Quarterly* 55.1;
it is reprinted here by permission of the Regents of the University of Arizona.

Library of Congress Cataloging-in-Publication Data
Grammer, Elizabeth Elkin, 1963–
Some wild visions : autobiographies by female itinerant evangelists in 19th-century
America / Elizabeth Elkin Grammer.
p. cm.—(Religion in America series)
Includes bibliographical references and index.
ISBN 0-19-513961-5
1. Women evangelists—United States—Biography—History and criticism.
2. Autobiography—Women authors.   3. Women evangelists—United States—History—
19th century.   4. Autobiography—Religious aspects—Christianity—History—19th century
I. Title.   II. Religion in America series (Oxford University Press)
BV3780 .G73   2002
277.3'081'0922—dc21   2002022038
[B]

1   3   5   7   9   8   6   4   2

Printed in the United States of America
on acid-free paper

for John Miller Grammer
and for our children
Zoita Elizabeth, Jessica Grace, and John Elkin

The grace of our Lord was poured out on me abundantly.
−1 Timothy 1:14

and in loving memory of my grandmother,
Jessie Louise Guthrie Rich

Acknowledgments

Each of the itinerant preachers whose autobiographies I examine in this book considered herself a pen in God's hands. I wasn't called to be such a pen, but I was lucky enough, in the years in which this book has taken shape, to have found myself and my manuscript in the *hands* of many people who have greatly enriched the pages that follow. Now I wish to give them thanks.

Without the love and support of my parents, this book would not have been possible. They fostered my love of reading from an early age and sacrificed much to send me to three remarkable schools where that love blossomed into my life's work. I know this book has been long in the making; I hope they will find it worth the wait.

Nor would it have been possible without the seven evangelists who graciously shared their *Lives* with the world. They have shown me, as they must have shown their nineteenth-century audiences, what a life of faith, wild visions, and itinerancy looked like; their lives as preachers and autobiographers have taken me places—intellectually and spiritually—that I never expected to go.

I would like to thank Sue Armentrout and Andrew Moser, at the University of the South, for their help in securing interlibrary loans over the last several years, saving me from extensive travels to libraries elsewhere. Tammy Scissom and the Print Services office at the university served me well all these years when my computer skills proved inadequate. I also received kindly assistance from the staff at the Bridwell Library of the Perkins School of Theology at Southern Methodist University, the Bentley Historical Library at the University of Michigan, and the American Antiquarian Society.

Dean Tom Kazee offered me a grant to cover child care expenses so I could spend some quiet hours in my office revising the book. The career women in this study, many of whom were also mothers, were rarely as fortunate in securing money, sitters, and time as I have been. I have been blessed by a host of women who have nurtured my children while I wrote this book. To the instructors at the Sewanee Children's Center and the University Day Care Center, and to Ellie Bostwick, Martha Lynn Coon, Rhonda Mims, Jeannie Williams, and Elizabeth Young, I offer here a heartfelt thank-you. I owe a special debt of gratitude to Elisha Hodge for her disciplined and loving care of my children over the last four years, and to Dessie Taylor for coming into our lives when we needed just the sort of wisdom, care, and friendship she gives so generously.

Randy Nelson and Max Polley, of Davidson College, deserve thanks for initiating the scholarly journey that culminated in this book. Along with many other professors there, they taught me well, challenged me always, and encouraged me to pursue graduate work. But their classes left me feeling torn between the disciplines of English and religion; I went through college never really knowing how to choose between the two. In graduate school, when I discovered autobiographical theory and the autobiographies of nineteenth-century itinerant women, I discovered I didn't have to.

Debbie McDowell, an extraordinarily inspiring teacher and critic, helped direct the dissertation that would become *Some Wild Visions*. It was she who introduced me to the autobiographies of Jarena Lee, Zilpha Elaw, and Julia Foote and thus set the book in motion; later she read the dissertation with a remarkable eye for that "busy intersection" of race, class, and gender. My greatest debt to her over the last decade, however, is for advice she gave me long ago: to begin a book, she reassured me, you need only questions, not answers. That liberating idea made all the difference.

The late David Levin generously offered to read these pages even after it appeared that I was not going to begin writing them before his retirement. He was, as so many of his former students in American literature have remarked, an "exemplary elder." I wish to express my gratitude for his close readings of earlier versions of these chapters; for his reserves of patience when I had difficulty putting a pen in my hand; for sending chapter 1 back to me (despite its many and glaring errors) with a note that read, "This is an excellent beginning. . . . I'm delighted"; for giving me, in his teaching and scholarship, a formidable model by which to judge my own; and for his many kindnesses in the decade in which I was lucky enough to count him as my mentor and friend. He is sorely missed.

Catherine Brekus and Nancy Hardesty read these pages with just the sort of eyes scholars dream of when they send their work out in search of an audience. Their responses were thoughtful, kind, and instructive. I wish to thank them especially for their challenge to consider these women's lives—and particularly their expressions of faith—on their own terms, as well as on mine and those of the academy. Cindy Aron, John Ernest, Susan Fraiman, and Alan Howard read and commented on the manuscript years ago. More recently, Virginia Craighill, Sarah Bell Earley, and Woody Register took *Some Wild Visions* into their wise hands. At a time when I wavered between certainty that the book was finished and certainty that it would never be, I so appreciated their encouragement, as well as their invaluable suggestions for fine-tuning my argument and the language with which I made it. As I struggled to complete this book with a kind of "feverish restlessness"—in the words of Zilpha Elaw—Cynthia Read and Theo Calderara, at Oxford University Press, were just the sort of editors I needed most: helpful when I called on them and patient when I did not. And it was a special pleasure to encounter, at Oxford University Press, my college classmate Christi B. Stanforth, whose title, "production editor," scarcely hints at the range of tasks she undertook to bring my manuscript to production.

So many people contributed to *Some Wild Visions* primarily by contributing to—and vastly improving—my state of mind as I wrote it. For their friendship, good cooking, and enlivening conversions, I thank Danny Anderson, Manette Ansay, Ann Arnold,

Henry Arnold, Julie Berebitsky, Virginia Craighill, Sarah Bell Earley, Tony Earley, Mary Grey Moses, Elizabeth Outka, Cheri Peters, Jim Peters, Barbara Prunty, Wyatt Prunty, Woody Register, Kelly Sundberg Seaman, Jake Smith, and, most especially, Julia Burnett Walker. I can never aptly convey my gratitude to Tom McDonald, Susan Ruby, Doru Deaconu, and all the folks at Small World Ministries for helping my husband and me answer the only *call* I believe I have ever received and forever changing our hearts and minds in the process. Your missionary work among the children of God is an example for, and a blessing to, us all.

When I began writing this book in 1993, I had no children; I wrote and revised it believing that these women must have longed to leave home and children and domestic chores for adventuresome public lives as preachers of the gospel. I assumed that their domestic lives were unsatisfying and that they must have desperately wanted a life—like my own—outside the home. I concluded, too facilely perhaps, that these women would do anything, even lie, to get one too. I knew the history of women who fought in the nineteenth and twentieth centuries for the right to leave their homes and difficult domestic work to engage in just the sort of stimulating life in public space I so easily occupied as a result. It goes without saying that I champion that right and continue the fight by studying here the books of women who struggled to live and write the unorthodox life. But I have come to believe that my situation in 1993 and my scholarly interest in feminist theories and histories—which long have led us to believe that a God-centered life cannot be a woman-centered one—somewhat distorted my initial readings of these women's autobiographies.

It is now the year 2002, and as I complete this book, I have three small children at home and some of the same attendant domestic duties and worries—though none of the severe financial hardships and class struggle—that must have plagued Zilpha Elaw, Laura Haviland, Jarena Lee, Lydia Sexton, and Amanda Berry Smith. I know now better than ever that a woman's work is *never* done. And yet were I called, as were the women in this study, to forsake it all, I do not believe I could. Since their arrival, Zoë, Jessie, and John have forced me to read these religious narratives with an eye peeled not only to the drudgery and boredom of a domesticity that is still often unrewarded and unacknowledged in our culture but also to the very real pleasures of a full house. When these women wrote about the "cross" they carried as they left their homes and families so that they could convert and care for the larger household of God, they were employing a useful cultural and literary strategy. But motherhood has led me to see that these women were describing, with this metaphor, a very real burden as well. My children have taught me much about the enormous depth of a faith to which these spiritual autobiographers attest, a faith that enabled them to take seriously Jesus' warning that "he that loveth son or daughter more than me is not worthy of me" and then to embrace what must have been a grueling, sometimes lonely—even when exhilarating—existence apart from loved ones at home. For these lessons, for enriching this book, and forever enriching my life, I thank my children.

I have spent the last year wondering how to thank my husband, John, for his help with this project. It seems hardly possible that the book would have been completed if not for his intellectual rigor, endless store of patience, quiet humor, and tenderness as I wrote and revised these pages. His engagement with and curiosity about my project surely equaled that with which he approached his own. I thank him for his willingness to sacrifice his own work, his leisure time, even his sleep, to help me begin to articulate the unusual and intriguing *Lives* that came into our own lives just weeks after we said "I do." He has graced these pages as he has graced my life—with honor, patience, and love.

With much pride and thanksgiving, then, I dedicate this book to my family. Never in my wildest visions did I see before me a household so gloriously full and fulfilling.

Contents

Some Wild Visions

Introduction

Stirring and Strange

Autobiographies of Nineteenth-Century Female Itinerant Preachers

> Say, *female stranger*, who art thou?
> That thus, art wandering through our land.
> Thy youth, thy sex, thy modest brow;
> Thy lonely state, may all demand.
> Why is it, thou has left thy home,
> With strangers only to sojourn?
> No friend attending,—but alone,
> Thou wing'st thy way, both night and morn?
> Has some wild vision, struck thy brain;
> To wander forth, from door to door?
> Whilst friends, afar, in grief remain,
> By restless, wayward fancy, bore?
>
> Poem by Judge —— to Miss M——,
> and afterward presented to Nancy Towle

Nobody has been able to learn for sure who "Miss M——" was, or how exactly she inspired Judge ——'s foray into verse.[1] But the judge was right later to give the poem to Nancy Towle, one of the seven American women whose evangelical careers and spiritual autobiographies I analyze in the present study. It describes Towle's life rather well, and very much in the terms Towle herself chose when she came to write her autobiography: she, like the others, led just the lonely, wandering, visionary existence described in the poem. But it probably describes even better the puzzlement that women like Towle provoked in those they met. Of the poem's seven sentences, five—including the last—are questions. None of them is answered; the identity and motives of the "female stranger" named in the first line are, at the end, as mysterious as at the beginning. Towle's decision to include the poem in her autobiography might be taken as her promise to answer the questions it raises: Who am I? What have been my motives? What "wild vision" has impelled me into the lonely, footloose, and unconventional life of a female itinerant minister?

An Age of Awakenings

The answer Towle and her sister itinerants insist upon is that God called them, often against their wills, often by way of wild visions, to leave their homes, their husbands, their families and friends, to wander the earth preaching the gospel. Another answer might be that evangelical religion "awakened" these and other nineteenth-century American women to the possibility of moving beyond the household and domestic service. The spiritual experiences of Towle and all the autobiographers under study here—Jarena Lee, Zilpha Elaw, Julia Foote, Lydia Sexton, Laura Haviland, and Amanda Smith—awakened them to the "healing balm" of salvation and then to the "cross" of being public, itinerant evangelists in a patriarchal culture that called them, in very different accents—because of race, class, and historical moment—toward private, domestic existence (Haviland 20). When Kate Chopin in 1899 suggestively entitled her one novel *The Awakening*, she called attention, if only ironically, to a phase of American history during which many women were converted, by the power of the Holy Spirit as they believed, to lives well outside the confines of patriarchal and domestic order.

The nineteenth century has been described by Perry Miller and countless others as the age of evangelical religion and its agent, revivalism. Though recent historians of American religion warn us that "there was no monolithic 'evangelicalism' in nineteenth-century America, and fault lines divided Protestants by region and class," it was nonetheless the "dominant expression" of Protestantism, and among the "most powerful social and religious movements" in the century (Brekus 16; Sweet, "Nineteenth" 875).[2] Evangelicalism and revivalism might have been, in the words of Miller, "the defining factor" of nineteenth-century American life: "We can hardly understand Emerson, Thoreau, Whitman, Melville, unless we comprehend that for them this was the one clearly given truth of their society. . . . For the mass of the American democracy, the decades after 1800 were a continuing, even though intermittent, revival" (*Life* 7).

Comprehending this "dominant theme" also provides the necessary context for understanding these evangelical women autobiographers, who entered the literary marketplace between 1832, when Nancy Towle published her *Vicissitudes Illustrated in the Experience of Nancy Towle, in Europe and America*, and 1893, when the itinerant preacher and missionary Amanda Berry Smith published *An Autobiography: The Story of the Lord's Dealings with Mrs. Amanda Smith, the Colored Evangelist*. With the exception of Amanda Smith, whose itinerant ministry began in 1870, each of these women left home to preach the gospel in the first half of the nineteenth century. The careers of Towle, Lee, and Elaw began in the 1820s and ended, so far as we know, before the Civil War; Foote, Sexton, and Haviland began preaching in the 1840s and continued to do so in postbellum America. Thus, while their lives spanned the entire century, their careers as messengers of the Word fall within the Age of Revivalism as defined by Timothy Smith in *Revivalism and Social Reform*. The Second Great Awakening in America is now generally recognized to have occurred between the 1790s and the 1840s (or 1850s if one includes the revival of 1857–58).[3] But as Smith convincingly argues, the religious awakenings of the nineteenth century did not end in 1858 but extended into the 1870s, and even beyond, with the flowering of the perfect love, perfectionist, or Higher Life movements involving not only Methodists but also New School Presbyterians, Quakers, Congregationalists, and Baptists.

Religion, central to the lives of many prominent men in the nineteenth century (we immediately think of Lyman Beecher, Peter Cartwright, Lorenzo Dow, Charles Grandison Finney, and Dwight Moody), was, perhaps, even more important for women. Historians have emphasized the degree to which prayer meetings, revivals, and Sunday church services were predominantly female affairs in the first half of the century; studies have shown "that women—mainly women under age thirty—comprised about two-thirds of those joining New Jersey Presbyterian, New England Congregationalist, and Southern evangelical churches during the Second Great Awakening" (Blauvelt 1). These statistics would not have surprised nineteenth-century Americans, who assumed that women, more emotional and passive than men, were naturally more religious as well: their submissiveness, in other words, made it easier for them to assume the posture necessary to be filled with the Holy Spirit. Thus has it often been argued that Christianity was the opiate by which women were comforted and encouraged to accept their subordinate position in society. Christianity was an outlet, a retreat from the inequalities of this world, which prepared women to cope with subordination; it was an escape valve for their discontent, a tool in the service of the dominant culture, for while Christianity may have altered women's interior lives within their own sphere, it did not affect their exterior lives.

My own sense of it, having spent some time with the spiritual autobiographies written by women deeply committed to evangelical Christianity, is a different one. These autobiographers—no less than religious men and women of all centuries—glory in the solace that their knowledge of God brings. "How vast a source of consolation did I derive from habitual communion with my God," remembers Zilpha Elaw; "to Him I repaired in secret to acquaint Him with all my griefs, and obtained both sympathy and succour" (58). And they record having learned Christlike meekness and humility in the face of opposition. Still, their autobiographies make clear that Christianity significantly marked their lives in ways that led them to reject their subordinate lot in the world and "to live deep," in Thoreau's phrase, "and suck out all the marrow of life" (66). Certainly, the autobiographies of these seven female preachers are not as dull or predictable as Estelle Jelinek implies when she dismisses them from her study *The Tradition of Women's Autobiography*, focusing instead on autobiographies that are "fortunately . . . more secular than religious in content" (94–95). Though conflicted over their decision to combat their culture's definitions of womanhood, none of these evangelical itinerants, unlike many famous women in the twentieth century, constructs herself as a "self in hiding" (Spacks, "Selves" 132). Here a useful contrast may be drawn between these women and their more radical, feminist sister, Elizabeth Cady Stanton, whose autobiography places her exceptional career as an advocate of women's rights within the context of her "ordinary" life as a wife and mother, thereby "counter[ing] the unidimensional public image of herself as a brilliant, argumentative, sharp-witted, unrelenting reformer from a prestigious upper-class family" (Jelinek, "Paradox" 71). These autobiographers do nearly the opposite, emphasizing their careers at the expense of their domestic lives though often using the *language* of domesticity to describe those careers. Even Zilpha Elaw, who believed a woman should be submissive to a husband's domination, implied something very different by writing an autobiography in which her husband is granted little textual space and her intense lifework expands to fill up the pages of her story.

According to Nancy Towle, Zilpha Elaw, and the rest, an experience of God offered them far more than mere compensation for their subordinate lot; rather, it enabled them to brave public scrutiny and engage in unconventional relationships and nontraditional work.[4] As the Methodist preacher and women's suffrage advocate Jennie Fowler Willing commented, Pentecost was "Woman's Emancipation Day" (qtd. in Schmidt, "Holiness" 825). And the holiness evangelist Phoebe Palmer, even with her "more domestic, middle-class model of ministry," regarded her famous Tuesday meetings—which began in the 1830s and continued even after her death in 1874, and which included men and women, ordained ministers, and laypersons—as an "equalizing process" (Brekus 338; Palmer, *Promise* 234). "The sects called evangelical," said Lydia Maria Child, "were the first agitators of the woman question" (356). Evangelical religion became the means by which women could measure the oppressiveness of their lives and at times overcome it. Authorized by God, these evangelical preachers found it easier to eschew marriage and domesticity in favor of an itinerant life that lay outside the safety, certainty, and closure—as well as the drudgery—that domesticity or domestic servitude promised northern women in the nineteenth century.[5] Their unmediated relation to God and Scripture gave them a subjective sense of freedom—they were not *of* the world but strangers—which empowered them to explore life beyond prevailing gender, class, and race hierarchies. "The shore is safer," they might have said with Emily Dickinson, "but I love to buffett the sea" (qtd. in Wolff 104).

None of this should be surprising. Historians like Catherine Brekus, Nancy Cott, Nancy Hardesty, Janet James, Dana Robert, Rosemary Ruether, Mary Ryan, Carroll Smith-Rosenberg, and Deborah Valenze have been arguing, for several decades, that evangelical religion, like bourgeois individualism generally, opened up a whole new world for northern women discontented with their roles as wives, mothers, sisters, and daughters.[6] Evangelical sects—with their ties to "religious dissent," and their desires to "preserve the element of 'protest' in Protestantism" and to "separate themselves from American culture by challenging its understandings of gender and race"—offered women an allegiance beyond the home, a new field in which they could become active, assertive, and relatively free agents responsible for nothing short of the redemption of the world (Brekus 78, 157).

Religion belonged, moreover, to a world somehow between the public sphere of men and politics and the private, domestic sphere, which was considered by many Americans the proper one for women. As recent students of the "social geography of gender" argue, religion belonged to what has variously been termed the social, civic, or informal public sphere, a space that—like front porches, camp meetings, lyceums, and even parades—mediated between the public world of government and the private world of the family (Matthews, *Rise* 117).[7] The postmillennialism of antebellum America made the once public and secular street a social and religious domain in which women could promote conversion and reform.[8] Evangelicalism, with its vast network of benevolent organizations, publishing concerns, and missionary societies, invited women to undertake new roles as social workers, teachers, managers, missionaries, and writers. The tenets of evangelicalism encouraged women to promote revivals through home meetings, prayer groups, and voluntary and mission work; they encouraged women to apply their skills and voices as exhorters within the church and as writers in such religious journals as *The Guide to Holiness*, *Women's Work for Women*, *Heathen Woman's Friend*, *Christian Palladium*, *Advent Harbinger*, and *Bible Advocate*.

My own interest in evangelical religion is a bit different from that of many historians and sociologists. They focus, quite usefully, on evangelicalism as a social movement of great importance. But, as Nathan Hatch argues, "The distinctive feature of American Christianity was not the surge of an impersonal force called revivalism, descending like manna from heaven, but a remarkable set of popular leaders" (*Democratization* 56). The popular leaders in whom Hatch is most interested are all reasonably well known:

Alexander Campbell, Elias Smith, Lorenzo Dow, Peter Cartwright, Billy Hibbard, and Lyman Beecher. But few of us have encountered women like Nancy Towle, Jarena Lee, Zilpha Elaw, Lydia Sexton, Laura Haviland, Julia Foote, or Amanda Smith. They were prominent in evangelical and revivalist circles of the nineteenth century, sufficiently so that they could expect readerships for their autobiographies; but they are virtually unknown in our own day.[9] Those who preached early in the century might even have been welcomed by some sects. According to Catherine Brekus,

> Populist and anti-intellectual, the Freewill Baptists, Christians, Methodists and African Methodists created a religious culture in which even the most humble convert—the poor, the unlearned, the slave, or the female—felt qualified to preach the gospel. . . . Influenced by the shortage of ordained ministers, the growing numbers of female converts, the turbulence of revival meetings, and popular beliefs in immediate revelation, they allowed hundreds of women to pray aloud, testify, exhort, and even preach in public, overturning cultural expectations of female silence. (145–46)

The seven women considered in this study, like women and many men in all periods of Christianity, were charismatic preachers who entered the ministry—and thereby overturned cultural expectations—by claiming an immediate experience of the divine and by demonstrating their "spiritual gifts." Their careers—and those of many female preachers like them—follow almost ritualistically similar patterns: after their conversions and visionary experiences in which they feel themselves called to preach, nearly all attempt to deny the claims of that experience. They find their calls, naturally enough, quite alarming: they have been commanded to deny both their own culture's assumptions about a woman's place and Saint Paul's proscriptions, in his letter to Timothy, of women's preaching. But the authority of God outweighs that of their parents, husbands, and friends, even that of their own consciences, which in many cases seem to assert quite forcefully their culture's prescriptive definitions of womanhood. Many of them, like many of their male counterparts, are able to make sense of their unwilling enlistment in God's service by invoking the biblical stories of Jonah and Jeremiah. Indeed, the beginning of these stories—the call and refusal to obey—has been described by Joseph Campbell as the archetypal structure with which all monomythic heroic tales begin. Often these women are afflicted with serious illnesses, which they interpret as chastening reminders from God of their unfulfilled obligations; they recover from these illnesses determined to resist no longer. Remarkably often, this resolution is abetted by the timely death of a husband who has forcefully personified the cultural suspicion of female preaching. Finally, unable to resist God's call, the women begin to preach the gospel in homes and at camp meetings, public assemblies, and churches, either as independent itinerants (Nancy Towle and Zilpha Elaw) or under the aegis of a particular sect, in most of these cases a Methodist or African Methodist Episcopal (Jarena Lee, Julia Foote, Lydia Sexton, Laura Haviland, and Amanda Smith), which would occasionally license—but not ordain—them to preach.[10] Having convinced local authorities of their divine sanction, they are pronounced "exceptions" to biblical and denominational proscriptions concerning women preachers. Like Nancy Towle, who once moved large crowds with her childhood theatrical performances, and who felt "a longing desire, to go into all the world and preach the Gospel to every creature," many women were permitted to fulfill their desires, use their talents, and preach in the wide world (Towle 10; Mark 16:15).[11] Thus did evangelical religion, against its own instincts and even against theirs, encourage these women to remake the world with their voices, to become preachers and "pen[s] in [God's] hand" (Jackson 107).[12]

Though my own literary orientation has led me to focus on seven women who wrote autobiographical accounts of their ministries, these were by no means the only women in the century whose spiritual gifts and determination led them to pursue adventurous careers as itinerant ministers.[13] Nor was the appearance of women on the public stage of nineteenth-century evangelical religion wholly unprecedented. Quakers had long considered women important disciples and missionaries who, like their male counterparts, undertook the work of the ministry as a part-time obligation (when the Spirit called) rather than as a full-time office; the eighteenth-century evangelist Elizabeth Ashbridge immediately comes to mind. Traveling by Quaker women in the eighteenth century, according to Rebecca Larson, was considered routine; she estimates that between 1700 and 1775 there were thirteen to fifteen hundred Quaker women preaching in the colonies and British Isles (63). Itinerancy and revivalism among the Separate Baptists, Freewill Baptists, and the New Light and New Divinity schools of the Congregationalists, Timothy Hall argues, persistently challenged not only spatial boundaries but social ones as well, encouraging some eighteenth-century women to step outside their "natural" station to lead praying societies and even, in a few cases, to exhort crowds. In 1741 the New Light exhorter Bathsheba Kingsley went so far as to steal a horse so that she might obey the "immediate revelations" she had received from God, revelations that called her to become an itinerant minister: as the revivalist Jonathan Edwards put it in his "Advice to Mr. and Mrs. Kingsley," she traveled "from house to house, and very frequently to other towns, under a notion of doing Christ's work and delivering his messages" (qtd. in Brekus 23, 24).[14] With the Second Great Awakening, as more and more women found themselves baptized by the Spirit, joining local churches, organizing praying bands and missionary societies, women were also awakened in greater numbers to the possibility of preaching the gospel. Louis Billington estimates that between "1790 and 1840 probably hundreds of women" preached, if only in a local church or revival, "grassroots practice" differing sharply from official or unofficial prescriptions against women's preaching (372, 381). Women took up careers as itinerant evangelists, often moving freely "between the Freewill Baptists, Christians, and a wide range of Methodist sects as opportunity occurred," the luxury of "settling"[15] in as pastors of particular congregations being an almost exclusively male prerogative (Billington 381).[16]

Because comprehensive church records from the nineteenth century are largely unavailable, because the role of women preachers was purposefully forgotten as once-radical sects became conservative denominations, and because most women preachers were neither licensed nor ordained and were often entirely unaffiliated, it has been difficult for historians to identify them, let alone document their activities. But the many names that have come down to us indicate that the experiences of Nancy Towle, Jarena Lee, Zilpha Elaw, Lydia Sexton, Julia Foote, Laura Haviland, and Amanda Smith were part of a significant phenomenon. A close reading of their life stories gives us, then, an appreciation for the lives of many nineteenth-century American women who dreamed of, and (despite much opposition) often succeeded in, becoming preachers of the gospel.

Introductions

Because the women whom I study are not well known, some introductions are in order. Jarena Lee was born on February 11, 1783, in Cape May, New Jersey. Her parents were free, but extremely poor, blacks who were forced to hire her out as a domestic servant at age seven to a family who lived sixty miles from their home. In 1804 she moved to Philadelphia, where she supported herself by working as a domestic servant. Though converted at the age of twenty-one, she continued to experience doubts about her salvation for four years, until a black man named William Scott informed her of a second blessing, that of complete sanctification,[17] which she subsequently attained, feeling at the time "as if [she] were in an ocean of light and bliss" (10).[18]

"Four or five years after [her] sanctification," or around 1811, Jarena Lee heard the voice of God calling her to preach the gospel (10). She applied for permission to Rev. Richard Allen, founder of the first independent black congregation and later the first independent black denomination in America (the African Methodist Episcopal or A.M.E. Church); he denied her request.[19] That same year she married Joseph Lee, "pastor of a Society at Snow Hill," and moved with him to Snow Hill, about six miles from Philadelphia, where she found herself so lonely and upset that she became ill (13). She recovered, knowing she had yet to obey the Lord's will that she preach. The next six years brought only tragedy: Lee's husband and four other family members died. In 1818 Lee returned to Philadelphia with two surviving children and requested Allen's permission simply to hold prayer meetings in her home, which he willingly granted. The following year, having heard her spontaneously exhort a congregation at Bethel, Allen supported her request to preach. Thus began an itinerant ministry to racially mixed audiences in the Mid-Atlantic region, the Northeast, and as far west as Ohio. In 1833, "laboring under the disadvantages of education," she hired an anonymous editor to "have a portion of [her journal] taken from the original . . . and corrected for press" (66). In 1836, and again in 1839, she printed for sale one thousand copies of *The Life and Religious Experience of Mrs. Jarena Lee, a Coloured Lady*, which is now considered to be the first extant personal narrative by an African American woman. In 1849, without the support of the African Methodist Episcopal Church, she published an expanded version of her life story, entitled *Religious Experience and Journal of Mrs. Jarena Lee*. Lee's movements after 1849 are unknown, as are the time and place of her death.

Zilpha Elaw was born around 1790 outside the city of Philadelphia to free black parents. Her mother having died when she was twelve, Elaw was hired out as a domestic servant to a Quaker family, in whose home she lived and worked until the age of eighteen. Her father died a mere six months after she left her home. During her teens she was converted by Methodists, and in 1808 she joined a Methodist society. At age twenty she married, regrettably, she came to feel, Joseph Elaw, a nonbeliever. With her husband she moved to Burlington, New Jersey, in 1811 and the following year gave birth to a daughter. At a camp meeting in 1817, she "became so overpowered with the presence of God, that [she] sank down upon the ground," feeling at the same time her spirit soaring to the sun and hearing a voice telling her, "'Now thou art sanctified'" (66). Shortly thereafter, Elaw's dying sister informed her that "an angel . . . bade her tell Zilpha that she must preach the gospel" (73). Elaw disregarded these instructions for several years, until she became seriously ill around 1819. Following her recovery, she felt divinely inspired to exhort at a camp meeting in the presence of a formidable group of ministers, an event that marked the beginning of her career as a preacher.

When Joseph Elaw died four years later, in 1823, Zilpha and her daughter were forced by financial necessity into domestic service. For two years she also attempted to run a school for black children, who were not allowed to attend Burlington's segregated schools.[20] Eventually, however, she was overwhelmed by guilt at having denied God's call; she left her daughter and began life as an itinerant evangelist, sometime in 1825 or 1826. Though she was associated with Methodists throughout her career, she preached independently, without denominational support, financial or otherwise, traveling from here to there, from slave states to free states, the itinerary being determined by "impressions" received from above. In 1840, having been "impressed" for years that the Lord called her to England, she sailed to London, where in 1845 she wrote and printed *Memoirs of the Life, Religious Experience, Ministerial Travels and Labours of Mrs. Zilpha Elaw, an American Female of Colour* as a token of her esteem, a souvenir of sorts, for her friends and followers there. After this point her movements, like Lee's, are unknown. Curiously, both Elaw and Lee were excluded from Susan Shorter's 1891 collective biography, *The Heroines of African Methodism.* They were, it seems, their own best, and only, historians.

Nancy Towle began her "Journey of Life" on February 13, 1796, in Hampton, New Hampshire (5). She participated in a revival at age twelve and began to reflect on the state of her soul; she was converted at age twenty-two by the Freewill Baptist evangelist Clarissa H. Danforth and baptized by Christian elder Moses Howe. Impressed with the words "Hearken, O daughters, and consider, and incline thine ear, forget also thine own people, and thy father's house," she realized she had been called to preach, a summons that both excited and distressed her for two years (11; Psalm 45:10). Though she had always believed there was nothing unscriptural about a woman's preaching, particularly "'in these last days'" on the eve of the millennium (when patriarchal restrictions could and should be abandoned), she was nonetheless reluctant to take up the cross, it being unseemly for a woman to wander the earth preaching (15; Hebrews 1:2).[21] But after a "visible decline in health," she finally left her father's home in 1821, took a teaching job to hide her real intentions, and began to preach as an independent itinerant, a task she continued at least for the next eleven years throughout the United States, Canada, England, and Ireland (17). Her evangelistic activities were recorded in both the *Christian Herald* and the *Morning Star* during the 1820s. After 1832, when she printed her autobiography at her own expense, and 1833 when a second edition was printed in Portsmouth, New Hampshire, her activities are unknown.

A contemporary of Towle and Elaw, though she began her ministry later than they, Lydia Sexton was born April 12, 1799, in New Jersey. Her father, a Baptist minister, died the following year, leaving her mother, Abigail Casad, to care for nine children. In 1811 the mother remarried, this time to John Wintermoot, also a Baptist minister and the father of seven children. Despite the protest of her biological children, Abigail sent them away to make room for the undisciplined brood of her new husband (51–52). Lydia spent a year with her Aunt and Uncle Casad, who treated her so poorly she willingly went to live with their neighbor, a Mr. Hand, whom she calls both her "keeper" and her "master" (65). In 1814 she left Mr. Hand and traveled with her brother Anthony to Ohio, boarding with him and other family members for the next few years and attending school. In 1820 she married the first of three husbands, Isaac Cox, who died two years later in an accident, leaving her with one son, born in 1821. After Isaac's death she eventually found herself "homeless, and almost friendless," so much so that she was forced to place her son, John, then three years old, with a "rich old man by the name of Kurtz" (156). In 1824 she married Moses Moore, a surveyor, with whom she had another son; the next year Moore died unexpectedly. Sometime later that year or in early 1826, Sexton managed to take back her firstborn son from Mr. Kurtz, despite Kurtz's opposition (161–67). In 1829 she married Joseph Sexton, with whom she lived for almost fifty years and bore three more children.

Sometime in the mid-1830s, Sexton was convicted of her sins at a "New Light" meeting.[22] She was then baptized by the Campbellites in the Miami River in Dayton, Ohio, but became somewhat "sickened" by the sect—because of "the everlasting ding-dong about 'the Word,' 'the Word,' and a continual warfare against discipline, and professing to be the only true church" (196). Eventually she joined the United Brethren Church, a German Methodist body. Shortly thereafter she received "a special call to the ministry" while attending a dance (199). She resisted the call for almost a decade and suffered tremendous guilt as a result. Finally, when one of her sons fell seriously ill, she made a covenant with God: should the boy survive, she would take up her cross. God spared the child, and Sexton began preaching sometime in 1843. Her itinerant ministry, primarily in the Midwest, continued until 1870, when she became chaplain of the Kansas State Prison in Leavenworth. In 1882 the United Brethren Publishing House considered her story central enough to its history to issue her autobiography. It is believed she died in 1892.

Laura Smith Haviland was born on December 20, 1808, in Leeds County, Ontario, Canada, the eldest child of eight in a family of dedicated Quakers. Her father was a minister and her mother an elder in the Society of Friends. In 1815 the family moved across the border to Niagara County, New York. Except for four months of public school in Canada, Haviland's early education took place at home; later she attended a Quaker school in Lockport, New York. At the age of thirteen, Haviland came under the influence of frontier revivalism that was then sweeping through western New York. Attending a Methodist prayer meeting, she was moved to contemplate the state of her soul; she was converted shortly thereafter, preferring the evangelistic and reformist tendencies of Methodism and heartfelt conversion of the revivalists to the formality of the Quakers. In 1825 she married Charles Haviland, a local Quaker farmer, with whom she had eight children. In 1829 she moved with him to a farm in the Michigan Territory, in the township of Raisin. Along with Elizabeth M. Chandler, Haviland organized the first antislavery society in Michigan. When they discovered that conservative Quakers there opposed their antislavery activity, the Haviland family resigned from the Society of Friends, an act that marked the beginning of Haviland's long career as an abolitionist and missionary. She and her husband opened a school on their farm for indigent children in 1837; in 1839, influenced by a brother who had attended Oberlin College, they turned it into a manual labor institution modeled on Oberlin principles, open to all regardless of race or sex; they called it the River Raisin Institute.

By 1844, at the age of thirty-six, Haviland was a minister in the holiness, abolitionist Wesleyan Methodist Church; she rejoined the Quakers only in 1872, when they began to embrace a missionary spirit.[23] In 1845 an epidemic of "inflammatory erysipelas" (or Saint Anthony's fire, a skin disease caused by a streptococcus) claimed the lives of

Haviland's husband, mother, father, sister, and youngest child. From then until the Civil War, Haviland committed herself to missionary work among blacks in the North and South. An avid abolitionist, she gave speeches, aided fugitive slaves, and even traveled in the South to promote the cause and help slaves escape. During the Civil War, Haviland considered it her mission to carry supplies to the front, to nurse Union troops, and to care for and give religious instruction to black children. In 1864 she became a paid agent of the Freedman's Aid Commission. And from that time until 1881, when she published the first edition of her autobiography, *A Woman's Life-Work: Labors and Experiences of Laura S. Haviland*, she continued her missionary endeavors among the freedmen and freedwomen, in schools, asylums, and orphanages, as well as endorsing the temperance crusade and the woman's suffrage movement. Her temperance work (like that of Amanda Smith) and her support of women's suffrage, along with her mentioning of Susan B. Anthony in her autobiography, remind us that though she ministered in an age of evangelicalism and revivalism, she also lived and worked into a later age in which some women began to look for political equality and authority in America. She died in Grand Rapids, Michigan, in 1898.

Julia A. J. Foote was born in 1823 in Schenectady, New York, to fervent Christians and former slaves who had purchased their freedom. Banned from Schenectady's schools, she was put to service with an influential white family so that she might attend a school in the country. At age twelve she returned home to care for her four younger siblings while her mother worked. At age fifteen she was converted and joined the African Methodist Episcopal Church; at age sixteen she was sanctified. In 1841 she married George Foote, a sailor, and moved to Boston, where she joined the African Methodist Episcopal Zion Church. Here she felt moved to testify to the joys of sanctification, despite her husband's opposition. Later Foote felt called to preach but was opposed by her minister. After considerable controversy, the minister tried to settle the matter by having her excommunicated. But Foote was not to be stopped. She began her ministry in Philadelphia, where she and several other women rented a hall and preached the gospel. Beginning in about 1845 she preached throughout upstate New York and later in New England, the Mid-Atlantic states, Ohio, Michigan, and Canada. Her husband, rarely mentioned in her autobiography, passed away sometime in the late 1840s or early 1850s. In 1851 she settled down in Cleveland owing to a "throat difficulty," not preaching again until 1869 as part of the Holiness Revival that swept through the Midwest in the early 1870s (224). For the next twenty-five years her activities are unknown. She died in 1900, having been ordained a deacon and later an elder in the A.M.E. Zion Church. Her autobiography, *A Brand Plucked from the Fire* (1879), did not fall into complete obscurity in the late nineteenth and early twentieth centuries; in 1894 Mrs. Nathan Francis Mossell included the book in a bibliography of African American publications entitled *The Work of the Afro-American Woman*.

Amanda Berry Smith was born into slavery on January 23, 1837, in Long Green, Maryland. Her parents lived on adjoining farms, owned by different masters, who allowed them to purchase their freedom as well as that of their five children. Despite his freedom, Smith's father was harassed by a group of white farmers who were disturbed by his once traveling out of state for over a week when the law forbade such lengthy trips by free blacks. Thus her parents moved the family to York County, Pennsylvania. Smith received some schooling when she was eight and later when she was thirteen, at which time she was put to service with the Latimers, the first of many white families for whom she would work as a domestic servant. She was converted in a Methodist church, but—unable to keep up her religious exercises on Sundays because of her strenuous duties in the Latimer household—she promptly "lost all the grace [she] had, if [she] really had any at all" (29). In 1854, at the age of seventeen, Smith married her first husband, C. Devine, an irreligious man prone, she later discovered, to drinking. In 1855, near death probably after childbirth, she had a vision of herself preaching before a large crowd and was reconverted sometime thereafter. Her first husband never returned from the Civil War, leaving her with a daughter, Mazie, her only child—out of five—to survive infancy. In 1865 she joined the Bethel A.M.E. Church in Philadelphia, the church that had been home to Jarena Lee half a century earlier. That same year she married her second husband, James Smith, a local preacher and ordained deacon at the Bethel A.M.E. Church, and moved with him to New York to find work.

In 1868, a year before both James and her youngest child would die, Smith learned of the blessing of sanctification, perhaps at one of Phoebe Palmer's Tuesday meetings; and at a sermon by John Inskip, the founder of the National Camp Meeting Association for the Promotion of Holiness, she received this "enduring grace," which she would later promote in Holiness camp meetings and revivals around the world (62). In 1870, at the Fleet Street A.M.E. Church in Brooklyn, Smith was called to preach, specifically to the people of Salem, New Jersey, and the Mount Pisgah A.M.E. Church. By 1871 she had reportedly converted 156 people there. From 1878 to 1890 she traveled abroad to England, Ireland, Scotland, India, and Africa, this time aligned with the white Methodist Episcopal Church. In 1892 she moved to Chicago to work with her friend Frances Willard of the Woman's Christian Temperance Union. At that time she also began composing An Autobiography: The Story of the Lord's Dealings with Mrs. Amanda Smith, the Colored Evangelist (1893) and publishing a monthly newspaper called The Helper. With the proceeds of the paper and her autobiography, along with contributions, she opened a school for black orphans in 1899, which remained open until 1918, when it was destroyed by fire.

In 1912 Smith retired to a home in Sebring, Florida, owned by her wealthy friend, the Ohio china manufacturer George Sebring, who had been sanctified through her preaching; she lived there until her death in 1915. Smith, more than any other woman in this study, achieved a degree of notoriety that prevented her accomplishments and her autobiography from slipping into obscurity. Her life has been the subject of two biographies—Life, Travels, Labors, and Helpers of Mrs. Amanda Smith, the Famous Negro Missionary Evangelist, written by Marshall W. Taylor and published in 1887; and, more recently, Amanda Berry Smith: From Washerwoman to Evangelist, by Adrienne Israel. Brief sketches of her life were also included in at least five collective biographies published by African Americans in the late nineteenth and early twentieth centuries.

Evangelical Autobiography and Gender

The spiritual autobiographies by these itinerants all reveal something of the democratic spirit of some Protestant sects (later denominations), which, theoretically at least, disavowed hierarchies, empowering every man and woman, educated or not, to interpret

Scripture and to bring about his or her own conversion. In *The Democratization of American Christianity*, Nathan Hatch focuses on the leadership of early-nineteenth-century evangelical movements because "the fundamental religious debates in the early republic were not merely a class of intellectual and theological differences but also a passionate social struggle with power and authority," which he convincingly uncovers (14). What Hatch fails to consider, however, and what these seven books stress, is the degree to which that "passionate social struggle with power and authority" was more than a battle between Charles Finney and Lyman Beecher; between the common man and the established clergy; or even among the various sects that vied for the souls of people like Elder Benjamin Putnam, who moved from the Baptists (by whom he was baptized), to the Freewill Baptists (by whom he was ordained), to the Christians, and, finally, back to the Baptists (by whom he was licensed to preach). One of the fundamental religious struggles of the eighteenth, nineteenth, and even twentieth centuries was between women who were called to preach and a culture that called them to remain silent. While their call to the ministry liberated female itinerants from the restrictive forms of womanhood by which many nineteenth-century women defined themselves, these autobiographies make clear that the authority conferred by "spiritual gifts" was never quite as secure, even among radical evangelicals, as was the authority given to men by a license to preach in a circuit or with ordination: which meant that a hierarchy of sex prevailed even among the most democratic of Protestant sects, both before and after these sects began acquiring social respectability and thus finding "spiritual gifts" to be rather embarrassing relics of former times.[24]

It is this gender hierarchy, and the response to it of the seven women under consideration here, that has primarily held my attention. I have been most interested in the similarities to be found in their spiritual journeys and autobiographies. Inevitably this means that some other issues pertinent to these books are consigned to the periphery of my focus and are in danger of being obscured. For instance, this is a study of three white women and four black women; doesn't race make for a difference between the two groups? Naturally it does: the black women, who were all at various times domestic servants as well as the keepers of their own homes, had a different relationship to the ideology of domesticity than did the three white women. And they all make an issue of race in their autobiographies (so, in a different way, do two of the white women, Laura Haviland and Lydia Sexton, who were active abolitionists). Like all African American women, Jarena Lee, Zilpha Elaw, Julia Foote, and Amanda Smith were confronted, as Anna Julia Cooper observed in 1892, by "both a woman question and a race problem" (qtd. in Foster, *Written by Herself* 10). Self-conscious about race, all four African American women report repeated encounters with a culture in which they were devalued and which considered them "curiosities" when they began to preach publicly (Sexton 251).

Jarena Lee proudly asserts her race and gender—and pointedly lays claim to an elevated class of women—in the title of her first autobiography, *The Life and Religious Experience of Jarena Lee, A Coloured Lady*. "No black woman, regardless of income, education, refinement, or character," Evelyn Brooks Higginbotham reminds us, "enjoyed the status of lady" ("African-American" 261). But Lee surely felt herself to be one, having discovered an inner strength and beauty in the "class" to which she belonged in Christ. Still, throughout her narratives she subtly calls our attention to what she suffered outwardly because of her color: she puts it mildly, for example, when she remembers a "most uncomfortable" trip on Lake Ontario where "they treated people of color very indifferently indeed" and a trip through the South where she was fearful of being enslaved despite being "fortified, for their laws, by [her] credentials, having the United States seal upon them" (72, 36). Though she never actively took up the abolitionist cause, she describes a meeting of an antislavery society "where [she] heard some very able discussions on the rights of the oppressed, and also clear demonstrations of the cruelty of the slaveholder" and later reports her regret at being unable to attend a convention of the American Anti-Slavery Society (72, 89). Though she speaks as well of her desire to preach "especially among [her] own people," she worked in a "countercultural" climate that looked toward "a more racially inclusive Christianity" in which she was free, as she frequently alerts us, to preach to whites, blacks, and racially mixed audiences (Lee 30; Brekus 156, 157). Perhaps most significantly, she emphasizes the intersection of race and Christianity when she expresses her support of Nat Turner and his rebellion: "In 1831, a young man who professed to be righteous, says he saw in the sky men, marching like armies, whetherit [sic] was with the naked eye, or a Vision by the eye of Faith, I cannot tell. But the wickedness of the people certainly calls for the lowering Judgments of God to be let loose upon the Nation and Slavery, that wretched system that eminated [sic] from the bottomless pit" (63).

Zilpha Elaw similarly insists upon recognition of her race and gender beginning with the title of her narrative, *Memoirs of the Life, Religious Experience, Ministerial Travels and Labours of Mrs. Zilpha Elaw, an American Female of Colour*. Traveling throughout the American South, as well as the North, she writes about the many fears and significant opposition she faced as a "coloured female preacher" (91). But she quite confidently declares that the "pride of a white skin is a bauble of great value with many in some parts of the United States, who readily sacrifice their intelligence to their prejudices, and possess more knowledge than wisdom" (85). God, on the other hand, makes no such sacrifice: "The Almighty accounts not the black races of man either in the order of nature or spiritual capacity as inferior to the white; for He bestows his Holy Spirit on, and dwells in them as readily as in persons of whiter complexion" (85). Elaw also berates the "pride of high-toned sensibility and civilization," which harshly judges African Americans for "an imperfect conformity to the politer standard of morals and tasteful delicacy" (118, 117). "The immoralities of the Abyssinian brethren, when they occur," she maintains, "are obvious and glaring, and are easily visited and purged by the discipline of the church; but those of more polished Christians too often flow in a deep and mighty under current," a current so deep that it cannot be altered without "crumbl[ing] to ruins every denominational superstructure in Christendom" (118).

Julia Foote begins her narrative with the story of her freeborn father's being "stolen, when a child, and enslaved" and of her enslaved mother's sufferings at the hands of a cruel master, who pursued her as a sexual object, and a cruel mistress who mistreated her because of it (166). As an adult, Foote's father purchased his freedom and that of his wife and first child. But they remained, as would their fourth child, Julia, enslaved by a racist culture, even in evangelical circles. Having joined the Methodist Episcopal Church, Foote's parents were "not treated as Christian believers, but as poor lepers" who were obliged to occupy certain seats in one corner of the gallery, and dared not come down to partake of the Holy Communion until the last white communicant had left the table. . . . This was one of the fruits of slavery. . . . How many at the present day profess great spirituality, and even holiness, and yet are deluded by a spirit of error, which leads them to say to the poor and the colored ones among them, "Stand back a little—I am holier than thou." (167)

These remarks remind us that evangelicalism's and revivalism's initial movement away from hierarchies of race was not a universal one. In 1851 Foote herself was invited to speak to a group of white Methodists, but because they refused to allow African Americans to attend the meeting, she refused to preach, Jesus having told his disciples to "preach the gospel to all" (222; Mark 16:15). Though her narrative is primarily about conversion, sanctification, and preaching, Foote takes time to lament the difficulties she faced because in her community "there were no schools where colored children were allowed" (170). At age ten, Foote lived with an "influential family" who managed to send her to a country school where she was "well treated by both teacher and scholars" (171). Later in the narrative, Foote writes that she still longed for more education, believing if she "were educated, God could make [her] understand what [she] needed" to gain religious maturation. But the teachers, Mrs. Phileos and Miss Crandall, were themselves oppressed by a "pro-slavery mob in Canterbury, Conn., because they dared to teach colored children to read" (184). Foote had to endure what she politely called "indignities on account of color" when attempting to travel around America, by stage or boat (see 215, 218, 224). Once she was even harassed in Baltimore by people who suspected she was a runaway slave. At the end of her career in 1879, Foote felt compelled to remark that "the monster, Slavery, is not yet dead in all its forms" (220).

An Autobiography: The Story of the Lord's Dealings with Mrs. Amanda Smith, the Colored Evangelist opens with an account of Amanda Smith's birth on a farm in which slavery was not dead in any of its forms. The autobiographer invites her readers, then, with the title and first chapter, to consider race as a significant category of analysis. Popularly known as the "colored evangelist," Smith, more frequently than the other black spiritual autobiographers in this study, documents the social, economic, and psychological hardships of growing up black in nineteenth-century America. Proud "to share" with other blacks "the great honor" of having "'come out of Egypt,'" the "birthplace of Moses, and the hiding place of the infant Jesus," she was "very well satisfied" with her "substantial color" of "royal black" (295, 117; Psalm 68:31). She knew by experience, of course, that many Americans did not share her pride in her heritage; so when asked if "all colored people wanted to be white," she responded with devastating understatement: "I, for one, praise Him for what He has given me, although at times it is very inconvenient" (117). Hence, in her self-portrait she writes about the hardships her family faced as free blacks, documents their participation in the Underground Railroad, records her difficulties making ends meet as a mother, defends herself against charges of being "a white folks 'nigger,'" provides numerous examples of the racism she faced within evangelical circles and when traveling in America and abroad, and draws on the language of slavery and race relations in her delineation of religious principles (117, 453). Amanda Smith's now famous rejoinder to those who considered hers an easy lot applies equally well to her black sister itinerants: "'If you want to know and understand properly what Amanda Smith has to contend with, just turn black and go about as I do, and you will come to a different conclusion.' And I think some people would understand the quintessence of sanctifying grace if they could be black about twenty-four hours" (116–17). As Smith professes here, conversion and sanctification enabled many African Americans "to define themselves not with respect to white power but to the divine" (Mathews, "Evangelical" 30). But writing in 1892–93, she no doubt despaired over the state of race relations in America. Her evangelical efforts to convert and sanctify blacks and whites had not led, as she—following Saint Paul—had hoped, to a world in which there was neither black nor white, in which "all [were] one in Christ Jesus" (see 185, 223, 226; Galatians 3:28).

Nor had "put[ting] on Christ" led to a cultural space in which "there [was] neither male nor female" (Galatians 3:27, 28). Often these women narrate stories in which the politics of gender overshadows that of race, despite the sometimes detailed and always moving descriptions of what were certainly more than mere "indignities" suffered by African American female itinerants because of color and class. For while black clergymen believed in and worked toward many reforms in this reformist age, a woman's right to ordination was not among them: the black church, no less than the white, was marked by sexism. "The [black] church, like the black community," writes Evelyn Brooks Higginbotham, "cannot be viewed solely through the lens of race" (*Righteous Discontent* 14). Thus the autobiographies by African American female evangelists, as Carla Peterson has said of Jarena Lee's, are "permeated by that tension between the heterogeneous sacred spaces of mystical vision and of the Second Great Awakening, and the institutional space of the A.M.E. hierarchy—a tension that not even the act of writing could reconcile" (87). All of these women, black or white, principally conceive of themselves as women of faith, authorized to preach by a loving and powerful God, and as women struggling against a predominantly male religious "establishment" (even when sects were barely established); all of them use their textual self-representations in defense of their own unconventional lives and a woman's right to preach the gospel. All of them to varying degrees participate in, rather than divorce themselves from, the dominant culture of white, middle-class America. "The dominant culture," as Elizabeth Fox-Genovese writes, "challenged women and members of other excluded groups to frame their own experience at least in part according to its norms" ("Between Individualism" 12). Even "when the radical voice speaks about domination," bell hooks theorizes, "we are speaking to those who dominate. Their presence changes the nature and direction of our words" (146). The "nature and direction" of these texts invite us, in other words, to read them through a lens of gender.

Indeed, it was the discovery of a degree of thematic and formal similarity among these works published over a seventy-year span, about preaching careers that began around 1818 and continued through the 1880s, that led me to group these women and their autobiographies together. This similarity, I was soon convinced, originated in the common experiences of these preachers as nineteenth-century women who wrote within a "web of significance" (in Clifford Geertz's useful phrase) with which they interacted on complex levels, borrowing, manipulating, revising (5). By recognizing and emphasizing this web and the commonplaces of women's self-writing here, I am not suggesting that differences among these women are unimportant, or that matters of "spirituality, race, and gender" should always be isolated from each other (LaPrade 67). As Candis LaPrade has argued about Lee and Elaw, it was "their deepening understanding of themselves in relation to God" that "empowered" all seven of these women "to voice their concerns about social and political problems as well [as] their own spiritual well-being" (67). And it is evident that their faith also made possible their efforts to search for and assert their identities in autobiography. Reading these women's *Lives* through a lens of gender should not obscure matters of race or of grace. Applications of other categories of analysis have been completed by William Andrews, Catherine Brekus, Joycelyn Moody, and Carla Peterson, and other such readings could usefully complicate the close literary analysis that follows. My business, though, is to identify the ways of writing that these women shared. I seek here to gain a sense of their common spiritual journeys and literary strategies as evangelical women writing autobiography.

These commonalities arose, as I have said, from their similar positions within the gender politics of their time. But to raise the issue of gender is to risk another misleading exclusion, because many men who worked as itinerant preachers had experiences of marginalization quite similar to those of these women, and many male itinerants who wrote autobiographies employed some of the same literary strategies as the women used in making sense of their experiences. They did so for some of the same reasons— "nineteenth-century evangelicals believ[ing] that a true Christian experience was a shared one"—as well as for some that arose from their entanglement in a different, masculine "web of significance" (Brekus 173; Geertz 5). Like the seven women considered here, several nineteenth-century male evangelists, for example, obviously discovered in opposition and singularity a virtue to be embraced in their literary productions. In his autobiography of 1831, the Freewill Baptist David Marks tells us that he experienced "persecutions, in which professed Christians of various denominations, have taken an active part," and that such persecution was "part of [his] salary," a "bless[ing]" from God (5, 114). He also tells us that his reputation as the "boy preacher" attracted people to his ministry out of mere "curiosity" (56). The Methodist Heman Bangs acknowledges in his memoirs that many people were motivated to attend camp meetings not to seek salvation but to satisfy a nagging curiosity (7–8). The Christian Abraham Snethen, popularly known as the "barefoot preacher," consciously made himself a curiosity to attract large crowds, often crowds of hecklers who carried guns and called him "a wolf in sheep's clothing" (135; Matthew 7:15). The same was true for Lorenzo Dow and the Methodist itinerant James Horton, both of whom proudly bore the label "crazy" throughout their careers, knowing that the label itself—and the behavior that provoked it—only served to increase their prestige (Dow 52). And quite commonly, male itinerants like John Colby, David Marks, Heman Bangs, and Lorenzo Dow—comparing themselves to Jonah, Daniel, and that "speckled bird" Jeremiah—profess that they, too, were reluctant to accept God's call to preach (Dow 11; Jeremiah 12:9).

To some degree, any person who undertook the life of itinerant ministry in nineteenth-century America invited the puzzlement and opposition of their more conventional fellow citizens. To an even greater degree, any preacher who paid attention to the prophetic books of the Bible could be expected to recognize this opposition as an important bona fides, a kind of credential legitimating one's own prophetic status, and thus to make the most of it in his or her textual self-representations. Male preachers recognized this just as readily as did female ones; accordingly, some of their autobiographies share formal features with those of these seven women. But there is an important difference between a male preacher who *chose* to be a "speckled bird"—who chose, that is, to eschew the more conventional forms of ministry available to him through the established churches—and a female preacher who could not, without abandoning her call altogether, have been anything else. Here I am interested in how these women attempted, in their autobiographies, to make sense, and even literary virtue, of this hard necessity.

To frame this study in terms of gender does not deny that these female preachers also share literary habits with writers, male and female, who were not itinerant preachers in the nineteenth century. But to study the writings of these women in relation to one another has its own utility. Doing so has enabled me to see how a specific group of evangelical women organized their stories throughout the century; how they negotiated cultural codes in the construction of their identity and place in American culture; how they used their autobiographies to protect, promote, and understand themselves; how, in other words, they wrote the self and sought author(ity), or, as Nancy Miller has said in another context, how these autobiographers "perform[ed] on the stage of [their] text[s]" (*Subject* 49).

An Anchor Sure and Steadfast

This is, then, primarily a literary study, about poetics as much as about politics or history. In each chapter I consider how these women—all of them what James Cox would call "naive autobiographers" (unlike autobiographers who were writers by trade like Henry James and Mark Twain)—use language, images, metaphors, and literary conventions in their attempts to justify and advertise themselves and in the complex task of understanding the self and representing it in autobiography (127). I do not dismiss the possibility of learning something factual about the lives of these women, and of nineteenth-century women in general, from these autobiographies. There is usually no way to check the facts they report: though nineteenth-century evangelicalism was in general well-chronicled, and though some women preachers found their way into religious periodicals, church records, and memoirs by men of the age, their lives come to us primarily through their own efforts toward publication. But whether or not the autobiographies are factually reliable, they inevitably tell us a kind of truth about the "lives and times" they describe. To read "autographically" with an emphasis on *auto* (self) and *graphe* (writing) is not to exclude *bio* (life), Porter Abbott argues, but to consider *how* these texts reveal their authors and their lives. "Autobiography," said Mark Twain, "is the truest of all books";

> for while it inevitably consists mainly of extinctions of the truth, shirkings of the truth, partial revealments of the truth, with hardly an instance of plain straight truth, the remorseless truth *is* there, between the lines, where the author-cat is raking dust upon it which hides from the disinterested spectator neither it nor its smell . . . the result being that the reader knows the author in spite of his wily diligences. (qtd. in Abbott 610)

Indeed, despite their many difficulties in converting unorthodox *lives* into completed *Lives*, these women succeed in presenting to us—or perhaps they fail in concealing from us—a revealing picture of their complex situation.

That situation began, perhaps, with their first "wild vision." Their ministries were "inspired" by God: to prove it, they write stories of revelations. Zilpha Elaw, for example, becomes assured of her salvation in a vision: "One evening, whilst singing one of the songs of Zion, I distinctly saw the Lord Jesus approach me with open arms, and a most divine and heavenly smile upon his countenance. . . . From that day to the present I have never entertained a doubt of the manifestation of his love to my soul" (56). Reading the Bible in her closet, she has no need to look outside herself for interpretation: "When I had been contemplating the wonderful works of creation, or revelation of the mind and truth of God to man, by the inspiration of his prophets, I have been lost in astonishment at the perception of a voice, which either externally or internally, has spoken to me, and revealed to my understanding many surprising and precious truths" (75). Even though these women knew that Satan "could transform himself into an angel of light for the purpose of deception"—that interpreting dreams, visions, and voices was dangerous business—they relied on themselves to comprehend and make use of these messages from God (Lee 10). Had these women looked to the outside world to explain their "internal prompting[s]," they might well have been told to scorn such visions, that the voice they heard *was* that of the devil.

And, of course, theirs were lives of faith. So quite naturally, they use their autobiographies—with remarkably similar scriptural language—to describe the rewards of experiential Christianity. In fact, though these women rarely *cite* the Bible, they *use* it extensively in their writings as an avenue toward self-definition. (I will take up this topic in detail in chapter 3, but throughout *Some Wild Visions*, I attempt to reveal—in parenthetical citations—the extraordinary role God's Word played in both their lives and their stories.) Many make use of the words of Isaiah to explain what life is like when nurtured by God: "Behold, I will extend peace to her like a river . . . then shall ye suck, ye shall be borne upon *her* sides, and be dandled upon *her* knees. As one whom his mother comforteth, so will I comfort you" (Isaiah 66:12-13). One winter in Philadelphia, Jarena Lee was much "afflicted"; "But in the midst of it [her] peace was like a river" (63). After living under a "dark cloud for more than three weeks," refusing to obey God's call, Zilpha Elaw felt chastised: when she chose finally to walk in the path God put before her, Elaw's "peace again flowed as a river on a calm summer's day" (88). When Julia Foote "surrendered [herself] and all [her] interests into the hands of God," she, too, experienced "peace flowing as a river, even to overflowing its banks" (191). These itinerants found in Christ a hope that would serve, as Saint Paul told the Hebrews, "as an anchor of the soul, both sure and stedfast, and which entereth into that within the veil" (Hebrews 6:19). "My hope bloomed with the glories of immortality and eternal life," Elaw assures us; "it was the anchor of my soul, sure and steadfast" (113). Or, as Foote tells her "Christian Sisters," "What though we are called to pass through deep waters, so our anchor is cast within the veil, both sure and steadfast? Blessed experience" (227). That "anchor" was a faith derived from the promises of their "only earthly treasure," the Bible: "No matter how the tempter would come," Amanda Smith remembers, "I stuck to the word, and would say, 'But it is the will of God.' And it seemed every time I would say it, it was like a girdle to my faith" (Towle, Preface 11; Smith 129).

But their actual situation, a situation, in fact, enabled by a very "sure and steadfast" faith, was that of being "unsettled." They were, in the first place, itinerant ministers, preachers who had no fixed congregation or pulpit but instead traveled, sometimes over extensive geographic areas, delivering their gospel message whenever and wherever they could. Unlike some women preachers who surrounded John Wesley and unlike the main group of itinerant ministers in the nineteenth century, the (exclusively male) Methodist, Baptist, and Christian circuit riders, these women were assigned no territories or itineraries. Like eighteenth-century itinerants—particularly Quakers—and even such nineteenth-century male itinerants as the famous Lorenzo Dow (who was once rejected by the Methodist conference and later refused to take a circuit), they followed their own instincts, or leadings of the Spirit, in plotting their travels. For long periods of their lives, they were homeless and alone. As Jarena Lee describes it, "[I] felt myself to be like a poor pilgrim indeed; wandering through this world so wide; having to travel among strangers, and being poor and destitute; I was sorely tempted. My money was gone, my health was gone, and I was measurably without a home" (61). Most of them were also "unsettled" in a metaphoric sense that was familiar to the nineteenth century: they were unmarried, having never married or having outlived husbands and not troubled to locate successors for them.

In their autobiographies these evangelists seem for the most part proud of their "unsettled" condition, offering it as evidence of their devotion to God and their adventurous spirits. Lee's description of her poverty and homelessness quoted earlier, for example, concludes with the following: "But I rested on the promises of God. . . . Without having a dollar to help myself, I saw the Lord would verify his promise, bless his name for it" (61). Being "unsettled" physically and materially was the very thing Lee needed to prove to her readers, and perhaps to herself, that she was authorized by God and "settled" in Christ, both now and in eternity. As Zilpha Elaw had discovered even before she became an itinerant preacher, being "settled" made it harder to trust in God: "After my dear husband was buried, and I had become a little settled, I rather leaned to my own understanding . . . nor did the blessing of my heavenly Father appear to prosper this course; for I was constantly obliged to be under medical treatment, and yet grew worse and worse" (85). Following Saint Paul, in his letters to the Corinthians, these women would all say, as Elaw does on the title page of her Memoirs, "our sufficiency is of God" (2 Corinthians 3:5). Indeed, how could they prove to themselves and their readers that they had "settled" faithfully in Christ if their "sufficiency" were elsewhere?

Still, their very movement across spatial boundaries, for their opponents at least, looked a lot like self-sufficiency and was easily interpreted as a symbol for the disorder such women wrought in their culture's carefully applied gender and racial hierarchies. After a long season in Philadelphia, Lee recalls that her "mind soon became oppressed and craved to travel"; she interpreted this "craving" as a sign from God that it was time for her to take up her itinerant ministry once again (40). While it is impossible to know for sure whether God had his hand in the workings of her mind, it is certainly possible to recognize that travel afforded Lee and her sister evangelists a life of mobility, independence, and public engagement unknown to most women of the century, with the exception of prominent reformers and lecturers such as Maria Stewart, Sojourner Truth, Susan B. Anthony, Frances Willard, and Frances Ellen Watkins Harper, as well as lesser-known actresses, circus performers, and foreign missionaries.[25] And just as they sought to unite the world under the leadership of Christ, so, too, did these preachers struggle to break down the social and cultural boundaries separating blacks and whites, men and women. As Donald Mathews argues, in giving its adherents "a common language that acknowledged a common experience and a common obligation," evangelicalism fostered communication among the races and sexes ("Evangelical America" 29). Told by God to "deliver a gospel message" to the richest white man in Burlington, Zilpha Elaw bravely entered the unfamiliar territory and led the family to conversion (68). Stepping into—and often struggling for—a pulpit, itinerant women challenged traditional authority and served as a model of change, as a new model of American womanhood, black and white: this one faithful, confident, adventurous, capable, ambitious, and wonderfully mobile.

The Itinerant Self

Their itinerant lives helped them poetically as well. To read these stories is to recognize that all of these women in fact did possess, in James Olney's words, an organizing "metaphor of self" by which to unify their autobiographies. *Itinerancy*, the literal subject of these autobiographies almost throughout, is their controlling, and richly meaningful, metaphor as well. All Christians, of course, are supposed to be itinerants, "strangers and pilgrims" wandering this weary land (Hebrews 11:13; 1 Peter 2:11). The journey motif so popular among Puritans living in an age of exploration and emigration was no less popular among nineteenth-century Christians. *The Pilgrim's Progress*, John Bunyan's classic seventeenth-century allegorical narrative of the Christian journey, was among the nineteenth century's best-sellers, common enough, for example, to be placed beside the Grangerfords' family Bible in *Adventures of Huckleberry Finn*. And as any reader of Bunyan knows, that story has a definite ending. Christian does not just march *around* the Slough of Despond and the Delectable Mountains: he marches *through* them on his way *to* the Celestial City. Most journeys, while they may take the form of a promiscuous odyssey, leading one to places not on a proposed itinerary, have an end, or at least most pilgrims have an end in mind when they set out.

Christians deeply committed to their faith, these seven women (no less than their male counterparts) would have identified the City of God as their ultimate destination. Though writing an autobiography primarily about her preaching "below," Zilpha Elaw frequently pauses to profess her faith in the resurrection: "My own soul was filled with heavenly hope, which maketh not ashamed; my affections were set upon things above; my treasure was in heaven" (113). Writing of her renewed evangelical labors during the Holiness Revival of the 1870s, Julia Foote concludes, "When I drop anchor again, it will be in heaven's broad bay" (226). The others all express, frequently, the same sincere commitment, making of itinerancy a figure for the journey to the next world.

Before each of them could freely depart for that world, however, she must devote herself to ushering in a millennial age. The evangelical journey would end, they all thought, if only they could complete the work of converting and reforming the democratic nation and the world. They would all agree with Lee's assessment of her itinerant ministry: "The happy seasons I have seen are ever memorable to me, and my prayer is, that all Israel may be saved, not only from the trials of life, but from the power of hell" (89). These itinerant lives, then, symbolize as well the "business" of America, a "Redeemer Nation."[26]

Though these women routinely deny having any aspirations for ordination, their life-writings make clear that they did think, if only subconsciously, of theirs as a journey toward distinction. While Julia Foote claims that "man's opinion weighed nothing with

[her]," her text and those of her sister itinerants tell another story, that of women seeking recognition, particularly from the male opponents who sought to thwart their evangelistic ministries (208). Their mobility is thus a figure for their ambitions in the world of nineteenth-century evangelicalism and revivalism, a world that had given them a nearly unique access to both freedom and authority.[27] This is not, by the way, to imply that their expressions of faith were insincere: their theological convictions were quite as real and meaningful as their very human desires for mobility, success, and recognition. Itinerant evangelism for these women was a result of their deep faith in God, but it was also what the "North" was to Frederick Douglass in his *Narrative* (1845): it was freedom, and gloriously was it embraced.

But Douglass learned that Mason and Dixon's line did not mark the end of the color line and found that nominal freedom carried its own disappointments. So it was with the freedom offered these women by itinerancy. They were disciples of Christ, but what did that mean for a woman in the nineteenth century, when most public disciples were men? They were rootless women, having left behind not only their geographic and familial roots but their cultural roots as well. Their experiential faith and the words of Scripture could repeatedly reassure them of their place within Judeo-Christian history; each preacher could comfort the inner self with her deep and visionary relationship with God. But what about the external self, the self that had to live in a particular time and place in America, with particular cultural, social, and political conditions? Though they could find a "center" in the pages of the Bible, where they could read about and identify with other marginalized, persecuted individuals of faith, they would remain primarily outsiders within the landscape of both evangelical and secular America. Thus one sees at work in these texts two selves: one lost in Christ and sufficient in him, and one called by her culture to speak its languages, and even, it seems to me, to think in its terms. These women wandered quite often to the center of their culture and borrowed there some of its most prominent discourses. They did so hoping to make familiar their wild visions; to satisfy critics and justify the unorthodox lives that they had been "impressed" to lead; and to give definition—pattern and meaning—to an itinerant existence that defied the popular stories of white and black womanhood in nineteenth-century America. Itinerancy finally becomes, then, in all these autobiographies, the figure for that cultural wandering and for the writing process this condition imposed on them: the need to invade the repositories of established cultural meaning, even as they occasionally invaded established pulpits, in search of authority.

What they found in those repositories, they made good use of: in their efforts to articulate a new woman's story and promote themselves, these evangelical autobiographers appropriate old, meaning-ful stories with which their nineteenth-century readers were familiar. By combining the "female" paradigms of domesticity, "male" discourses of individual assertion and competitiveness, and biblical paradigms of the reluctant prophet and suffering savior, these writers simultaneously inhabit and subvert many assumptions about gender, race, and class. As Sidonie Smith argues in *A Poetics of Women's Autobiography*, "Fashioning her own voice within and against the voices of others, [the female autobiographer] performs a selective appropriation of stories told by and about men and women. Subversively, she rearranges the dominant discourse and the dominant ideology of gender, seizing the language and its powers to turn cultural fictions into her very own story" (175). In doing so, these writers give us an example of the powerful tension found in all autobiographical narratives: the tension, that is, between self-creation and the social construction of identity. This is not to suggest, however, that the women under study here were simply passive instruments being written upon by the central languages of their culture. Though their autobiographies illustrate the degree to which we are all constructed by history, culture, and language, they also demonstrate the degree to which a self-conscious architect can guide this "construction." "The other side of the unsettling notion that the self depends necessarily and helplessly on language for its creation," says G. Thomas Couser, "is that the vast repertoire of the language gives the self a high degree of freedom and flexibility" (250).

But one organizing metaphor of self (even a particularly good one) does not make a finished narrative, and the figure of itinerancy partly sabotages all these writers' gestures toward narrative order. The damage becomes especially evident near the end of their stories. "Endings" would have been a problem for these writers in any case: though they were all sincere in their expectations of the "last days" that they saw looming in the not-so-distant future, and of a final anchorage in heaven, for narrative purposes these "ends" are nearly useless. Their books could not, of course, end with death and resurrection; the telos of an autobiography is necessarily the moment of its composition, not the end of the author's life. And as for the kingdom of God on earth, like all their predecessors and successors in the continuing labor of Christian reform, these evangelists failed to bring it about, though not for lack of trying. They must end their stories, as they may well have ended their lives, still "strangers and pilgrims," pursuing an ending that kept receding before them as they moved. But these itinerant women, unlike some other Christian autobiographers, were also denied many of the merely secular and historical "endings" toward which they might have directed their stories. Though some white women had made enormous gains during the second half of the nineteenth century, their efforts for political equality little affected the lives of poor itinerant evangelists, white or black, who continued to walk outside the halls of power throughout the century. And as Carla Peterson argues in her study of nineteenth-century African American women writers and public speakers, "If such liminal spaces functioned as centers of empowerment . . . they also remained sites of oppression, separating the women from their 'homes' and 'native' communities, forcing an unfeminine exposure of the body, and thus further reminding them of their difference" (19-20). Though itinerancy symbolizes the freedom of these women's novel lives, it also reminds us of their exclusion from the centers of power in a culture that aggressively resisted the changes their mobility represented.[28]

Operating largely outside of institutional frameworks, and thus lacking the biographical and narrative landmarks (the occasions of public achievement and success, moments of unmistakable *arrival* from which autobiographical narratives usually issue and toward which such narratives usually proceed), these women were thus doomed to be "unsettled" in another sense, one that is revealed in their autobiographies more or less in the way Mark Twain has in mind in the passage I quoted earlier—revealed, that is, in spite of the authors' efforts to conceal it. Ultimately, the "remorseless truth" is that these autobiographers—though empowered by visions, Scripture, prayer, and faith in another, better world—were finally unable to make complete sense of their lives using the terms available to them in this world, in the dominant culture through which they moved and by which they were judged. Thus the freedom of itinerancy came at a high price: not far beneath the surface of these confident spiritual autobiographies, one can hear the voices of female itinerant preachers who wandered the margins of that culture seeking, but never really finding, a way back into *its* center.[29]

The hope of any autobiography is to tell a unified story that somehow represents the unified self behind it. The autobiographer, no less than the novelist, writes in search of both the story and the meaning. The search can be an easy one for the autobiographer whose life (or whose sense of the life) accords fairly closely with some established bio-graphical paradigm. If your story is one of "Conversion," of "Education," of secular success (or, for that matter, failure), of triumph or disgrace, then your culture provides you with an abundance of precedent to guide you in laying out the plot and meaning of your experience. But what if your life is one for which no single precedent fits exactly? By what will you be guided in tracing a plot, and discerning a meaning, in the welter of remembered facts that are the raw materials of autobiography? How will you undertake the "pre-autobiographical" task of conceiving a single, coherent self whose story is to be told?

This was the predicament of these women, and it was one that few of them com-pletely solved. Therein lies the deception, the concealment, in their autobiographies. For they wrote their books, sometimes at considerable length. They gave them titles that promise not only the facts about the "Ministerial Travels," "Labors and Experi-ences," "Vicissitudes"—and, in nearly every case, the *Life*—of the author, but the moral meanings of those as well. They claim to offer texts that are, as James Cox has phrased it, "equal" to the selves behind them (128). But all of them found this task difficult.

Of course, to some extent all of us make sense of our lives, unorthodox or not, by weaving an identity out of borrowed threads, out of the cultural materials at hand. And there is a certain freedom in not having a particular story to live out, a certain liberation in escaping cultural plots. The *stories* these women construct show us, however, how much the loss of—or the inability to discover—a representative *life story* is the loss of a useful fiction, the loss of a totalizing self-knowledge that enables men and women to give order to the chaos of existence. Ultimately, these *itinerant* autobiographies movingly reveal, if only "between the lines," what it was like to be an *itinerant* woman in nine-teenth-century America trying to make sense of the rootless life to which she had been converted and called, scouring the cultural landscape for precedents and paradigms with which to organize her story, and seeking a comfortable position of authority both in the evangelical world through which she traveled and in her writing. Wandering outside woman's sphere and never fully accepted in man's, these preachers were in some sense lost in American culture. Neither a comfortable sense of self nor a comfortable position in the evangelical landscape was available to itinerant women who felt forced to keep going and going. "When, oh! when will the day arrive that I can cut loose from the cares of the world and see heaven in view and experience glory in my soul," writes a seemingly exhausted Lydia Sexton (568). But like her sister evangelists, she believes she must "keep the ark moving" (568).

This is the place to mention, then, that Nancy Towle chose to place "the Judge's" interrogatory poem—"Say, female stranger, who art thou?"—near the end, rather than the beginning, of her autobiography. Her autobiography had succeeded in exploring the "wild visions" that initiated her restless journey far from home; indeed, it had suc-ceeded in reproducing some sense of her identity to her readers: she was an utterly unique and yet representative disciple of Christ, a woman characterized by a combination of motherliness, victimization, independence, competitiveness, and courage. But such a woman, Towle seemed to be acknowledging, might nonetheless have remained an enigma, even to "judges" who had reviewed all the evidence presented in her narrative. Her story was such a strange one that it inevitably generated for its readers more questions than answers. To many of them, who were "grieved" and disturbed by the itinerant women in their midst, the author was fated to remain, like the other six itinerants with whom she keeps company in these pages, a "stranger."

1

Breaking Up Housekeeping

Female Evangelists and Domestic Ideology

In my very Infancy, I had an awful regard for religion & a great love for
religious people, particularly the Ministers, and sometimes wept with Sorrow, that I was not a boy that I might have been one.

Elizabeth Ashbridge, *Some Account of the Fore Part*
of the Life of Elizabeth Ashbridge

Ah was born back due in slavery so it wasn't for me to fulfill my dreams of
whut a woman oughta be and to do. Ah didn't want to be used for a work-
ox and a brood-sow and Ah didn't want mah daughter used dat way neither. . . . Ah wanted to preach a great sermon about colored women sittin'
on high, but they wasn't no pulpit for me.

Nanny, in Zora Neale Hurston, *Their Eyes Were Watching God*

For I think that God hath set forth us the apostles last . . . for we are made
a spectacle unto the world, and to angels, and to men. . . . Even unto this
present hour we both hunger, and thirst, and are naked, and are buffeted,
and have no certain dwelling-place.

1 Corinthians 4:9-11

In 1855, having joined the African Methodist Episcopal Church, Amanda Berry experienced a remarkable vision: she saw herself preaching the gospel before a large crowd.
It seemed an unlikely notion, and not only because female preachers were rare in the
United States in the mid-nineteenth century. She was, for one thing, a backslidden
Methodist who felt she had lost most of the grace she received upon conversion; she
was also the wife of an irreligious man and the mother of his child—indeed, the vision
came to her as she was recovering from childbirth. Her responsibilities to her family
would seem to have had a prior claim over any call to go forth and preach. God, it
seems, could hardly have chosen a less likely candidate.

But when her first husband, C. Devine, never returned from the Civil War, Berry
saw the chance to effect a kind of compromise with God: instead of becoming a
preacher, she would marry one—James Smith, a "local preacher" of the Bethel A.M.E.
Church—achieving what many Protestant women in the nineteenth century thought
of as their best opportunity to do God's work: "One reason for my marrying a second

time was that I might have a Christian home and serve God more perfectly. . . . I had seen and known the influence of a minister's wife, and how much she could help her husband or hinder him to a great extent in his work. Mr. Smith said that was just the kind of wife he wanted" (57–58). "Marrying a minister," Leonard Sweet suggests, "was more than a blessed alternative to domestic humdrum and the humbug of social formulas, and more than the right to pick up the crumbs and bones of religious opportunity that dropped from the table of a husband's ministry. It was a passport to influence, deference, and power" (*The Minister's Wife* 8).[1]

But Amanda Smith's husband, at least in her estimation, turned out to be demanding, unsympathetic, and self-centered, and she never had the opportunity to gain "power" as a minister's wife. James Smith was devoted neither to God—his religious profession, she discovered, was entirely fraudulent—nor to his family: on several occasions he deliberately declined, or so she maintains, to provide even basic support for her and their children. He had nothing but scorn for her lingering desire to preach.[2]

Then, as is so often the way in the lives of these female evangelists, destiny took a hand. Thus does Smith usher her second husband out of her life and autobiography: "My husband, James Smith, was formerly of Baltimore, Md. He was for many years a leader of the choir of Bethel A.M.E. Church, in that city. Afterward he moved to Philadelphia, and was ordained deacon in the A.M.E. Church. He died in November, 1869, at New Utrecht, N.Y." (96). Smith's mastery of tone here is perfect and devastating; writing in an age that loved nothing more than a lachrymose deathbed scene, she sends her husband of five years[3] to his reward with all the passion of an overworked obituary writer. His inadequacy as a husband and a religious leader is underlined by Smith's dry irony. The passage continues: "Since then I have been a widow, and have traveled half way round the world, and God has ever been faithful. He has never left me a moment; but in all these years I have proved the word true, 'Lo, I am with you always, even to the end'" (96; Matthew 28:20). The contrast between her "faithful" God and her faithless husband is clear enough. By choosing at last to heed the call God issued years before, Smith had in effect married a third time, and successfully at last. She found in her life as an itinerant evangelist the best of both worlds: the freedom of a single woman, able to travel the world with perfect autonomy, following only the promptings of the Spirit; but also the security of a married woman, blessed with the most dependable of protectors and providers, a supporter rather than an enemy of her secular and spiritual ambitions.

Smith's brief account of her two unhappy marriages, and of her final acceptance of God as her provider and protector, repeats a pattern that may be found in all the autobiographies under study here; indeed, Smith's book, coming late in the tradition, reads almost like a synoptic version of the autobiographies that came before. Many of them involve a husband who is either irrelevant to the major narrative, like Smith's first one, or important only as an impediment to his wife's ministry, like Smith's second. And nearly all of them dispose of these husbands through the expedient of untimely death: a death that leaves the widow free to pursue her call to preach. Nearly all of them, that is to say, create and then dissolve an apparent conflict between domestic obligations and God's uncompromising call.

Domesticity in Black and White

To recognize this pattern in these autobiographies is to see the close connection between them and the enormously powerful nineteenth-century ideology of domesticity, by which many white, northern, middle-class women defined—and many other women measured—their lives. Itinerancy, obviously, put the women in this study at odds with an ideology whose central symbol was the home. Indeed, the itinerant lives led by these women, considered as cultural texts, as well as the *Lives* written by them, undermine domestic obligations and conventions systematically. Yet rather than reject domestic ideology out of hand, they ultimately, and successfully, transform it into a metaphoric discourse, a language that speaks to their own needs to lead "strange," mobile lives beyond the four walls of home.

This ideology has been ably described by the historians Nancy Cott, Glenna Matthews, Mary Beth Norton, and Barbara Welter. Let me briefly summarize their findings. In the eighteenth century, production in America was largely centered in the home, with most Americans living and working on farms rather than in cities. Husbands and wives worked together, producing food and clothing sufficient for the family's use. This arrangement meant that women shared in the economic functioning of the household. The onslaught of the industrial revolution and market capitalism, however, brought vast economic change to the new nation. Between 1780 and 1835, New England moved away from an agriculturally based economy to a more commercial and industrial one. Families moved to urban areas in greater numbers. Goods such as candles and cloth that were once produced by women in the home could now be easily and cheaply purchased in the market. Job opportunities lured men—and young, single women—away from the home, but most middle-class white women, though they were now freed from the responsibility of producing essential household goods, still remained at home working as housekeepers and mothers. Black women and poor white women were excluded from this transformation; some worked hard for wages, many still worked hard beside their husbands and brothers, and many were enslaved. Middle-class wives and husbands, mothers and sons, daughters and fathers, however, were now—with few exceptions—separated geographically into what became known in the literature of the day as the domestic sphere and the public sphere.

And an ideology quickly arose to explain these overwhelming economic changes to the nation's white middle class: the cult of domesticity and the related one of true womanhood. "The canon of domesticity," Cott argues, "encouraged people to assimilate such change by linking it to a specific set of sex-roles. In the canon of domesticity, the home contrasted to the restless and competitive world because its 'presiding spirit' was woman, who was 'removed from the arena of pecuniary excitement and ambitious competition'" (*Bonds* 67). Matthews adds that "turmoil and instability in the Jacksonian Age of the 1830s penetrated into a wide range of institutions and created great concern about social cohesion. . . . Not surprisingly, the home came to be seen as an especially potent symbol of integration at this time, valuable because it seemed to represent a haven of stability" (10). The home was the place to which men could return for solace after a hard day in the competitive countinghouse that America had become; it was the place from which America's socialized citizenry would emerge, young children having been nurtured and educated there by their mothers, who were practically and theoretically, if not legally, in charge of the home.[4] These women, though no longer producers in the household economy like their eighteenth-century foremothers, now became highly valued members of the culture because as wives and mothers they preserved the future of the nation in their new, politicized home. And although this domestic ideal, Donald Mathews argues, "eventually became a boundary to be maintained, rather than a quality to be prized," it "offered [women] honor and respect equal to that of men" (*Religion* 112). That respect was primarily relational: women were defined as daughters, sisters, wives, and mothers.

By 1850 the domestic sphere was thoroughly sentimentalized in literature as the locus of all that was good and moral and Christian about American culture. And just as the home became sentimentalized, so the women in charge of it became idealized in the ideology of true womanhood. Reading the popular literature of the day, Barbara Welter found that true women were above all else pious, pure, submissive, and domestic. Piety associated with women was nothing new to the nineteenth century. As early as the mid-seventeenth century, New England clergymen had begun to notice that the majority of their members were women. In 1692 Cotton Mather, commenting on the phenomenon in his *Ornaments for the Daughters of Zion*, proposed that women's participation in matters of religion stemmed from the pain they suffered as the daughters of Eve; such suffering led them to God for comfort (42). He also speculated that women simply had more time than men to devote to religion. By the eighteenth century, Enlightenment thought, with its separation of reason and emotion, the former highly valued and associated with men, the latter devalued and associated with women, asserted that women were more "naturally"—because more emotional—religious than men. Nineteenth-century thinkers adopted this view. "Christianity," Annie Wittenmyer argued in her popular *Women's Work for Jesus* of 1871, "comes to women with stronger claims than to men, because they are more spiritual, and have larger ability to apprehend its deep meaning and respond to its demands" (108). Women's faith is "quick, spontaneous, sincere, complete"; "little disturbed by theological controversy, not unsettled by varying theories, not startled by novel discoveries, she believes and enters into rest" (Wittenmyer 75-76). And as Welter discovered when analyzing the language of nineteenth-century hymns and revivals, "whether in the divine or human order, woman was constantly urged to be swept away by a torrent of energy, not to rely on her own strength which was useless, to sink into the arms of Jesus, to become absorbed and assimilated by the Divine Will" (*Dimity* 93). Historians of American religion concur that women in the century did become so absorbed, if not in the Divine Will, then at least in religion. Religion, it is argued, became "feminized."[5]

Purity was an essential virtue of true womanhood. Only women as pure as Samuel Richardson's Clarissa Harlowe could marry, and only married women and mothers could enjoy the privileges of domesticity. It was as wives and mothers that women could best be useful, demurely "influencing"—rather than debating—husbands in the home. But it was submissiveness—and by extension reticence, helplessness, and a complete lack of anger and ambition—that was the most important virtue of a true woman. "Men," Welter notes, "were supposed to be religious, although they rarely had time for it, and supposed to be pure, although it came awfully hard to them, but men were the movers, the doers, the actors. Women were the passive, submissive responders" (*Dimity* 27-28).

Women, many believed, were different from men; hence, they belonged to a different sphere, one that would preserve their delicate nature, one that would best make use of their difference. The ideologies of domesticity and true womanhood—which dovetailed nicely with the biblical injunctions of Saint Paul—then, fully explained the century's need for and glorification of separate spheres—one public and gendered male, one private and gendered female—which "provided a secure, primary, social classification for a population who refused to admit ascribed statuses, for the most part, but required determinants of social order" (Cott, *Bonds* 98). And though the cult of domesticity and true womanhood are often thought of as midcentury ideologies, clearly the "cultural prescriptions/proscriptions of true women as demure, compassionate, and soft-spoken fully spanned the nineteenth century (and still persist today)" (Moody 30).

For the many daughters of Eve who found themselves not so very different from the sons of Adam who felt called to preach, the dominant culture offered a choice: lead quiet lives in the home, repress aspirations for an existence beyond its walls, and keep passions and frustrations in check, or risk alienation and marginalization from the only spatial and social "place" that lent status—security and definition—to white, northern, middle-class American women. In the words of the prominent minister Lyman Beecher, "There *is* generally, and should be always, in the female character, a softness and delicacy of feeling which shrinks from the notoriety of public performance. . . . No well-educated female can put herself up, or be put up, to the point of public prayer, without the loss of some portion at least of that female delicacy, which is above all price" (qtd. in Miller, *A Claim* 50).

Now the ideology I have been describing possessed great explanatory and regulative power for many white women of the nineteenth century. But for the purposes of this study—half of whose protagonists are black women, and most of whom were poor—it is essential to recognize its usually unstated racial and class dimension. We need to recognize, that is, the complex and ironic relationship of excluded groups, especially African Americans, to the social order defined by domesticity. Under the ideologies of domesticity and true womanhood, all women were not created equal. "While free black people could marry, their participation in the institutions of parenthood and family," historians concur, was "severely compromised by their impaired civil states" and, particularly, by the discrimination and exploitation they faced in the marketplace (Tate 25). And as Jacqueline Jones argues, after the Civil War "whites feared that black people's desire for family autonomy, as exemplified by the 'evil of female loaferism'—the preference among wives and mothers to eschew wage work in favor of attending to their own households—threatened to subvert the free labor experiment" (45). All four of the black women in this study, for example, were born to poor parents who found it necessary to hire them out as domestic servants despite their tender ages, which made them prone, as Julia Foote's story illustrates, to physical and psychological abuse.[6] Two of them report how financial struggles as adults again forced them into service, Zilpha Elaw before her marriage and again after the death of her husband, Amanda Smith while married to and following the demise of James Smith; and both Elaw and Smith had to board their daughters or put them into service, a not uncommon answer to poverty among free African Americans before and after the Civil War.[7] Smith's financial situation often forced her into domestic service where her daughter Mazie was not welcome. She "boarded her . . . here a while and then there" (57). "Sometimes [Mazie] was well taken care of and at other times she was not," Smith remembers, "and when I would go and see the condition of my poor child, and then had to turn away and leave her and go to my work I often cried and prayed; but what could I do more?" (57). Later, when Smith traveled with the McGraw family to their new home in Wheatland, Maryland, she took Mazie and her six-month-old baby, Nell, with her, but the situation was difficult at best and ultimately devastating: "I had to do all the cooking for the house, and eight farm hands, beside helping with the washing and doing up all the shirts and fine clothes and looking after my children. . . . My baby seemed to get along nicely for the first three weeks, then she was taken sick with a summer complaint, and in six weeks I had to lay her away in the grave to await the morning of the Resurrection" (59-60). Not long thereafter, Smith's husband would lose his position as coachman to an Irish immigrant who was willing to work for lower wages. The oppression of black men clearly made it difficult for them to function effectively as heads of households, the sort that Amanda Smith longed for. These African American evangelists, then, like most black women of the century—slave and free—could not have been accustomed to the "radical split equating private with home and public with work" popularized by domestic ideology (Collins 47).[8]

In addition to the crippling effect of poverty on the creation and maintenance of the "traditional" home and family presided over by a "politicized" mother, crude stereotypes of black womanhood further alienated black women from the cults of domesticity and true womanhood. Unlike white women who were defined in the literature of the day as pious and pure, black women—slave and free, before and after the Civil War—were alternately characterized as immoral, lascivious, aggressive (Jezebels, whose sexuality ensured that their bodies would be protected neither by law nor by an ideology that idealized motherhood) or, at the other extreme, as extraordinarily submissive and nurturing (Mammies, who lavished attention on the white families who enslaved or employed them).[9] "Feminine attributes and functions of the black female body," Carla Peterson writes, "were . . . commonly represented in degraded terms as abnormal excessive sexual activity; and, when superimposed on masculine ones, led to the creation of a complexly ambiguous portrait of the nineteenth-century black woman" (20). Pejoratively defined by images that originated in, but were never contained by, the geographic or temporal borders of slavery, black women were excluded from the gendered ideologies that gave meaning to the lives of middle-class white women.

That is not to say, however, that black women were unaware of the ideologies of domesticity and true womanhood or that they rejected the dominant discourse out of hand. As Frantz Fanon persuasively theorizes in *Black Skin, White Masks*, "Every colonized people . . . every people in whose soul an inferiority complex has been created by the death and burial of its local cultural originality—finds itself face to face with the language of the civilizing nation; that is, with the culture of the mother country. The colonized is elevated above his jungle status in proportion to his adoption of the mother country's cultural standards" (18). Nineteenth-century black women, struggling to be acknowledged by the dominant culture—to be considered human by the colonizers—not surprisingly found bourgeois gender conventions particularly attractive, and particularly useful. Their relationship to the cult of domesticity was, then, like that of poor white women, one of desire.[10] Many black women hoped that by situating themselves within a cult that promised middle-class white women respect and power (albeit secondary), they could combat the dominant culture's enslaving stereotypes, protest racist and class injustice, and ultimately achieve full citizenship in the republic.[11] Both Harriet Jacobs, a fugitive slave, and Harriet Wilson, a Northern free black, for example, insist in their autobiographical narratives that the quest for freedom is a quest for a home, an ideal household, a sanctuary from violation, racial abuse, and economic exploitation, a place presided over by woman. Jacobs and Wilson were not alone in this quest for a situation idealized by the canons of domesticity. The personal writings of many free, nineteenth-century African American women, Frances Foster argues, reveal a desire for domestic authority ("Neither" 128).[12]

And as Martin Delany's *The Condition, Elevation, Emigration, and Destiny of the Colored People of the United States*, published in 1852, illustrates, black men similarly adopted the dominant culture's gendered language of domesticity as part of their emancipatory discourse. Black women, Delany argued, should confine themselves in their own homes:

> We do not say too much, when we say, as an evidence of the deep degradation of our race, in the United States, that there are those among us, the wives and daughters, some of the *first ladies* . . . whose husbands are industrious, able and willing to support them, who voluntarily leave home, and become chambermaids, and stewardesses. . . . We have nothing to say against those whom *necessity* compels to do these things, those who can do no better; we have only to do with those who can, and will not, or do not do better. The whites are always in the advance, and we either standing still or retrograding. (198–99)

The position of the entire race, Delany maintained, depends on the position of its women: "Our *best ladies* being washerwomen, chamber-maids, children's traveling nurses, and common house servants, and menials, we are all a degraded, miserable people, inferior to any other people as a whole, on the face of the globe" (199). Delany's expectations were shared by many African Americans. As James Horton discovered when exploring gender conventions among free blacks,

> Black liberation was often defined in terms of the ability of black women and men to become full participants in American life. Ironically, this not only meant the acquisition of citizenship rights, almost all of which were applied only to men, but also entailed an obligation to live out the gender ideals of American patriarchal society. . . . All women were expected to defer to men, but for black women deference was a racial imperative. (*Free People of Color* 116)

The necessity of combating the "black image in the white mind," of proving their humanity by proving their "whiteness," led black men like Delany to define black women according to the sexist ideology of middle-class whites; their efforts to elevate or "uplift" the race seemed to mandate their obeisance to the dominant culture and its ideologies of gender.[13] Black men began to interpret a woman's movement beyond the home—even into what historians now call the "informal" public sphere—as a transgression against the entire race. Amanda Berry Smith's decision to become an evangelist was further evidence of the degradation of all African Americans.

Escaping Domesticity

It is clear enough that the evangelical women whose autobiographies are considered here lived their lives largely in defiance of the ideologies of domesticity and true womanhood that dominated the mid-nineteenth century and whose influence extended well into the twentieth century. Their careers read almost like deliberate renunciations, point by point, of those ideologies. And, as historians have recently begun to recognize, these preachers were not alone in this renunciation: "Despite the rhetoric of separate spheres, women were active participants in shaping civil society. An ideology of domesticity may have shaped women's self-perceptions, but it did not determine their destinies" (Brekus 13).[14] Though most of these itinerant women were at some point married, the circumstances of their lives eventually led them into experiences not contemplated by the marriage plot—abandonment, widowhood, unavoidable self-reliance. Many of them finally lived out a kind of anti-marriage plot: the major phases of their lives—their careers as preachers—begin where the marriage plot leaves off. Their real stories begin where they ought to end, with the protagonist married and securely ensconced in what looks like a happy home. God's call and the failure or inability of the husband to act his part in the domestic arrangement push plot beyond the conventional ending and ultimately require the protagonist to reverse the terms of the conventional story of courtship. Hers becomes a progress away from marriage, security, and institutionally sanctioned purity and toward the unsettled condition of a single woman, the insecurity of homelessness, and the "promiscuity" of a woman who regularly presents herself in public. Stepping outside the profile of true womanhood, these heroines traduced its most sacred terms: they were not passive but active, seeking confrontations with both Satan and secular opponents; they exerted their moral influence not by the indirection of example and insinuation but by direct exhortation of the wicked.[15] And, most obviously and most important, they were compelled by their circumstances to replace the central metaphor of *home* with the countermetaphor of *homelessness*, or itinerancy, as their religious communities called it. So far as one can determine, there was no particular system or method behind these inversions of domesticity, and—if the autobiographies these women wrote are at all reliable—many of them regarded their forcible ejections from the domestic ideology with considerable alarm and confusion. God's call, or circumstance, thrust them into unmapped territory, a kind of ideological vacuum that provided few referents by which to make sense of their lives.

Of the writers under study here, Nancy Towle seems to have found this vacuum least uncomfortable. Printing her autobiography, *Vicissitudes Illustrated in the Experience of Nancy Towle, in Europe and America*, in 1832, Towle appears to have experienced few qualms while boasting of her extraordinarily unconventional life far outside the "required determinants of social order" (Cott, *Bonds* 98). Reading her story, one would hardly be aware of her culture's idealization of domesticity and woman's place in the home, either as a personal experience or as a ruling ideology, for Towle is noticeably silent on the issue. She admits an initial reluctance to preach, doubting her ability to promote "God's righteous cause"; and she claims to have worried briefly about her ability to "face a frowning world" and "endure" the life of "a solitary wanderer through the earth, far, far, from every friend, and no more a certain dwelling place, beneath the sun" (12; 1 Corinthians 4:11). But she never once questions whether public preaching is a justifiable pursuit for women, particularly "'in these last days'" before the millennium (12, 15; Hebrews 1:2). Towle would have been aware of a conflict between her public calling and the domestic commitments of most women of her age—an age, after all, in which nine out of ten American women were married, and in which single women "were institutionally marginal to the increasingly nuclear family of the bourgeoisie, and ideologically marginal to Victorian social beliefs, which stressed the biologically determined female role of marriage and motherhood" (Smith-Rosenberg, *Disorderly Conduct* 160). Perhaps this explains why a reluctant Towle experienced a "visible decline in health": "While I saw my flesh decaying, and eternal things, as it were, impending, with how much more comparative ease, said I, could I now resign my life . . . than to go up and down the earth, to be made a gazing-stock to an ill, misjudging world" (16, 17; Hebrews 10:33). But Towle recovers, becomes a teacher "as a sort of screen," and begins to preach with the support of female preachers among the Freewill Baptists (19). Though she admits that her first attempt to preach to a large assembly failed because of her "fear of man," she continues in the work out of a great desire to prove the validity of her call: "I desired now to live especially for one thing," she assertively pronounces, "to vindicate my own cause to the world of mankind, and to see the host of gainsayers confounded before the LORD" (22). Late in the autobiography she mentions the case of Mrs. Elice Miller Smith, according to Towle the most admired female preacher of her day: "Since her *confinement* by marriage," Towle reports, Smith "had not that religious enjoyment which she formerly had known" (184, emphasis added). Towle, whose divine call came in the form of a "longing *desire*" to preach, is obviously glad to have avoided Smith's fate, glad to have "forsake[n] [her] kindred and [her] home, and through the waste-howling desert of a sinful world, '*testify the*' GLAD TIDINGS '*of the grace of God*'"(11; Deuteronomy 32:10). But she makes relatively little of this escape, concentrating matter-of-factly on her ministerial labors and plainly expecting her readers to do the same.

But Towle was preaching and writing early in the century, when women were a prominent part of the evangelical landscape. Numerous sects battled for control of the nation's Christian population, availing themselves of any tools they could find, even women preachers. According to Brekus, "By 1830, female preachers were more visible, more popular, and more aggressive than ever before" (276). Towle, more than any other autobiographer in this study, frequently mentions the names of famous women preachers she meets in her travels, names she expects her readers to know: Clarissa Danforth, Martha Spaulding, Judith Mathers, Elice Smith. Such women met with opposition, but in an age in which preaching was frequently authorized by prophetic gifts rather than education, in which millennial expectations led male leaders to see the nation and the century as exceptional and therefore not subject to the strictures of tradition, in which lay leadership was an important part of the sectarian movement, women preachers with an authoritative call from God were unusual but not aberrant.[16] Towle published her autobiography just before the sects that relied on female preaching—the Methodists, Freewill Baptists, and Christians—began to envision "their small, countercultural churches" as "successful denominations" with an educated ministry (Brekus 271). Adopting the dominant culture's proscriptions of women's public speaking, these sects began to oppose the gifted women who, quite "ironically," had "helped build their sects into respectable, middle-class institutions that no longer welcomed their labors" (Brekus 284).

The African Methodist Jarena Lee, though her first autobiography appeared in 1836, just four years after Nancy Towle's, seems almost to have inhabited a different age, one in which the claims of "spiritual gifts" were becoming enfeebled, and those of domestic confinement were gathering strength. Lee's autobiography reveals a condition of cultural displacement that was little known to Towle but was the common affliction of all the other women under study here.

From life by A Harfy.

Printed by PS Duval.

MRS. JARENA LEE.

Preacher of the A. M.E. Church.

Aged 60 years on the 11th day of the 2nd month 1844.

Philada. 1844

Jarena Lee. Frontispiece to *Religious Experience and Journal of Mrs. Jarena Lee* (1849). Courtesy of the American Antiquarian Society.

Lee responds to this sense of disorientation by placing at the center of her narrative the conflict that created it. In both versions of the autobiography (*The Life and Religious Experience of Jarena Lee, a Coloured Lady*, printed in 1836 and 1839, and the *Religious Experience and Journal of Mrs. Jarena Lee*, printed in 1849), she personifies the authority of domestic ideology in two major characters, her husband and the Reverend (later Bishop) Richard Allen. Sometime around 1811, Lee reports, she heard a voice commanding her to "'Go preach the Gospel!'" (10; Mark 16:15). She took this voice to be that of Satan; so she went to a "secret place" and applied to God for advice, whereupon she saw "the form and figure of a pulpit, with a Bible lying thereon" (10). Though interpreting this vision was easy enough, mounting a pulpit and preaching the gospel would be far more difficult. For the path to the pulpit was first obstructed, at least as Lee tells it, by the imposing figure of the Reverend Richard Allen, then minister of the Free African Society, soon to become the Bethel African Methodist Episcopal Church. And Richard Allen, when asked if Lee could preach, said no.

Meanwhile, Lee reports, she married the Reverend Joseph Lee, whereupon it became necessary for her to "remove" from her home in Philadelphia, where she had experienced "sweet fellowship" with a congenial band of fellow Methodists, to the nearby village of Snow Hill, where she knew no one but her husband (13). The suggestive verb "remove" might remind us of that prototypical narrative of Indian captivity, *The Sovereignty and Goodness of God . . . Being a Narrative of the Captivity and Restoration of Mrs. Mary Rowlandson*, in which each stage of the heroine's forced journey from her Christian home into the godless wilderness is termed a "remove." Lee's removal to Snow Hill serves in her autobiography as a figure for a general loss of control that necessarily attends her participation in the marriage plot: once married, she becomes an object, moved by her husband's needs and desires rather than her own. And Lee's account of her sojourn in Snow Hill, of her marriage to Joseph Lee, and indeed of all her struggles against the ideology that made it difficult for her to accept God's call, does essentially comprise one long story of "Captivity and Restoration."

Of course, it is not simply the coercive power of Joseph Lee and Richard Allen that enforced this captivity; Lee recognizes that she herself had internalized the domestic ideology, creating a psychological problem that prevented her from answering the call: she is initially "glad to hear" that the Methodists disapproved of women's preaching (11). But as a narrative strategy, she personifies that ideology in those two patriarchs. The text of her autobiography becomes at last an instrument of her revenge on them: the seven years of her marriage to Lee, the birth of her children, and her continued frustration by Richard Allen are shrunk to fit a single chapter, entitled "My Marriage"; it sits, like a pause for breath, between two longer ones: "My Call to Preach the Gospel" and "The Subject of My Call to Preach Renewed." Lee invites us to recognize that the marriage plot and all that went with it caused her eight-year failure to obey God's call, and caused, moreover, the dissipation of her "holy energy" (11). Like Mrs. Elice Smith, Jarena Lee found that domesticity and religious energy did not easily mix.

Lee's textual revenge is actually even more complete than it first appears, for only three of the ten paragraphs in "My Marriage" actually concern her life with Joseph Lee. The rest is devoted to "restoration," a process that begins when—as occurs over and over in these autobiographies—the frustrated female preacher falls into "a state of general debility . . . so much so that [she] could not sit up" (14). In all likelihood, William

Andrews speculates, Lee suffered a nervous breakdown, paralyzed by a situation that frustrates her deepest desires; in any case it was a "sickness," Lee remembers, from which "I did not expect to recover, and there was but one thing which bound me to earth, and this was, that I had not as yet preached the gospel to the fallen sons and daughters of Adam's race, to the satisfaction of my mind" (14).[17] The rest of "My Marriage" is strategically devoted not, as the chapter title would imply, to domestic matters regarding her husband and children but to the completion of her "restoration"—that is, the untimely deaths of her husband and four other family members, which moves the now chastened Lee to follow God's injunction at last.

Free to leave Snow Hill, a sorrowful Lee returns to Philadelphia, at which point in the autobiography she begins to narrate a powerful victory for herself. Moved by "a fire shut up in [her] bones," a holy energy that threatened to destroy her if it were not released, Lee finally extracts from Richard Allen permission to hold prayer meetings and to "exhort" the children of God (15; Jeremiah 20:9). But a year later, dissatisfied with her home ministries and still anxious to try her hand at preaching, she stands up in the middle of a service at Bethel and spontaneously—at least that is how she puts it in her autobiography—exhorts the congregation. We can only wonder how much her exhortation was a "supernatural impulse" and how much was a deliberate calculation on the part of a woman long denied her goal of preaching (17). Certainly, the scene in the autobiography calls our attention to her deep faith, but it also demonstrates quite forcefully her resourcefulness and her desire to interrupt, literally in this case, the dominant discourses that would deny her voice.[18] Whatever the cause, the tactic works: Bishop Allen is so impressed by her words that he finally grants her permission to preach the gospel (and, indeed, supports her throughout much of her career, traveling with her and inviting her to preach at conferences, giving her appointments to preach at Bethel Church, interceding on her behalf in the face of opposition, and caring for her son during her travels). "I now began," Lee writes, "to think seriously of breaking up housekeeping, and forsaking all to preach the everlasting Gospel," which indeed she does from 1818 until at least 1849 (18). Thus, with God's help and by her own willingness to confront her patriarchal captors, is Jarena Lee "restored," not, as in Rowlandson's case, to the "House-keeping" from which she can, as Moses admonished, "'Stand still and see the salvation of the Lord,'" but to the itinerant life that had been in her dreams long before her removal to the domestic fires of Snow Hill (Rowlandson 111, 112; Exodus 14:13).

From this point on in the 1836 narrative and particularly in the 1849 edition, Lee insists on her status as an untrue, undomestic woman. The second edition is five times longer than the first, but it contains no more information about Lee's personal or family life. The eighty-odd additional pages are devoted to her evangelical labors, one of which, interestingly, was to preach to her husband's former congregation in Snow Hill (33). Though Lee writes about periodic reunions with her mother, sister, son, and grandchildren, and expresses "relief" when her son recovers from a serious illness, she does not—at least in the pages of her autobiography—"grieve with him in later years over the untimely deaths of his children" as Carla Peterson maintains; she reports their deaths matter-of-factly, reminds herself and her readers of the wisdom of relying on "God's Will," and then goes about the business of reporting her evangelical labors (C. Peterson, 74; see Lee, Religious Experience 91, 88, 96). And though she may have "maintained close parental ties with her son," she does not emphasize strong familial bonds in her story (Peterson, *Doers* 74). The meaning of her life, the autobiography's structure suggests, inheres not in the domestic sphere, not even in her undoubtedly close relationship with God, but in her successful career as an itinerant preacher, as a lone woman bearing the word of the Lord across the threshold of the home, across the racial and gender boundaries that warned her to keep quiet and keep still.

The *Lives* of Zilpha Elaw, Julia Foote, Lydia Sexton, Laura Haviland, and, as I described at the beginning of the chapter, Amanda Berry Smith follow a similar pattern of captivity and restoration. All but Lydia Sexton and Laura Haviland narrate their struggles with disagreeable husbands who oppose their ministries; Foote's husband even threatens to imprison her in a "crazy-house" (196). All save Towle (who never married) and Sexton (whose husband was extraordinarily supportive of her mission, staying at home with their children, maintaining their household, and often traveling with her) structure their stories to show how the death of a spouse and God's persistent demand that they "break up housekeeping" facilitated their exit from the constraints of domesticity and their entry into an adventuresome preaching career (Sexton 368). At times in these narratives the relationship between the evangelist's frustrated will and the husband's untimely death starts to look like cause and effect: when Zilpha Elaw details her husband's opposition to her new role as "public speaker," we are not surprised to hear her immediately report, "My poor husband's health about this time began visibly to decline" (84). Elaw goes on to say that God rescued her from her work in domestic service and in teaching—indeed rescued her from debt—by forcing her to preach: "my captivity," Elaw joyously announces, "vanished" when she decided at last to take up the cross and preach the gospel (88). Awakened, then, to a living God and to her own inner resources, each of these women identifies herself as a preacher who knows how to enter the competitive world of nineteenth-century evangelicalism. "Breaking up housekeeping" inevitably leads Jarena Lee, Nancy Towle, and the rest of the women in this study to break up what Nancy Miller calls the cultural "plots and plausibilities"—the fictions, in this case of domesticity and true womanhood—that hold women captive ("Emphasis Added" 339).

Having effected that escape, these autobiographers are able to write identities for themselves that must have astonished adherents to the literature of true womanhood. The women who appear in these autobiographies are not the submissive, selfless, demure creatures described in the sentimental novels of the day. In arguing this I take issue with Jean Humez, who, in her study of five black nineteenth-century women preachers, maintains that conversion led to a "conquest of angry, malicious, revengeful feelings, as well as fear, and replacement of those with 'love for God and all mankind'" ("'My Spirit Eye'" 134). Certainly the black women in my study, and their white contemporaries as well, seem fearless, and as evangelical Christians, they claim that "conversion manifests itself in all kindness and love, happiness and sunshine to all" (Sexton 357). Once converted, Elaw reports that she was able to meet her mistress's "reproofs without the exhibition of [her] former resentments and saucy replies" (58). But these autobiographies, including those also studied by Humez, also reveal a strain of anger and assertiveness that even conversion and a visionary relationship with God could not erase from their lives or stories.[19]

In her autobiography of 1882, Lydia Sexton, for example, portrays her relationship with her mother as far from the ideal one described by the ideology of true womanhood. Her widowed mother hastily remarried in 1811 and agreed to adopt her husband's children and "shove off" her own (64). Lydia was sent to the home of her uncle Jacob Casad, where she was treated as a servant. At this point in the narrative, Sexton reports, "I thought it very strange that mother should shove me off in this way. Orphans indeed, without father or mother, know the cold world has but little sympathy; but for a mother with ample means at her disposal to treat me thus was a mystery to many more than myself" (64). But later in the text, concluding an account of her mother's death, she loses her struggle to keep resentment beneath the surface: "Fare thee well, mother dear," she writes; "rest in peace in thy deep, damp, dark grave" (174). To be sure, she quickly recovers her composure: "I trust," she continues, "thy released spirit is enjoying the society of the just made perfect, the glorified spirits, and best of all, our dear Redeemer" (174). But it is clear that Sexton viewed the autobiography as an opportunity to release her own spirit, and to settle a score or two as well. Of Henry Enoch, a relative by marriage and by all accounts a reprobate, Sexton writes, "I should bury his foibles in oblivion and proclaim his virtues on the house-tops if he had any" (181). Much later in the autobiography, after she has begun describing her work as an itinerant preacher, she asks the reader to "imagine [her] feelings" when she is denied a license to preach by the United Brethren and another man takes credit for her labors: "There stands the man who boasts before conference of having taken sixty members into the church, when God had made me the instrument in his hand of doing that same work. For my work, which was reported by him, he is honored; and the recommendations held by me, who did that work, are laid on the table" (401). A pious woman, Sexton assures us, need not be self-effacing.

Similarly, Julia Foote still seethes with anger and a desire for revenge years after her own confrontations with the Reverend Beman and the men of the African Methodist Episcopal Zion Church. Threatened with excommunication from her church for her professions of holiness and desire to preach, she requests an "impartial hearing" from the Conference: "In my simplicity, I did think that a body of Christian ministers would understand my case and judge righteously" (207, 208). She finds, however, that in the Conference justice is reserved for men. Borrowing the language of the *Dred Scott* decision of 1857, a decision she expected her black brethren to remember, she insists on her rights and calls attention to the slavery of sex: "My letter was slightingly noticed, and then thrown under the table. It was only the grievance of a woman, and there was no justice meted out to women in those days. Even ministers of Christ did not feel that women had any rights which they were bound to respect" (207). As a character in her story, Rev. Beman, moreover, has no rights Foote is bound to respect. Portraying him as a weak patriarch fearfully clinging to his pulpit, Foote achieves, if not justice, then a textual revenge not only on Beman and the men of the A.M.E. Zion Church but also on the ideologies of gender that would excommunicate women from the communion with a wide world beyond the home.

But of course their most notable act of self-assertion, the most striking attack on the ideologies of domesticity and true womanhood, was the publication of their autobiographies, stories that enabled them once again to seize a pulpit, to reinterrupt the dominant discourses that denied them a place and a voice outside domesticity. "To justify the unorthodox life by writing about it," Nancy Miller suggests, "is to *reinscribe* the original violation, to reviolate masculine turf": "To build a narrative around a character whose behavior is deliberately idiopathic . . . is not merely to create a puzzling fiction but to fly in the face of a certain ideology (of the text and its context)" (*Subject* 52, 26). These autobiographers would have understood that assertion; writing in the nineteenth century, they would have known, "as would any literate woman, expressive restrictions so stringent and so ingrained that they amounted to a culturally endorsed and culturally monitored feminine community of expression" (Dobson xii). Women were welcome in the literary marketplace, but all traces of women's independence or deviance from gender norms were to be studiously erased from their manuscripts. To do otherwise was to risk becoming, in the words of Nina Baym, "the occasion for a generalized gender terror" (*Novels* 266). This was, as we have seen, a risk they were willing to take. They understood that "writing–for publication–represents entrance into the world of others, and by means of that passage a rebirth: the access through writing to the status of an autonomous subjectivity beyond the limits of feminine propriety" (Miller, *Subject* 55). For Nancy Towle, autobiographical writing was more than a useful means by which to convert others; she speaks of her writing as a pious Christian might have spoken of the Bible: it "had been," she confesses, "a sort of life-buoy to me; both upon the land, and on the sea" (109).[20] It was, moreover, a source of pride for this itinerant evangelist who vainly admits that she harbored great hopes of meeting in heaven everyone who had "seen the '*Vicissitudes Illustrated of my Life*'" (11).

Though no doubt aware that many Christians simply published their private journals in the nineteenth century, most of these women attempted to organize their journals into autobiographies proper, a genre they recognized as more self-assertive and more public (masculine) than the diary. However, for all but Sexton, Haviland, and Smith, who wrote in the latter half of the century and found publishers for their books, the quest to communicate with the world through the written word was not easy. For example, Jarena Lee's status as the first woman licensed to preach under the auspices of the African Methodist Episcopal Church would seem to have lent her story historical, even institutional, significance. Yet no publisher, evangelical or otherwise, offered to publish her autobiography. Publishers were unwilling to support literary endeavors that would re-create and *fix* in print a woman's "original violations" of man's spatial and social turf. But Lee, Towle, Elaw, and Foote were undeterred by this absence of support. They issued their stories at their own expense, thereby demonstrating an extraordinary degree of confidence in themselves and in the value of their unorthodox experiences as Christian women. Julia Foote, writing in 1879, even asserts that her book is no less important and meaningful than the Word of God: "If anyone arise from the perusal of this book, scoffing at the word of truth which he has read, I charge him to prepare to answer for the profanation at the peril of his soul" (226). Confident in their ability to bear not only the "Word" of God but also their own words, these seven, decidedly undomestic women entered the literary marketplace with texts that *call* us to reconsider our image of the woman writer in nineteenth-century America.

The Household of Faith: Rewriting Domesticity

Breaking up housekeeping, these female evangelists also broke away from an ideology that had confined them spatially, socially, and culturally. They went on, as we have seen, to write autobiographies that not only suppress references to the domestic but also call attention to behavior "unbecoming" a woman (Elaw 131). Itinerant preachers, they were literally and figuratively "homeless," having taken seriously both the command of Christ—"he that taketh not his cross, and followeth after me, is not worthy of me" (Matthew 10:38)—and the words of the apostle Paul, who enjoined them to "be not conformed to this world: but be ye transformed by the renewing of your mind, that ye may prove what is that good, and acceptable, and perfect, will of God" (Romans 12:2). "Perhaps many will think," Sexton acknowledges of her decision to preach, "that I should have consulted my husband first; but I realized the full import of these words, 'He that loveth father, mother, brother, or sister more than me is not worthy of me.' I felt indeed that the ratio of my temporal to my spiritual duties was no less than that of time to eternity" (226; Matthew 10:37). These women knew well that she who lost her life—with its familiar patterns and identifiable meaning—for the sake of Christ, would find it (Matthew 10:39). "When supreme self is melted away by faith," Laura Haviland learned, "our spiritual vision becomes clearer" (12).

Ultimately, and inevitably, however, Nancy Towle, Jarena Lee, and their sister itinerant evangelists *were* lost without some familiar cultural referent that applied specifically to women of nineteenth-century America, despite the clarity of "spiritual vision." "To the extent that the autobiographical text can be thought of as a mirror," Margo Culley argues, "it is a mirror gazed at in public" (9). Indeed, no matter how courageous and independent these itinerant preachers were, they never could cease to see themselves through the gaze of a demanding, critical public, which found in women's "immodest" appearances on public stages cause for great alarm. These autobiographers were intensely aware of the suspicion that they excited in their public: knowing well how a woman's appearance in the pulpit would be received, they routinely claim to shrink from God's call because of their fear of public scrutiny or, as they so often put it, because of their "fear of man," their "man-fearing spirit" (Towle 22; Sexton 217; Proverbs 29:25). Having rejected the plot for which many poor black women longed and by which many nineteenth-century white women were defined, these female itinerants were no doubt fearful that they were in a sort of no-(wo)man's-land, being neither male nor female. And they would face countless hecklers who would tell them just that: you are "not a woman," the A.M.E. preacher Jarena Lee was told, "'but a man dressed in female clothes'" (23).[21] Or as an opponent of women's preaching put it to Lydia Sexton (of the significantly denominated United Brethren), God made "'roosters to crow, not hens'" (396).

The hectoring, critical voices of their enemies were sometimes echoed by inner voices, speaking in similar accents. "I thought," Sexton reports, "if I were only a man it would be no hardship to me, nor even a cross, to preach, but rather a pleasure. But for me, a woman, to preach, even if I could; to make myself a subject of ridicule and comment among my friends and kindred": "Thus for ten long years did I debate and falter and hesitate, and, like Jonah, trim my sails for Tarshish" (213). Lydia Sexton refers here to a fear common among prophets of all ages, common in fact among many of her male contemporaries, who quite naturally felt somewhat unprepared for a task that would render them socially marginal, but her comment reminds us that women called to preach faced a challenge that a Jonah, Lorenzo Dow, David Marks, or Heman Bangs could hardly imagine. "Forsaking *all* to preach the everlasting Gospel" surely meant more to these women than leaving home and family; it meant—as Jarena Lee discovered when she was accused of being a man in disguise—forsaking their very identities, particularly their sexual identities (Lee 18, emphasis added). And for the African American women in this study—Jarena Lee, Zilpha Elaw, Julia Foote, and Amanda Smith—it meant the loss of an identity that they had only begun to negotiate with the dominant culture, which had long regarded black women as just the sort of "grotesque" creatures who would immodestly expose themselves before a "promiscuous" assembly. In the words of Hazel Carby, "They had to define a discourse of black womanhood which would not only address their exclusion from the ideology of true womanhood but, as a consequence of this exclusion, would also rescue their bodies from a persistent association with illicit sexuality" (32). Failing to conform to the standards of domesticity, black women risked confirming the racist stereotypes that they and their black male contemporaries struggled to defeat.[22]

No matter how radical, then, each of these autobiographers ultimately availed herself of a publicly accessible and publicly valorized language, which in the case of nineteenth-century women meant the language of domesticity and true womanhood, a language broadly employed by all manner of women who left their homes to engage in the "business of benevolence," to work for social reform, to promote women's rights, and even to work with men in the Civil Service (Ginzberg 36).[23] They could hardly have done otherwise. Though these preachers, unlike their more domestically-minded sisters, claim to have no home in the world, to be "strangers in a strange land," they necessarily participated in a historically specific context (Exodus 2:22, 18:3). "Whatever else modern anthropology asserts," Clifford Geertz has argued, "it is firm in the conviction that men unmodified by the customs of particular places do not in fact exist, have never existed, and most important, could not in the very nature of the case exist" (5). Or, as historian Elizabeth Fox-Genovese puts it, "We know ourselves through the languages available to us and the languages that we know inescapably influence what we perceive ourselves to be" ("Between Individualism" 25). Though these daring women clearly conceived of their autobiographies as opportunities to voice a critique of the ideologies of domesticity and true womanhood—to "reviolate masculine turf"—they inevitably borrowed the culturally familiar ("customary") language of domesticity in their efforts both to understand and "know" themselves and to justify their lives to an age that regarded them with considerable suspicion. Thus domesticity, forcibly ejected from these women's lives, found its way back into their *Lives*, providing there a necessary element of narrative style and structure.

A case in point is Zilpha Elaw's spiritual autobiography, *Memoirs of the Life, Religious Experience, Ministerial Travels and Labours of Mrs. Zilpha Elaw, an American Female of Colour*, published in London in 1846. The bow that Elaw executes in the general direction of domesticity is a relatively simple maneuver, though an effective one. Rather than quarrel with her culture's expectations for women, she freely embraces them. Even after leading an exciting and independent life as an itinerant minister both in America and in England, Elaw maintains throughout her autobiography that women are by nature inferior to men and in need of their supervision.[24] She insists that she "never durst take any important step without first consulting [her] superiors," nor "could [she] possibly understand how [her] ministry . . . involved any dictation or assumption of authority over the male sex" (69, 147). She lashes out with particular vigor against independent women who do wish to rule both themselves and men: "the fancied independence and self-control in which they indulge," she insists, "has no foundation either in nature or Scripture"—those seemingly unambiguous textual guides to God's will (61). And unlike many of her contemporaries, she makes little effort to reinterpret Paul's strictures against female preachers: "In the ordinary course of Church arrangement and order," Paul's words apply. However, she continues, "the Scriptures make it evident that this rule was not intended to limit the extraordinary directions of the Holy Ghost, in reference to female Evangelists, or oracular sisters"—directions such as she herself had received (124). She accepts her culture's rules about the subordination of women and claims for herself the status of exception. A true woman's place, Elaw maintains, is in the home, where she is governed by men, defined by relations, and responsible for the socialization of America's children; but in her own highly unusual case, these restrictions do not apply because she has been chosen by God. She frees herself from the restrictions against women posited by Paul and the ideology of domesticity while simultaneously, by failing to critique Paul's restrictions, reinscribing herself within that ideology.

It is an Emersonian moment in the autobiography—and found in the autobiographies of many of her contemporaries and many of her medieval visionary foremothers, a moment no doubt common to visionaries of all ages. And, like Emerson's ideology of liberation, it is simultaneously conservative and radical. It does not challenge hegemonic conceptions of women's roles in nineteenth-century culture; most women, according to Elaw, should be guided by "nature and Scripture" to piety, purity, submissiveness, and domesticity. And it is certainly elitist, for are not those elevated by the "Spirit" an elite, a righteous remnant? And yet it is revolutionary; for who might not be called to that elite, and what changes might it not accomplish, on the authority of the "Spirit"?[25]

In fact, though Elaw tries hard to avoid treading on the general rule of women's silence, she ends up doing exactly that. Her autobiography in many ways undermines the stance she so persistently and forcefully maintains. Susan K. Harris, in her study *19th-Century American Women's Novels: Interpretive Strategies*, gives us a way to consider the paradox of Elaw's narrative. Borrowing from the work of Roland Barthes, Jacques Derrida, and Gerald Prince, Harris persuasively argues that the oft-belittled nineteenth-century sentimental novels can be and were read "in a multilayered, gender-specific mode" (30). In other words, these novels function for the reader on two levels. There is the "cover story," which presented to the public the hegemonic ideology of domesticity and true womanhood; but there is also a subversive plot, in which this ideology is undermined. In Susan Warner's *Queechy*, for example, the cover story of a young, orphaned heroine rescued from a life of hard work and poverty by marriage to a wealthy English gentleman is at odds with the bulk of the novel, which emphasizes the girl's courage, strength, and competence in the face of seemingly countless difficulties.[26]

A similar montage of cover story and subversive story can be found in Elaw's spiritual autobiography. The cover story presents a woman no different from her readers in accepting her subordinate position in her household, even to the point of "meekly" and "silently" coping with her husband's challenges to her religious authority (63). But the narrative as a whole describes a powerful, visionary woman who traveled extensively, withstood excessive opposition, and entered the public sphere through her preaching and her writing. She titles her work *Memoirs of the Life, Religious Experience, Ministerial*

Travels and Labours of Mrs. Zilpha Elaw, and, as in all the autobiographies in this study, the travels and labors dominate the text. Fully two-thirds of the autobiography is given over to mind-numbingly detailed accounts of Elaw's travels in America and England and of her tremendous success therein. She assures us that she had no part in choosing a career beyond the home and that she has never been other than a "true" woman—both in her relations with her male superiors and as a "vessel designed for honour, made for the master's use" (66). But the text, whose 110 pages are taken up mainly with the travels of a highly independent and adventuresome woman, betrays these assurances. What she gave with one hand to her century's idealization of the domestic sphere—and women's submission within it—she took away with the other.

In the autobiographies of Jarena Lee, we can see a slightly more sophisticated version of Elaw's approach. Lee, too—though fully capable of deconstructing the Pauline prohibitions against female preaching—at times claims to be simply an exception to generally valid restrictions on women's lives. She reminds skeptical readers that "as unseemly as it may appear now-a-days for a woman to preach . . . nothing is impossible with God" (11; Luke 1:37).

But *explaining* God's radical plots was, if not an impossible, then surely a daunting assignment. It could, for example, impose embarrassments to which the author can respond only with silence. Lee, for instance, tells us at the end of "My Marriage" that she has two surviving children. One she never again mentions in either edition of the autobiography; we never even learn the sex of the child, let alone its name or what became of it. The other, a son, she left with her mother when she took to the road as an itinerant preacher. We hear of him thrice more, once when he commences his education with Bishop Allen, again when he is converted, and when Lee sorrowfully writes about the death of his child. These odd silences about her children and family life surely reveal Lee's defensiveness about her willed homelessness in a culture structured by the gendered division between work place and home place, about her decision to ignore the pleas of a Martin Delany and "voluntarily leave home."[27] Perhaps Lee found that "while the culture tolerated and . . . even admired writers who were also mothers, it denied these women the possibility of recording their struggles as mothers. The myth of maternal love rendered such a record taboo" (Reimer 208).[28]

The one instance in which Lee violates this taboo is telling. Apologizing to her readers for leaving her son behind so that she can attend to the business of God, she begins speaking from a rhetorical space within the cult of domesticity: "During that time I kept house with my little son, who was very sickly. About this time I had a call to preach at a place about thirty miles distant, among the Methodists, with whom I remained one week, and during the whole time, not a thought of my little son came into my mind; *it was hid from me*, lest I should have been diverted from the work I had to do, to look after my son" (18, emphasis added). Lee carefully selects the passive voice here. Her audience must not think that she deliberately put aside thoughts of her ailing son. She is not an unnatural mother. Without help and compulsion from God, the ultimate patriarch, who called her to "keep house" with "the fallen *sons and daughters* of Adam's race," she would have been unable to forget her own son (14, emphasis added). What looks like independence on her part, she assures us, is really just the opposite. Living outside the cults of domesticity and true womanhood, whose dictates applied primarily to northern, middle-class, white women, Lee here lays claim to the dominant culture's rhetoric and maneuvers, in the course of this apology, to a new space on the margins of those ideologies. She reconstructs herself as a "coloured lady" so that she locates and occupies, for a time, a cultural corner where the otherwise separate spheres overlap.[29]

This was the territory Lydia Sexton searched for in her 1882 autobiography. Her 655-page tome hides behind a subtitle forty-five words long, not one of them, oddly, a first-person pronoun: *The Story of Her Life through a Period of over Seventy-two Years, from 1799 to 1872. Her Early Privations, Adventures, & Reminiscences. Clouds and Sunshine, As Child, Wife, Mother, and Widow; As Minister of the Gospel; As Prison Chaplain. Her Missions of Help and Mercy.* This onomastic overload, whether written by Sexton or her publisher, certainly de-emphasizes the unfeminine assertion of self that autobiography necessarily entails. By virtually compelling us to think of her in terms of her relational roles, this title seeks to assure readers that Sexton occupies comparable positions in the private domestic sphere. Her careers as minister and prison chaplain were secondary, and even they, the title's final words suggest, are in woman's proper sphere of "helpmeet." But the length of the title betrays a certain defensiveness; it invites us, moreover, to consider her autobiography, like Elaw's, as multilayered, to keep an eye peeled for the subversive plot beneath the "cover story" of Sexton's domesticity. And, in fact, the auto-biography does finally emerge as the story of a woman who *shed* her relationships to make room for her lifework; Sexton deletes, as it were, her personal life to make room in the text for her career. She writes so little, for example, about her husband, Joseph Sexton, that we are left to imagine him rather as Hawthorne imagined Ann Hutchinson's husband, "who is mentioned in history only as attending her footsteps, and whom we may conclude to have been (like most husbands of celebrated women) a mere insignifi-cant appendage of his mightier wife" (23–24). Sexton's autobiography seems to imply what Margaret Fuller said explicitly in 1855: "If any individual live too much in rela-tions . . . he becomes a stranger to the resources of his own nature" (119).

Still, Sexton dutifully and lengthily recounts for her readers her reluctance to obey God's command that she preach, because "that was not woman's place"—either spatially or so-cially (208). "Woman," Sexton argues to herself, "was made a helpmeet for man, and she ought to know she was not called on to help in the ministry" (368). Thus had she been taught to think, by the ideology of domesticity and, of course, by the King James Bible and nearly two thousand years of Christian patriarchal misinterpretation of Hebrew Scrip-ture. But Sexton, extraordinarily, was able to recognize her imprisonment within that ideology and was able to recognize the ideology itself as a cultural construct: "I was so fixed in my ideas and conceptions of my duties and sphere of action by my early training, that my prejudices yielded very stubbornly to my convictions—indeed little short of alarm at my very unpardonable neglect of Christian duty" (208–9). To recognize one's preju-dices as such is not necessarily to dismiss them, as Sexton appears to have realized; her prejudices, like most, including those of her imagined readers, prove rather stubborn. But to recognize the *constructedness* of such prejudices *is* to open up the possibility of *recon-structing* them, which turns out to be the project of Sexton's long autobiography. Since neither "prejudices" nor "convictions" will give way entirely, Sexton's job—both in living her life and in writing it—was to manage some negotiation between them.

Torn between those two powerful motives, Sexton took up her cross and entered the ministry only after suffering ten years of poverty, "despondency," and, finally, the ill-ness of her son (223). "I surely felt," she reports, "this affliction to be a dispensation toward me, and that if I permitted the love of my family to intervene between me and the full performance of my duty one of the idols of my heart would be torn away from me" (223). God would spare her child only if she left her home and family to preach his word. And so this loving mother reluctantly agrees to accept her "duty" beyond the home, to embark upon a highly public life, for eminently domestic reasons. "If I could feel that I could reach heaven," she confesses to her husband after she began preaching without his knowledge or consent, "I would prefer to die now than to preach; but for me there was no peace in time nor eternity aside from the performance of duty in the work my Master had assigned me" (226). By arguing that she accepted God's call both to save her family and to obey her father in heaven, she simultaneously endorses and violates the domestic creed, and justifies her own departure from it, indeed uses the very terms of the creed to effect that departure.

Having learned this useful maneuver, Sexton employs it repeatedly in the text. When another son, Thomas, dies, Sexton is absent on a speaking tour. And though she was undoubtedly overwhelmed by such a loss, she tells her readers that she had to continue to preach. Sexton defends her absence, when a Mrs. Hammond, who had "all the warm emotions of a mother's love but without the pressing call of the Spirit to the ministry," criticized her (343). She does so, however, not as a radical bourgeois individualist might, with protestations of her rights as woman, but with an appeal to the sovereign God who called her away from the son she loved, an appeal that inventively invites her readers to consider domesticity as more than a literal condition. Domesticity could be used in her autobiography, quite effectively, as a metaphor to explain both her work and the purpose of evangelicalism. As she informed Mrs. Hammond,

> if you were working for God, in a work that would tell to your advantage and the advantage of hundreds of others of the *human family in time and eternity*, or if thereby you were an instrument in the hands of God in waking them up to see their dangerous condition by nature and practice . . . if your motive-force was to promote the glory of God and the salvation of never-dying souls, you would then feel as I do. (343, emphasis added)

Both her faith in God's call and her command of domestic ideology make it possible for her to order her life—and even cope with her losses—by accepting an essentially new set of priorities. At another point in her text, Sexton writes that she has heard news—false, as it turns out—of her son Zadok's death. Rather than stop preaching and head for his home, she "attend[s] to [her] Master's business," keeping the preaching appointment she had made, knowing that she would be accused of being an "unnatural mother" (590). Sexton abandons her family, but only to be a dedicated spiritual mother to all humankind in this millennial age. She employs the language of domestic ideology that placed motherhood at the center of all that was good, even as she rejects the role that language would prescribe for herself. She discovers a place on the frontier between the sphere of domesticity and that of the informal public. Like most evangelicals, male and female, she compliments older women in the field by calling them "Mothers in Israel," a term which assured readers that she had not strayed far from Scripture or from the popular ideologies of the day: Mothers in Israel "helped to spread the Christian faith through their nurture of the family of God" (Sexton 190; Brekus 151). The term also, and significantly, however, implied that they were women of valor and strength: the two women in the Bible given this title were "powerful women who took on leadership roles outside of the patriarchal household" (Brekus 152; see Judges 5:7; 2 Samuel 20:19).[30]

What Sexton is developing is not so much a rejection of domesticity as a radical redefinition of it: her "domestic" obligations to the children of God continually push her outside the confines of her actual home. Preaching primarily in the 1840s and 1870s, Julia Foote develops this strategy fully, in her autobiographical sketch, *A Brand Plucked from the Fire* (Zechariah 3:2), published in 1879. Foote embodies the claims of domesticity in her husband, an unsanctified man who opposes both her profession of sanctification and her call to preach. She finds herself torn between her religious beliefs and her domestic obligations, between God and her husband. Should she be a true woman, pious in the home, obedient to Saint Paul, and submissive to her husband, or a faithful visionary, obedient to God who called her elsewhere? Should she meekly abandon her call to preach the gospel or boldly pursue it? "It was difficult for me," writes Foote of her relation to her husband, "to mark the exact line between disapprobation and Christian forbearance and patient love" (197). But God provides her with the verbal formula that dissolves this conflict: "'For thy Maker,'" he tells her, "'is thine husband'" (197; Isaiah 54:5). With this phrase Foote states the theological solution toward which all her sister autobiographers had been groping. Borrowing a figure from the Bible, she reconstructs the canon of domesticity, transporting it from the realm of social prescriptions to that of metaphor. Once this transformation is effected, literal domestic relations virtually disappear from Foote's narrative: George Foote, for example, reappears only once, when Julia—with her grief notably restrained—reports his death at sea. He is replaced by another demanding patriarchal authority, another master and husband, but one who provides for and protects his "wives" who are busy *mothering* "the human family in time and eternity" (Sexton 343). Foote mothers this family even in the autobiography, where she frequently addresses "Dear children," "Parents," and "Mothers" (170, 172, 179). Long stretches of the autobiography are then devoted to elaborating this brand of domesticity. Foote's God, for instance, is not only a husband but also a lover: Describing one particularly wild vision, she writes, "My hand was given to Christ, who led me into the water and stripped me of my clothing, which at once vanished from sight. Christ then appeared to wash me, the water feeling quite warm" (203).

"Thy maker is thy husband," God tells Foote; therefore, the whole world is "home," and every converted soul is a son or a daughter. The elaboration of this pattern is the work of many of the autobiographies under consideration here. Many evangelical sects, "searching for the right words to explain their position in American culture, . . . chose to describe themselves as 'families' linking believers together in closely knit communities" (Brekus 154).[31] Even Zilpha Elaw, who never quite rejects the literal meaning of domesticity, is happy enough when circumstances lead her into the realm of this popular evangelical metaphor: "I was now accounted a full member of the [Methodist] society, and privileged with the communion of the Lord's Supper. In *this happy home* I continued nearly seven years, and only parted from it when I left my situation. In the year 1810, I surrendered myself in marriage to Joseph Elaw" (61, emphasis added).[32] Elaw is forced out of this happy and blissful home temporarily, during her thirteen-year marriage to Joseph Elaw, but after her husband's death, God replaces him admirably. The "household of faith" is able to supplant all other social connections for her: "Knowing myself to be an adopted child of divine love," she remembers, "I claimed

God as my Father, and his Son Jesus as my dear friend" (106, 60). Such a family, unlike the literal one to which she "surrendered," is infinitely capacious; each new convert is invited in. Having converted a young woman who had once opposed her, Elaw concludes: "Thus one of my enemies became my child in the gospel, and my sister in the Lord" (106). So, too, does God become a father and husband. During her baptism she finds herself "completely lost and absorbed in the divine fascinations" (61). These fascinations, like Foote's, are marked by a most certain passion and sensuality: "An overflowing stream of love filled my soul, even beyond my utmost capacity to contain, and I have thought, when in such ecstacies [sic] of bliss, that I should certainly die under them, and go to my heavenly father at once . . . for I could not imagine it possible for any human being to feel such gusts of the love of God, and continue to exist in this world" (58).

It is Amanda Berry Smith, as I suggested at the beginning of the chapter, who made the most of this literary strategy of "marrying" God and placing him at the center of her "domestic" life in her *Autobiography* of 1893, just as she may well have benefited most, psychologically speaking, from the "gusts of the love of God" that blew her way after her conversion and sanctification. Born a slave and forced into domestic service throughout much of her life, Smith found her difficulties increased by her marriage to James Smith, who would not provide for her, if we believe Amanda, or could not, as was often the case among free black laborers discriminated against and economically exploited in nineteenth-century America.[33] The contrast between Smith's hapless spouse and her divine provider and protector is marked. Upon the death of one of her babies, Smith believes that her "husband would meet [her] at the cemetery, as it was but a short distance from where he lived. I hoped he would be able to come that far; but no, he was not there. O, I could not describe the feelings of that hour. *God held me Himself*" (125, emphasis added). Even stronger is the contrast between James Smith's stubborn will, which usually frustrates Amanda's, and God's benevolent will, which invariably coincides with that of his servant. Early in her narrative, Smith tells us that she trusts God so much that despite her poverty she abandons her decision to accept a position as servant, when the Lord says to her, "'Go Preach,'" "for it was not the will of the Lord for me to confine myself as a servant in any family, but to go and work in His vineyard as the Spirit directed me" (148, 149).[34] At one point Smith badly wishes to stay in a home that boasts a luxurious featherbed, but she dutifully submits the matter to God— who turns out precisely to share her taste in sleeping arrangements. "Oh," Smith exclaims, "how wonderfully God provided for me" (257).

God's extraordinary, husbandly solicitude for his evangelists is one of the most common ideas in these autobiographies. He not only provides for them economically and ensures their comfort but also, at least as these autobiographers recall things, is not at all backward about protecting them from their many enemies—an astonishing number of whom seem to have experienced extreme misfortune not long after offending a female evangelist. The God of these narratives is the God who addresses his righteous remnant in chapter 54 of Isaiah, one of the most frequently quoted and paraphrased chapters in these autobiographies: "No weapon that is formed against thee shall prosper; and every tongue *that* shall rise against thee in judgment thou shalt condemn" (Isaiah 54:17). When Lydia Sexton is "abused" by a Brother S. and some other Copperheads "on account of [her] Abolitionism," she simply trusts the Lord to "bring him down into the pit of destruction" (540; Psalm 55:23). A bit later Brother S. quarrels with his church, and the members refer the dispute to God for disposition: "When they arose [Brother S.] was as pale as death. Within one week he was a corpse. Somehow or other many in that community thought it was a providential interposition" (540–41). The antislavery activist and preacher Laura Haviland, who often refers to the timely deaths of slave owners, writes also of a man who had been "empowered to arrest [her]," but who "died of cholera—a singular coincidence" (205). Merely to disagree with these women, it seems, was to risk serious trouble with their divine protector.

Such a protector was a useful thing to have, for the world of itinerant ministry was a surprisingly violent and dangerous one. Abraham Snethen reports that "men usually brought their guns to church with them, and many times did they shoot at a mark while I would be preaching, and sometimes they would curse me to my face, calling me a wolf in sheep's clothing" (135; Matthew 10:16). Such an environment occasionally called for decidedly "masculine" responses. Peter Cartwright—a thoroughly pious Methodist, to all appearances—proves that his is a manly pursuit when he recounts several instances when he found it necessary to wade into a crowd of listeners, locate the heckler who had disrupted his sermon, and beat the miscreant senseless.[35] Afterward his sermons would proceed, usually without further disturbance. Cartwright's solution to the problem of opposition was usually unavailable to female evangelists, and the ideology of true womanhood, with its demand of silent suffering and endless forgiveness, would have forbidden it in any case. But with their usual resourcefulness, these women discovered when writing their lives other ways of punishing their opponents, ways that positioned them, as was so often the case, both inside and outside the dominant cultural paradigms of the day.

Lydia Sexton, for example, uses her autobiography to document a protracted conflict with a preacher who once supported her, but then entered a formal complaint against her at the quarterly conference. She decides that she must confront him in person—"Either myself or somebody else must be condemned"—but God directs her to Scripture: "For it *was* not an enemy *that* reproached me; then I could have borne *it*. . . . But *it was* thou, a man mine equal, my guide, and mine acquaintance. . . . As for me, I will call upon God; and the Lord shall save me. . . . But thou, O God, shalt bring them down into the pit of destruction: bloody and deceitful men shall not live out half their days; but I will trust in thee" (424; Psalm 55:12–23). Here she finds courage in typology (a strategy I will discuss further in chapter 3). And as Brekus contends, while "this violent God held little appeal for liberal, reform-minded Christians . . . he clearly served the psychological needs of female preachers. Longing for the reassurance that God would punish their adversaries, they searched for evidence of his anger as well as his compassion" (215). Sexton can easily rely on God to "sustain the right and put down the wrong" and remain at the same time true to Catharine Beecher's strictures against woman as combatant (424). Rather than always speak of their anger and frustrations directly, Sexton and her sisters also displace those "un-feminine" emotions onto God, thereby achieving outside the domestic sphere the gendered division of labor that prevailed inside it. They would have the reader believe that *they* do not punish the hecklers who disrupt their worship services, the male clergy who shut them out of their meetinghouses, or husbands who refuse to support their calling or oppose them outright. The response, though fully justified, is God's. Once again these autobiographers enjoy both the security of domestic conventions and the freedom to reinterpret them radically.

What these books do, then, is reject the apparent, literal meaning of the "text" of domesticity but then rescue that text—and their own autobiographical texts as well—by recasting it as metaphor. Rather than try to ignore the vast cultural consensus amid which they had lived all their lives, they attempt a radical reinterpretation of domesticity—a potentially subversive rereading of a canon whose apparent meaning they could not accept but whose authority they could not altogether reject.

Your Daughters Shall Prophesy: Rereading Scripture

To understand their project in these terms is to recognize perhaps surprising affinities between these American "Bible Christians" and the biblical "Higher Critics" of Göttingen and elsewhere, whose challenges to the literal reliability of the Bible were among the scandals of the age. Some of these evangelists—despite their exclusion from formal theological training—actually do attempt a bit of Higher Criticism, though they question not the authority of the Bible, in the manner of Strauss and Renan, but its interpreters. Struggling to maintain their positions as itinerant preachers, the women in this study often look to the prophet Joel: "I will pour out my spirit upon all flesh; and your sons and your daughters shall prophesy" (Lee epigraph; Sexton 253-54; Joel 2:28). And, as these women knew, Joel's prophecy did come to pass on the day of Pentecost (Acts 2:16). Many remind their readers that "God hath chosen the weak things of the world to confound the mighty" (Elaw 92; 1 Corinthians 1:27), that "nothing was impossible with God" (Lee 11; Foote 200; Luke 1:37), and that God must not be "straitened" [sic] (Lee 11). They argue, in other words, that they were exceptions to Paul's injunction for women to "learn in silence with all subjection" (1 Timothy 2:11).

While eighteenth-century women had to transcend their gender in order to preach, to be in Paul's words "neither male nor female," many of these itinerants "affirmed that women had a right to preach as *women*," and they turned to the Bible for evidence (Galatians 3:28; Brekus 14, 15). Using a familiar phrase from the Gospels, Sexton argues, "Make sport and laugh as we may, we cannot revoke God's decrees; for it is said that heaven and earth shall pass away, but the word of God shall endure forever" (254).[36] These seven women recognized, however, how easily the word of God could be misappropriated by men who would bring "disjointed passages out of Scripture to bear them out" (Foote 193). As a result they were often forced, like Jarena Lee, to document their labors as evidence that God has called them to preach: "If he has not," Lee asks, "how could he consistently bear testimony in favor of my poor labors, in awakening and converting sinners?" (12).

But Julia Foote writes that she was often distressed by the fact that a woman called to preach "will be believed [only] when she shows credentials from heaven" (209). Such distress leads her to search the Bible for precedents of women's prophesying and preaching, thereby anticipating the revisionary acts of twentieth-century feminist theologians.[37] She would have agreed with Zilpha Elaw, who confidently claims that "the illumination which accompanies our perusal of the Scriptures" is in direct "proportion to our measure of grace," a measure that Elaw believed she had: "The Scriptures ever develop new and surprising truths to the regenerate soul" (132). In a chapter entitled "Women in the Gospel," Julia Foote assures her readers that she has discovered a number of such "truths," stemming from the fact that not all translations of the Bible can be trusted: "The same word, which, in our common translation, is now rendered a 'servant of the church,' in speaking of Phebe (Rom. xix. 1. [*sic*]), is rendered 'minister' when applied to Tychicus. Eph. vi. 21" (209; Romans 16:1). Nancy Towle analyzes the various uses of the word *prophesying* in the Bible, particularly as they applied to women: "I hence became satisfied for myself," she confidently records, "that according to the Scriptures the word 'prophecy' implied not only the foretelling of future events, but often related to public testimony . . . whether produced by the energies of either sex, male or female" (15-16). The Protestant Reformation had empowered them to interpret God's word—in its various translations—for themselves, to their own "satisfaction" (Lee 14).

Angered by those who would have it that women in the Bible *prayed* and *prophesied* but never *preached*, several of these women look to other authorities. Towle juxtaposes her interpretations with those of the itinerant Lorenzo Dow, who, in a prefatory letter to her autobiography, provides substantial evidence from the Bible of women's preaching. Towle also draws upon the authority of "Commentary on Holy Scriptures," by the well-known English critic Adam Clarke (1762-1832), whose work was widely reprinted in the United States and beloved by Methodists and women for its favorable interpretations of passages of Scripture that related to a woman's right to preach: "'That no preacher can do more, every person must acknowledge,'" Clarke argued; "'because to *edify*, *exhort*, and *comfort*, are the prime ends of the Gospel ministry, If *women*, thus *prophesied*; then women preached'" (Towle, Preface 9).[38] Confronting an elder and opponent in Salem, "West Jersey," Jarena Lee, too, calls upon Clarke: "And here let me tell the elder . . . I have heard as far back as Adam Clarke's time, his objections to female preaching were met by the answer—'If an ass reproved Balaam, and a barn-door fowl reproved Peter, why should not a woman reprove sin?' I do not introduce this for its complimentary classification of women with donkeys and fowls, but to give the reply of a poor woman, who had once been a slave" (23).

Most often, however, these women had no need to rely on the scholarship of others. "Did not Mary *first* preach the risen Saviour," Jarena Lee asks her readers, "and is not the doctrine of the resurrection the very climax of Christianity . . . ? Then did not Mary, a woman, preach the gospel? For she preached the resurrection of the crucified Son of God. But some will say that Mary did not expound the Scripture, therefore, she did not preach. . . . To this I reply, it may be that the term *preach* in those primitive times, did not mean exactly what it is now *made* to mean" (11-12). These women urge their readers to remember that "the first preachers of the resurrection were women" (Elaw 132). Lydia Sexton, fearful of becoming a female preacher, claims to have opened her Bible hoping to find there evidence *against* female preaching, evidence that would "justify [her] conduct" in refusing God's call, but she is sorely disappointed: "As I perused my blessed Bible I saw that in all ages of the world the good Lord raised up of his own choosing, men, women, and children, Miriam, Deborah, Hannah, Huldah, Anna, Phebe, Narcissus, Tryphena, Tryphosa, Persis, Julia, the Marys, and the sisters who were workers with Paul in the gospel" (214). Taking up her Bible the morning after she had taken up her cross to preach, Sexton is directed to the passage "'Arise and thresh, O daughter of

Zion'" and "felt renewed"; having searched the Bible, she could now easily see that she was just one such daughter who had arisen to thresh at God's command (226, 227; Micah 4:13).

Less often, these women defend their right to preach by referring to their foremothers in the eighteenth century, usually Sarah Crosby and Mary Bosanquet Fletcher, the pious Methodist who was recognized as a preacher by John Wesley and whose "life story became must reading in nineteenth-century American Holiness circles" (Hardesty et al., "Women in the Holiness Movement" 228).[39] Though there were numerous women in America as well, in both the eighteenth and nineteenth centuries, who preceded these seven preachers in the field of evangelism, they never call upon them, as Jarena Lee and others call upon Fletcher, as evidence that preaching by women was not "something new" (Lee 38).

They do, and significantly, apply forceful cultural critiques to the biblical precedents that their research uncovers. "When Paul said, 'Help those women who labor with me in the Gospel,'" Foote caustically observes, "he certainly meant that they did more than to pour out tea" (209; Philippians 4:2–3). Like many of the women in this study, Foote understood that Paul's injunction for women to "be in silence" was *never* meant to apply to all women (1 Timothy 2:12). Rather than reject the Bible in the manner of an Elizabeth Cady Stanton, Foote reinterprets it, at once challenging the patriarchal misreadings of Scripture that oppose her right to preach and critiquing her culture's ideology of domesticity, which restricts women to a superficial life—by millennial Christian standards—of drawing-room rituals and household chores. Disturbed by a woman who had a "talent" for preaching but lacked the courage to "break up housekeeping," Lydia Sexton makes use of Scripture to show why women must make use of their talents: "Oh, how I wish [Sister Elizabeth Fox] would cut loose from every incumbrance and go into the work in good earnest. . . . What a pity that such talents should be buried in a napkin!" (368, 522). Women "impressed with the call to the ministry" should no more bury their skills than servants, according to the familiar parable, should hide their "talents" or "pound[s] . . . in a napkin" (Sexton 522; Matthew 25:25; Luke 19:20). In the final chapters of her autobiography, Foote includes, in a somewhat unusual gesture for evangelical autobiographers, several exhortations, one specifically addressed to her "Christian Sisters," whom she calls forth to labor for God: "Sisters, shall not you and I unite with the heavenly host in the grand chorus? If so, you will not let what man may say or do, keep you from doing the will of the Lord or using the gifts you have for the good of others. . . . Be not kept in bondage by those who say, 'We suffer not a woman to teach,' thus quoting Paul's words, but not rightly applying them" (227). Nancy Towle, writing almost fifty years earlier, blames education for a lack of spiritual gifts among women and hence in churches generally; women, she believes, are taught to see themselves as subordinate and hence unfit for anything but domestic rituals. Echoing the radical eighteenth-century feminist Mary Wollstonecraft, Towle concludes with the following promise: "'I wish to deliver up my life, a sacrifice, for one, towards remedying these evils; and seal my testimony, as with my blood, in vindication of the rights of woman!'" (241).[40] She prays for the day in which "the Lord [will] raise up a host of *female warriors*,—that shall *provoke* the opposite *party*, from their *indolence*,—and in too many instances, far—*unlawful traffick*, of the *Word of God!* Amen" (Preface 9). There is a difference, each of these women knew, between mere servility and true Christian servanthood.[41]

I Feel at Home, Thank God, in Every Place

More commonly, though, these women undertake what might be called a "Higher Criticism" of their own cultural paradigms, especially that of domesticity. The ideology of domesticity was, like the Bible, a canonical text that they could neither abandon nor take at face value. And so in their autobiographies they attempt a kind of Bloomian "strong misreading" of that text—in their cases a misreading motivated by political rather than Oedipal anxiety. Their culture presented them with an ideology whose central symbol was the home, the locus of social and moral stability in a world otherwise characterized as "heartless." The central personage of this ideology was a wife and mother, situated securely in the home, dispensing hot food and moral education in equal measure. She was supposed to be a "true woman," which is to say morally alert, powerful in her own way, but passive, conciliatory, and private; she worked her will upon the world by indirection—by personal example and subtle insinuation. Considered as a narrative, her story was governed by the marriage plot. The lives of these seven American women, on the other hand, were governed, they would remind us, by God. But the stories they came to write were necessarily influenced by the domestic ideology that governed the perceptions of many nineteenth-century men and women. Their unorthodox careers took these "female strangers" beyond the bounds of hearth and home and led them to *convert* the language of domesticity and true womanhood into a most useful metaphoric discourse. This discourse served them well in their efforts to *justify* their lives and, at the same time, lay claim to some place—if only at a crossroads of the various gendered and racialized spheres—in American culture.

Carolyn Heilbrun, in her pathbreaking feminist study *Writing a Woman's Life*, disparages women who merely "put God or Christ in the place of man," for "the results are the same: one's own desires and quests are always secondary" (21). No doubt she would find in these narratives ample justification for this judgment, for all of them—whatever radical intentions they attempt to disclose—end up doing so in profoundly conventional terms. Whatever "wild visions" these evangelists may have experienced, when they came to write about them, they found available only a very old and very familiar language with which to do the job. Though their lives were highly independent, their life stories are often sometimes the opposite, woven from those "webs of significance," those ideologies, that bound other nineteenth-century women. As Clifford Geertz argues, "Culture is not a power, something to which social events, behaviors, institutions, or processes can be casually attributed; it is a context" (14). These women necessarily speak from that context; they speak, moreover, a language in which all words, as Bakhtin says, are necessarily "half someone else's" (293): "The word does not exist in a neutral and impersonal language . . . but rather it exists in other people's mouths, in other people's contexts, serving other people's intentions" (294). As a preacher and author, Elaw longed for a "pure language, unalloyed by the fulsome compliment, the hyperbole, the tautology and circumlocution, the insinuation, double meaning and vagueness, the weakness and poverty, the impurity, bombast, and other defects, with which all human languages are clogged," pure words that could help her express her unorthodox life and her close relationship with God (74). But such a language is "unknown to mortals" (74). Foote also confesses her disappointment in language: "I would that I could tell you a hundredth part of what God has revealed to me of his glory, especially on that never-to-be-forgotten night when I received my high and holy calling. The songs I heard I think were those which Job, David and Isaiah speak of hearing at night upon their beds. . . . Certain it is, I have not been able to sing it since. . . . When I tried to repeat it, it vanished in the dim distance" (227). Unable to render their visions fully, let alone the unusual nature of their nineteenth-century lives, these preachers write books that at times read like so many issues of *Godey's Lady's Book*, one of the preeminent texts of the cult of domesticity. God is a husband, lover, father, master. They are mothers, converting the souls of men. They are pens in God's hand.

It is important, though, to recognize how emphatically these women themselves would have rejected Heilbrun's accusation. The central facts of their lives, their faith in God and love for his children, did not reduce these women to a secondary position; rather, God empowered them and filled them with a peace that they could not derive from their culture. "Oh, what a fountain is opened for cleansing!" Laura Haviland exclaims after her conversion; "My peace was like an overflowing river. It seemed as if I could almost live without breathing—my tears were brushed away by the breath of heaven" (20; Isaiah 66:12). "I was the recipient of many mercies," Foote reflects, "and passed through various exercises. In all of them I could trace the hand of God and claim divine assistance whenever I most needed it. Whatever I needed, by faith I had" (222). These itinerants acknowledge that their eccentric lives were thrust upon them by the Pentecostal power of a heavenly father, but they also want us to know that they greatly benefited from this imposition, that they reveled in the adventurous lives he required of them. In fact, because his imperatives coincide so closely with their own, they need not—in Heilbrun's phrase—"erase all their own desires" from their autobiographies in order to write God in (48). Marriage to God, these texts insist, actually frees the heroine from what Heilbrun calls the "lifetime of marginality" that followed marriage to most nineteenth-century men (21). As Julia Foote explains in the midst of her struggles with the men of the A.M.E. Zion Church, "I saw, as never before, that the best men were liable to err, and that the only safe way was to fall on Christ" (208). Or as Margaret Fuller wrote, "I wish Woman to live, *first*, for God's sake. Then she will not make an imperfect man her god, and thus sink to idolatry" (176). God, that is to say, rewrites these women's lives, but somehow his act of assertion does not preclude—indeed, it is the condition of—their own similar acts. He encourages them to reject the plot written for them by their culture in favor of a radical one of his own design, and in doing so he empowers each of these women to write her own story.

To be sure—God having failed to provide them a radical language in which to record their radical lives—they had to make do with the familiar discourse of domesticity. Without it, in fact, they could hardly have made their stories intelligible, to their readers or even to themselves. But they used this inescapable network of meanings for their own purposes. Though they speak in the language of their day, the ideas, the lives, and the stories that language reveals are revolutionary: "While it may resemble the colonizer's tongue, it has undergone transformation, it has been irrevocably changed" (hooks 150). They take the word, appropriate it for their own uses and "populate it with [their] own intention[s]" (Bakhtin 293). As we have seen, one of their first tasks as preachers and autobiographers had been to "repopulate" the Word of God, which had long been "half someone else's," had long "served other people's intentions," had long been appropriated in arguments against women's preaching (Bakhtin 294). Even Christ, Jarena Lee sarcastically remarks, had long been "half someone else's": "If the man may preach, because the Saviour died for him, why not the woman? seeing he died for her also. Is he not a whole Saviour, instead of a half one?" (11).

By claiming this "whole Saviour"—by marrying him and placing him at the center of their lives—these women make "the world their household," the pulpit their kitchen, and their readers their family.[42] "I feel at *home*, thank God, in every place," Towle professes, "and nevermore, than when urging my flight with the utmost speed, from city to city—whether by land, or by sea" (Preface 11). By "mis-reading" the dominant discourses of their day and generations, Towle and her sister autobiographers convert a gendered ideology into a vehicle of liberation. Their doing so can help us remember that a radical subjectivity need not be oppositional, that even a dissent fully involved in the "over-populated" language of the dominant culture may articulate, powerfully, the desires of powerless people.

2

Feverish Restlessness and Mighty Movement

Female Evangelists in the Marketplace of Salvation

For *no rest* can I find in body or mind, but in the place I took when my soul
was liberated from condemnation the second time, which is to use my hands
in wielding the quill, my tongue in sounding salvation publicly; and devot-
ing my soul, body, and spirit, entirely to the dear Redeemer of them all.
    Harriet Livermore, *A Narration of Religious Experience in Twelve Letters*

What had I on earth to do
With the slothful, with the mawkish, the unmanly?
                                        Robert Browning, "Asolando"

Many shall run to and fro, and knowledge shall be increased.
                                        Daniel 12:4

At the beginning of her *Religious Experience*, Jarena Lee describes her conversion as a
contest between action and passivity. Passivity, she tells her readers, is a condition of
sinfulness. Paralyzed by "the weight of [her] sins" and "not knowing how *to run* immediately to the Lord for help, [she] *was driven* of Satan, in the course of a few days, and
tempted to destroy [herself]" (4, emphasis added). Passivity in the matter of salvation is
dangerous business: it leaves one vulnerable to the actions of Satan. "To run" is to take
charge, to educate herself about the new dispensation, to seek "a knowledge of the being
and character of the Son of God" (8).
    And having learned to run, she appears reluctant ever to stop. Lee must have taken
seriously the words of Isaiah, who said, "How beautiful upon the mountains are the
feet of him that bringeth good tidings, that publisheth peace . . . that saith unto Zion,
Thy God reigneth!" (Isaiah 52:7, emphasis added). "Who knows," Frederick Buechner
writes, "in what inspired way the heart, mind, spirit of the herald came to receive the
good tidings of peace and salvation in the first place, but as to the question whether he
would actually do something about them—put his money where his mouth was, his shoe
leather where his inspiration was—his feet were the ones that finally had to decide. Maybe
it is always so" (*Wishful Thinking* 31). Lee's feet, her autobiography suggests, had clearly
decided. She reminds us, on almost every page, how far her feet carried her during a
particular day. She writes on one occasion, for example, "From this place I walked twenty-
one miles, and preached with difficulty to a stiff-necked and rebellious people" (23). Lee
was evidently fascinated by her mileage totals and had no doubt that her readers would

be as well: "I have travelled, in four years, sixteen hundred miles and of that I walked two hundred and eleven miles, and preached the kingdom of God to the falling sons and daughters of Adam, *counting it all joy* for the sake of Jesus" (36, emphasis added; James 1:2). In 1835 alone, she reports, she "travelled 721 miles, and preached 692 sermons"; in 1836, 556 miles and 111 sermons (77). She kept up this relentless pace of travel and preaching because, she says, she "felt still more like wearing out in the service of God," or because, as she claims in the conclusion to her autobiography, she "felt it better to wear out than to rust out—and so expect to do until death ends the struggle" (77, 97).

This urge to wear out the reader with statistics is not peculiar to Jarena Lee; all the women in this study (and many male evangelists as well) feel a powerful imperative to quantify their lifework. They write tales of extraordinary productivity. Nancy Towle reports midway through her autobiography that she had traveled fifteen thousand miles and escaped countless dangers, which she carefully chronicles for her readers. Later in the book, having concluded the text once and returned to it after a printer's lengthy delay, she could not resist the urge to add another statistic: in that year alone she had traveled five thousand miles as an itinerant preacher (227). Most of her autobiography is a report of her movement from place to place—from "Newbury, Haverhill, Bradford, and Portsmouth" in the winter of 1826, then on to Hampton, British America, England, and New York (35). At times she chooses to summarize the challenges inherent in her life's work:

> The language, of the great Apostle to the Gentiles, I could adopt, and say, "I have been in perils of waters, in perils of robbers, in perils of my own countrymen, in perils by the heathen, in perils in the city [etc.] . . .—and unto this present hour, I have no certain dwelling-place." I had been in prisons, and prison ships. I had been amidst showers of stones, powder, fire, snow-balls, ice, & c. & c. I had been before a "Bar of Justice," a lonely foreigner. I had been saluted by the roar of cannon, and other implements of war. I had been on the raging oceans tossed,—amidst cold, wintry-winds, and chilling storms;—half-stiffened, with cold,—half-stifled with smoke; and with constant heaving by sea-sickness, scarce able from my hard pillow, to raise my head. (106–7; 2 Corinthians 11:26; 1 Corinthians 4:11)

As if this exhaustive account of her sufferings while traveling were not enough, near the end of the work, she once again calls our attention to her labors as a female itinerant:

> During the space, that I have travelled, to and fro, in the earth; I have been in *labours more abundant*. Besides my travels, in much painfulness, cold, hunger, thirst, and nakedness: I have sometimes spoken, from six to eight times a week, for months in succession: and seldom, less, than one hour, upon the stretch. With much exhortation and prayer, for individuals; not unfrequently till midnight, and in some instances, till the dawn of morning. I have also kept a diary; in which I have sometimes written, large portions, for every day: with hundreds of letters, in the course of a year. Moreover, I have been from first, to last, the orderer of my own apparel: not only the making, but in a great measure, the cleaning thereof. And, in addition to all this; I may add, in truth, and verity, "these hands of mine have often ministered to the necessities of those that were with me; and to others." (227–28; Acts 20:34)

Towle protests here that hers has been a life well spent. Despite the passivity implied in the title *Vicissitudes Illustrated in the Experience of Nancy Towle*—a book not about her but about what happened to her—Nancy Towle depicts herself as active and assertive, a woman who knows how to *add* miles traveled, souls converted, and personal sacrifices to her autobiographical *account.*

You Will Be Useful: Producing the Millennium

This literary strategy of depicting themselves as poor, overworked, tirelessly active itinerants can be explained in part by the context in which these women worked and wrote, that of nineteenth-century evangelicalism. The Arminian tendencies of evangelicalism and the methodologies of revivalism spoke forcefully of the need of individuals to be active agents in the conversion process. And as Timothy Smith long ago argued, evangelicalism, with its millennial expectations, called its adherents to public action, despite its emphasis on the inner spiritual life. Evangelicals throughout the century saw themselves as responsible for preparing America and the world for the Second Coming of Christ. Though some historians of American religion regard the "Age of Reform" as an antebellum phenomenon, it in fact continued, Edwin Gaustad argues, throughout the century. Gaustad concedes that "changing the hearts of men" was the principal business of postbellum evangelists; but "even those concerned primarily with private morality and personal sin agreed that group action against sin was occasionally desirable" (*Religious History* 228, 231). In the words of Nancy Towle, "This New-World . . . [was] designed for very rapid advances of the Redeemer's Kingdom" (235). Though disagreeing about just what "action" meant—was it witnessing for Christ Jesus, speaking out against slavery, or campaigning against rum, Romanism, and rebellion?—all evangelicals were sure that it was necessary. Premillennialists and postmillennialists alike believed they were living in the momentous "last days."

Conversion—even for evangelist and missionary Amanda Smith, whose rebirth and call came after midcentury—brought peace of mind, not peace of body, or at least that is how she tells it in her autobiography: conversion required her to embrace the ethic of "usefulness." An article of Protestant faith in general, this ethic was revived among evangelical Protestants. "If filled with the Spirit," Charles Finney told his audiences in 1835, "you will be useful" (*Lectures* 118). Anyone who has read much evangelical literature will recognize the movement's favorite word. It appears in sermons, essays, autobiographies, and book titles. In 1843, Sarah R. Ingraham, seeking the title that would sum up the life of the evangelist and reformer Margaret Prior, could imagine nothing more evocative than *Walks of Usefulness.*[1] In addition to its intrinsic merits, the ethic of usefulness also dovetailed nicely with the anti-Catholicism of most evangelicals, the congenital indolence of Catholics being an article of evangelical faith. Recording her visit to Rome, Amanda Smith denounces Catholic priests, who "had never done a day's work in their lives" (289). Or, as Nancy Towle disdainfully exclaims half a century earlier, "I could hardly see, how it was possible, Christians should be so idle!" (180).[2] Evangelical Christians were called to enter with all the energy they could muster the race of voluntarism, benevolence, and reform that swept the nation. In the words of Ernest Lee Tuveson, "The incessant busyness of the people in the millennium—engaged in 'industry,' in making inventions, in public service, and the like—constitutes one of the greatest contrasts between the holy utopia and the old idea of a 'world-sabbath' of rest and rich rewards. Carlyle's command 'Work!' looms over the Happy Time" (194).

Tuveson's comment reminds us that the ethic of usefulness was not confined to Americans or evangelicals but was a feature of the Victorian Age, a period that, most scholars agree, spanned at least three generations in the Anglo-American world, approximately from the 1830s through the turn of the century; the period thus encompasses the autobiographies and the preaching careers of all but Nancy Towle, whose itinerancy and writing seem to have been confined to a period of about twelve years, from 1821 to 1833, when a second edition of her *Vicissitudes Illustrated* was printed.[3] Jarena Lee's determination to wear out rather than rust out "until death ends the struggle" recalls Tennyson's Ulysses (who preferred to "shine in use" rather than "rust unburnished") and Browning's remarkable promise that, on reaching heaven, he would "fight on . . . there as here" (Lee 97; Tennyson 167; Browning 1211). Female itinerant preachers were not immune to this injunction to "Produce! Produce!," believing with Carlyle that "man is sent hither not to question, but to work" (*Sartor Resartus* 998; *Characteristics* 968). Significantly for our purposes, the ethic of usefulness was also a prominent feature of African American discourse in the nineteenth and early twentieth centuries. Struggling to be accepted by the dominant culture, the black male and female elite adopted the evangelical and Victorian rhetoric of usefulness: African Americans were told again and again, in the words of Martin Delany, to "prepare for usefulness—the day of our Elevation is at hand—all the world now gazes at us" (193). Preoccupation with work for the kingdom among female evangelists, in other words, should come as no surprise; living and preaching in the context of such millennial energy, they were part and parcel of a busy age.[4]

Not that these women were likely to beguile their idle hours, even if they had any, with forays into the philosophy and poetry of their age. They were, as they often profess, "Bible Christians."[5] For their injunction to constant labor they need only look to Carlyle's source, the New Testament: "I must work the works of him that sent me, while it is day: the night cometh, when no man can work" (John 9:4; see also Ecclesiastes 9:10). Zilpha Elaw's *Memoirs* demonstrates how seriously female evangelists took those words of Saint John; the night looms over her autobiography, as it must have loomed over her life: "My earthen vessel was continually exhausted, and as continually replenished; my bodily frame was often wearied in the service of my Saviour, Proprietor and Lord" (127). And Elaw is quick to provide her readers with detailed accounts of that service. "I had an extensive circle of young ladies who were constant attendants upon my ministry," she writes; "these manifested great diligence in their pursuit of the higher attainments of experimental spirituality. . . . the avidity with which they drank until they were filled with the Spirit, and the wonderful revelations God was pleased to manifest to them, provoked me *to run forward in the heavenly race* with increased earnestness, lest they should overtake, and leave me behind them" (119, emphasis added). The autobiography is clearly one long paean to the day well spent. She wishes to document, at almost every turn, her extensive labors:

> During my sojourn in England, I have preached considerably more than a thousand sermons. I have expended all my means in travels of no little extent and duration; devoted my time, employed the energies of my spirit, spent my strength and exhausted my consti-

tution in the cause of Jesus; and received of pecuniary supplies and temporal remunerations in comparison with my time and labours a mere pittance, altogether inadequate to shield me from a thousand privations, hardships, target fires, vexatious anxieties and deep afflictions, to which my previous life was an utter stranger. (158)

Thus does Elaw conclude her *Memoirs* and summarize her fifty-six years, diminishing here the privations we know she suffered in her "previous life" in order to accentuate the adverse conditions under which she so intensely labored as an itinerant preacher. An unusual calculus is at work here: what looks like failure—poverty and the deprivation that comes with it—is really success in accounting the life of a female itinerant working in an age of usefulness and productivity.

The reader who has got this far in Elaw's autobiography of 1846 hardly needs the life summary just quoted. Having made our way through nearly interminable catalogues of places visited and souls saved, we nod our heads in weary assent as she assures us that she "had not been an idle spectator in [her] Heavenly Master's cause" (158). I quote one segment of her twenty-page account of her ministry in England:

On the 27th, I went to Glossop to preach three anniversary sermons. . . . the anniversary was a delightful day; and numbers found it good to be in attendance. I preached again on the following evening, and the place was excessively crowded: on the day after, I returned to Manchester. On the 5th of December I went to Stockport to preach some charity sermons; and the crowd was so great, that it was with great difficulty I reached the pulpit; many hundreds of persons were forced to retire who could not gain admittance. I preached again on the 8th, and spent a very happy week there in visiting the brethren and sisters, and returned again to Manchester. On the 10th, I went to Hollingsworth. (150-51)

There is an odd sort of artfulness in these accounts. Extraordinarily lengthy and strung together with colons and semicolons, Elaw's complex sentences (used throughout the autobiography) provide us—our own strength failing as we stumble across the endless expanses of rough prose—a direct experience of this "day of feverish restlessness and mighty movement" (Elaw 51-52). The reader, propelled forward by the syntax, is granted no opportunity to pause; Elaw demands that we adhere to her own seemingly relentless pace. Hurried through her itinerary, only the most critical of readers would recognize her sly omission of November 30 through December 4, and December 6, 7, and 9, days in which she perhaps *was* "idle" in her Master's cause.[6]

This strange autobiographical premise (which I will address again in chapter 4) that an author could represent her life by compiling her itineraries seems to have suggested itself to female itinerants, and to many of their male evangelical contemporaries, throughout the nineteenth century. Julia Foote, in a chapter entitled "Work in Various Places," for example, lists her preaching engagements with little or no accompanying detail: "On the 28th we went to Snow Hill, where we spent one Sunday. We visited Fethersville, Bordentown, Westchester, and Westtown, all to the glory of God. . . . July 20th we left for New York, stopping at Burlington, Trenton, Princeton, Rahway, Brunswick and Newark" (219). Foote writes as though the substance of these travels will little interest her readers; what they want to know, she believes, is how much and how far she traveled.

Even Lydia Sexton's 655-page autobiography, written in 1882, sometimes reads like a mere collection of itineraries, held together with the bare minimum of narrative glue:

"From there I went to Iroquois county, Illinois. I held a meeting in the Longshore neighborhood, and had a good time. I then went to the Kenoyer neighborhood—in Indiana—to make arrangements to go to Kansas. I sold our place in Jasper County, Indiana; then went to Milford, Warren County, and held meeting there; thence I returned to Kenoyers, Newton County, Indiana. I intended to start from there to Kansas" (586). Neither here nor elsewhere in the autobiography does Sexton pause to reflect on her inner spiritual life; it would seem, from passages like this, that she hardly ever paused at all. She represents herself as the tireless itinerant whose life would be nothing at all were it not for her work and travel, her "travail," to borrow the original sense of the word. Like their many sisters of the spirit, and like Paul before them, they "travail[ed] in birth" for countless "little children" "until Christ be formed in [them]" (Galatians 4:19; Elaw 101).

To reinforce these tales of productivity—of travel and travail—Julia Foote and Laura Haviland make use of descriptive titles. Foote may well have been, as the title of her autobiography contends, "A Brand Plucked from the Fire," but the passivity implied in this biblical verse in no way characterizes the life work she describes in her autobiography (Zechariah 3:2). The final third of the brief text is devoted to her work: "The Lord Leadeth—Labor in Philadelphia," "A Visit to My Parents—Further Labors," "Continued Labors—Death of My Husband and Father," "Work in Various Places," "Further Labors—A 'Threshing' Sermon," and "My Cleveland Home—Later Labors." Even inattentive readers could hardly fail to draw the moral of this story. Laura Haviland called her narrative *A Woman's Life-Work: Labors and Experiences of Laura S. Haviland*, a title that impressed the Methodist pastor F. A. Hardin for its sheer appropriateness: "The title by which Mrs. Haviland is pleased to call her narrative is itself a most fitting introduction, for it heralds the contents of the coming volume" (Preface to 4th edition). The title notifies us that the story we are about to encounter is not about being but doing. Indeed, the text surveys one "laborious field of labor"—Haviland's revealingly redundant term—after another (210). She had led an extraordinarily active life—running her late husband's farm, founding a school, working on the Underground Railroad, and risking her life doing "Sanitary Work" during the Civil War—and her chapter titles, like Foote's, drive the point home: "An Ohio School-Teacher," "The Underground Railway," "Fugitive Slaves Assisted," "Christian and Educational Work," "Hospital Work," "Sanitary Work," and "Home Mission Work."

Like Elaw, Haviland chose not to write about time spent at home; she considered domestic matters unimportant to her life story and perhaps uninteresting to her reform-minded audience. At the end of chapter 8, for instance, she manages to summarize three years of "home work" with the following: "I spent nearly three years looking after the best interests of my children, and making preparations to re-open Raisin Institute, for the moral, intellectual, and spiritual improvement of our youth" (210). And she reminds us in the preface to the third edition of the *Life-Work* that though her life has lasted more than seventy-five years and though her volume now stretches to 554 pages, both are unfinished. There is more work to be done and duly recorded; her life continues beyond the conclusion of her story. Only death or the appearance of Christ could really bring an end to the important work that lay before her. In fact, these tireless itinerants may have written their autobiographies so that even death would not bring an end to their labors: As Zilpha Elaw remarks, "These humble memoirs will doubtless continue to be read long after I shall have ceased from my earthly labours and existence" (160).

Living and even dying are, it seems, synonymous with working. The "I" of these narratives, though capable of movement and achievement, has no inner life to speak of (which is not to say, of course, that the narrator has no inner life, but simply that she chooses not to share that inner life directly with her readers). At times these autobiographies read like so many tales written by the boot in Monopoly. Though these autobiographers listen to and obey the voice of God, they rarely, as in the tradition of much Protestant autobiography, plumb the depths of their experience for evidence of their salvation. Their life stories are almost the mirror opposites of that famous autobiography in the Puritan tradition, Bunyan's *Grace Abounding to the Chief of Sinners.* Where Bunyan devoted two-thirds of his story to his agonizing self-scrutiny and protracted conversion, most of his nineteenth-century female successors pay only lip service to this important part of Puritan spiritual autobiographies. The Puritan emphasis on the doctrine of predestination leads Bunyan into a torturous quest for evidence of his salvation, so much so that his modern reader must wonder how he ever survived the ordeal: "How can you tell you are Elected?" he asks, "and what if you should not? how then?" (21). "By these things," continues Bunyan, "I was driven to my wits end, not knowing what to say, or how to answer these temptations . . . for that the Elect only attained eternal life, that I without scruple did heartily close with all: but that my self was one of them, there lay all the question" (21). That question dominates his autobiography, which, as the title suggests, is not about *his* work but the Lord's. And that work, consuming most of the story, impresses the reader as having also consumed a considerable portion of the life itself. Bunyan, moreover, studiously avoids references to specific units of time, preferring instead the vague "in these days," or "all this while," or "a long while," or "for some years." His conversion gains a sort of timeless quality; this is the story of everyman's salvation through faith.

For Nancy Towle, Jarena Lee, Laura Haviland, and the rest, life's meaning inheres in a profound commitment to God through faith, but they equated their faith with works, a typically Arminian position. Or, rather, "like other evangelical Protestants in nineteenth-century America, they measured their faith by their works: they believed that true Christians should help the 'sinners' in their midst, not ignore or condemn them" (Brekus 290). Salvation and work were, to begin with, endless processes, never to be finished this side of the grave. In both worldly and heavenly matters, these women appear to be unacquainted with the idea of completion (one reason, no doubt, why they had trouble ending their autobiographies, or even their sentences). But the call to ceaseless labor, and the energy to perform it, were for these women—as they were for Weber's Puritans—both the means of salvation and the surest signs of it. To have felt, at the advent of old age or simple exhaustion, that enough was enough would have been troubling indeed. To quit "running" was to surrender all.

This explains, I think, what might appear to be an odd feature of these autobiographies: their treatment of the experience of conversion. The reader who approaches these narratives expecting a detailed account of a protracted conversion will be startled by how quickly they cover what is often the climax of spiritual autobiographies. Laura Haviland remembers her early religious experience—as a Quaker longing to be a Methodist—and conversion on pages 15 to 20 of her nearly 600-page *Life-Work.* Lydia Sexton's conversion by the New Light Christians takes up a mere 5 pages of her 655-page narrative. Julia Foote gives over several pages to describing her several false starts toward conversion; the conversion itself—in which she falls to the floor unconscious, convicted of her sins, and awakes "with rapture too deep for words"—is described in 2 pages (181). Zilpha Elaw's conversion account most resembles Bunyan's; she reports seasons of engaging in sin, seasons of reflection and weeping and contrition, seasons of backsliding, and a gradual work on her soul by the divine. Assurance follows this gradual work in the form of a vision in which a man in a "long white robe . . . stood with open arms and smiled upon [her]" while she was "milking the cow and singing" (56). "After this wonderful manifestation of [her] condescending Saviour," she obtains the "peace of God which passeth understanding" (57). Jarena Lee also constructs her conversion account around the prescribed feelings of guilt. Upon hearing a Presbyterian minister read a Psalm-like rhyme on original sin,[7] Lee is struck by the weight of her sins; later, in the congregation of the Reverend Richard Allen, Lee is moved by the words of Scripture to "forgive *every* creature" and is overcome by a wild vision: "That instant, it appeared to me, as if a garment, which had entirely enveloped my whole person . . . was stripped away from me . . . when the glory of God seemed to cover me in its stead" (5). Though she continues to be buffeted by Satan until the moment of her sanctification and refers to her conversion for several more pages, the moment of conversion itself ends here on the third page of her autobiography.[8] Nancy Towle reports her conversion almost in passing; with stock religious language she tells her readers that she was converted by the Freewill Baptist preacher Clarissa H. Danforth and baptized by a "Christian" elder. Then she, like all the evangelical autobiographers under consideration here, moves on to more important matters. This is not to say that conversion was unimportant in these women's lives; it was undoubtedly a pivotal moment in their religious experiences, the beginning of their "sure and stedfast" lives of faith and ultimately of their lives as itinerant preachers (Hebrews 6:19). But when they came to construct themselves in their autobiographies, conversion seemed less important than their evangelical labors.[9]

These women, like their male contemporaries, were licensed to minimize the narrative length of their conversions by nineteenth-century evangelical theology and revivalist methodology. While many Protestants have accepted a complicated morphology of gradual conversion "marked by clearly defined stages" of preparation and self-scrutiny, accounts of nineteenth-century revivals are full of stories of men, women, and children converted in an instant by God (Sharrock xxvii).[10] For both English and American Puritans, conversion was a long, anguished process, and even afterward no one could be completely sure of election. This notion of conversion began to erode as early as the eighteenth century as many American ministers began to emphasize, in the manner of Jacobus Arminius (1560–1609), the role human beings played in their own salvation. By the nineteenth century, Arminianism was no longer the heresy of the early seventeenth century; it was, for most sects and denominations, the way to salvation. The famous "new measures" of the nineteenth-century preacher Charles Finney, which evangelistic itinerants gladly employed, were designed to promote conversion as a conscious decision of the will, perhaps evolving out of an emotional crisis—what the Puritans would have disparagingly called "a faire and easie way to heaven."[11]

Holiness advocates, following efforts of American Methodists to revive Wesley's interest in Christian perfection, made the achievement of sanctification similarly easy:

it, too, was a instantaneous work of grace received by faith.[12] Methodist Phoebe Palmer used her Tuesday prayer meetings and numerous publications to convince her audiences that conversion and sanctification were matters of will. With her Arminian altar terminology, regarding the second blessing of holiness or sanctification, she declared that under the new dispensation one simply placed oneself and everything in one's life— worldly goods, health, children, spouse, reputation, even fear of public speaking—on God's altar in the name of Christ. The altar—which was Christ himself—sanctified the gift. With "faith that God had promised sanctification and would honor that promise based on the work of Christ already completed" and with an "immediate public confession that one had received the blessing," one began a life "of full Christian commitment" (Hardesty, *Your Daughters* 40). Palmer's New Testament theology, borrowed from the Book of Hebrews, turned an Old Testament image into a metaphor and plan for sanctification (see Hebrews 13:8-12). As Palmer writes in *The Promise of the Father*, "While I have thus kept my unworthy offering on the *Christian's altar*, presenting myself a *living* sacrifice to God, I have not dared to dishonor Christ, by doubting whether the offering is 'wholly acceptable unto God.' In view of the *medium* through which it is being continually presented, that is, *through* Christ, I dare not doubt" (204). Whether by emotional crisis, act of will, or, even in the manner of Horace Bushnell, by "Christian nurture,"[13] conversion and sanctification need not be, evangelicals continually preached, the protracted affair of John Bunyan and most of his American contemporaries. Conversion, no longer a mysterious process in need of careful delineation, could be dispensed with quickly and never referred to again. And these autobiographers are happy to do so; their real interests, like those of most evangelical Christians, are in recording the postconversion struggles of "working Christians."[14] "It can be stated almost as a law of spiritual autobiographies," in the words of G. A. Starr, "that the greater the attention paid to events before conversion, the less emphasis given to what happens afterwards, and vice versa" (46). Evangelical Christians, focusing on the propagation of the gospel, tend to be among those who concentrate on "what happens afterward."

Though Laura Haviland's story takes place within the context of her religious conversion, the conversion itself was important only because it taught her that she could not serve God "in a silent, quiet life" (30). She took this discovery to heart, working and speaking daily on the behalf of poor, sick, illiterate, disfranchised Americans. A Quaker-born Methodist, she led prayer meetings, preached, and organized church groups wherever she traveled, though usually under no particular denomination. But, unlike her sister itinerants, Haviland did not believe conversion would solve America's problems, particularly those of slavery and race relations. For most evangelicals, William McLoughlin argues, "the road to the millennium lay through God's reformation of the human heart. All man-made efforts of social reform, as the French Revolution demonstrated so forcefully, were sheer folly" (Introduction 12-13). Haviland did not expect— as did Harriet Beecher Stowe, Julia Foote, Amanda Smith, and countless other evangelical Americans—that missionary endeavors aimed at saving souls would rid the country of prejudice and poverty, even though her own conversion had put an end to her prejudice against the Irish. Perhaps, too, working and writing from about 1840 to 1880, Haviland was influenced in her ministry by the increased prominence of the cult of domesticity and the resulting backlash against women as speakers. Though she labored for the Wesleyan Methodists, one of several Methodist splinter groups that was "more tolerant of female preaching" at midcentury, she would also have been aware that even among radical evangelical sects like the Christians, Freewill Baptists, and Methodists, a "Mother in Israel or Sister in Christ was [no longer] a crusading evangelist who traveled from town to town preaching the gospel, but a Sunday school teacher, a temperance reformer, or an antislavery activist who deferred to the authority of her local pastor" (Brekus 295, 294). Other women in this study who preached at midcentury or later seem to have been less troubled by the rising tide of domesticity in choosing how to live their lives, though, as we have seen, they did find its tenets useful in writing their autobiographies. That tide may have influenced Lydia Sexton's decision to accept a post as a prison chaplain near the end of her career in 1870. And it may have encouraged Amanda Smith to become involved in the temperance crusade and to spend much of her life as a missionary abroad. But both Smith and her African American predecessor Julia Foote also continued to preach as itinerants after midcentury because of their participation in the Holiness revivals that stirred the nation beginning in the 1870s. Laura Haviland, however, devoted herself to saving souls through reform, not just through conversion and sanctification; hence, in her ministry the gospel was at all times supplemented by food, clothing, and practical aid, particularly to slaves and freedmen and freedwomen. It was, it seems, a gospel her readers understood and appreciated; the autobiography closes with an appendix of testimonials, the last of which from George Clark sums up Haviland's brand of Christianity: "I received a letter from John G. Whittier not long since, in which he . . . spoke of the thrilling interest with which he read your 'Woman's Life-work,' and added that 'the world sadly needed more such examples of practical Christianity.'"

Amanda Berry Smith's autobiography, written at the end of the century and documenting a career that began after the Civil War, is something of an exception to the pattern of accounting I have been describing. Not a defense of "practical Christianity" or a tedious record of miles traveled, Smith's book is, nonetheless, the story of a committed evangelist, zealous in her mission to convert the world to Christianity. Smith concludes her autobiography with numerous testimonials to what one admirer called her "untiring labors," of which her readers would by that point in the text be well aware (467). In America, she tells us, she preached—as would most female itinerants in the latter part of the century—primarily at holiness camp meetings, which necessarily involved intensive work over a three- or four-day period. At one such meeting she was asked to go "to a little quiet meeting in a cottage"; that little meeting, Smith reports, turned into an evangelistic marathon in which "more than a score of souls were swept into the fountain of cleansing" (187). Smith gave herself up to the work for the entire afternoon. "Most of the time," she remembers, "I stood on my feet and exhorted, and sang, and talked, and prayed. When I got out and went to start home, I could scarcely walk. I was thoroughly exhausted. I had a cup of tea, and lay down a while, and was ready for another pitched battle. Glory to God!" (187). Smith, not unlike a soldier, is both enervated and energized by her efforts. She is at pains to depict herself as an overworked, exhausted evangelist in a cosmic drama; at the same time, she is unable to deny the intoxicating effect of such "battles." Here the mere contemplation of another war for souls, despite her bodily weakness, sends her into a fever of excitement.

Laura Haviland. Courtesy of the Bentley Historical Library, University of Michigan.

As the preceding story attests, Smith does document her work and productivity as an evangelist. But for the most part she eschews the literary techniques that her sister evangelists employed in their quest to write the productive life. She does not, however, reject the quest. Though Smith describes her book as the "simple story of God's dealings with a worm," the plot of *An Autobiography* is anything but simple, and she is no worm (505-6; Psalm 22:6). By painstakingly depicting her warfare with her chief antagonist, Satan, Smith convinces her readers that she was far from idle. To cite only one example: after receiving her call to preach the gospel, Smith hears a voice commanding her to go to Salem, New Jersey, to preach. Having contemplated the command for several weeks, Smith finally decides to go and is immediately "attacked" by Satan, who tells her that she goes only "to look for a husband" (134-35). Clearly disturbed by this pronouncement, Smith cries to Satan that he lies. But her "Accuser" continues to "harass" her so much that she turns to the Lord in prayer. She goes on in the autobiography to give a lengthy account of her discussion with God, who finally convinces her that he "would go with [her]" (135). Such three-way debates among Satan, God, and Amanda Smith occur repeatedly in the *Autobiography* and evidently took up a good part of Smith's life and energy. Between listening to and answering Satan's accusations and conveying her distress to God, the weary evangelist rarely had a free moment. With both the devil and the Lord demanding her undivided attention, making even the simplest decision could be an exhausting ordeal. "Persons often ask me," she confides, "how I came to think of going to Africa"; these persons, one speculates, may have regretted their curiosity, for what follows is a highly detailed account of Smith's debate with God on the subject. Similar stories introduce her trips to England, India, and a great many camp meetings and revivals in America (215; see also 206, 243, 282). In these accounts Smith converts what most of us would call introspection—that idler's ploy to avoid work?—into an objective struggle. Far from pursuing a life of ease and "loaferism"—and thereby, according to the white middle class, "subverting the free labor experiment"—Smith invites us to regard this African American life as one of usefulness and productivity (J. Jones 45). By writing her life as one endless psychological drama, Smith both fills out her five-hundred-page autobiography and convinces her readers that mental struggles with Satan are at least as strenuous as the physical labors of her more decisive colleagues.

Numbering Israel: Women in the War for Converts

Satan was not the only rival who dignified, by resisting them, the productivity and competitive labors of these evangelists. There were also the male preachers of other sects and denominations. As Nathan Hatch convincingly argues in *The Democratization of American Christianity*, behind the Evangelical United Front lay a religious environment of intense sectarian competition and entrepreneurship.[15] American Protestantism in the first half of the nineteenth century embraced the "new democratic vocabularies and impulses that swept through American popular cultures": the result, democratic dissent and its corollary, the "splintering of American Protestantism" (7, 64). This was an age of fervid competition among Baptist, Methodist, and Christian sects—the big winners in this war for converts—and also among Congregationalists, Presbyterians, and Episcopalians, who were, for a time at least, stunned at being no longer "the center of the culture" (Hatch, *Democratization* 61).

Throughout his *Autobiography*, published in 1856, the Methodist itinerant Peter Cartwright recounts feats of remarkable preaching that enabled him to garner converts from other sects, thereby increasing both the size of the denomination and his reputation. Preaching once to a Baptist congregation, Cartwright recalls his success: "A great many of *their members* gave up Calvinism, close communion, and immersion, and joined the Methodist Church; and *we took possession* of their meeting-house, and raised a large society there that flourishes to this day" (82, emphasis added). Cartwright's imperialistic language—"we took possession of their meeting-house"—hints at the intense competitiveness that the evangelical wars fostered. And his use of the plural pronoun "we" suggests that he was always a team player, exerting himself for God no doubt, but also for the Methodists: "*We*," writes Cartwright, "had a little Book Concern then in its infancy. . . . *We* had no Missionary Society. . . . *We* had no pewed churches. . . . *we* had no instrumental music" (61, emphasis added). One senses that Cartwright would have enjoyed his triumphs less had there been no Baptists and Calvinists to discomfit by his efforts.

It is true that evangelicalism and revivalism were partly unifying forces in American religion, the Age of Reform in nineteenth-century America being marked by nondenominational efforts to remake America and the world for the Second Coming. Evangelicals were united by their opposition to traditional Calvinist orthodoxies, their acceptance of Arminianism, their appeal to the common people, and their millennialist vision of America as, in the words of Tuveson, the Redeemer Nation. Some evangelicals, calling for a return to a more primitive Christianity, claim to have opposed the sectarian division in their midst, and many write about preaching to people from various religious backgrounds or no background at all. Baptized in the Church of Christ, John Colby often preached to Methodists and Baptists, and though he tells us in his autobiography of 1815 that he did seek to convert the misguided Quakers, he appears less anxious to attract converts away from other sects. Too, there were preachers like Lorenzo Dow who, having become a "leper" among the Methodists, chose to go it alone (Dow 124). As he puts it in his autobiography, "Some Methodist local preachers treated me cool, and strove to shut up *my* way; but God opened *my* way . . . and at Frankfort *I* got the *state house*: and at Lexington *I* got first the court house, then a play house, and afterwards, the Methodists opened to *me* their meeting house" (144, emphasis added). He concludes by noting, almost as an afterthought, that "in several meetings, God was with *us*" (144). Indeed, this most successful of evangelists transformed himself, quite literally, into a household name: historian Jon Butler comments that he was "so well known as a Methodist itinerant that it was commonly said parents named more children after him than after any other figure except Washington" (*Awash* 241). He became a force unto himself, an *I* with little need for denominational support or control: "There is no question that he preached to more people, traveled more miles, and consistently attracted larger audiences to camp meetings than any preacher of his day" (Hatch, *Democratization* 36).

But most male itinerants, representing a particular sect or denomination, did participate in the war for converts. The Methodist Elbert Osborn remembers one particular conference in which "Bishop George" was disappointed in the small "net gain of between six and seven hundred" members (120). While the bishop was willing to concede that "the tide of immigration, constantly flowing to the west, accounted in part for the smallness of this increase," he also "urged" the itinerants in his midst "to consider" the possibility that they were to blame (120). The Methodists would have had "larger accessions of genuine converts" if the itinerants had more "zeal and faithfulness" (120). Even Dow initially participated in just the sort of warfare Hatch documents: "During my stay in these two circuits, in ten months," Dow reports, "about six hundred were taken into society, and as many more went off and joined the Baptists and Presbyterians" (50). Elder Benjamin Putnam, who joined a Baptist church in 1820, penned his autobiography for the sole purpose of revealing—and persuading his readers to accept— "His Present Views of Divine Truth," as well as "the dark and bewildering paths of error" along which he walked when he preached for the Freewill Baptists and Christians (subtitle, 6). Abraham Snethen, who worked among the Christians, writes that he and his brethren were "bitterly persecuted" in Indiana: "We were scattered over a wide scope of country, and we met with great opposition everywhere. The severest trials came to us, from the Methodists, Campbellites, and though they were bitterly opposed to each other, they would join their forces in persecuting us" (227). George Brown, originally a member of the Methodist Episcopal Church, remembers well his doctrinal quarrels with the Presbyterians: "In all, I preached six carefully prepared sermons on the points of difference between Methodism and Calvinism. This ended our troubles with our Calvinistic brethren, for they drew off to another place, and we pursued our own course in new efforts to evangelize the wicked world" (102).

Female preachers, no less than their brethren, enthusiastically took part in this culture of competitive individualism and accounting. They were motivated by faith, by a sense of urgency and millennial zeal, and by "wild visions" that called them also "to evangelize the wicked world." But they were motivated as well by a desire to promote themselves, to show Americans with their lives and in their autobiographies that they had a right to preach: they could prove it by demonstrating how effectively they could compete with—and often defeat—men in the war for converts.

Thus the competitive religious environment of the nineteenth century is often figured in their autobiographies in terms of gender. Because their work was seldom encouraged by church officials, several of the women in this study refused to join a particular denomination, preferring the lives of independent itinerants. Nancy Towle prided herself on her ecumenism, on her "wish to be free from party spirit, and to love Christians of every order" (231). Those women who were affiliated with a particular denomination were so only in the loosest of senses. Though Jarena Lee initially received much support from Bishop Richard Allen, returning to Philadelphia in 1835, she was "debarred from [her] own Church as regards this privilege [she] had been so much used to" (77). She was scorned by the A.M.E. Church under the leadership of Bishop Daniel Payne, who believed in an educated ministry, "objected to the enthusiastic clapping, dancing and shouting he witnessed in church meetings," and "opposed . . . female preaching" (Brekus 295). Denied positions of power and authority within the institutional church, these women do not claim, in the manner of Peter Cartwright or Abraham Snethen, to have stolen converts from another sect. Nor do they situate themselves, like Elder Benjamin Putnam or George Brown, within the prominent sectarian theological debates of the century. While their male contemporaries were at war with Calvinist orthodoxy and battling numerous sects for control of the populace, these women were involved in a passionate social struggle for legitimacy and power. Their competitive instincts, even early in the century when female gifts were encouraged by some, were most aroused at the prospect of converting difficult congregations, sinners who had proved too hard-hearted for male evangelists.

On one occasion in Reading, Pennsylvania, Jarena Lee reports that she was opposed by "Rev. James Ward, a colored Presbyterian," who "was so prejudiced he would not let me in his pulpit to speak" (44). Finally, a "sister" interceded on her behalf, and though "the men of color . . . remained idle in the enterprize," Lee triumphantly records, "*we* got possession and *we* had a large concourse of people" (44, emphasis added). "We," in this case, being the black sisters of the congregation.

In Africa in the mid-1880s, the "colored evangelist" Amanda Smith is opposed by a Brother Ware, who is suspicious of female preaching. Smith's anger at this gendered opposition stirs her to divulge, subtly, her success in his absence: "Brother Ware did not get back for six weeks; so we had full swing, and God was with us. When he did come, how surprised he was. Every Sunday, prior to his coming, a number were taken in. The first Sunday after he came he took in nine or ten; I don't know what the number was exactly" (450). Even those nine or ten, we gather, were carried in by the momentum of Smith's efforts, not by Ware's inferior preaching. Smith stops short of giving us the total number of souls saved through her ministry: "I never like to number Israel," she explains; "the record is on high" (450).

Her reticence on this matter is unique among the women under study here. The others show a considerable knack for numbering Israel; for the most part converts exist in these works to be claimed and counted, not understood. "Some *thousands* have I seen," proclaims Nancy Towle, "*made the sharers* of redeeming grace; and many more of every nation, I expect to see added to that number, should I continue here below" (Preface 11). The passive voice suggests the modesty one might expect of a mere instrument of God's redemptive power, a passive witness to a miraculous revival of religion. But the ambiguity of the passage bears further scrutiny. Towle might well be saying that she fully expects to see more conversions, should she live; if she does not live to see them, someone else might. Towle's optimism about further conversions might also be read as conditional: the revival will continue only "should I continue here below." Whose converts are these "thousands"? By the end of this passage, God seems to be sharing the credit with Nancy Towle, who is undeniably proud to report her accomplishments. Later in the autobiography, Towle unambiguously announces the success of her evangelistic efforts. In Lubec, she writes, "I labored incessantly for the space of ten weeks; and *saw myself*, in the end, 'from the joy of many,' *abundantly crowned*" (39, emphasis added; Isaiah 60:15). She also reports that once she packed her bags and left Painsville when it became clear to her that the elders there opposed preaching by women. She goes on to proclaim that her leaving in fact did much harm: the ministers could effect no revival without her.

Jarena Lee and Zilpha Elaw punctuate their autobiographies with stories that demonstrate their abilities to effect "prosperous" times with their preaching (23). A "wonderful shock of God's power was felt" here; "considerable weeping and a profitable waiting upon the Lord" were experienced there as Lee evangelized congregations (20, 27). "Melting, sin-killing, and soul-reviving time[s]" were the norm, not the exception, of Lee's career (22). Zilpha Elaw tells us, after describing the crowds that attended her ministry in Portland and the conversions of two men there, that she cannot include the "other instances of the Lord's especial favour to me" because the "limits" of the volume "require their omission" (120). But throughout the autobiography, despite the limits of space, she does manage to convince us of the power of *her* word. Though her sense of herself as a prophet, as God's mouthpiece on earth, moves her to proclaim that her "'sufficiency is of God,'" modesty does not prevent her from rejoicing in her continued success and subtly calling attention to the "numbers," the overflowing "crowds," the "hundreds of persons" who, due to her popularity, "could not gain admittance" to the overcrowded halls (epigraph; 150–51; 2 Corinthians 3:5).

Lydia Sexton, who served God as an itinerant preacher from 1843 until 1870 when she became a prison chaplain, is even more self-asserting than her sister autobiographers, boldly declaring her many successes. She describes how a Brother Wainscott, with whom she had numerous conflicts, claimed in conference to have added sixty-two new members to the church. "The truth is," Sexton asserts, "that was about the number I had taken into the church; and I don't think he had taken in one." "What advantage it could be to him to dissemble in this way I could not understand," Sexton writes, "only by his report of work he improved his chances for *preferment*. At any rate, he came off with flying colors. I believe there was a resolution passed in that annual conference year for every local to keep a strict account of how many members they should receive into the church during each year. I thought then, and think now, that the resolution passed; and I think that honor should rest where honor is due" (399–400). Sexton lays claim to the honor due her for her many accomplishments in the evangelical wars. She wants to "come off with flying colors" and improve her chances for "preferment." And strict accounting, she hoped, was just the way to do it.

Sexton was probably familiar with the words of Charles Finney, America's grand revivalist (and formerly a lawyer), who called his readers to evaluate ministers according to the number of souls (or "cases") saved: "He is the more wise, by how much the greater is the number of sinners that he saves. A blockhead may indeed now and then stumble on such truth, or such a manner of exhibiting it, as to save a soul. . . . But the amount of wisdom is to be decided, 'other things being equal,' by the *number* of cases in which he is successful in converting sinners" (*Lectures* 183).[16] At one point in her autobiography, when contemplating how the validity of one's religious "calling" is to be determined, Sexton positions herself securely in Finney's world. Quantifiable success, she suggests, is the only reliable measure of a legitimate call: "If you determine that there is no acceptable preaching only through a called ministry, who will arrogate to himself the power to determine the calling—seeing that none are invested with miraculous power? But should you deny that there is any divine authority by which the word is to be preached, why not offer the most encouragement to those who may labor the most successfully" (255). Her autobiography makes clear that female preachers deserve such encouragement. "I never preached at a place without having the satisfaction to learn that they desired me to return. I mention this," Sexton apologizes (somewhat boastfully), "only as a matter of encouragement to some of my sisters who feel that they have a call to the ministry" (367).

Clearly, identity for these female itinerants did not derive from their attachment to a particular sect. It derived most obviously from their sustaining relationships with God. But it stemmed as well from their keen sense of themselves as "women preachers" (Sexton 336). Having abandoned their homes and the sphere of domesticity that offered them the possibility of prestige based on relationships with fathers, husbands, brothers, and children, these women embraced instead what David Potter calls the principle of mobility (105). The chance to define themselves and prove their worth must have been compelling for women accustomed to having their status handed to them in accordance with their roles within the home. It must certainly have been compelling for the black women in this study, all of whom were defined not only in relation to men but also in accordance with the many racist stereotypes that permeated the culture.

And yet, as fulfilling as life in the competitive evangelical world could be, women participated in the world of mobility with a handicap. They were permitted to travel about the evangelical landscape and sometimes to preach inside churches and other public spaces; at times they were supported by men in the ministry.[17] Even so, they were never more than what Patricia Collins calls "outsiders within," women occupying a paradoxical space both inside and outside the center of the dominant culture, in this case as expressed in the evangelical tradition that alternately accepted them and their spiritual gifts and told them to keep silent (94).[18] This paradoxical space, where they were both welcomed and opposed, made quantification all the more important in the *Lives* of "female strangers"—or, as Bishop George would have it, Christian merchants—who wanted to be acknowledged, understood, and found worthy (Towle 254). They "numbered Israel"—just as they borrowed and revised the language of domesticity—in an effort to negotiate their status within the dominant culture. Though evangelical theology made it possible for them to take their own conversions for granted, these women found it difficult to feel completely "justified" in their new public roles as preachers, given the widely accepted admonitions of Saint Paul, the cult of domesticity, and the culture's complex and often contradictory definitions of black womanhood. In this respect their situation differed from that of their male counterparts and competitors. A man like Peter Cartwright had no need in his autobiographical account to overemphasize conversions wrought and miles traveled in the service of the Lord (though he occasionally did so); he need only gesture toward his rise to authority within the Methodist Episcopal Church—from itinerant, to elder to presiding elder—to reassure himself and his readers of his worthiness. A committed Protestant, Cartwright would never complacently indulge himself with the notion that the great race for souls had finally been run; he could, however, look back over his career, his part of that race, and say, in effect, "I have arrived." But these female itinerants had no such honors and promotions to point to. Their careful cataloguing of activities and travels were what they needed instead, proof of their value in the public (masculine) world of evangelical religion.

The difficulties, for female evangelists, and the need for such proof, became greater as the century wore on. At midcentury, when the age of competition among sects drew to a close, the struggle of female itinerants intensified. As the dissenting sects themselves began seeking respectability, their former indifference to female preaching hardened into more or less official proscription. The more a group becomes integrated within the dominant culture, sociologists agree, the less it is able to review and critique the values of that culture. Evangelical churches felt compelled, as they moved into the social mainstream, to accept their culture's assumptions about the roles of women.[19] Jarena Lee's activities, I have noted, were "severely curtailed" after Bishop Richard Allen's death in 1831 and particularly with the rise of the influential Daniel Payne (C. Peterson 75). In the second edition of Lee's autobiography, published in 1849 and covering the years immediately before and after Allen's death, she found it necessary to write what some scholars have called a mere travelogue, a day-by-day listing of her labors. Perhaps, Carla Peterson suggests, Lee "turned to literary composition as a supplement to her evangelical activities . . . in an effort to erase her 'public' bodily self and silence the 'private' voice of religious ecstasy in favor of a more 'public' language that she hoped would legitimate her preaching in the eyes of institutionalized religion" (78). So, too, did Lydia Sexton, Laura Haviland, and Amanda Berry Smith. Each of these women published her *Life* after the Civil War, and each went to greater lengths, literally, to depict herself as a zealous, tireless, and successful worker. Despite preaching and writing after the emergence of the women's rights movement, they seem to have felt the same pressure as their predecessors to prove their worth to the men who denied them traditional, authoritative accolades. The more radical feminists (like the Grimkés, Fanny Wright, and Abby Kelley) who emerged as early as the 1830s actually turned the public *against* less radical "biblical feminists" and preachers. According to Brekus, feminist reformers "caused such a furor that *any* woman who spoke in public, even a theological conservative, seemed inherently dangerous" (281). For competitive female itinerants, the race continued, and their "arrival" at the "Evangelical United Front" was forever deferred.

Accounting for Oneself in the Marketplace of Salvation

To notice the language of "net gains," "larger accessions," and "strict accounts" in the writings of a Bishop George, Lydia Sexton, and Charles Finney—and, more generally, the emphasis on competition in the autobiographical writings of male itinerant evangelists—is to recognize a resemblance between nineteenth-century evangelicalism and the commercial world that existed in America and abroad. Both gauged success by volume and had been doing so since the mid–eighteenth century.[20] The predominant philosophy of the marketplace, of course, was one of competitive individualism. And historians of American religion, following Weber, have long debated the relationship among nineteenth-century evangelicalism, revivalism, and the capitalist marketplace. "The clergyman and theologian of evangelicalism," Martin Marty argues, "progressively identified himself with competitive individualism at the expense of community" (*Righteous Empire* 110). William McLoughlin takes that argument a step further, seeing in evangelicalism the cornerstone of capitalism: "Both as motivation and as rationale evangelical religion lay behind the concept of rugged individualism in business enterprise, laissez faire in economic theory, constitutional democracy in political thought, the Protestant ethic in morality, and the millennial hope in the manifest destiny of white, Anglo-Saxon, Protestant America to lead the world to its latter-day glory" (Introduction 1).[21] Sociologist George Thomas claims that both republicanism and revivalism were "isomorphic" with individualistic nationalism. They were, in other words, mutually influential. According to Thomas, revivalism "grounded and legitimated the identities and rational activity of the petty capitalist and citizen":

Rational evangelism defined the individual as one who autonomously makes decisions and acts according to rational laws within a mechanical universe. This both supported and was supported by the impersonal rational calculation and authority of market and polity. . . . The revivalist message was cognitively compelling because it corresponded to their everyday experience as shaped by the dominant cultural myth of individualism. (82–83)

It is important to remember here Perry Miller's words of caution concerning this tendency to view "the revivals as only a device in the capitalistic expansion—as though revivals did no more than set Max Weber's 'Protestant Ethic' on fire in primitive America" (*Life* 12). Still, even Miller believed that revivalism was not "unrelated to national and economic concerns" (*Life* 12).

Certainly, measuring the ability to "sell God" was a central feature of the eighteenth-century evangelistic ministries of the Grand Itinerant, George Whitefield, and his nineteenth-century American heirs. Though "commercial aspects of religion are traceable in any century," it was Whitefield who first saw the need to transform religion into something "popular," something that "would compete in the marketplace for its own market share" (Moore, *Selling God* 7; Lambert 68). As Harry Stout argues in *The Divine Dramatist: George Whitefield and the Rise of Modern Evangelicalism,*

Americans and Britons were caught up in a "consumer revolution" stimulated by vast increases in manufacturing, capital, and leisure time. This trend would not become general until the nineteenth century, but already by 1750 the seeds were sown, first in London and then outward. Inevitably this revolution created what the historian T. H. Breen has called a "shared language of consumption," which increasingly characterized society in the impersonal market-driven terms of producer and consumer, buyer and seller. (xvii)

And Whitefield quickly learned how to advertise his ministry by calling attention to his productivity: "Size was the confirmation he needed. Throughout his transatlantic career, Whitefield legitimized his novel and challenging ministry with numbers. His ubiquitous audience estimates—recorded even when Scripture texts were not—constituted not only evidence of hubris but a badge of legitimacy" (Stout 74–75). His "press agent" William Seward—and later Whitefield himself, writing in the third person—"sold Whitefield to readers" by giving them "a statistical report of his activities, indicating he was onshore thirty-three days, traveled 'hundreds' of miles, preached fifty-eight sermons, attracted crowds up to twenty thousand, and collected 'near 500 pounds sterling'" (Lambert 54, 57–58). Not surprisingly, the use of such marketplace strategies would only explode in the world of nineteenth-century American evangelicalism, particularly after the disestablishment of state churches. As R. Laurence Moore argues, "Something important happened in the United States when religion could no longer be defined by legal privilege. It had to sell itself not only in the competitive church market but also in a general market of other cultural commodities"; "Supposedly an item that promoted culture in Arnold's sense, religion looked for ways to appeal to all consumers, using the techniques of advertising and publicity employed by other merchants" (*Selling God* 11, 6). Charles Finney's *Lectures on Revivals of Religion,* for example, is all about marketing and persuasion, providing its readers with a plan for mass-producing (selling) religious conversions.

The women in this study, no less than Finney, understood that they worked and wrote in a complex marketplace, a new society in which Christian sects and denominations participated, if not fully, at least in part. "The creation of this new society" in the first half of the nineteenth century, Barbara Epstein notes, "was accompanied by the development of a new set of values: individual achievement was held to measure individual worth, and wealth, power, and fame were taken to be measures of achievement" (67). It was "the era of the 'self-made man,' when aristocratic privilege could finally be challenged on a wide scale by individuals with talent, opportunity, and the capacity for simple hard work" (Poovey 124). It was also, as Martin Delany reminded African American men in 1852, an era in which "white men are producers—we are consumers" (44). The remedy, Delany insisted, was the adoption of a philosophy of competitive individualism: "Let each one make the case his own, and endeavor to rival his neighbor, in honorable competition" (45–46). Delany called black men to go out and become productive, self-made Americans, at the same time that he exhorted black women to stay home and adhere to the ideologies of domesticity and true womanhood. But black and white women alike no doubt knew that "in spite of the oft-cited Victorian idealization of motherhood, *reproduction*—childbearing and childrearing—commanded little respect in a society dedicated to *production*" (Reimer 207).[22]

The urge, on the part of female itinerants, to emphasize the number of miles they traveled in the course of a day, a year, or a career, to call attention to the hours they spent on their feet imploring the sinful, the hardships they suffered traveling from place to place, and, of course, the number of converts they garnered along the way can also be explained, then, by their entry into the public marketplace of nineteenth-century America. There they confronted on a larger scale the values of competitive individualism, productivity, and quantification, virtues so useful to men like Whitefield in the previous century and so revered in their own. One could even argue that several of these women *anticipate* (and some of them survived into and wrote within) the period Howard Mumford Jones aptly called the "Age of Energy." According to Jones, new national markets together with countless inventions and industrial innovations in the period between the Civil War and World War I called for an intensification of the midcentury virtues with which Towle, Lee, and Elaw were familiar. The predominant values of the marketplace in the first half of the century—entrepreneurship, competitiveness, and productivity— remained the same in the second, in an epoch that became much engaged with Darwinian rhetoric; they were, however, judged on a wholly different scale.[23] This was an age that worshipped energy, "the power by which anything or *anybody acts effectively to move or change other things or persons*" (H. M. Jones 104–5, emphasis added). It was an age characterized by vast increases in industrial output (industrial energy), the rise of yellow journalism (stylistic energy), the accelerated careers of successful Americans as diverse as Annie Oakley and John D. Rockefeller Sr. (personal energy), and the excessive and extravagant living of the wealthy (recreational energy). It was the age of the celebrated Corliss engine on display at the Philadelphia Centennial, and of the even more famous dynamo encountered by Henry Adams at the exposition in 1900. It was an age in which America's long love affair with mobility intensified: "Mobility, which had been the mark of a westering society from the beginning, became an absolute virtue in an industrial democracy wherein mechanism put a special premium on speed and movement and a special disadvantage on standing still" (H. M. Jones 145). It was also, I would add, an age in which some daring women preachers continued to greet the world with all the energy, output, excess, and mobility of the new industries, the new journalism, the new careers, even the new engines. Though Towle, Lee, and Elaw did not publish their stories in the second half of the century, this context can, I believe, be retrospectively and usefully applied to their works. The culture that Jones describes did not grow up under General Lee's heels at Appomattox. As George Thomas and studies of Whitefield's career and writings remind us, both the marketplace and the culture of evangelicalism and revivalism were influenced by a philosophy of individualism long before 1865.

The second half of the century, in particular, was also marked, in the words of Robert Wiebe, by its "quantitative ethic": "It seemed that the age could only be comprehended in bulk. Men defined issues by how much, how many, how far. Greatness was determined by amount, with statistics invariably the triumphant proof that the United States stood first among nations" (40). The impulse to quantify, the exuberant desire to recount and celebrate the sheer unprecedented magnitude of industrial output was, as Susan Strasser argues in *Satisfaction Guaranteed: The Making of the American Mass Market*, a common cultural reflex in the age of mass production and mass consumption. Indeed, Foote, Sexton, Haviland, and Smith, all of whom wrote and preached during the latter half of the century, were witnesses to vast changes in the commercial economy. New products, even new kinds of products, demanded new habits. New habits necessarily required new marketing techniques. Americans had to be convinced that they needed and wanted the consumer goods that were now being produced on a massive scale. The National Biscuit Company, for example, devoted itself to what we would call "product education" to sell its packaged cookies and crackers (Strasser 34–35). Others promoted their products by invoking the theme of modernity in their advertising. Try our products, our new Gillette razor blades, they preached, and become a modern American. "Other companies," Strasser notes,

> put a strong emphasis on *converting* the population to the modern ways of mass production and factory-made goods, using images that ranged from fanciful to factual and inviting the public to observe mechanized processes. Some literally *celebrated the "mass" in "mass production," bragging about the size of their output* and the enormities they distributed, and *insinuating that everybody was buying their product.* (112, emphasis added)

Quaker Oats advertised in 1895 that its goods were "'Shipped in Train Loads'"; Wrigley's, with an even surer instinct for the vivid image, told consumers that the Illinois Central line carried sixty thousand boxes, or "'2,500 cubic feet of space, one solid mass of chewing gum'"; Waterman's campaign theme for the marketing of its fountain pens read "'A Million a Year'" (qtd. in Strasser 112, 113). These companies sold products by selling productivity. Buy our products, they argued, because we make so many of them. The "primary goal" was not, as it might seem, simply "to promote mass production but to sell goods" (Strasser 123). Their campaigns implied the insatiable demand that mass productivity required.

Now evangelicalism and the revival were in most respects antimodern, warning against materialism and selfishness, and by their emphasis on individual responsibility in conversion, they pulled against the implicit corporate demand that one surrender individuality and become one of the vast, faceless army of gum-chewing, fountain pen–using consumers. And yet by an odd cultural determinism these female evangelists ended up imitating—some of them even anticipating—the techniques of modern mass marketing in those "advertisements for themselves," their autobiographies. This is not to say that Towle, Lee, or Elaw (who wrote during the first half of the century) knowingly looked ahead to the Industrial Revolution that accelerated after the Civil War or that any of these women were preaching and writing *of* the market. With the exception of Laura Haviland, these preachers struggled with poverty, and all were antimaterialistic. In the words of Jarena Lee, who was often "poor and destitute," "We, as a people, are generally poor and cannot support so many changes of fashion. . . . One of our preachers left us on the promise of forty dollars per year. Poor man, he was like Simon Magus who perished with his money" (61, 50; Acts 8:9–24). Nancy Towle shows utter disdain for people who enter the ministry as "bigoted, selfish-hireling[s]" (216). Though she would not have considered herself a "selfish-hireling," Lydia Sexton admits that "a little more liberality about paying [her] . . . would have promoted the Master's cause and no doubt eased many a conscience" (350).

Many of these female itinerants, moreover, were not just poor but consciously opposed the market. Many of them deliberately imitated Quaker styles of dress to emphasize their disdain for the materialism that consumed the nation. "I had my outfit," Smith remembers of her trip to the A.M.E. General Conference in Nashville; "a pretty tan dress, with a drab shawl and bonnet to match. I thought I was fine; but bless you, I found I did not shine in that land, worth a nickel; for my people, as a rule, like fine show" (201). And many respectfully followed the words of Jesus, who called them, in no uncertain terms, to give up the "glutted cares of this world" (Lee 92). Jarena Lee was even reluctant to sell her own book, fearing that to "sell them appears too much like merchandize" (77). Zilpha Elaw refused to accept a house a gentleman offered to buy her: "I dared not, like Demas, forsake my itinerating ministry, to love this present world: nor was filthy lucre the object I had in view in the service of the gospel" (100; 2 Timothy 4:10). Still, it should be noted that these female autobiographers borrowed the language "of the market" because they were necessarily "in the market" (Lambert 9). Like "Whitefield's commercialization of religion," their use of market language—whether they wrote in the early part of the century when the market revolution was gaining momentum or late in the century when it was exploding—"need not suggest a secular orientation" (Lambert 51). In the words of R. Laurence Moore, "In American life, religion had to become a commodity, but that did not make it peanut butter," chewing gum, fountain pens, or Quaker Oats (*Selling God* 145).[24]

Female itinerants throughout the century, when they heeded the call to leave the father's (or husband's) house and enter the father's marketplace, faced a marketing dilemma. Though several of these women were associated with sects that "through their distinctive rituals and practices, especially female preaching, . . . tried to draw firm boundaries between their pure covenanted communities and the sinfulness of the secular world," all of them discovered a need to sell themselves and their right to preach to their readers (Brekus 155). Though Jarena Lee had close ties with Bishop Richard Allen and the A.M.E. Church, she tells us that she faced much opposition on account of her gender *even before* the once-dissenting A.M.E. Church sought to become a respectable denomination. Nancy Towle began preaching as early as 1821, but she never found a sect that would support her ministry wholeheartedly. Thus, these autobiographers, like the new inventions and new products of the century's end, needed new marketing techniques. For in addition to selling religion in a market in which too few people knew the doctrine of free will and too few had been born again, they were also demonstrating the efficacy of a woman's preaching and asserting her right to move freely in the sphere of the "informal" public. Their strategies, they realized, demanded more than simple product education. Instructing the public about the rights of women to preach the gospel—rights derived from biblical precedent—could only be part of the campaign. Anticipating the competitive spirit of Wrigley's, Quaker Oats, or even the nation itself, they launched an attack on their opponents by selling their productivity. I walked miles and miles, preached for days on end, endured numerable privations, and converted a quantifiably large number of sinners, they tell their readers again and again. The marketing technique of quantification enabled these women to protest the superiority of their ministries and to assert that theirs were ministries "sealed" by God: Who could question the power of numbers? (Elaw 91, 148, 155).

In the first half of the century, female itinerants in effect were marketing a new product, and their autobiographies were central to the marketing strategy. Though these were not the first women to preach publicly, they were "cut off from their collective past" and hence "struggled to defend their right to preach without ever realizing that others had fought the same battles before them" (Brekus 15). These autobiographical advertisements were not only for themselves—some of them published their stories near the ends of their careers, too late to benefit from them personally—but also for all women called to preach the good news. Sadly, few women heard them. Amanda Berry Smith appears to have known nothing of her African American foremothers who preached the doctrine of sanctification at camp meetings years before. Thus even Foote, Sexton, Haviland, and Smith would strike a similar promotional chord in their autobiographies, though precedents for women in the ministry were numerous by the 1880s. The socialization of once-radical sects, which encouraged denominations to adopt the dominant culture's ideologies concerning women's behavior, forced these autobiographers to *account* for their unorthodox lives, to engage the competitive marketplace in defense of "female strangers," a *product*, as it were, that had never really caught on in the masculine world of institutional Christianity.[25]

Ultimately, though, female preachers faced something more serious than a marketing problem when they tried to claim their places in the evangelical landscape. They were involved in what Robert Wiebe has called the "crisis in values" of the latter half of the century (40). "As the network of relations affecting men's lives each year became more tangled and more distended," he argues, "Americans in a basic sense no longer knew who or where they were. The setting had altered beyond their power to understand it. . . . For lack of anything that made better sense of their world, people everywhere weighed, counted, and measured it" (42–43). This crisis was the source, he concludes, of the half-century's "quest for goodness in bigness" (41). Ultimately, a version of that crisis must have been the source as well of the uncertainty which led these autobiographers—narrating their journeys far beyond the familiar domestic sphere into a world that sometimes made little sense—to weigh, measure, and otherwise quantify the results. Their doing so was their effort to clarify the meaning of that world, for themselves and for others like them who were similarly confused. There seemed to be many of these. Julia Foote, for instance, remembers meeting three women who, though called to preach the gospel, "were very much distressed and shrank from their duty" (210). She encouraged them in their calling by offering to "procure a place and hold a series of meetings" of which she would "take charge" (211). Jarena Lee tells us that she helped a woman "who seemed very zealous": "I asked permission to take her into the pulpit, which was granted, and she spoke much in the spirit of God—which was attended with power" (61). When conducting a worship service, Lydia Sexton asserts, she "never invite[d] ministers into the pulpit, except women-preachers" (336). Lee, Foote, and Sexton offered, in other words, to guide women in this new and often hostile environment.[26] And to guide themselves and their readers to an understanding of "who they were," these seven women wrote "masculine" stories of productivity. Totaling the number of miles traveled in a given year, counting the number of converts attributed to their preaching, or simply recalling their untiring efforts for Christ's sake and recording it all in their autobiographies, they believed, would prove useful in their efforts to understand, define, and advertise themselves.[27] They resorted to quantification in an attempt to measure, almost literally, the unorthodox life.

Those Were Wonderful Days

"The grand theme of American autobiography, almost its fixation," Herbert Leibowitz argues, "is the quest for distinction, a quest that has shaped and deranged American identity throughout our history" (xix). Although one could take issue with Leibowitz's monolithic approach to American autobiography, certainly the pursuit of distinction is a prominent theme in that literary tradition. The evangelical autobiographies considered here were obviously "shaped and deranged" by a desire for recognition, so much so that they write the genre not as self-presentation in the spirit of a Rousseau or even as self-interpretation in the spirit of Bunyan; they write autobiography as self-justification.[28] This is an identifiable tradition of the genre. Its participants include fugitive slaves, defeated generals, disgraced politicians, and convicted felons, all feeling themselves unjustly indicted by what one of them called "the court of public opinion," and all eager to vindicate themselves in that court if no other.[29] Georges Gusdorf contends that this urge to write a "revenge on history" is one of the "elementary motives" of almost all autobiographies: "No one can better do justice to himself than the interested party," reflects Gusdorf, "and it is precisely in order to do away with misunderstandings, to restore an incomplete or deformed truth, that the autobiographer himself takes up the telling of his story" ("Conditions" 36).

That many autobiographers avail themselves of the opportunities offered by the genre to set the record straight, to create or preserve for posterity a particular image of the self, can hardly be questioned. But *levels* of defensiveness surely vary, depending on the autobiographer's status within his or her culture. Cardinal Newman could write an *Apologia Pro Vita Sua* in the confident expectation that his readers would recognize his importance and care about his quarrel with Charles Kingsley. American fugitive slaves, in contrast, felt an obligation not only to advance a cause but also to claim the attention of a public whose interest and sympathy could not safely be assumed. The evangelists in this study—though their chances of a fair hearing were no doubt greater than those of escaped slaves—likewise could not write from a simple desire "to do away with misunderstandings" or "to *restore* an incomplete or deformed truth." But autobiography could serve these seven women in their quests for distinction or perhaps just simple recognition of their unusual, visionary lives. Though authorized by God, they look as well to the dominant culture for authentication. Their autobiographies were their last weapons—their last acts or actions, to borrow the words of Elizabeth Bruss and Porter Abbott—in this important quest.[30]

In delineating a "poetics" of women's autobiography, Sidonie Smith argues that the very task of writing autobiography places all women in a double bind. An androcentric genre, autobiography demands that she speak as a "representative man": "Repressing the mother in her, she turns away from the locus of all that is domesticated and disempowered culturally and erases the trace of sexual difference and desire" (*Poetics* 53). According to Smith, what they create is not so much a self-made woman but a self-made man; they take their "place on stage, not as Eve, but as Adam" and thereby perpetuate woman's disempowerment "by accepting the fiction of man as the more valued ideal for which to strive" (*Poetics* 53). These autobiographies do tell the story of women who are struggling to make it in a man's world, in spaces where neither a woman's body nor her voice was legitimate. One reads in these books protestations relevant on an American Adam's stage: I am ever-mobile, hardworking, competitive, and successful. And these female evangelists might even have apologized for such protestations had they thoroughly understood the ways in which they wrote themselves into the dominant, masculine spirit of nineteenth-century America. They might have said, in other words, though our experiences of conversion and sanctification, our visionary relationships with Christ, and our sincere faith in the truths of Scripture lead us *away from the world* into "an ocean of light and bliss," our human nature often, and necessarily, carries us *back to it* (Lee 10).

Presenting their readers with tedious accounts of their efforts to establish Christ's kingdom on earth, these autobiographers appropriate the values of the marketplace—even as they argue against them—in an attempt to assert themselves in the marketplace of salvation. The women in this study often encountered a world in which their limitations were presumed: as a wry Lee writes, "We fell in with the elder of the circuit, who spoke to me in a cold and formal manner, and as though he thought my capacity was not equal to his" (22). Storing up tales of productivity, these autobiographers write narratives marked by a certain degree of frustration: no matter how much they quantify their work, their record really does count only "on high." One cannot help but read between the lines of these books a weary story of women who participated in a war for converts side by side with male itinerants but were never adequately honored in this world. As female itinerants they were permitted to participate in the ideology of success, but for them, unlike their male counterparts, productivity had to be its own reward.

But to interpret these *Lives* solely as accounts of frustration and weariness, as narratives about exceptional women struggling to become exceptional men, is to miss half the point. These "feverishly restless" autobiographies also articulate stories of women thrilled to experience the life of a pioneer, stories of female itinerants prepared to embrace the competition, excitement, and even danger that traveling a continent unknown to women could bring. Unlike the lives of most of their female contemporaries, theirs were, like "the map of America" in the nineteenth century, "full of blank spaces that had to be filled" (Boorstin 223). As Nancy Towle remembers, "I felt desirous to fly from pole to pole; and if I had a thousand tongues, I thought I would freely wear them out, in proclaiming to all the kindred of the earth, Jehovah's boundless love and grace!"

(23). Surely Towle celebrates here the active, itinerant life that lay before her, the opportunity to insert her voice in the evangelical competition of the day, and the chance to write her own life's script. Indeed, the philosophy of rugged individualism, regardless of its limitations, regardless of its being a "male-identified ideal," offered these women a chance to make use of their boundless energy, to define themselves in ways most women could not. One could argue with Robert Nisbet that "the philosophy of individualism may be said to have had a kind of pragmatic value in an age when the traditional primary relationships were, if anything, too strong, too confining" (205). "How powerful," Towle reflects near the end of her autobiography, "must be that charm, to engage and to continue for a succession of years, a female, in such a warfare as this!" (228). "That charm" is surely her Lord Jesus Christ, but situated as it is in a lengthy paragraph about her competitive spirit, endless labors, and self-sufficiency, this exclamation invites her readers to consider the possibility that she is charmed by the warfare itself. These women could exhaust themselves for the sake of their Lord and then, as Jarena Lee puts it, "[feel] happier than a King" (27). Though their participation in the myth of competitive individualism may have reinscribed these preachers and their female readers in a position of powerlessness, the myth also afforded them much that confinement in strong, traditional relationships could not. While their opportunities for advancement were necessarily limited within the marketplace of nineteenth-century American religion, these women remind us that they, too, were Americans who welcomed mobility—literal and figurative. They wanted to participate in the "advent of a social order of competition, self-expression, and free enterprise" (Hatch, *Democratization* 14). Together with the writing of autobiography, the religious economy gave them the opportunity to assert themselves in this new order, if not fully, at least in part. "Those were," Amanda Smith recalls of her times at Holiness camp meetings, "wonderful days" (187).

3

Nothing Succeeds Like Failure

Singularity and the Uses of Opposition

In the day of this book hungry hearted people found the experience and went into their homes, work, and churches to witness often under severe opposition. This opposition made glowing, powerful, exemplary characters of the grace of full salvation.

Henry Shilling, 1955 preface to *Forty Witnesses* (1888)

Yea, and all that will live godly in Christ Jesus shall suffer persecution.

2 Timothy 3:12

I have made thee this day a defenced city, and an iron pillar and brasen walls against the whole land, against the kings of Judah, against the priests thereof, and against the people of the land. And they shall fight against thee; but they shall not prevail against thee; for I am with thee, saith the Lord, to deliver thee.

Jeremiah 1:18-19

For a short period in her career as an itinerant minister in the 1820s, having abandoned the comforts of home, family, and community, Nancy Towle enjoyed the company of Elizabeth Venner. Venner was a young woman whom she had met and befriended in Canada and who subsequently became her traveling companion. But after several years, Venner, weary of the unpredictable itinerant life led by her friend, tearfully parted with Towle and returned home with her brother. "Here I was called," Towle writes, "to the most bitter trial, as I thought, that I had ever experienced: i.e. the parting with my Elizabeth" (83). In the *Vicissitudes* Towle confesses that Venner's departure left her so lonely that she decided to overtake her former companion and even traveled with her again for a time, unable to endure the pain of parting with the only close friend mentioned in her autobiography. Ultimately, however, their paths did diverge, and from then on, Towle reports, she traveled for the most part alone: "I therefore now saw myself again a lonely traveller in the earth; and that, let others do as they would—to me 'no cross on earth, would be no crown in Heaven'" (83). Indeed, she concludes her narrative by announcing her intention to continue flying solo: "I can seldom find a female that has courage sufficient,—or, if she has that qualification, she has not grace proportionate" (239).

Towle's decision to reveal her strong feelings for another human being is nearly unique in the autobiographies under study here: these itinerants rarely write about feeling lonely, in part because they were, as we have seen, extraordinarily busy, and in part because they were rarely alone. Before the Lord introduced Towle to Venner and thereby answered her prayers for a "fellow-helper in the truth, and in the Vineyard of the Gospel," she tells us that the Freewill Baptist preachers Almira Bullock, Hannah Fogg, Judith Prescott, and Mrs. Quinby "strengthened [her] hands much, in the Lord, and exhorted [her], to patient continuance in doing well" (42, 21). Towle also records having traveled at times with the itinerant preachers Martha Spaulding, Sarah Thorton, Betsey Stuart, Eliza Barnes, Harriet Livermore, Susan Humes, Jane Perry, and the "beloved sister Judith Mathers" (37). Lydia Sexton frequently traveled with her husband, and Laura Haviland worked with other women, particularly during the Civil War. Julia Foote mentions the "very dear sister, Ann M. Johnson" who "accompanied" her to the General Conference in Pittsburgh and elsewhere in her travels and "the dear sisters [who] accompanied [her] to Flatbush" (212, 216). Her frequent use of the first-person plural pronoun in her book tells us that she often traveled with others, but seldom does she tell us who her companions were or what the nature of their relationship was. Jarena Lee "enjoyed good seasons" with Zilpha Elaw and "precious seasons" with sister Lydia Anderson, sister Mary Owan, and others (Lee 88, 21). Once, when Lee found herself particularly depressed, she was comforted by "relating the feelings of [her] mind to a sister who called to see [her]" (24). At that very moment, she writes, "I was overwhelmed with the love of God and souls. I embraced the sister in my arms, and we had a melting time together" (24–25). Like all itinerants, as I noted in chapter 1, Lee belonged to and worked for the larger family of God. Often this family could be counted on to fill these faithful hearts with "peace" and lead them back to the "throne of love" when "the hosts of darkness were arrayed against" them (Lee 25). Indeed, many women relished the social aspects of Christianity that had been "revived" in nineteenth-century America, and before they began their careers as itinerants, several of the preachers in this study confess that they enjoyed the intimacies afforded by praying bands, missionary societies, benevolent circles, and the like.[1] Julia Foote tells us that before she began preaching she "belonged to a band of sisters whom [she] loved dearly" (200); Jarena Lee, Zilpha Elaw, and Amanda Smith similarly report how praying bands and other spiritual groups once afforded them much pleasure and support. Donald Mathews attributes this affection for the black Methodist class or society to the fact that it was the "concrete place in which *communitas* was acknowledged," the liminal place "in which the ordinary rules of the world did not apply" ("Evangelical America" 30).

But "breaking up housekeeping" to become an itinerant preacher meant leaving such societies behind (Lee 18). Nor could the groups of preachers who so often traveled together provide itinerant women with the sort of bonds one can derive in class, community, family, and friendship. These women were, then, primarily "sisters" in "spirit"; they could play little part in that "female world of love and ritual" so well documented by Carroll Smith-Rosenberg and others. And, as Towle's account makes clear, at times their separation from that world could be acutely depressing. Though Lee could find comfort in the arms of a "sister" who could carry her back to the "throne of love," she still occasionally found it difficult to preach, "perhaps," she reflects, because of her "feelings of loneliness in the world" (25, 33). Despite traveling in the company of many sisters and brothers of the spirit, Lee felt alone, having embarked on a journey that necessarily diminished the possibilities of nurturing relationships and put her at odds with many men and women in her culture. Laura Haviland no doubt spoke for many evangelical itinerant women when she confessed, "I often felt myself a stranger in a strange land, and yet I was never alone. . . . the dear Savior was near at hand" (404). God was, and had to be, their principal companion.

Thus these books primarily narrate the lives of loners. "Like Joseph," Zilpha Elaw remembers, "I was hated for my dreams; and like Paul, none stood with me" (83; Genesis 37:5-11; 2 Timothy 4:16). "Let me admonish you," Emerson told the Harvard divinity graduates in 1838, "first of all, to go alone" (113). None of these women could have heard that message—they would have been intensely aware of their exclusion from places like the Harvard Divinity School—but all of them mastered the doctrine and applied it consistently in their lives and writing. They learned it, at least in part, in the same place Emerson did: in the long-standing Protestant tradition of spiritual individualism. Rejecting the church as mediator between humankind and God and between humankind and God's Word, the Reformation radically altered the way the Western world viewed the individual. The individual had stepped outside the bounds—and the protection—of the catholic community into a reformed faith in which men and women were responsible for ascertaining their own spiritual condition through relentless scrutiny and introspection; salvation was a matter for each individual and God.

I do not, however, want to overstate this point. Though it fostered the belief in "a whole society mainly governed by the idea of every individual's intrinsic independence both from other individuals and from that multifarious allegiance to past modes of thought and action denoted by the word 'tradition,'" Protestantism did not relinquish, as Emerson later would, a sense of community in religious worship (Watt 60). "Conversion as a liberating experience," Robert Bellah notes, "was always balanced by the coordinate concept of covenant, which implied a definite set of obligations between God and man and between man and man" (18-19). As they sailed for America, the Puritans were urged to consider these communal obligations: John Winthrop, in his sermon "A Model of Christian Charity," asked that as "fellow members of Christ" they "account [themselves] knit together by this bond of love. . . . for the work we have in hand . . . is . . . to seek out a place of cohabitation and consortship" (89).

By the time of the Great Awakening in the eighteenth century and, to a greater degree, by the turn of the nineteenth century, this equilibrium between conversion and covenant had been upset by the surge of revivalism that flowed through the nation. Eighteenth-century "New Lights," such as the famous Jonathan Edwards, who emphasized the importance of religious affections and personal religious experience, "inadvertently dismantled the social hierarchy that had once underpinned their communities of faith" (Brekus 44). Orthodox Calvinism's insistence on the total depravity of humankind and subsequently on unconditional election and irresistible grace gave way in the nineteenth century to an evangelistic theology with a decidedly Arminian cast. Individuals were no longer told that original sin rendered them unable to effect their own conversions; rather, they were encouraged to become the agents of their own salvation. Charles Finney's theology, for example, much like the New Divinity theology taught at Yale, was meant, in matters of faith and morals, to make individuals free agents who could readily respond to the new measures created to assist in converting Americans. "Nothing," Charles Foster writes, "so frustrated a revivalist as to enter the anxious room only to find its occupants agreed in Augustinian piety that they were utterly unable to do anything about their own salvation and therefore had no responsibility in the matter" (262). Reforming Calvinists hoped to equal the success of the Freewill Baptists and Methodists—both of whom stressed free will—in the nineteenth century.[2] By placing the individual conversion experience at the heart of religion and reemphasizing both the individualization of conscience and the reformed belief in unmediated interpretation of Scripture, the new measures and new theology of revivalism embraced an ideology of individualism. This is not to say that evangelicalism lacked a sense of community, any more than the New England Puritans lacked a sense of the individual. The communal and reformist fervor of nineteenth-century lay societies is well documented, as is the communal nature of the revivals. But the emphasis had shifted from one to the other. As Horace Bushnell would note in his *Christian Nurture* (1861), revivalism brought about a "fictitious and mischievous individualism" that really lacked the ability to sustain community as individualism became more and more the ideology of the dominant culture (31).

The female evangelists considered here were sincere and faithful Protestants. But their understanding of Protestant individualism served other purposes as well. As I argued in the last chapter, these women "feverishly" participated in—and made good literary use of—their culture's idealization of productivity and competitive individualism, and its belief in quantification as a reliable measure of success. But by deploying that American rhetoric of success—by presenting themselves as fantastically productive spiritual capitalists, providing salvation in quantity—they had involved themselves in an extraordinary dilemma. By their constant resort to merely statistical measures of evangelical success, they inevitably obscured the individual aspect in the drama of salvation: if the only meaningful record of a revival is an accounting of the sheer number of sinners who stepped forward to be saved, then one saved soul is (as far as we readers are able to discern) more or less like another. None of these writers would have denied that each member of the vast crowds they attracted had a dramatic and meaningful spiritual autobiography to recount. And yet, as Joyce Warren and others have argued, "The individual who is so intent on establishing his own persona cannot look outward" (13). These "female strangers" do look outward at the God who can be found in these books "tapping on [their] shoulder[s]," reassuring them of an abiding connectedness (Lee 33). But the techniques of self-advertisement to which they felt driven required them to obscure the drama and meaning in those other stories of connection and to subsume them under a mere statistical summary. Thus one of the imperatives of these autobiographers becomes the paradoxical struggle against a logic they themselves have set in motion, straining to exempt themselves from a dispensation they themselves have helped create.[3] This imperative sometimes gives these autobiographies a disorienting double vision: even while these women stress the assembly-line routineness of the conversions they worked, they use their *Lives* to raise themselves above the mass of lives around them.[4]

Climbing in the Steepest Place

Lydia Sexton's autobiography (appropriately subtitled *Her Early Privations, Adventures, and Reminiscences*) serves as a good example. Early in the book, she revisits for us a scene in which as a child she "perform[ed] a great exploit": "Immediately in the rear of

[Mr. Hand's] house, there was a high mount, with almost a perpendicular face fronting the premises. No person had ever ascended it more than a few yards. I took a fancy I would climb that mountain in the steepest place. All laughed at me when I talked of such an adventure, telling me that no human foot had scaled that precipice, and they thought never would" (66). Thus begins her account of what she comes to view as a defining moment in her life, the one in which she begins to distinguish herself from her compatriots. In the tradition of Petrarch's ascent of Mount Ventoux in 1336, she climbs her mountain "because it is there" (Asher 1050). Petrarch, however, hastily descended the peak after opening his copy of Augustine's *Confessions* "to a passage of exacting relevance, reproaching those who would sooner admire landscapes than scrutinize their souls" (Asher 1050). But Sexton is untroubled by the conflict between "aesthetic gratification" and "contemplative inwardness" (Asher 1050). She climbs her mountain not to see but to be seen, to stand out by doing what had not been done before.

The adventure is treacherous, and at times the child fears for her safety, particularly when she comes to a fifty-foot rock that stands between her and the mountaintop. Nothing, she wants us to know, protected her from the "abyss below" (67). Determined to "go up or die in the attempt," she manages to climb the rock, placing her toes in a "small seam" that ran its length (67). But then she discovers an even more formidable obstacle, for behind the scrub oaks "[is] a lair which look[s] like the nest of some wild beast of the forest" (67). At this point, exhausted and alone, Sexton turns to God, "confessing [her] sins and pleading with him to have mercy on a poor orphan that had so presumptuously risked her life, and that, too, on his holy Sabbath" (67). She is caught between the proverbial rock and a hard place, in this case between a duty to confess her unchristian presumption, self-reliance, and pride, and a rather touching desire to boast of her youthful triumph.

Of course the foolish youthful act is a commonplace in spiritual autobiography, and many of the classics in the genre make good use of it. In the *Confessions* Saint Augustine remembers stealing a piece of fruit, demonstrating—to the satisfaction of the mature, Christian autobiographer—the fact of innate depravity; Wordsworth remembers stealing a rowboat and seeing Nature itself darken in response to this stain on his childish innocence; and Benjamin Franklin remembers stealing a pile of building stones in order to construct a fishing pier, establishing early on his habit of performing useful works. Sexton's account likewise anticipates something of her mature life and thought. In the next chapter she addresses the queries of readers who might see only folly and childishness in this adventure on the mountain. Had she learned nothing from the feat, Sexton argues, her readers would be right in judging her. But, protests the autobiographer, "I learned from it the philosophy of success, trust, and perseverance" (69).

It is a philosophy of individualism that, as the autobiographer makes plain, guided her throughout her tumultuous career, from the 1840s through the 1870s, as an itinerant minister and prison chaplain. And it is a philosophy to which she repeatedly refers in her autobiography. Throughout the narrative she adverts to the metaphor of the mountain climb to describe her challenges and successes: "When I was notified of my election as chaplain of the state prison in Kansas, I said to myself, Is not the mountain too high and steep for my ascent? . . . Trusting in the providence of my heavenly Father, I undertook the perilous task" (69). Here, as with the actual mountain of her youth and with all the metaphoric ones that come later, God seems merely a helpful assistant,

Lydia Sexton. Frontispiece to *Autobiography of Lydia Sexton. The Story of Her Life through a Period of over Seventy-two Years, from 1799 to 1872* (1882). Courtesy of the American Antiquarian Society.

a kind of Sherpa guide, in adventures of which she is the unrivaled heroine. Sexton revels in detailing stories of her triumphs despite overwhelming opposition and peril, only barely remembering, as if by force of habit, to thank God for his contributions to her success.

These obstacles play a large part in her narrative. Sexton, as we have seen, makes clear that her decision to undertake an evangelical career in the 1840s was fiercely resisted by her family. Her mother-in-law for a time "bitterly opposed" her mission; her family refused to attend her preaching engagements, thinking "it a disgrace for [her] to go about preaching" (234, 240). So often did she encounter opposition from the congregations to whom she preached that she came to expect it and often traveled to meetings in a state of deep anxiety. On one such occasion, she was invited to assist at a protracted meeting in Piqua, Ohio, where "all were strangers" (290). The night of her journey, she dreamed of a black snake blocking her path. "I thought there were a great many people around," Sexton remembers of her dream,

> but none of them appeared to show the least solicitude for my safety, not even to warn me, but rather that it might strike me. I seemed to be going before the rest of the company which increased the danger to me. I took up a stone and threw it on the serpent. The serpent floundered and rolled and hissed and died. . . . I dreamed still further that we went to another point, and there found a nest of them, all knotted together like Caput Medusa. With heads protruding, they were hissing and darting at me with their forked tongues, I picked up a ponderous rock; and letting it fall on them, it crushed them all. (290-91)[5]

Sexton, interpreting the dream according to "the old and familiar German rule," believes she will "triumph over the enemy," who indeed does turn up in Piqua in the form of a woman who "devoted her time in 'looking daggers at [Sexton]'" (291, 293). Anyone familiar with this tradition of women's autobiography and with Sexton's youthful achievements can guess the outcome: the woman, affected by Sexton's preaching, repents and, concludes Sexton, "by the word of truth from the rock that was hewed out of the mountain the head of the adversary was crushed and victory obtained" (293). Sexton had climbed another mountain, had conquered yet another of the "persecutor[s] of preaching women" who fill the pages of this autobiography (358). As mentioned earlier, many of these were men within the church establishment, who aggressively opposed her mission and her request for a permanent license to preach. Undaunted by such sexist assumptions, Sexton continues to assert herself, demonstrating her capabilities, rising above her audience, as a child on a mountain, as an adult in print.

Indeed, her mountaineering adventure should be read as a figure for the autobiography itself: she pens her life story—which at 655 pages is itself a mountainous affair—as she climbed that dangerous precipice, not only in Christian humility but also from an irrepressible desire to be noticed. Writing and publishing the *Life* are clearly central episodes in the difficult project of asserting her right to individuality—and to individualism, or the free play of such individuality—in a culture in which individualism was predominantly a masculine prerogative. Sexton's successful, if somewhat foolhardy, mountain-climbing adventure invites us to recognize the author as an individual struggling to create and maintain a separate identity.

It invites us, moreover, to read her story in terms of a poetics of space. Sexton was familiar, as we have seen, with the century's ever-pervasive cult of domesticity. She would have "sigh[ed] over" the prescriptive literature of domesticity and true womanhood that aimed, Margaret Fuller said, to "fit Woman for heaven" or "fit her to please, or, at least, not to disturb, a husband" (157–58). Climbing to the top of a dangerous precipice, and then foregrounding it in her autobiography, Sexton engages in a ritual of reversal, in which proscriptions of women's participation in more "masculine" dramas are suspended, if not altogether overturned. She shows us that she is *fit* for more than household dramas, that it is her place to *disturb* a mother-in-law, an outraged minister, and a culture that called her to remain in her place at the bottom of the mountain. Written into the early portion of her voluminous narrative, her youthful adventure is more than an introduction to a resourceful, self-reliant heroine. It warns her readers that this is a book about power struggles, about who will be on top and who will be in control. Having witnessed her determination and combative spirit in childhood, we know Sexton will not be deterred by the obstacles placed in her path by a patriarchal culture.

Taking the Highest Seat

Sexton's mountaineering adventure serves as a perfect metaphor for the lives of all the women in this study: facing formidable obstacles and finding themselves in highly visible situations on revival platforms and in church pulpits, they, too, make the most of the opportunity rather than repenting the danger. By emphasizing their "failure" to be accepted in the world of nineteenth-century American culture, they "succeed" in the autobiographical task of creating and preserving a self.

Nancy Towle, near the end of her autobiography, published in 1832, reflects on a lifetime of antagonism and forcefully compares her lot to that of her male counterparts: "Neither, is such an host of the sons of Belial—the Reverend Clergy, or the worldly-wise, of every description, to pitch battle against them, a thing for which they look" (228–29). Male itinerants, while they may have experienced opposition particularly in the early years of the century, did not *look* for it.[6] Female evangelists, on the other hand, expected it at every turn; it was part of their itinerant landscape. Towle lived with a gnawing expectation of opposition from men. It was, she professes, a female itinerant's special mission to be in turn the thorn in the side of the established clergy: "I believe that *females* are sent into the harvest of the Lord Jesus, more especially to provoke the idle shepherds to more earnest endeavours for the good of souls, and the promotion of the 'word and kingdom of the Redeemer,' over the world" (81).

Early in her autobiography Towle declares that she ignored the church's opposition to female preachers, forging ahead, if quietly at first, with her career in the itinerant ministry in the 1820s because she was "satisfied with [her]self" (15). Nonetheless, she repeatedly documents the "*warfare*" to which she was subjected as a female preacher, and she regards herself and other female itinerants as "*warriors*" (228; Preface 9).[7] That warfare began, as noted earlier, even before she renounced her father's house to preach the gospel: long before she faced her first heckler, her first dismissive male clergyman, she had to confront her own inner qualms about the unconventional life to which she felt called. Having internalized her culture's prescriptions for women's behavior, she entered the ministry only after experiencing two years of inner conflict and illness. Towle was bothered by the phantom that Virginia Woolf—borrowing the title of Coventry Patmore's paean to married bliss—called *The Angel in the House*, the phantom that Woolf said "bothered me and wasted my time and so tormented me that at last I killed her . . . in self-defense" (236–38). Towle defends herself equally well in the pages of her personal narrative. She tells us, for example, that in Ithaca, New York, she outwitted a clergyman who, though he had agreed to let her speak, refused at the crucial moment to give over his pulpit to a woman. Like other male evangelists who appear in these stories as antagonists, he clearly saw the pulpit as the locus of his power, and perhaps of his masculine identity. Alert to the relationship between particular places and the construction of gender, Towle gleefully reports, "I disappointed him, for I stepped, without hesitation, into the pulpit—which very much diverted, the whole assembly!" (154–55); she went on, she tells us, to preach over an hour. The episode is the equivalent of Sexton's mountaineering adventure. In both cases the heroine raises herself, literally as well as figuratively, above the mass; in both she becomes, by her boldness and ability, the focus of everyone's attention. The scenes, clearly tenacious acts of insurgency in which the women actively resist oppression, serve the heroines in the complex task of self-creation and promotion. Both women lay claim to a new "place" in their culture—on a mountain, in a pulpit—unwilling to be consumed either by the mass culture of American revivalism in which they participated or by their culture's gendered expectations. One might be reminded here of Peter Cartwright's forceful seizure of the Baptist meeting-house; but Towle's brand of imperialism clearly serves her not in some sectarian rivalry but in her own "pitched battles" both to seize a place for herself and to establish and maintain a separate identity.

This last point is important because Towle refused to be a warrior for any particular sect: she remained an independent itinerant throughout her life, not wishing to be controlled by hierarchical church authorities. "I am therefore," she proudly proclaims, "still, a citizen of this world; but bound to a better country; and accountable to no mortal, for my procedure—nor hath any human being, any control over me" (232). Having defined herself by opposition, she has no wish to obscure this contrast by joining a particular sect. In effect, she creates a world in which few are allies and all are potential enemies. She rejects religious hierarchies and forms, we must believe, for the same reason that many other Protestants have: because they threatened to obscure her vision of God. But they would also necessarily have obscured our vision of her. By categorically rejecting the domination that might come with membership in a particular sect, she ensures, among other things, her own distinct identity. She is the champion of her own cause; rather than serve some large establishment, she becomes an establishment unto herself, serving only God. Indeed, she marks herself as an individualist of Emersonian scope by insisting throughout her autobiography that she also opposes a "systematical mode of procedure, in the ministry" (7). She refuses to become the sort of believer who "by a constant adherence, to a round of customary devotions, and a habitude of borrowing for a prop, the sentiments of other Authors . . . deprives himself of that spiritual light . . . which it is the exalted privilege of every believer to enjoy" (7–8). She anticipates here Emerson's statement in "The American Scholar": "I had better never see a book than to be warped by its attraction clean out of my own orbit, and made a satellite instead of a system," and again in 1838 in his address to the Harvard Divinity School:

"Whenever the pulpit is usurped by a formalist, then is the worshipper defrauded and disconsolate" (68, 109). Towle herself is an independent agent neither "fettered by forms" nor defeated by enemies (188-89).[8] Returning home to preach and shrinking from the task, knowing that there her "name was now cast out as evil," she nonetheless asserts herself forcefully "to vindicate [her] own cause to the world of mankind" (21, 22). She is "willing to have *a place*, upon a *level with the rest*" at a particular church, but, she professes, rather than "seem to any, like a coward, I took the *highest seat*" (29, emphasis added).

This technique—of defining the self in terms of the obstacles it overcomes—is a familiar one to students of the novel. And it is deployed to similar effect by nearly all the women under study here, as it was by many Protestant autobiographers. They render the character unique by consistently placing her in opposition to individual antagonists and to her culture at large. As described in previous chapters, many evangelical preachers encountered resistance from opponents of revivalism and religion in general. Women, however, had the added cross of being assaulted because of their sex: "A female preacher was a religious outsider in a way that a male preacher could not be" (Brekus 160). Willingly and openly challenging the gender and racial norms of nineteenth-century America, these autobiographers found themselves in a useful literary position. They stepped outside their homes, experienced opposition, and subsequently found it easy to define themselves as individuals apart from—figuratively and sometimes literally above—their contemporaries.

Detailing a life of constant warfare proved useful in another sense, for it enabled these women to summon the adventurous muse, to give a narrator (seemingly a centered, peaceful, and loving human being) and a narrative (ostensibly about "enter[ing] into the rest of full salvation") dramatic energy (Foote 213). For, as Frederick Buechner writes, "nothing is harder to make real than holiness. Certainly nothing is harder to make appealing or attractive" (*Clown* 18). Nothing, one might add, is harder to make interesting in narrative. Like the domestic romance, these autobiographies "proceed on a logic of action rather than on a logic of discursive ideas"; they must, therefore, "depict situations which are less than ideal. In a perfect domestic situation, no action would be necessary or even desirable; and without action the novel is tongue-tied" (Spengemann, *Adventurous Muse* 73). The same can be said of religious autobiography. Spiritual writers of all ages have worried about the need to make objectively real struggles that are by nature subjective and invisible. The problem is not, of course, insurmountable. If, like Petrarch writing an account of and confession for his ascent of Mount Ventoux, these women could render their spiritual, psychological, and material opponents "as fierce as battlefield foes," then their autobiographies "could compete with [their] martial analogue in meriting historical commemoration" (Asher 1057). They could compete with the tales of adventure—the historical romances, the captivity and epic narratives—that were, along with domestic fiction, staples for the nineteenth-century American reader.

Their doing so in their autobiographies places these women in a rare position in American literary history. For the literary figures whom they most resemble are the heroes of the "classic" American novels of their day: they are kindred spirits of James Fenimore Cooper's Natty Bumppo and Mark Twain's Huck Finn, self-reliant and independent loners. The stories of these isolatoes have often been taken as the quintessential American narratives: fierce individualists realizing themselves against the background of raw nature, in constant conflict with a society intent, as Huck Finn puts it, upon "adopt[ing] . . . and siviliz[ing]" them (362). Such legendary figures, writes Constance Rourke, "appeared always as single figures, or merely doubled or multiplied, never as one of a natural group, never as part of a complex human situation, always nomadic" (144). They were primarily white men: "Women, blacks, Indians, and other 'others' had no place in the drama of American individualism" (Warren 4).[9] As Nina Baym instructs us in "Melodramas of Beset Manhood: How Theories of American Fiction Exclude Women Authors," because few women in the nineteenth century, and certainly few African Americans, had the necessary freedom and mobility to pursue an individualistic quest, this American script was largely unavailable to American women writers. But Nancy Towle, Jarena Lee, and the rest at times tell precisely this "masculine" story. Though they insist that their "liberty" came from God, these autobiographers also insist on their independence and individuality.[10] They represent themselves as singular heroines—"speckled birds"—struggling for self-definition (Elaw 59; A. Smith 108; Jeremiah 12:9).[11]

Satan and Lesser Adversaries

Jarena Lee recognized the literary opportunity afforded her by the opponents she faced in her three decades of preaching under the aegis of the African Methodist Episcopal Church. The first of these is formidable indeed: Satan, "the enemy of all righteousness," attempts to thwart her conversion, even to the point of tempting her to commit suicide: "No sooner was the intention [to kill myself] resolved on in my mind, than an awful dread came over me, when I ran into the house; still the tempter pursued me" (5). "That night," continues Lee's vivid account, "I formed a resolution to pray; which, when resolved upon, there appeared, sitting in one corner of the room, Satan, in the form of a monstrous dog, and in a rage, as if in pursuit, his tongue protruding from his mouth to a great length, and his eyes looked like two balls of fire" (6). We cannot know what actual visionary experience inspired this account, nor is it my intention to evaluate its spiritual and psychological validity, but Lee surely understood its dramatic potential. Though she never describes scaling a mountain in the manner of the young Lydia Sexton, she does "totter" at the "edge" of many a "precipice" (6). By demonstrating her equanimity in this confrontation, she elevates herself for her readers and proves herself a heroine of remarkable scope, an Odysseus battling horrific monsters (6). Scenes like this one assure us that Lee faced very real terrors in her "state of conviction," a state in which she was "permitted" to encounter "evidence" of the "Bible account of a hell of fire, which burneth with brimstone" (7, 6; Revelations 21:8). Such scenes also make vivid for her readers her experience of contending constantly against an amorphous, impersonal consensus that a "poor coloured woman" had no business doing what she was doing (18). For in this autobiography Satan invariably speaks in behalf of the patriarchal religious establishment, which viewed black women like Lee with grave suspicion.

Not surprisingly, many black women, following a centuries-old Christian tradition, personify a hostile culture—or whatever they consider the enemy—in the menacing figure of Satan. Zilpha Elaw writes of "agonizing conflicts" with this "unwearied adversary" (Elaw 83). And, like that of her human opponents, his is a voice of conservatism; he speaks for the many Christians who were suspicious of the blessing of complete sanctification—it reeked of antinomianism and arrogance—and appalled by women preachers. Following her sanctification in 1817, Elaw feels called to speak to families about salvation, visit the sick, and engage in other such traditionally female ministries. "But," Elaw writes, "Satan at length succeeded in producing a cloud over my mind, and in damping the delightful ardours of my soul in these blessed labours, by suggesting, that I ought not to make so bold a profession of an entire sanctification and holiness of spirit" (67). And it is Satan who instigates opposition to her call to preach the gospel. Though sanctioned by her ministers, Elaw's ministry is undercut almost before it begins, Satan having wrought jealousy among her Methodist class members, friends who subsequently abandoned her. Her theology, however, absolves these people of blame: the ultimate source of all her trials is the devil, who "never fails to find a pretext by which to inspire his agents with opposition against the ministry which is of God" (Elaw 155).

To argue that these women found in confrontations with the devil a useful literary strategy is not to say that these confrontations with and renunciations of Satan in their writings are not essential elements of their faith; renouncing the devil has been a feature of baptismal and confirmation services in Christian churches for centuries. "Put on the whole armour of God," Paul told the Ephesians, "that ye may be able to stand against the wiles of the devil" (Ephesians 6:11). "If sinners wanted to be born again," nineteenth-century evangelists believed, "not only did they have to beg Jesus for mercy, but they had to do battle with Satan, the terrifying 'deceiver' and 'seducer' who wanted to drag them into everlasting torment in hell" (Brekus 209). Satan was, for each of these women, a real oppressor. He is an ever-present threat, against which they must "watch and pray, and on [their] God rely" (A. Smith 18). The devil ignores the "worldly-minded," Charles Finney acknowledged: "But spiritual Christians he understands very well, are doing him a vast injury, and therefore he sets himself against them" (*Lectures* 118). In the words of Brekus, "At a time when Satan was losing his hold on the public imagination," in the early nineteenth century,

> lower-class evangelicals were too aware of the reality of human suffering to question their faith in his literal existence, and in contrast to many prosperous, middle-class Americans, they imagined him in vivid personal terms as "a cruel tempter, a malicious accuser, and a wretched liar." Struggling to understand how a loving God could permit the existence of slavery, black women in particular seemed to see Satan prowling in every dark corner. (209)

Curiously, it was Amanda Smith, writing at the *end* of the century, who saw Satan prowling about most often. Like Virginia Woolf's phantom, Satan sometimes "sets himself against" Amanda Smith as the voice of her own inner qualms. No less than Nancy Towle, though writing sixty-one years later and forty-five years after the first women's rights convention at Seneca Falls, Smith appears to have suffered anxiety in her efforts to create and preserve an authentic existence outside the parameters known to most black women. Her "struggle for individuality," like that of all women autobiographers, "is complicated by the power of those culturally prescribed norms of female identity" (Smith, *Poetics* 10). Amanda Smith writes, for example, of one particularly agonizing occasion, in which she is invited to go to England, but refuses to pray about the matter because it is "well enough for swell people to go," but not for the "colored washwoman" (242). Later, impressed that she must go, she is suddenly attacked by Satan, who argues from the point of view of the century's definition of womanhood, which Smith, despite her independence, has internalized. "'What about your child?'" he asks (245). Questioning the "propriety" of leaving Mazie, Smith is confronted by Satan, who forces her to envision the worst: "I saw myself on the steamer in a big storm, and the ship wrecked. . . . Then my daughter got the news, then I saw her frantic and wild with grief!" (245–46). Making Satan a prominent character in her autobiography, Smith renders many subjective conflicts as objective reality, making them understandable to her readers. And like Sexton's mountaineering or Towle's conflicts with vigilant guardians of the pulpit, her dramatic battles with Satan help Smith establish herself as a heroine in print. In this instance, as in others, confronting Satan in her *Life* enables her, moreover, to express, and then distance herself from, the anxiety inherent in an unorthodox life that certain identifiable opponents, but more importantly a faceless consensus, condemned as immoral.

And there was another, and related, benefit to this literary strategy: characterizing Satan as a patriarchal oppressor offers Smith a veiled means of dissent. Facing and conquering the "tempter" gives Lee, Elaw, and Smith a ritualistic means by which to profess hostility, if only quietly, toward the hierarchical elements of their culture that repeatedly challenge their rights to be successful itinerant evangelists (77). Once Satan tries to prevent Smith from exhorting and distributing religious tracts to upper-class white men: "The Devil said, 'That is a white gentleman, and he will curse you'" (107). But Smith resists Satan's efforts to thwart her ministry and offers the man a tract anyway. Though "thoroughly astonished," the young man is "pleasant and courteous," and, as Smith later learns, the tract helps him find "peace and joy in the Lord" (107). Here Smith defeats Satan, crosses the boundaries of race, class, and gender, and labors to *free* white Americans from *enslavement* to racial prejudice, a task that she, like most nineteenth-century evangelicals, believed could be accomplished only through heartfelt conversions.

Smith understood well the metaphoric potential of the dialectic between freedom and slavery in American history. She opens her autobiography with an anecdote about a slave owner—"a professed Christian, and a class leader in the Methodist Church"—who was "so blinded by selfishness and greed" that he risked his life to reenslave two boys "who sought only for freedom" (18). She concludes the vignette with a spiritual moral that could be applied to all Christians: "How selfishness, when allowed to rule us, will drive us on, and make us act in spirit like the *great enemy of our soul*, who ever seeks to recapture those who have escaped from the bondage of sin" (18, emphasis added). Here the "great enemy" takes the form of a cruel slave owner, relentlessly pursuing his slaves even as—or, rather, because—they cross over into a state of freedom. Giving over part of their autobiographies to this enemy, Smith and the other black women under study here forcibly, if indirectly, enter their voices in the political struggle against domination.[12] These narratives by black women are clearly situated, then, in the tradition of nineteenth-century African American autobiography, for by recounting both the heroine's flight from the bondage of sin to the freedom of salvation and her quest for independence and power in their culture, they resemble slave narratives.

Indeed, throughout her autobiography Amanda Smith defines her spiritual struggle—and those of the people she seeks to convert—as an ongoing battle between slavery and freedom. The metaphor is as old as Christianity itself: "And ye shall know the truth, and the truth shall make you free" (John 8:32); or, in the words of Peter, "While they

Amanda Berry Smith. Frontispiece to *An Autobiography: The Story of the Lord's Dealings with Mrs. Amanda Smith, the Colored Evangelist* (1893). Courtesy of the American Antiquarian Society.

promise them liberty, they themselves are the servants of corruption: for of whom a man is overcome, of the same is he brought in bondage" (2 Peter 2:19). And the metaphor is common in these and other spiritual autobiographies. Julia Foote, in language familiar to students of fugitive slave narratives, describes her quest for sanctification as a struggle for freedom: "I had wandered in the wilderness a long time, and now that I could see a ray of the light for which I had so long sought, I could not rest day nor night until I was free" (185). Or, as Amanda Smith asks rhetorically, "I longed for deliverance, but how to get free" (30). The metaphor was, historians of black religion argue, a psychologically and politically potent one for blacks, before and after the Civil War. Freed from bondage to sin, blacks were also freed to experience their "ultimate worth as one of the chosen of God" (Raboteau, "Black Experience" 193). Because many African Americans "made no distinction between sacred and secular," the metaphor was clearly political in its capacity "to support [both] slaves in the act of rebellion by flight" and freedmen and freedwomen in their resistance to charges of biological inferiority and institutionalized discrimination (Mathews, *Religion* 198; Raboteau, *Slave Religion* 305). Northern black evangelicals, both in their war against slavery and racism *and* in their promotion of moral reform, mobilized themselves with the rallying cry, "What shall we do to end slavery?" (Raboteau, "Black Experience" 192).

A "Bible" Christian, Smith would have been quite familiar with the paradox of freedom and slavery found in the writings of Paul: "For he that is called in the Lord, *being a servant* is the Lord's freeman: likewise also he that is called, *being* free, is Christ's servant" (1 Corinthians 7:22). Born into slavery in 1837 and only provisionally free even in the 1890s, she would have been all too aware that Paul's paradoxical terms had very real consequences for African Americans in the nation's political and social climate. "I often say to people," Smith explains, "that I have a right to shout more than some folks; I have been bought twice, and set free twice, and so I feel I have a good right to shout" (22; 1 Corinthians 6:20, 7:23). As a child Smith lived in a station of the Underground Railroad; she once saved a sister who had been sold into slavery; and she spent much of her life barely making ends meet as a laundress. Certainly she repeatedly encountered racism—on omnibuses; in churches; in Phoebe Palmer's famous Tuesday meetings, where she met women who were "uncomfortable" in her presence; at camp meetings, where she often had to perform domestic service for rich white attendees, where she was "told to sit down" and let others speak first, and where she had to "learn obedience of the powers that be"; and even in England, where white evangelicals worried that her going to the famous Broadlands' Conference would spoil and "make [her] proud" (119, 263). As this rather short list reveals, Smith experienced the slavery of poverty and racism almost as often as she experienced the freedom and love of a living God. She preached in the last quarter of the century, an age known, in the words of Rayford Logan, by its "betrayal of the American Negro." The last decade of the century, when Smith published her autobiography, was characterized not by the redemption of America and the end of racism but by disfranchisement acts, segregation laws, and the ritualized lynching of black men. Living and writing in such an age, Smith understood the beauty of holiness because she had experienced firsthand the chains of bondage. Conceivably, then, she better understood—and thus made more use of—the literary strategy of writing Satan into her *Life*: at a time in which racial codes were both more rigid and complex, perhaps she had to search harder for a method by which to dramatize a life that may well have been one long negotiation—was it between Satan and God, or among complicated racial, gender, and class hierarchies around the globe?—for selfhood.

Most often, of course, these evangelical women preachers contended with opponents more mundane, though no less "masterful," than the "Old Accuser" himself. Most of these opponents were contemporary preachers, men who coveted the pulpit as a privilege of their gender; most, moreover, were never absolved of blame. As noted in chapter 1, in Jarena Lee's autobiography that opposition is first personified in the Reverend

Richard Allen, whom she petitioned in 1811 for permission to preach within the fold of the Free African Society, and later within the African Methodist Episcopal Church. Allen's biographer reminds us that the bishop "gave [women] the opportunity of exercising their talents and encouraged them to be useful in the service of the church," and Lee credits him with helping her and her son *after* she gained permission to preach (Wesley 195-96). But Lee's purpose in portraying Allen in the chapter entitled "My Call to Preach the Gospel" is not to balance his defects with virtues; she presents him simply as an enemy seeking to thwart God's plan for her life. After being impressed to preach, Lee tells us that she sought permission to move within the "sphere" of the African Methodists but was rebuffed by Allen, who informed her that his "discipline knew nothing at all about [women preaching], that it did not call for women preachers" (11).[13] When her call was rejected, Lee writes, "that holy energy which burned within me, as a fire, began to be smothered" (11; Jeremiah 20:9). The biblical metaphor is well chosen, for it calls attention to the history of women in the church who were repeatedly told to "be in silence" (1 Timothy 2:12). Just recapturing this moment in her autobiography offends Lee so much that she launches into a page-long exhortation on the rights of women to preach: "O how careful ought we to be, lest through our by-laws of church government and discipline, we bring into disrepute even the word of life" (11). She wants us to know that Allen was not entirely successful at smothering her voice. And eventually, she reports, he granted her permission to preach in 1819. The occasion of his change of heart forms one of the more remarkable episodes in the autobiography. The Reverend Richard Williams, Lee remembers, "lost the spirit" in midsermon. His text, ideally for Lee's purposes, is Jonah 2:9: "But I will sacrifice unto thee with the voice of thanksgiving; I will pay *that* that I have vowed. Salvation *is* of the Lord." Among the congregation, even more ideally, is none other than her nemesis Bishop Allen. So, in the spirit of Nancy Towle, Lee rises from her seat, gains the attention of the crowd, and expounds upon her own Jonahesque failure to answer God's call, regardless of such worldly obstacles as the presumably discomfited Allen: "I told them I was like Jonah; for it had been then nearly eight years since the Lord had called me to preach his gospel . . . but that I had lingered like him, and delayed to go at the bidding of the Lord" (17). Allen responded to the incident—thus perhaps confirming his biographer's portrait of an essentially benevolent man—by giving Lee what she wanted.

The bishop is quickly succeeded by other opponents. Lee was supported in her ministry by many male preachers, and she credits them throughout her autobiography. Once, for example, she notes that the "preachers generally were very kind to me. Both white and colored" (54). And often she recounts times when she was welcomed and helped in her travels by circuit preachers and "brothers" in the church. But she also writes, on practically every page, about her conflicts with male adversaries who are, she emphasizes, later "turned out of the Church" or made "an example of" (44, 37). At times she prefers to acknowledge the opposition in passing. "On Wednesday night," she writes of an incident in 1823, "I spoke to the people at Trenton Bridge, and notwithstanding the opposition I had met with from brother Samuel R—, then on the circuit, the Lord supported the 'woman preacher' and my soul was cheered" (33). In these instances she pays tribute, as it were, to her opponents, masterfully heightening the level of her success by showing her readers what she was up against. Lee's more cowardly opponents, she reports, often failed to show their faces, preferring simply to lock her out of the appointed meetinghouse. Another "antagonist, who was ready to destroy [her] character . . . sent a letter to Pittsburg to stop [her]" (54–55). After encouraging this man to "throw away his prejudices," Lee turns to Bishop Allen: "I felt under no obligation to bear the reproaches of progressing Preachers; and I wanted it settled at Conference. But it was looked upon with little effect by the Preachers and Leaders" (55).

So relentless was the opposition she faced even among African Methodists that she considered leaving them, or so she tells us (in perhaps an excess of pious martyrdom), "lest some might go into ruin by their persecutions of me" (24). Lee portrays herself as a "Sheep among Wolves"—a female itinerant at odds with the irreligious, racist, and sexist elements of her culture (59; Matthew 10:16): "At times I was pressed down like a cart beneath its shafts—my life seemed as at the point of the sword—my heart was sore and pained me in my body" (24; Amos 2:13).[14] Her choice of biblical metaphor is again apt, for the word "pressed" evokes its etymological offspring "oppressed" and "depressed": "Something pressed," Marilyn Frye reminds us, "is something caught between or among forces and barriers which are so related to each other that jointly they restrain, restrict, or prevent the thing's motion or mobility" (2). As a "poor coloured woman" struggling to succeed as an itinerant preacher, Lee probably suffered from what today we would consider a severe depression (18). Nevertheless, she lets us know that she reentered the battlefield: "Let the servants of Christ gird on the armor," Lee instructs her fellow itinerants, "and 'listen to the Captain's voice: Lo I am with you always, even unto the end'" (32; Matthew 28:20). Drawing here on a particularly masculine metaphor from the Old and New Testaments, she dramatically presents herself as a Christian soldier doing battle with her culture's basic assumptions.[15] She creates herself in her autobiography not only as a mother nurturing the family of God but also as one who invariably outwits those dominating figures—Bishop Allen, Brother Samuel—who threaten to "sivilize" her and deconstruct the autonomous selfhood she sought in her itinerant ministry and in her autobiography. It is one of the great ironies of her career, then, that Lee's opponents ultimately handed her the literary technique with which she could guarantee that autonomy; she seized it in her literary self-representation as a means of individuation.

Julia Foote goes much further than Lee in detailing her primary antagonists' "opposition to [her] lifework" (205). The Reverend Beman's opposition eventually assumes such proportions in Foote's account that she professes, perhaps hyperbolically, to be an Ishmael, engaged in battle with *all* men: "It is no little thing to feel that every man's hand is against us, and ours against every man, as seemed to be the case with me at this time" (208; Genesis 16:12). No doubt Foote felt that she had no ally but God: some of her friends, like most of Elaw's, "said [she] was too forward"; one preacher told her that she was "too young to read and dictate to persons older than [herself]"; and influential ministers in the African Methodist Episcopal Zion Church—men "who had been much blessed"—put her through "fiery trials" (200, 188, 208). Foote, however, informs us that she was not a woman who would be easily deterred: "Though my gifts were but small, I could not be shaken by what man might think or say"—even by what her husband would say (189; see also 204). In the autobiography she depicts her spouse as another figure who is alarmed by her newly acquired independence; he responds to her deviance from culturally prescribed modes of female behavior by labeling her "mad." Threatened both by her desire to preach publicly about the blessing of complete sanctification and by the self-assurance such holiness gave her, he warns that he will commit her to a "crazy-house," where, forced back into the role of dependent Other, she would be duly disciplined and excluded from further excursions into what he considered the territory of men (196).[16]

Julia Foote would hardly have been surprised by her husband's allegations and threats, for early in the century revivalists like Charles Finney insisted that such charges were common in—perhaps even definitive of—the experience of spiritual Christians. Male itinerants, like "the crazy man" Lorenzo Dow and "crazy [James] Horton," were proud of the charge, believing that the "label confirmed rather than denied [their] religious calling" (Dow 40; Horton 52; Butler, *Awash* 241). Anticipating Michel Foucault's analysis of the cultural construction of sanity, Finney warned his audiences in 1835: "If you have much of the Spirit of God, it is not unlikely you will be thought deranged, by many. We judge men"—and particularly women, he might have added—"to be deranged when they act differently from what we think to be prudent and according to common sense" (*Lectures* 115-16). Perhaps that is why Foote, despite the opposition encountered, never questions her sanity; rather, she reads her husband's threat as a mere desire for social control and, moreover, as evidence of her own sanctification. As she defiantly concludes, "Though opposed, I went forth laboring for God, and he owned and blessed my labors, and has done so wherever I have been until this day" (209).

Historians of religion have well documented the extent to which female preachers—and secular feminists as well—participated in a kind of warfare in their efforts to cross the culture's racial and gender boundaries. We know that these women did not invent the conflicts that they carefully emphasize in their autobiographies. From their writings, we also know that despite the forceful efforts of angry hecklers and stubborn clergy to create a disabling environment, these women were not paralyzed by the challenges put before them. We can even speculate that such constant warfare had some psychological benefits. One might recall what Ralph Ellison's Invisible Man said of his battle with "Monopolated Light & Power": "It allows me to feel my vital aliveness" (7). Though these women would confess to have been "so overwhelmed with the love of God, that self seemed annihilated," their autobiographical rendering of self proves otherwise (Elaw 61). Arrested in England for "obstructing the way and making a disturbance" as she preached the gospel, Nancy Towle tells us that she was anything but upset. Rather, she welcomed the opportunity to show her strength and to challenge the image of American womanhood as frail and passive. Eventually acquitted in court, Towle reports that she hastened back to the town center to pick up where she left off, to give them "a sample for once, that 'American females, are not all of them, cowards'" (63). Neither she nor her sister autobiographers preserve the self, as Barbara Rigney has said of characters in many feminist novels, by withdrawing from threatening situations; they do so, rather, by actively seeking them out. Their world seems like Emerson's, in which the self survives only by conquering the world around it: the alternative to climbing the mountain is being crushed by it. Without exception these narratives follow a heroine who sheds her relationships and—without even the aid of a Chingachgook or a Queequeg—pursues an unquiet life of constant movement, much opposition, and even some danger.

Speckled Birds and Gazing Stocks: Making Sense of Marginality

And yet, as Nancy Towle so movingly shows us when she writes of her friendship with Elizabeth Venner, shedding relationships was never easy. Singularity and the opposition it provoked, while assets in the making of selfhood, or in the *marketplace of autobiography*, might also be psychologically disorienting for these women, who were often, in the words of the evangelist Harriet Livermore, "too much exposed," "spectacle[s] to angels and men" (12, 15; 1 Corinthians 4:9). But all of these women were ultimately able to find—or perhaps they always knew—the virtue of such exposure and the persecution that accompanied it. What Paul wrote to the Hebrews about the descendants of Abraham, these itinerant autobiographers learned to apply to themselves: with their faith they had seen the "promises . . . afar off, and were persuaded of *them*, and embraced *them*, and confessed that they were strangers and pilgrims on the earth" (Hebrews 11:13). These "female strangers" knew that God had made them "a defenced city, and an iron pillar and brasen walls against the whole land" and that God would "deliver" them from their enemies (Towle 254; Jeremiah 1:18-19). Reading themselves in Scripture, these women discovered another means of understanding, defending, and even promoting themselves and the "spectacular" lives they were called to lead.

Though her autobiography demonstrates that she obviously enjoyed the freedom of itinerancy, Amanda Smith's text also reveals that she felt lost at times as a black female leaving the safe harbor of private life in 1870 and attempting to navigate the waters of a primarily white, primarily male, and primarily middle- and upper-class Holiness sea. Smith and her sisters could always be comforted by the word of God. Facing opposition in her quest for sanctification, Smith reminds us that she knew where to drop anchor:

> When Satan would suggest, "You cannot expect such a blessing," I stood on these words, "But it is the will of God. He is my Father. And He said in His inspired word, through His Apostle Paul, it is the will of God. And I am one of His legitimate children and a rightful heir, and I propose to have my rights out of the will, if all the rest of the heirs get offended." When I anchored there, somehow I seemed to get help. (129; see Hebrews 10:9-10)

So, too, did Julia Foote: "The glorious wave of holiness . . . sent me to sea once more with chart and compass. 'The Bible is my chart; it is a chart and compass too, / Whose needle points forever true'"(226). But these autobiographies make clear that even the most faithful and sincere Christian pilgrims could easily lose sight of that "chart and compass" and hence feel anxious about their public journeys, particularly when the marginal sects that once permitted their movements had become established denominations that frowned upon women's public speaking. These preachers were "strangers in a strange land" even as late in the century as the 1870s—when Foote, Sexton, and Haviland were continuing their labors and Smith was beginning hers—when the women's movement had begun to challenge the cult of domesticity's hold on the American imagination (Elaw 138; Exodus 2:22).

Though Amanda Smith chose a combative life as a captain in God's industry and remained enthusiastic about that choice throughout her life, she was also pained both by her high visibility on the evangelical stage and by the isolation and sense of placelessness that accompanied it. She tells us that for a long time she was distressed by the notoriety afforded her as she crossed the dominant culture's boundaries. In Holiness and revivalist circles, she stood out as "the black woman" (280). At one particular revival, Smith writes, she could get no rest, despite her many attempts to "slip" away from the onlookers who followed her: "Sometimes I would slip into a tent away from them. Then I would see them peep in, and if they saw me they would say, 'Oh! here is the colored woman. Look!' Then the rush!" (183). She resorts to hiding "out of sight" under a friend's bed, though even there she only narrowly escapes these would-be ferrets, who insist on uncovering "'the colored woman'" (183). Only when the coast is clear does Smith emerge from the tent and complain to Sister Clark: "'The people have followed me about all day, and have stared at me. Somehow I feel so bad and uncomfortable'" (183).

Jarena Lee similarly documents the extent to which she was burdened by the gaze of the curious. Of a trip to Portsmouth, Lee writes, "It was altogether a strange thing to hear a woman preach there, so it made quite an excitement, which made my labor very heavy, as the people were all eyes and prayed none" (87). Objectified in the white field of vision, Smith and Lee—though preaching at least twenty-five years apart—are "see[n] constantly" and "recognize[d] immediately"; like inmates of Bentham's Panopticon, they suffer the anxiety and discomfort of being in "a state of conscious and permanent visibility" (Foucault, *Discipline* 200-201).[17]

Zilpha Elaw remembers being objectified, particularly, though not exclusively, when preaching to slaves and slave owners. "The novelty," she writes of her preaching in Alexandria, Virginia, "had produced an immense excitement and the people were collecting from every quarter, to *gaze* at the unexampled prodigy of a coloured female preacher" (91, emphasis added): "There were some among the great folks whom curiosity induced to attend my ministry; and this formed a topic of lively interest with many of the slave holders, who thought it surpassingly strange that a person (and a female) belonging to the same family stock with their poor debased, uneducated, coloured slaves, should come into their territories and teach the enlightened proprietors the knowledge of God" (92). "I became such a prodigy to this people," Elaw recalls, "that I was *watched* wherever I went" (92, emphasis added). Throughout America and England, she was "the woman," "the dark coloured female stranger," who intrigued the curious who came en masse to hear her preach (112).[18]

But the incessant surveillance that initially makes Smith "feel so bad and uncomfortable" and imprisons her in an odd game of hide-and-seek is made in these autobiographies to serve not the dominant culture, with its ever-vigilant guards, but the "transgressors," the "madwomen" in that culture's attic. Each of these women was a "seeming curiosity" (Sexton 251). Upon notification that "a woman was to preach, the people would come running and walking and riding,—any way to get there,—just from pure curiosity to hear a woman preach" (Sexton 367). And that curiosity often led to conversions: "'I am so glad I went to hear *a woman preach!*'" Sexton remembers one onlooker shouting after hearing her (303). Again and again, these women tell us, their status as "curiosities" in the evangelical marketplace helped them achieve the quantifiable success I described in chapter 2.

It would also, and significantly, help them achieve self-understanding. When Amanda Smith turns to Sister Clark to complain about the discomforting "gaze," Clark counsels her, "Don't you know the Bible says, 'You are to be a gazing stock?'" (184; Hebrews 10:33). There is, Smith discovers, a story that could "give shape to" the imprisoning experience of objectification (Christ, *Diving Deep* 5). Biblical precedent empowers Smith to make sense of the gaze that sought to control her. In the Book of Hebrews she could read her own experience: she, too, was called to remember "days, in which, after ye were illuminated, ye endured a great fight of afflictions; Partly, whilst ye were made a gazingstock both by reproaches and afflictions" (Hebrews 10:32–33). If she encountered ugly stares from curious onlookers at revivals and mission trips, if she felt guilty about publicly exposing her body before white and black, male and female alike, she had the satisfaction of knowing she was in good company: she was now a member of a prestigious club of individuals who were paradoxically marginal and powerful. "They shall," she learns, "look on him whom they pierced" (John 19:37). Finding refuge in the Bible, she need no longer seek it under beds. Her confidence renewed, Smith embraces her marginal status and shouts, "'I have got the victory! Everybody come and *look at me!*'" (184, emphasis added). "The field of battle having been marked out," to borrow the words of Frantz Fanon, "[she] entered the lists" (114). Thus does she critique the politics of the gaze and dismantle its power to render her self-conscious about her bodily presence in public spaces, to make her a "docile object" of power. No longer questioning her position onstage—am I taking up too much space? is my place here legitimate?[19]— Smith and her sister autobiographers *revive* the gaze in their autobiographies so as to comment upon, ironize, and resist its power to objectify them. As writers, they appropriate it for their own use; laying claim to the gaze of onlookers, they invert its power to dominate.

Smith could, then, with palpable pleasure recall her appearance at the A.M.E. Church Conference in Nashville: "I was quite a curiosity to most of the visitors, especially the Southern brethren, in my very plain Quaker dress: I was eyed with critical suspicion [sic] as being there to agitate the question of the ordination of women. All about, in the little groups that would be gathered talking, could be heard, 'Who is she?' 'Preacher Woman.' 'What does she want here?' 'I mean to fight that thing'" (200). Overhearing these conversations, Smith must have wondered whether they were referring to the ordination of women or to the "preacher woman" herself when they announced their intentions "to fight that thing." On another occasion, Smith remembers encountering polite but forceful opposition from a group of wealthy white women who "advise" her not to attend the evangelistic meetings being held by Hannah Whitall Smith, even though she had been invited by Hannah's husband, Robert Pearsall Smith: "'There will be,'" she is warned, "'a great many very wealthy ladies in from Germantown and West Philadelphia, and Walnut Hills, and the meetings are especially for this class'" (197). But Smith, who usually avoids "going where she was not wanted," decides on this occasion to obey the promptings of the Spirit rather than the warnings of the race- and class-conscious and slips into the meeting (197). "And now," reflects Smith of her efforts to blur the boundaries of race, class, and gender, "instead of Amanda Smith, *the colored washwoman's* presence having a bad effect on a meeting where ladies of wealth and rank are gathered to pray and sing His blessing, they think a failure more possible if the same Amanda Smith, *the colored woman,* cannot be present" (198, emphasis added). Because of her status as a poor, black washwoman, she is gazed upon by middle- and upper-class whites. And because of her profession of holiness, she is "a speckled bird" even "among [her] own people" (108; see also 146, 204; Jeremiah 12:9). Pierced on every side, Smith could take comfort that hers was an old story; that, ironically, far from standing alone, an Emersonian individualist, she was representative, a player in an age-old typological drama. "I belong," she tells us, "to Royalty, and am well acquainted with the King of Kings" (198; 1 Timothy 6:15; Revelations 17:14, 19:16).

Appropriating biblical paradigms is similarly comforting and liberating for Lydia Sexton, who recognizes in each experience of "censure and ridicule" her own acquaintance with the King of Kings (336). In one particularly revealing chapter of her autobiography, she tells us how on the road to a preaching engagement in Crawfordsville, Indiana, she "stopped to take dinner with a family," who could not take their eyes off her (251). Though accustomed to such usage, in this instance "[her] feelings were overcome while meditating on the many opposing elements that seemed to meet [her] on every hand" (251). "Although there was nothing in their treatment that would warrant such melancholy," Sexton remembers, "yet in this instance as in many others, I realized the cross that seemed to bear so heavily upon me, until I could in spirit and in truth sing: 'Must Jesus bear the cross alone, / And all the world go free; / No, there's a cross for every one, / And there's a cross for me'" (251–52). Though the scrutiny, poverty, and seemingly endless opposition she encountered occasionally overwhelmed her with a sense of isolation and exhaustion, she assures her readers that such a heavy load warranted not lamentations but the singing of a well-known hymn, with its joyful, and rhythmically iambic, acceptance of suffering.

Indeed, all these women had a resource that secular autobiographers and rebels lacked: a way of making sense of their marginality. Christians had, in the example of their creed's founder and the many prophets who preceded and disciples who followed him, an alternative geometry in which difference was not deviance, in which the margin *was* the center. Narrating the life as conflict was thus much more than a means by which women could create and preserve a certain individuality and force recognition from their culture; it was also an avenue into biblical typology, where they could gain a much-needed self-understanding. "Experience," writes Ursula King in *Women and Spirituality*, "includes social pressures, constraints, and opportunities," as well as "inner thoughts and feelings," and "at the deepest spiritual level we must inquire what meaning we can discern in the intricate web of our experience and whether we can find in it a pattern, a direction or an orientation which seems to make sense" (87). Nineteenth-century American culture failed to provide these women with an adequate framework in which to understand their experiences. Hence, as described in the last two chapters, they situated themselves on the margins of the ideology of true womanhood and resorted to quantification in an attempt to anchor their conduct in both the century's valorization of domesticity and its ethics of success and competitive individualism. They did so to prove the propriety and the quality of their work to any rational reader and to measure their unorthodox careers. In leaving behind what Barbara Welter calls the "standardized" experience of domesticity, these itinerant women also turned to biblical precedents in discerning the meaning of their intricate lives (*Dimity* 18). They looked to the oldest prescribed roles available to them, standardized experiences that gave them both freedom from traditionally female roles and the comfort of knowing they "belonged." The Bible, in other words, became for these preachers what Patricia Collins in another context calls "a 'safe space' for self-definition" (95). Looking to Old Testament prophets and New Testament disciples, these *rootless* itinerants discovered that they were not really pioneers after all: they were deeply *rooted* in a powerful and empowering tradition. The mountains they crossed each day on their journey through enemy territory had been mapped long ago. The topography was familiar: they need only retrace it in their autobiographies to impress themselves and their readers that they were far from lost.

Retracing her steps in the Bible, Zilpha Elaw finds herself. Having been appointed to preach in the afternoon at a "union," or nonsectarian chapel, Elaw is naturally upset when one of the chapel managers "advises [her] not to enter the pulpit" (108). And though she is later asked by the deacons "to ascend the pulpit according to the recent arrangements," she is ultimately "shut out" by the other ministers in charge, a result, she believes, of "gospel rivalship" (108-9). The experience does not shut her out, or up, completely. She has a place in the world of distinguished prophets; she locates herself securely in the Book of Ezekiel: "The Lord said unto me, 'It is enough; I will take thee away from them, and I will put bands upon thee, and thou shalt not go out amongst them; and I will make thy tongue cleave to the roof of thy mouth, that thou shalt be dumb, and shalt not be a reprover to them, for they are a rebellious house. But when I speak unto thee, I will open thy mouth'" (109; Ezekiel 3:25-27). And that is exactly what happens. Struck "with a very severe fit of illness," she is "dumb to them indeed"; and once recovered she returns to the chapel not at all surprised to find the people "extremely anxious" to hear her preach (109-10). Elsewhere in the autobiography, Elaw seamlessly incorporates the language of well-known scriptural passages into her own sentences: "Although I had been sick and laid aside for a time, I lost nothing . . . it was merely a furnace, in which my heavenly father saw the necessity of my being placed for a time" (93; Daniel 3:19-27); "He preserved me in my going out and my coming in; so that the production of the documents of my freedom was not once demanded during my sojourn on the soil of slavery" (99; Psalm 121:8); "When I was a child, I thought as a child; and often wondered how the ancient servants of the Lord knew the will of God in reference to their movements in life" (102; 1 Corinthians 13:11).

In fact, biblical typology is so embedded in these narratives that they resemble a palimpsest. The particular books of the Bible to which these writers naturally gravitate and which they trace in their autobiographical acts are strikingly visible. In effect, these autobiographies are written *over*—both in the sense of writing on top of and in the sense of revising or updating—the Bible. Several of these women, as noted in chapter 1, preface their works with passages from the Bible that call attention to the history of women's prophesying and leadership.[20] But these autobiographers also quote the Bible on almost every page, often without quotation marks or citations, so much so that many readers might not recognize how often these women write what was for them an everlasting, ever-living *Word*—the "word made flesh" (John 1:14).

Describing her call to preach, Jarena Lee situates herself squarely in the tradition of Old Testament prophecy, specifically in that of Jeremiah and Isaiah. Told by a voice to "Go preach the Gospel!" Lee responds in the manner of Jeremiah, who pleads that he is but "a child": "'No one will believe me,'" she cries (10; Mark 16:15). But the voice returns, "'Preach the Gospel; I will put words in your mouth, and will turn your enemies to become your friends,'" which God did (10; Jeremiah 1:9).[21] Still, as a black woman, Lee necessarily approached her public duties with a certain amount of fear and trembling. Like the prophets with whom she identifies, and like many African Americans subordinated under slavery and institutionalized racism, Lee stammered, or so she implies, when required to speak in public, displaying that "fear-induced hesitation," which often characterizes efforts both to challenge and to "anticipate the response of the dominant" (Scott, *Domination* 30). Stammering is a biblical figure found throughout the Old Testament, in relation to Moses and to the Hebrew prophets. It reappears in the writings of religious figures of all ages, particularly among men and women who see themselves as divinely inspired prophets but who, like Moses and Isaiah, are reluctant to speak. Nancy Towle, like Isaiah, refers to her "stammering tongue," and Zilpha Elaw acknowledges how "inspiration" enabled her to overcome her fear of preaching in public: "My tongue was set at liberty, and my heart was enlarged; and I was enabled to preach with more fluency and copiousness than ever before" (Towle, Preface 11; Isaiah 28:11, 33:19; Elaw 88). Yet unlike many subordinate groups facing a dominant power, Towle, Elaw, and Lee had the advantage of being inspirited by a higher authority. "Aided from above" throughout her career, Lee concludes the first edition of her autobiography by merging her voice with that of Isaiah (20). She establishes her authority and proclaims her linguistic freedom: "My tongue was cut loose, the stammerer spoke freely" (20; Isaiah 32:4).

Even Laura Haviland, whose causes were mainly political and who rarely uses religious and biblical language in her writing, was aware of the rhetorical advantages of placing herself within a particular biblical paradigm. Like many of the women in this study, she frequently refers to her Lord as the "God of Daniel"; given her confrontational experience in literal, and figurative, battlefields, she reads in Daniel a figure for her own embattled existence (216). Undertaking a daring mission to deliver sanitary and medical supplies to Union troops during the Civil War, Haviland reports that guerrillas threatened to capture the boat on which she was traveling. Approached by the colonel who was worried about his female passengers, Haviland fearlessly responds, "'The God of Daniel lives at this hour . . . and in him I trust'" (284). By depicting the Civil War and its aftermath as her "lion's den," Haviland completes the paradigm, aligning herself with the heroic prophet himself (435–36). Recounting her missionary work among freedmen and freedwomen following the war, Haviland again finds use for the figure of Daniel in the lion's den:

> While pursuing this work our lives were daily threatened, and some had fears of another riot. One Union woman on our block told me that she had often spent sleepless nights on our account. She had heard such frequent threats that "Nigger teachers should be cleared out, as well as free niggers," that she expected every day would be our last. . . . But I told her I did not believe we should have another riot; I believed the God of Daniel was able and willing to protect us, and that in him was my confidence. (437)

It makes sense that Haviland and other women preachers of the nineteenth century should choose to identify with the Book of Daniel. Looking back on their lives, they probably felt as though they had often been in the lion's den with him or the fiery furnace with Shadrach, Meshach, and Abednego. They must also have recognized in that prophetic book themes that they wished to emphasize in their own sacred texts. Like Daniel's, their lives were filled with visions and dreams that only they could rightly interpret. Like Daniel, they were part of a righteous remnant who knew the power of God to protect. Like Daniel, a pious Jew living under the persecution of Antiochus

Epiphanes (167–164 b.c.), they were unduly opposed.[22] But like King Belshazzer, they "saw the writing" on the wall and were obedient to their God and confident in his power to save (Foote 201; Daniel 5:17).[23]

How Nobly Women Suffered: The Uses of Martyrdom

And yet, though they recognized in Daniel a kindred spirit, the story these autobiographers tell ultimately conflicts with the central message of the Book of Daniel. Many readers have been inspired by the book's prophecy, for Daniel tells how faithful Jews triumphed over their enemies by relying on divine aid, and in an apocalyptic vision it predicts a consummation when the saints shall have victory. The book would therefore have resonated for embattled women looking to the day when they, too, would be victorious over the dominant culture of nineteenth-century America. But these women seem to find a certain pleasure in suffering the fiery furnace and the lion's den; there appears in their writings something of a dependence on persecution. Like the female autobiographies discussed by Doris Sommer, these writers "value marginality as a mark of personal distinctiveness rather than as a measure of political inequality" (130). "Opposition," in the words of R. Laurence Moore, "gives value to struggle and inculcates self-confidence" (*Religious Outsiders* 35).[24] Reading their own lives in terms of biblical precedent enabled them, as we have seen, to make sense of a journey that seemed, if analyzed from the point of view of the dominant culture, heretical or at best unorthodox; looking to the prophetic roles of Jeremiah, Isaiah, and Daniel, however, a preacher like Jarena Lee knew exactly where she fit in. She could take pride in the persecution she suffered as "a poor coloured woman" (18); for, explains Lee, "The ministers of Jesus must expect persecution, if they would be faithful witnesses against sin and sinners" (32). Excluded from the halls of worldly power, denied institutional recognition for their achievements, these itinerant preachers who had abandoned domesticity (and thus were already self-marginalized) do not simply expect persecution. They actually pursue what Moore calls "outsider strategies"; they willingly suffer persecution—and privilege it in their narratives—for martyrdom, even of a figurative sort, had its own rewards (*Religious Outsiders* 46).

Of course, to say that they valued marginality is not to say that they were indifferent to, or failed to protest, the many inequities in the business of converting souls. As bell hooks observes, "Understanding marginality as a position and place of resistance is crucial for oppressed, exploited, colonized people" (150). These autobiographers can even be called "feminist" in the sense described by Elaine Showalter in *A Literature of Their Own*, both in "protesting" the social roles thrust upon them and in "advocating" the rights of women to preach as women, "including a demand for autonomy" (13).[25] When these women recount lives of endless conflict, their implied critique of the patriarchal system that hinders them is clear enough; "Of the other sex," protests Nancy Towle in a long diatribe against an unequal system, "though three-fold the natural vigor, whereof to boast, it is seldom expected that they will go, without some suitable mode of conveyance, or without purse and scrip, at hand. Nor is it expected, that after their strength is quite exhausted, for the good of souls, that they then (to appear decent) must make, clean, or repair, some article of apparel, for themselves, before renewing again, the heavy struggle" (228). Nancy Towle's autobiography—like those of Sexton and Haviland, who supported the women's rights movement—must be read in part as a discourse of resistance against the marginal existence forced upon her by the evangelical establishment and the culture in which it was situated.

And yet despite Towle's angry critique of the discrimination she faced in the evangelical marketplace, there is an obvious note of boasting here. She assumes a mask of victimization, wishing to impress us with the degree to which she is marginalized. Zilpha Elaw refers to herself so often as an "unworthy instrument," a "poor, coloured female," a "feeble . . . earthen vessel," a "humble agent," and a "poor weak female" that one cannot help but wonder if she is not *asserting* her marginalization; at one point in the book, she uses such labels nine times in just three pages (89, 92, 104).[26] Julia Foote, writing thirty-odd years after Elaw and almost fifty years after Towle, even engages in what one might call competitive marginality. Comparing the trials of her ministry with those of women entering the ministry in 1879, when her autobiographical sketch was published, she writes: "Dear sisters, who are in the evangelistic work now, you may think you have hard times; but let me tell you, I feel that the lion and lamb are lying down together, as compared with the state of things twenty-five or thirty years ago" (214). She distinguishes herself from these late-nineteenth-century evangelists who, it seems, don't know how easy they've got it. At best she and her sister preachers were gazed at and misunderstood; at worst they were opposed and called "crazy," despite all the quantifiable success they document in their narratives.

So they decided to make a virtue of it. Had these women lived in sixteenth-century Spain, they might have shared Saint Teresa's dream of traveling with her brother "to the country of the Moors, begging our way for love of God that we might be there beheaded" (4). Traveling throughout England and America in the first half of the nineteenth century, Nancy Towle had no need to dream of or beg for trouble. The "heavy struggle" she endured in England and elsewhere gave her a grand opportunity to suffer martyrdom for her convictions (228). She "rejoiced" in being arrested for her public preaching not only because it enabled her to prove woman's courage but also because therein lay the "prospect of becoming a 'prisoner' for Christ Jesus sake, and the Gospel" (63). "A prophet," Zilpha Elaw remembers, "is not without honour, save in his own country" (83; Matthew 14:57; Mark 6:4; John 4:44). Rather than sink beneath the weight of suffering, all these women could "rejoice in persecution" (Foote 189). Foote could recognize in her life story a thread of martyrdom that connected her to a long line of Christian heroines: "In the early ages of Christianity," Foote proudly announces, "many women were happy and glorious in martyrdom. How nobly, how heroically, too, in later ages, have women suffered persecution and death for the name of the Lord Jesus" (209).[27]

Foote and the others are hinting here at a point made recently by Sidonie Smith: that, though martyrdom has never been an exclusively female pursuit, it may, by virtue of its "exaggeration of the quintessential model of the feminine," have held a special significance for women (*Poetics* 10). As Smith argues in her discussion of the poetics of women's autobiography, "self-abnegation" is rhetorically useful "for a woman who would dare to speak, even to instruct, in a church and culture that suspected and rigidly proscribed such individualistic and atypical activities in women" (*Poetics* 10). She refers here to the autobiography of Catholic pietist Jeanne Marie Bouvier de la Motte (Madame Guyon), whose work is marked by its many references to victimization and which was, significantly for our purposes, enormously popular among nineteenth-century evangelical women.[28] One could argue that in appropriating models of willing victimization in their construction of public female identities—in "cloth[ing] their resistance and defiance in ritualisms of subordination"—these women were in danger of losing even the "informal" power they had garnered in the evangelical marketplace (Scott, *Domination* 96). Though they could, as I argued in chapter 2, easily prove that their power was "effective," quantitatively speaking, by failing to champion the cause of institutional ordination for women and mobilize themselves accordingly, in effect they "reaffirm[ed] men's official rule as powerholders" and perpetuated their own powerlessness (Scott, *Domination* 52).

James Scott's work on the politics of disguise invites us, however, to consider the possibility that the act of effacing self into a powerful and empowering tradition of biblical typology was a means—risky though it may have been—by which these preachers could begin the process of transforming their lives from "sites of domination" into "sites of resistance" (Collins 102). "Most of the political life of subordinate groups," Scott argues, "is to be found neither in overt collective defiance of powerholders nor in complete hegemonic compliance, but in the vast territory between these two polar opposites" (*Domination* 136). "Not wholly exempted from those trials and persecutions, which are the common lot of the servants of Jesus," these women could feel assured that their careers were legitimate and valuable; hence, they were empowered to go forth "laboring for God" (Elaw 104; Foote 209). Portraying themselves, in the words of Madame Guyon, as "victim[s] incessantly offered upon the altar to Him who first sacrificed himself for love," they could justify their individualistic behavior, keep censure at bay, and even, it would seem, gain approval from an evangelical audience who would recognize in such suffering the marks of a saint (qtd. in Weintraub 224). Remembering a surprise visit from the Mitchel family with whom she was reared, Zilpha Elaw draws a deliberate parallel: "They came to me with presents, as did the wise men who came to the infant Jesus and his mother, and presented them with frankincense and myrrh" (80). Surely no reader could miss the point of this simile.

The Bible, in other words, was more than a safe haven for self-definition. It offered these autobiographers more than a way to make sense of their marginality: its familiar topography afforded them obvious ways to *make use* of it.[29] Typologically speaking, their singularity was an asset; biblical roles lent them an authoritative status that would clearly be destroyed by the sort of recognition church officials could bestow. It should come as no surprise, therefore, that none of these itinerants ever write about actively seeking ordination, though Sexton did request a "license" from the United Brethren.[30] "Satisfied with the ordination that the Lord [gave them]," Amanda Smith and the many preaching women who went before her were empowered to see their calls as incontestable: "Before thou camest forth out of the womb I sanctified thee, *and* I ordained thee a prophet unto the nations" (Smith 204; Jeremiah 1:5). Smith could readily deny charges that her desire to participate in the General Conference of the A.M.E. was based on some hidden agenda to press for women's ordination. Her voice was authorized by a more powerful, more prestigious conference: "He knew that the thought of ordination had never once entered my mind, for I had received my ordination from Him, Who said, 'Ye have not chosen Me, but I have chosen you, and ordained you, that you might go and bring forth fruit, and that your fruit might remain'" (200; John 15:16). Much earlier in the century, Nancy Towle claims to have refused letters of recommendation from two local preachers, deciding simply to rely on God: "This I believed I should do; as what I had begun, I was conscious God had required of me, and that every tongue hence, that should rise up against me in judgment, HE would put to silence, or condemn" (22; Isaiah 54:17). And Zilpha Elaw tells us that she was once accosted by two policemen who demanded to know "what authority [she] had for preaching" in the streets (142). A gentleman in the audience responded on her behalf, saying, "'She has her authority in her hand . . . the Word of God'" (142). Julia Foote's authority, she learned in a remarkable vision, was in her heart. As she remembers in her autobiography, she became "lost to everything in this world" after being approached by "a supernatural presence"; in the course of the vision, her "hand was given to Christ, who led [her] into the water and stripped [her] of [her] clothing" (202, 203). After being "changed into an angel," Foote watches Christ "write something with a golden pen and golden ink, upon golden paper. Then he rolled it up, and said to [her], 'Put this in your bosom, and, wherever you go, show it, and they will know that I have sent you to proclaim salvation to all'" (203). Later, she recalls, she looked for the "letter of authority" only to discover that she had no need for any letter or license: "it was," she proudly asserts, "in my heart, and was to be shown in my life, instead of my hand" (203). Institutional ordination could only be a hindrance to these female prophets: better to be free of official organizations than be deprived of the satisfaction and psychological benefits of knowing that one's call is superior, even if ultimately derivative, that one's *ordination* is definitive while that of the male clergy might well be counterfeit.[31]

Elaw and her sister itinerants knew that the crown of thorns was theirs; they knew as well how to claim it. Leaving behind the prescriptions for woman's behavior in nineteenth-century America and the proscriptions concerning women's preaching in the New Testament, they accepted instead the prescriptive "consequences of having the Spirit" outlined for them in biblical typology and, more recently, in Charles Finney's *Lectures on Revivals of Religion*: "If you have much of the Spirit of God," they well knew, "you must make up your mind to have much opposition, both in the church and the world. Very likely the leading men in the church will oppose you. There has always been opposition in the church. So it was when Christ was on earth" (117). Or, as Lydia Sexton puts it, borrowing the words of a persecuted and imprisoned William Penn, "No cross no crown" (Sexton 368).[32] Convinced of the paradoxical power of marginality, these "seeming curiosit[ies]" discovered in their singular physical appearance and the opposition such bodily difference provoked an easy means of distinguishing themselves (Sexton 251). Though their culture found in their gender and racial identities biological inferiority and cause for discrimination, familiarity with the Christian tradition of discipleship, prophecy, and martyrdom encouraged these women engaged in the task of self-construction ultimately to embrace the often humiliating and cruel discrimination that came their way.[33] Foregrounding their marginal and oppressed status in their autobiographies, they could put "ostensibly selfless testimony to an exactly contrary purpose"; in other words, advertising themselves as martyrs, they could achieve the much-desired, much-deserved prestige they had long been denied (Asher 1058).

All of this is to say that, though these autobiographers were sincere in resenting their exclusion from power, that resentment was complicated by their awareness of the advantages of martyrdom: it provided a safeguard against the moral dangers posed by success and power. Thus the ceiling on success that they repeatedly bemoan in their narratives was actually a safety net, preventing these productive people from slipping all the way into the competitive ethic of success, a guarantee that no matter how much they accomplish, how effectively they compete, in the end they would remain the martyrs and outsiders, the "strangers and pilgrims," that Christian souls are called to be (1 Peter 2:11). Though they might relish their minor triumphs over their oppressors, the final victory promised in Daniel must be, for their purposes, indefinitely postponed.

4

A Poetics of Itinerancy

Evangelical Women Writers and the Form of Autobiography

How shall we sing the LORD's song in a strange land?

> Psalm 137:4

Like a man lost in woods, more than once she had doubled upon her own track.

> Herman Melville, "Benito Cereno"

Well, what design and whose?

> Ralph Ellison, *Invisible Man*

When, in her seventy-third year, Lydia Sexton came at last to publish her autobiography, she felt compelled to begin with an apology to her readers. The apology was for the relative brevity and incompleteness of her account; the full record of her life was found "too lengthy" by her publisher, who insisted that the manuscript be cut back to a mere seven hundred pages (iii). Her faith in the stamina of these readers is remarkable, though by no means inconsistent with the pattern established by most of the autobiographers studied here. But even more striking is the method Sexton employed to make the required cuts. To another writer the publisher's harsh edict might have necessitated a laborious process of culling, but she was able to make the reductions by the simple expedient of subtracting "ten years of history" from her life story, thus excising from it "much pleasure, much work and success," and also the death of Joseph Sexton, her "dear companion for nearly half a century along life's pilgrimage" (iii). There is nothing to indicate that she eliminated these pages because they seemed less important than others; indeed, nothing to suggest that any particular editorial criteria were employed in making this emendation. She cut her manuscript like a deck of cards, shipped the larger portion off to the United Brethren Press, and saved the remainder for a better day.

That Sexton felt able to do this without disturbing the symmetry of her account certainly tells us something about her sense of the autobiographer's craft. Imagine the *Confessions* breaking off just as Augustine begins to doubt the teachings of the Manicheans, or the *Education* with Adams contemplating the dynamo, and the point is made: the autobiographies that traditional theorists of the genre think of as "classic" have an apparent narrative shape, tending toward closure.[1] The disappearance of a concluding hundred pages would have been disastrous. But Sexton was right nonetheless: there is no reason to suppose that the missing ten years of her narrative would have lent anything more than volume to the whole document. For Sexton's autobiography has a beginning, but nothing one could mark as a climax or end.

Composing by Addition

In this respect, Sexton is at one with her "sisters of the spirit"; most of the autobiographers considered here were unable to impose—no matter how hard they tried—narrative order on the events they relate. Literary scholars are familiar with the idea of parataxis, with what Northrop Frye in *The Secular Scripture* calls the "and-then" narrative, as a feature of medieval and renaissance romance and of picaresque fiction. But few of them, I daresay, have read anything like several of these autobiographies, in which the suppression of narrative markers (crises, turning points, beginnings, middles, and ends) could almost be considered a rigorously enforced aesthetic principle. I quote at random, for example, the opening sentences of several paragraphs in Jarena Lee's *Religious Experience and Journal*:

> June 24, I left the city of Philadelphia to travel in Delaware State. . . . In July I spoke in a School house to a large congregation, from Numbers xxix, 17. . . . The next place I visited was Newcastle. . . . From here I proceeded to Christine. . . . Another family gave me the invitation to attend a prayer meeting. . . . I left Mrs. Ford's and walked about three miles to St. George. . . . At Smyrna I met brother C. W. Cannon. (25–26)

Or consider this from the *Vicissitudes Illustrated in the Experience of Nancy Towle*, published in 1832:

> I went to Chepachet village, and on Sabbath day, I spoke at the different meetings, by exhortation, & c. which was agreeable to the most; but Universalists grumbled, and made quick-step homeward. I proceeded on to Burrelville, where I found many, that were brought to the Lord, by the instrumentality of J. Colby and C. H. Danforth. . . . there I made a second appointment to preach (as it is usually termed) and spake with a good degree of enlargement, to the satisfaction, I believe, of all that heard. . . . I was now greatly encouraged to hope, that if faithful to God, my labors would be crowned with abundant success, where ever I might go. I went in the next place to a village called Blackstone, and spoke in a steeple-house, to some hundreds, with a tolerable degree of freedom. I visited a female minister, of the Society of Friends, (M. Batty,) and was invited to speak with her, on a funeral occasion, which I did, I believe to her surprise. I then went to Pawtucket, and took for a companion in travels, Martha Spaulding, (of the F. Baptist order) who thought herself called to the work of the Ministry. We travelled for some weeks together, in Gloucester, Foster, Killingly, (Con.) Scituate, Johnston and Smithfield, in these places, severally, we had access to large auditories, alternately, every day. (23–24)

The reader can take my word for it that similar passages could be supplied to demonstrate the same mannerism in Zilpha Elaw's *Memoirs* or Lydia Sexton's or Amanda Smith's autobiographies. This is parataxis with a vengeance, a nearly complete refusal of what we conventionally think of as the responsibility of a narrator. One is tempted to credit these writers with the invention of a new sort of narrator, the autobiographer alienated from her own life story, which is left to tell itself without benefit of her ordering intelligence.[2]

These books do, as I say, have clear beginnings: conviction, conversion, sanctification, and the call to preach. Take Nancy Towle's *Vicissitudes*. As I noted in the introduction Towle tells us that she began to reflect on her salvation at a revival in her home of Hampton, New Hampshire, at the age of twelve. At age twenty-two, she was converted at the Inn at Northampton by Clarissa H. Danforth. Baptized at a later date by Moses Howe, an elder in the sect called "Christians," she then began to feel "a longing desire" to preach throughout the world (10). Experiencing "*the Word of the Lord as fire shut up in [her] bones*," she "*longed to speak that [she] might be refreshed*" (11; Jeremiah 20:9). Despite this urge to preach, however, she remembers being tempted by Satan to question the legitimacy of her call and encouraged by friends to engage in more worldly pursuits, and becoming ill as a result. Finally, on April 20, 1821, three years after her conversion, Towle reports, she left home, though with lingering doubts, and began to preach the gospel.

Here, on page 19 of her almost-300-page narrative, she begins the account—or, rather, accounting—of her evangelical labors, which I discussed in chapter 2. And from this point on the narrative assumes the paratactic plot I noted earlier: "I went. . . . I proceeded. . . . I visited. . . . I then went." She composes her spiritual narrative as one might compose a list. To be sure, there are places in the autobiography that seem activated by narrative energy, where she interrupts this breakneck pace of reporting her engagements to tell a story and to reflect upon its meaning or significance. She develops her arrest in England for disturbing the peace, drawing from the event two lessons: all disciples must suffer for Christ's sake, and she is no coward. The protracted illness and death of her father receive much narrative attention; Towle recognizes the value of a sentimental deathbed scene for any nineteenth-century spiritual narrative. And she pauses to fume about the material conditions of England's poor, the "cruel oppression and distress," and to prophesy the inevitable fall of such tyranny, an event that shall precede the "REDEEMER's Kingdom" (76-77, 75). Yet even in such episodes, when she turns away from her travels to focus on a particular event or expound upon an issue of interest, she often winds up writing in a "serial" or "additive" fashion.[3] Notice what happens when Towle, near the end of her autobiography, attempts a summing up of her career: "Besides my travels, in much painfulness, cold, hunger, thirst and nakedness: I have sometimes spoken, from six to eight times a week, for months in succession" (227). But then the paratactic itch seizes her: "I have also, kept a diary. . . . Moreover, I have been from first, to last, the orderer of my own apparal. . . . And, in addition to all this; I may add, in truth and verity, 'these hands of mine have often ministered to the necessities of those that were with me; and to others'" (227-28; Acts 20:34).

Indeed, Towle was virtually paralyzed by this habit of composing by "addition," so much so that she found herself almost unable to finish her autobiography. In the preface to *Vicissitudes*, Towle apologizes for the length of her story; she had meant to write a mere twenty-page pamphlet, "but things have had such a termination, that I have been drawn,—or rather driven, quite beside my own designs, even to the lengths you here survey. . . . The greatest difficulty with me, here has been, to keep my pen within due bounds;—having such an abundance, that I wished to reveal, and of which, the *narrow limits* first surveyed for this,—would not admit" (Preface 6). Towle's paratactic method became especially problematic as she tried to prepare her story for publication: the narrative's infinitely receding ending eluded her time and time again. Traveling to

Nancy Towle. Courtesy of Virginia Taylor.

Charleston, South Carolina, in 1832, to visit her brother's grave and being denied access to all public places in which to preach, she decided at last to publish her manuscript, having no immediate call to preach elsewhere. The previous year, during a prolonged illness, Towle confesses, she had been concerned that her "valuable writings" would not be published "to the world" (109). She had concluded, however, that it would not be "consistent with Jehovah, to take [her] away in the integrity of [her] heart; ere that work had been completed": God would not "cut [her] off in the completion of it" (109). And yet "completion," though she devoted considerable time to it, proved extraordinarily difficult for Towle; she was unable to give her work over to a printer, "not feeling liberty to put [her] writings to the press" (116). One year and one hundred pages later, Towle again "completed" her writings and delivered her manuscript to James L. Burges of Charleston for printing. Two months later, still residing in Charleston because of the printer's many delays and apparently unable to resist such a glorious opportunity, she again took up her pen and added another twenty-five-odd pages to the manuscript.

The A.M.E. preacher Jarena Lee, whose paratactically organized autobiography I quoted earlier, had many of the same troubles. She began her career as an itinerant minister around 1819, when Richard Allen, bishop of the African Methodist Episcopal Church, finally recognized her spiritual gifts and granted her permission to preach. In 1836, she "felt under much exercise to print a book" and was encouraged to do so by both Allen and the "Rev. R. R—" (77). At her own expense she had one thousand copies of *The Life and Religious Experience of Jarena Lee* printed in Philadelphia. Three years later in Cincinnati, her "pamphlets went off as by a wind"; encouraged by an elder, she had another thousand copies printed for sale (85). But printing the book at her own expense, she had to keep it short.[4] She does convey the hope, however, that another volume "may at some future day be published," which indeed it was (*Life* 48). In fact, we know about the publishing history of the first volume only because in 1849 Lee decided to issue a revised edition of her spiritual narrative, the "narrow limits" (in Towle's words) of the first having been found inadequate to contain the story of her life. Over five times the length of the first edition, which had covered only the first two years of her ministry, the 1849 *Religious Experience and Journal of Mrs. Jarena Lee* covers the years 1783 to 1842. Like Nancy Towle, Lee printed her first narrative in midcareer; she was fifty-three and had been an itinerant for about sixteen years. Thus it is not surprising to find that both women felt the urge to update their original stories.

Because autobiography—unlike biography—can never tell the story of a "completed" life, many autobiographers have found themselves irrepressibly moved to take up their pens again to extend what they—and their readers—once may have considered a "fixed" account of the life. Beginning in 1855 and continuing to his death in 1891, P. T. Barnum repeatedly "amended his Life," "tinkering" with the 1869 edition for years and issuing three major versions of his life story, each one more "inclusive" though not necessarily more "comprehensive" than the last (Couser 62, 61).[5] Between 1845 and 1881, Frederick Douglass similarly published three versions of his life story, even revising the last one, *Life and Times of Frederick Douglass*, again in 1892 to include "his complete history to the present time." Should he go on living, this subtitle suggests, booksellers might well have in hand yet another, "more complete" history. The list could go on: Benjamin Franklin, Willie Morris, Frederick Buechner, and Maya Angelou, whose life has become nothing short of "an autobiographical project" (Fichtelberg 213). All of these writers and their proliferating texts remind us, as G. Thomas Couser writes, that "an autobiography—unlike, for example, a novel, which aspires to a timeless wholeness—can be periodically supplemented as long as one lives. Indeed, an autobiography virtually *demands* to be serially composed because its authority—whether as an icon of its subject or an index of its author—begins to diminish the moment it is 'finished'" (62). Autobiography, in the words of William Spengemann, "is not a reflection of the life but something added to it, not a picture, but an action, which can neither stand still long enough to see the life whole nor pursue its own movement to a point of certain rest" (*Forms* 109).

But rather than undertake the arduous process of revision—of publishing, in the manner of Barnum or Douglass, a "new" life—Jarena Lee opted to revise her narrative by cutting and pasting. Rather than rewrite *The Life and Religious Experience of Jarena Lee* in light of her experiences from 1821 (the last year discussed in the 1836 edition) to the present (1849), Lee basically removed the three concluding paragraphs of this first narrative and, picking up where she left off, added seventy-five pages of new material culled from her journal. She then tacked the original three concluding paragraphs to the new material and added a brief postscript. And, as William Andrews noted when selecting the shorter, 1836 edition for inclusion in *Sisters of the Spirit*, much of the interpolated material reads like a travelogue.[6] Despite all this, Lee must conclude the revised edition, *Religious Experience and Journal of Mrs. Jarena Lee*, in 1842, seven years before the date of publication. Somehow her devotion to detail, her inability (or refusal?) to edit and choose, left her once again unable (or determined not?) to bring her life story up to date.

If we believe that Lee was in control of this process of cutting and pasting, that she found the three concluding paragraphs of the earlier edition still adequate to convey her sentiments thirteen years later, then we have every reason to expect Lee to produce yet another, more "complete" narrative, for the claim made in the first edition still stands in the second: "I cannot go through with the whole of my journal, as it would probably make a volume of two hundred pages; which if the Lord be willing may at some future day be published" (97). Nor is that declaration our only reason to hope for another edition of Lee's story. The paratactic plot of both autobiographies primes her readers not only to expect more from her *life* but also to want more of the autobiography. In each edition Lee leaves her readers hanging in midlabor. Even in the earlier edition, in which she more carefully balances the conventional stages of a spiritual narrative—awakening, conversion, call, and ministry—the text, though it climaxes with her call and triumphant exhortation in the presence of the bishop, has no real denouement. In the 1836 edition, we leave Jarena Lee stopping off at Dennis Creek, where she "spoke to a large congregation of various and conflicting sentiments" and "a wonderful shock of God's power was felt" (48). She concludes the narrative of 1849 with a brief accounting of the life she led after 1842 and the life she intends to lead in the future: "My health being very much impaired, I knew not but that I should be the next one called away, but the Lord spared me for some other purpose, and upon my recovery I commenced travelling again, feeling it better to wear out than to rust out—and so expect to do until death ends the struggle" (96–97). She leaves us expecting another "I then," wondering if indeed the paratactic style that predominates on the sentence and paragraph level will apply as well to the narrative as a whole. Will Lee, in other words, update her incomplete, unfinished narrative for us once more?

Invisible Narrators

This habit of composing by addition, of refusing to prioritize and edit a lifetime of activity, demands some explanation. For the habit was not universal: though Julia Foote turns to parataxis in two chapters—significantly titled "Continued Labors—Death of My Husband and Father" and "Work in Various Places"—for the most part she chooses to summarize her labors, confidently telling her readers that she "visited too large a number of places to mention in this little work" (216). Why did her sister evangelists not avail themselves of that expedient? Were they simply incompetent storytellers? It seems unlikely; though we know little of their reading, we can be sure of their familiarity with that great compendium of compelling narrative, the Bible. It is true that some books of the Old Testament—Numbers, Kings, 1 and 2 Chronicles, for example—have an additive style, but it seems unlikely that these autobiographers sought to imitate the "and then" formula found there. And it is clear, at various points in all these accounts, that they were familiar with the conventions of spiritual autobiography, which have given any number of inexpert writers the wherewithal to make their lives read like stories. Why did these women not benefit similarly? Though this question is a difficult one— and though the answers remain speculative—several possibilities do suggest themselves.

One has to consider, for instance, the formal effects of relying heavily on private ministerial journals in converting the *life* into the *Life*. Lee quite frankly calls the second edition of her autobiography, *The Religious Experience and Journal of Mrs. Jarena Lee.* Lydia Sexton suggests that she wrote her book with a memorandum of her life's work in front of her. And Zilpha Elaw humbly refers to her autobiography as a mere "outline of [her] religious experience" (160). Though journals and diaries, as Georges May reminds us, are themselves "autobiographical" and deserve to be considered as such, being at one end of a broad spectrum that also includes autobiographical fiction and poetry, journals clearly differ from what we have been taught to think of as "formal" (i.e., retrospective) autobiography.[7] As a daily record of one's activities, less personal and introspective than the diary, the journal is necessarily serial, each new entry an "addition to" and only rarely a "revision of" the previous day's record, each entry a discrete unit forming ultimately a discontinuous rather than coherent narrative whole with a distinct pattern. But to say that merely delays our asking the inevitable question: Granting the usefulness of these journals as aids to memory, why did these writers choose, in the words of Harriet Livermore, to "journalize," rather than transform the diaries, as countless other autobiographers have done, into shaped narratives (228)?[8]

Given the extent to which publishing—particularly an autobiography—involved an even greater assertion of self in the public sphere than preaching God's word, these women's lack of strong editing may be related to their discomfort, conscious or otherwise, with the authorial role itself. Though this was an age in which women authors were thriving in the literary marketplace—the century's three best-sellers were written by women—it was also an age in which women entered the literary world at their own risk, forced to apologize for daring the public domain and constrained by any number of "expressive restrictions": "They did have voices," writes Joanne Dobson of nineteenth-century women writers, "yet as individuals they were expected to maintain a decorous silence within their texts, in essence, to become 'invisible ladies,' manifesting nothing that would reveal to the world the presence of any passion or aspiration beyond the ordained" (57). But how can a "lady" write an autobiography and remain "invisible"? Though these seven women had long flouted genteel conventions in their lives, they may well have been uncomfortable doing so in their autobiographies.

They knew, moreover, that their "commission"—in preaching and perhaps even in writing—"was from heaven" (Foote 208). "Ordained" by God, they considered themselves passive vessels for his word. They *needed*—just as some of their male contemporaries *wanted*—to prove that "the good Master filled [their] mouth[s]" and that "the Spirit of the Lord was there also, to direct and bless and own his word" (Lee 26; Elaw 104). All of these itinerants denounced ministers who read prepared—and hence uninspired—sermons. And as Donald Mathews argues, "Substance for early Methodists . . . was the spoken word, the event and act of preaching and responding"; thus he is not at all surprised to discover that the journals of many circuit riders, male and female, are "often merely reports of places visited, texts preached, and appointments kept" ("Evangelical America" 19). Christians who *experienced* Scripture as the *living* word of God—as the "flesh" that "dwelt among [them]"—these women would have taken to heart this passage from Matthew: "For it is not ye that speak, but the Spirit of your Father which speaketh in you"; not you that write—they might have added—but the Spirit of your Father that writes in you (John 1:14; Matthew 10:20). Just as Elaw claimed to be a "mouth for God," so, too, would she claim to be a "pen in God's hand" (Elaw 89; Jackson 107).

Indeed, many of them claim that the "divine spirit poured into [their] mind[s]" not only as they preached but also as they "journalized" (Elaw 95). "Glory to God," Jarena Lee exclaims, "for what my heart feels while I use my pen in hand"; and later, "Praise God for I feel the unction from on high, while I hold my pen"; and yet again, "While my pen moves my heart burns with love to God" (56, 79, 82). This feeling of power that overtook her as she wrote, however, was balanced by a feeling of inadequacy: "So great was the joy, that it is past description. There is no language that can describe it" (10). Each of these women confesses that the "manifestations" of God that she experienced, the wild visions that filled her days, were "at the last, unutterable" and "indescribable," in a way that their literal journeys were not (Elaw 57).

Zilpha Elaw readily admits that God did not grant her the "privilege of self-direction" in designing her travels; similarly, he may have granted her little in designing her memoir (102). Or perhaps she shaped her narrative to make it *appear* as if she had little self-direction, to emphasize the fact that she was a pen in God's hand (102). Catherine Brekus contends that female preachers may well have written "monotonous" autobiographies "for the sake of appearing objective" (171). Certainly the reportorial style that these women use—and perhaps even borrow from male contemporaries—would be one way to de-emphasize the very independence that itinerant preaching readily gave them and to remind readers that they are not subjects, but objects, "impressed" and "moved" by God, women who traveled an "orthodox" path no different than that of male itinerants (Brekus 171). Sharing the title page with God, however, is problematic for any author: there is much authority in this configuration, but it is not theirs. Perhaps, then, these women found themselves clearly outranked by their collaborator, crowded out of their own books and forced to become "invisible" narrators. And to the extent they do, they call attention to a theoretical issue at the heart of all autobiography: to what degree does any autobiographer, male or female, religious or irreligious, "control" or "pen" the content and form of his or her narrative?

Some feminist scholars have popularized the notion that women's autobiographical writing is necessarily fragmented, discontinuous, repetitive, formless. Living fragmented lives, they say, women have no choice but to write formless autobiography: social experience determines literary expression. Many women have chosen the diary form, according to Norine Voss, because autobiography "poses the problem of welding both private and public experience"; women, however, "relegated to the private realm of home, personal relationships and emotion," enter the public domain of autobiography only at their own "peril" (226). "Diaries, letters, and journals" are, moreover, "accessible forms for women whose emotional, intellectual, and practical lives are fragmented by domestic responsibilities that leave them little leisure time to contemplate or integrate their experiences" (Jelinek, *Tradition* 104). A prominent aspect of "woman's work experience is its fundamental 'interruptibility,'" says Josephine Donovan: "This phenomenon contributes to the structure of women's artistic labor just as it does to their household labor, and it also contributes to a consciousness that is aware of contingency, that perceives itself bound to chance, not in total control" (102). "Even in . . . autobiographies proper," Jelinek maintains, "a disjunctiveness persists" (104). Women's lives, that is, are more formless than men's and also afford less leisure for the imaginative discovery of form.

No doubt, as I have illustrated in the previous chapters, these itinerant women, perhaps even more than the women who stayed at home, led extraordinarily busy, genuinely fragmented lives. Certainly they perceived their lives as contingent and beyond their control, for some of the same reasons as their more domestic sisters and, as we have seen, for fundamentally different ones, too. And in this time of "feverish restlessness and mighty movement," these women may well have been simply too busy ushering in the millennium to be bothered with the immense editorial task of *re*-reading and integrating the experiences recorded in their journals and then composing a more shapely narrative of their lives (Elaw 52). As an outraged Nancy Towle so forcefully communicates to her readers, female itinerants, in addition to fulfilling their many engagements around the nation and abroad, had to be their own domestic servants: they had no wives at home mending their stockings before another long journey. Such an untidy life might well necessitate an untidy *Life*, unless, of course, the storyteller is willing to falsify the nature of her existence. Perhaps, then, we need to consider the degree to which these formless autobiographies serve as a figure for the actual and cultural rootlessness of the female itinerant lives they detail. No less than the *Book* of Margery Kempe, these narratives mirror "the jumbled rush of experience as it must have been lived and certainly as it is recollected" (Smith, *Poetics* 82).

But this explanation—in the case of these female autobiographers, at least—only partly accounts for the paratactic, "itinerant" form of most of these autobiographies. Though Elaw's serving as a "mouth for God" who directed her complicated movements across the landscapes of America and England tells us something about her situation as an autobiographer, it does not fully explain the problems she faced as a female author and itinerant evangelist in the nineteenth century (89). To suppose that the serial form of these women's autobiographies emerged solely from the serial, spirit-directed life oversimplifies what is certainly a most complex social and literary problem. Anyone who has taken up Lydia Sexton's 655-page tome, or Amanda Berry Smith's *Autobiography* (506 pages), or Nancy Towle's *Vicissitudes* (250) will doubt, prima facie, that these autobiographers lacked time or energy for writing. Though all of them were spectacularly busy, most of them tell us that they experienced periodic lulls in their evangelical careers, during which they composed and published their books. Nancy Towle notes in her *Vicissitudes* that she often took the opportunity provided by illnesses to devote herself to her writing: she had trouble keeping her "pen within due bounds," not finding time to write her story, a labor she considered as important as her other evangelical endeavors (Preface 6). And to those who believe women are almost incapable of writing orderly narratives, we can cite the experience of Susan Waugh, who discovered the opposite when teaching women's autobiographical writing workshops: "Even those who had lived for many years the fragmented lives of traditional women were not prisoners of a common subject, style, or form. The form of a life does not inevitably dictate the form of the autobiography" (151). Felicity Nussbaum's study of eighteenth-century women's autobiographies suggests, moreover, that twentieth-century women are not alone in their ability to write autobiographies "that display narrative closure" ("Eighteenth-Century" 153).

Indeed, many spiritual autobiographers (male and female), even some who were itinerant evangelists, have been able and willing to lend structure to their lives, to "make manageable and intelligible the sheer flux of events," or, in the words of John Sturrock, to "use time instead of giving in to it" (Starr 36; Sturrock 56). Most have been able to reduce their Christian pilgrimage to its bare essentials; with James Fraser of Brae, they could say, "I shall reduce what I have met with to these eight heads" (qtd. in Starr 39). We have, moreover, examples of other itinerant ministers—George Brown, Peter Cartwright, Charles Finney, Elbert Osborn, and Benjamin Putnam, for instance—whose lives were very nearly as chaotic as Towle's or Lee's but whose autobiographies, formally speaking, are little like theirs; though all these men do periodically lapse into a paratactic mode when describing their travels or revivals, for the most part they order their lives, both before and after they become itinerants, into coherent autobiographies. The mere circumstance of a busy life does not fully explain the apparent formlessness of these women's books.

One possibility, of course, is that the women in this study did not think the books were formless; they might have supposed that the serial and repetitive record of miles traveled, sermons preached, and souls saved *was* a form, and a familiar one. And the later writers might have read the early ones and learned therefrom a model of autobiographical expression. Or any of them might have taken inspiration from some of the male itinerants (about whom more later) who wrote similarly structured autobiographies. Personal narratives by Heman Bangs, John Colby, David Marks, and others were apparently as well distributed as were the works of these women, and it seems almost certain that at least some of the women were familiar with such models. Did they, lacking other models, simply assume that all autobiographies were composed thus? I suspect that there is some merit to this idea; the existence of these male precedents would, at the very least, have reassured women who for whatever reason could do no better. Given the extent to which itinerants, according to Methodist itinerant Elbert Osborn, quite commonly "scattered [books] through the land," it is likely that most of these women would have been familiar with the hybrid form of spiritual autobiography-travelogue (23).[9] It is a bit harder, though, to believe that they *knew* no better; nineteenth-century women, if they were literate at all, were likely to have read not only David Marks and Heman Bangs but also several more distinguished practitioners of the autobiographer's or biographer's craft like Bunyan who were able to create narratives that look much more like stories. Too, they might have been familiar—and in any case we can be—with the several male itinerants of the day who did *not* write additive autobiographies. Why did men like Cartwright, Brown, and Finney not follow the "form" pioneered by Colby, Marks, and others? What permitted them to escape it, when virtually no itinerant women did so?

Success Stories: How Some Male Evangelists Wrote Their *Lives*

Perhaps this is the place to acknowledge that, for some critics of autobiography, the question should be disallowed or at least ruled out of generic bounds. There is a well-established argument to the effect that these "repetitive serial representations of particular moments held together by the narrative 'I'" are not autobiographies at all (Nussbaum, *Autobiographical Subject* 18). According to Jerome Buckley, "The ideal autobiography presents a retrospect of some length on the writer's life and character, in which the actual events matter far less than the truth and depth of his experience. It describes a voyage of self-discovery, a life-journey, confused by frequent misdirections and even crises of identity but reaching at last a sense of perspective and integration" (39). Georges

Gusdorf similarly argues that "autobiography . . . requires a man to take a distance with regard to himself in order to reconstitute himself in the focus of his special unity and identity across time" ("Conditions" 35). To fulfill the "Conditions and Limits of Autobiography," a text, in other words, must be well made: "An autobiography cannot be a pure and simple record of existence, an account or a logbook: on such and such a day at such an hour, I went to such and such a place. . . . A record of this kind, no matter how minutely exact, would be no more than a caricature of real life; in such a case, rigorous precision would add up to the same thing as the subtlest deception" (42). Flourishing his abstract ideal of autobiographical art, Gusdorf denies that formless narrative really deserves the name of autobiography. Similarly, John Sturrock has written that "an autobiography written without hindsight—put together, that is, from notes written over many years and never afterwards revised—would be a curious document certainly, but also a perverse one" (56).[10] I myself find such exclusionary practices unhelpful and indeed likely to produce circular arguments about autobiographical form, ruling out of bounds narratives that might enrich our sense of the range of autobiographical expression.[11] I find it more useful to place these women's works in comparison to the "well-wrought" specimens that conventionally define the genre, and try to understand the differences. Putting aside the question of whether a formless narrative deserves the name of autobiography, I prefer to consider empirically what these writers do, and to continue pondering what their motives might have been.

We might begin by comparing them to the books which—in aspiration, at least—they seem most closely to resemble: the autobiographies composed by male itinerants like George Brown, Peter Cartwright, and Charles Finney. As a Christian pilgrim who found it necessary to keep track of his journey to Newcastle and Philadelphia no less than his own progress through the Slough of Despond and Vanity-Fair, the pioneering Methodist circuit rider Peter Cartwright was nonetheless able to lend narrative shape to his repetitive, fragmented life. He manages to organize his peripatetic existence into thirty-four somewhat discrete chapters in his *Autobiography* (1856), ranging in subject matter from his parentage and conversion to slavery in the church, the formation of circuits in the West, and his continued success as itinerant evangelist and later as presiding elder. I say "somewhat" because Cartwright the storyteller does not allow the organizational mechanism of discrete chapters to obliterate the "jumbled rush" of his itinerant experiences. The chapter entitled "Sermon on Baptism at Camp-Meeting," which begins with a humorous account of winning a bet with a "spunky Methodist widow," also includes other curious incidents from camp meetings of 1822, a digression on unsanctified wealth in the church, and concluding reflections on the success of Methodism in the West (154). These digressions, however, are not far-flung; Cartwright manages to avoid the parataxis that dominates Jarena Lee's narrative by focusing on a particular time frame in each chapter, by culling only a few incidents from the period in question and enlarging them into shapely scenes. His ability to prioritize his experiences and, in his words, to "embody them here as well [he] can" enables him to recount a life that must at times have seemed as paratactic as that described by Lee (160). George Brown, a Methodist itinerant and later founder of the Methodist Protestant Church, similarly manages to order his *Recollections of Itinerant Life* into memorable scenes of his conversion, pioneer life, service in the War of 1812, and active participation in the divisive controversies within the M.E. Church over chattel slavery and the "enslavement" of lay members at the hands of powerful bishops. Though he reminds his readers of the new assignments he receives at yearly conferences, he rarely "journalizes" and occasionally even recognizes—or creates—important turning points in what will become his *Life*: "Thus I entered the service of Christ," he tells us, "on the 21st day of September, 1813, just one year after I entered the service of my country, under General Harrison" (63). Though certainly episodic, *Passages in the Life and Ministry of Elbert Osborn, an Itinerant Minister of the Methodist Episcopal Church*, also for the most part eschews the paratactic mode that dominates so much of Jarena Lee's narrative. Instead, Osborn constructs an autobiography that calls our attention, on the one hand, to the many books he read as a child that "had so much effect on [his] heart and conscience" and, on the other, to the many influential preachers he met during his years as an itinerant minister (48). People and their biographies, Osborn's autobiography suggests, were more important in his development than the itinerary that filled his days and only occasionally fills his autobiography (see, for example, pages 88–92).[12] An itinerant evangelist and revivalist for much of his life, Charles Finney was able to organize his life story into a linear narrative replete with a beginning (his birth, education, and conversion), a middle (his calling to be a missionary and his subsequent success as the prominent revivalist of the Second Great Awakening), and an end (his fame and popularity as a revivalist, professor of theology, and college president).

What was it that permitted these men to do this? They had, it seems to me, at least two advantages that would be important for any autobiographer.

The first great asset that men like Brown, Cartwright, and Finney possessed, and perhaps their most important one, was the availability of distinguished literary models upon which their own narratives could be patterned. The importance of such models is, I suppose, clear enough. The form of one's life never simply reveals itself to any of us, even to a spiritual autobiographer, who, no less than the novelist, "draws out of the flux of events a coherent pattern" and then fits the details of the life into it (Olney, *Metaphors* 45).[13] And "to the extent that autobiography, like any narrative, requires a shaping of the past, a making *sense* of a life, it tends to cast out the parts that don't add up . . ." (Miller, *Subject* 58). Nor is the job of "casting out" those parts or "drawing out" that pattern undertaken entirely by the author's private imagination; for most autobiographers, as for other writers of narrative, the facts must be fit, with more or less success, into plots whose broad outlines are largely determined in advance by cultural expectation. To be recognizable as a "story" at all, an autobiographical narrative must assume a shape familiar to its readers. "To a wholly new sensational or emotional experience," James Olney writes, "one can give sufficient organization only by relating it to the already known, only by perceiving a relation between this experience and another experience already placed, ordered, and incorporated" (*Metaphors* 31). Thus the importance of models and precedents for autobiographers like Brown and Cartwright.

By the nineteenth century there were, of course, plenty of models upon which a prospective autobiographer might draw. Without attempting a structuralist anatomy of all possible autobiographical forms, we can all think of some important ones that were familiar to both readers and writers in nineteenth-century America. Two that are most relevant here are the conversion or education narrative and the record of accomplishment or success story.[14]

By the 1860s, when Finney wrote his spiritual autobiography, the story of conversion had long been rehearsed in the tradition of spiritual autobiography that originated with the fourth-century *Confessions* of Saint Augustine. In Augustine's narrative we find the Pauline paradigm of spiritual progress that will inform—to varying degrees—virtually all Christian spiritual autobiographies: I was lost and now I'm found, conversion being the climactic experience of one's life and narrative. The Reformation brought with it a renewed interest in spiritual diaries and autobiographies, the reformed faith's emphasis on the individual's responsibility in ascertaining his or her own salvation through introspection having imbued the old form with increased significance. Recording the minute occurrences in one's life and relating those details to one's spiritual progress would be of obvious use in understanding and evaluating the work of grace upon one's soul. Protestantism's belief, moreover, in the universal nature of the work of salvation, "that spiritual life varies little from man to man," further stimulated interest both in the writing and, more particularly, in the private circulation or publication of spiritual autobiographies (Starr 17). And, of course, the widespread publication of such narratives in turn heightened the already conventional and formulaic nature of the genre. Thus the reformed practice of introspective spiritual autobiography began to acquire a particular shape: like Augustine, the narrator details his or her unregenerate life—John Bunyan's love of Sabbath sport, for example, paralleling Augustine's stealing of pears. The narrator experiences growing anxiety about his or her state of sinfulness and is ultimately convicted of sin; at the climax of the narrative, the repentant author is converted, prior to which he or she, overwhelmed by feelings of helplessness, often falls into a state of despondency, even physical illness; finally the justified narrator concludes by outlining the fruits of his or her personal religious experience, this being, in the case of ministers, their calling and resultant pastoral work. The basic pattern is, thus, one of crisis, resolution, and closure.

With the rise of evangelical religion in Britain and America in the late eighteenth century, the form of spiritual autobiography was revived, and also significantly transformed. The conventions and shape of the Puritan "life accounted for"—"the life examined, interpreted, justified, and shaped into a transmissible *account*"—remained largely unchanged: but a new emphasis had been added (Aldrich 18). No evangelical autobiographer would be able to summarize his or her work as John Bunyan had on the title page of the first edition of *Grace Abounding to the Chief of Sinners*:

> Wherein is particularly shewed, The manner of his Conversion, his sight and trouble for Sin, his Dreadful Temptations, also how he despaired of Gods mercy, and how the Lord at length thorow Christ did deliver him from all the guilt and terrour that lay upon him. Whereunto *is added*, A Brief Relation of his Call to the Work of the Ministry, of his Temptations therein, as also what he hath met with in Prison. (Emphasis added)

Bunyan devotes the bulk of his narrative to detailing his sinful life and protracted conversion, merely "adding" on a relation of his ministry. But most evangelical autobiographers reverse the proportions; conversion and sanctification tend to occur quite early on, and the bulk of the text is dedicated to a narrative of the successful evangelical labors that followed.[15]

When this transformation occurred, some spiritual autobiographers found themselves involved in a second autobiographical pattern, and one for which American writers like

Brown, Cartwright, and the others had strong precedents available. This pattern was the narrative of success, of which *The Autobiography of Benjamin Franklin* is a classic example. The plot of this narrative is a fairly simple upward trajectory: the protagonist begins poor, with few prospects, and ends up successful, having gained at least acclaim and perhaps wealth as well, but in any case is eminent enough to expect an interested readership for the autobiography. This may be the most common form of American autobiography; other examples, after Franklin's, include Frederick Douglass's *Narrative*, P. T. Barnum's many autobiographies, Booker T. Washington's *Up from Slavery* (whose title summarizes the success plot succinctly), and many others. It is also the form of practically all the popular, often ghostwritten autobiographies of sports heroes, movie stars, and tycoons. Even *The Education of Henry Adams*, that celebrated narrative of failure, depends on the standard success narrative for its ironic effect.

Now Brown, Cartwright, and Finney were undeniably famous and successful men; more important, for the purposes of autobiography, their successes were empirically verifiable: they not only had converted many souls but also had been rewarded for these conversions by an uninterrupted ascent through the hierarchy of the institutional church. Thus they each had at their fingertips both the confidence and a convenient means by which to give shape to their lives. They could punctuate their narratives by reference to officially conferred certificates of achievement and worth. They could display a kind of trophy case that, if arranged chronologically, provided a narrative skeleton on which an autobiography could be laid out. Cartwright had no need to impose a pattern on his life; out of his rootless existence there emerged an overarching pattern of yearly and quarterly attendance at regional and general conferences of the Methodist Episcopal Church, of participation in the important religious debates of his day, of institutional acknowledgments of his many successes. George Brown, D.D., could easily organize his *Recollections* by calling our attention to his yearly assignments to new circuits, to his election on several occasions to the position of presiding elder, to his efforts to reform the M.E. Church and to found the Methodist Protestant Church, and finally to his rise to the presidency of Madison College, where he would become a spokesman for an educated ministry. Charles Finney could similarly draw out of the flux of his experience a pattern of ascent from boyhood through conversion and calling to renowned revivalist and champion of the "New Measures" that would redeem the world. He could mark the success of these new measures by organizing "his story" around the revivals he orchestrated: his table of contents reads, "Revival at Antwerp . . . Revival at Gouverneur . . . Revival at De Kalb . . . Revival at Western," and so on. Brown's and Cartwright's positions within an organized and hierarchical church structure and Finney's standing as America's grand revivalist gave them the coordinates by which to plot the "upward trajectory" that the success narrative requires. The progress of their lives, in other words, lent itself to a familiar, culturally validated story.

And, as James Olney astutely recognizes, "Our sense that there is a meaning in something . . . comes only when the elements that go to make up that thing take on a relation to one another; in other words, the meaning emerges with our perception of a pattern" (*Metaphors* 30–31). Out of a chaotic life of travel and preaching engagements, Cartwright could discover the significance, the meaning of his life: he was not simply moving *around* the West; he was moving *up* in the West, from lowly itinerant to presiding elder to historian. Finney's many travels around the "burned-over district" were not evidence of his rootlessness—or lack of place—in his culture but of his deep roots, his authoritative position in American religion and culture.

Hence the second great asset that these autobiographers possessed: a secure justification for writing at all. To write an autobiography is, after all, a remarkable assertion of one's own importance; an autobiographer is implicitly telling readers that they should cease attending to their own lives for a time and instead contemplate his or hers—and that they will be improved for having done so. Eminent men by the time they wrote their autobiographies, Brown, Cartwright, and Finney were able to justify their self-assertion and at the same time humbly to deny it. Cartwright disclaims the intention of writing his own life, except as an incidental feature of a larger and less self-interested project. "The history of my life," he assures us, "as one among the oldest Methodist traveling preachers west of the mountains" is "necessarily connect[ed]" to the "history of the rise and progress of the Methodist Episcopal Church in the great valley of the Mississippi" (11). I am not really an autobiographer at all, in other words, but merely a historian using, for convenience's sake, the *form* of autobiography. Even Cartwright's most recent editor introduces the book as "one of the outstanding historical records of a heroic era in the life of the United States and of the Christian Church" (9). His is not simply the story of a man; it is the story of an "authority," a man called upon to write the account of a significant movement within American religious history. The Reverend John Scott, D.D., when writing the introduction to George Brown's *Recollections*, assures us of Brown's "eminence" as a student of the Bible, "philosophical thought," and "Christian theology" (vii). And, like Cartwright's, his autobiography can be read as history, as a record of significant sectarian debates within the Methodist Episcopal Church and the splintering of that denomination in the nineteenth century. "The recollections of such a man," Scott argues, "dating back to the commencement of this century, and coming down to the present time, connected, as they are, with great social and religious changes and important ecclesiastical reforms, in which the Author bore a prominent part, can not fail, we think to interest and instruct the reader" (ix). The same is true of *The Life Experience and Gospel Labors of the Rt. Rev. Richard Allen*, the autobiographical narrative of the founder of the African Methodist Episcopal Church. The subtitle of Allen's memoir reads, "To Which Is Annexed the Rise and Progress of the African Methodist Episcopal Church in the United States of America." Finney adopts a similar strategy in authorizing the act of autobiography. His *Memoirs* is a "history" of "those revivals with which [his] name and labors have been connected": "it is thought that the truth of history," Finney apologizes, "demands a statement from myself of the doctrines that were preached, so far as I was concerned, of the measures used, and of the results of preaching those doctrines and the use of those measures, as they have been manifest to myself and others for many years" (2). His mission is as much to defend one last time the new measures of revivalism as to shape a narrative of his life.

These men justifiably saw themselves as figures of authority when they sat down to compose their autobiographies. And their readers, as they knew, saw them in the same way, so that they were able to preface their stories with a humble disclaimer: they have been, in Cartwright's words, "unceasingly importuned" to make their "Lives" available to the public (11). "Some of our beloved bishops," Cartwright professes, "book agents, editors, and old men, preachers and private members, as well as a host of our young, strong men and ministers, who are now actively engaged in building up the Church, have urged me to undertake this sketch of my life, and I have not felt at liberty to decline" (12). Of course, it is a convention of autobiography to begin with an apology for undertaking such a self-assertive act. It was also, and perhaps significantly, a convention of American electoral politics in the eighteenth and nineteenth centuries: even the most naked office-seeker must treat his candidacy as a highly unwelcome burden, imposed by well-meaning "friends." By observing this convention, the candidate assured the public of his freedom from dangerous ambition and egotism; more subtly, he also implied that his constituency was already in place, merely awaiting his reluctant arrival at the head of the parade. Finney and Cartwright and Brown took up their pens assured of their position at the head of just such a parade or, at the very least, of what the editor of Frederick Douglass's *My Bondage and My Freedom* calls "the existence of a commendable curiosity, on the part of the public" (viii).

The trajectory of their lives had led to a position—the one the autobiographer occupies when writing—of eminence. This, too, gives writers like Brown and Cartwright a valuable narrative tool. For it is an odd fact about autobiography that its narrative pull—on the writer as much as on the reader—is just the opposite of that exerted by other kinds of narratives.[16] Writers of such a narrative already know the ending—know where they are when they set about writing, and know *why* that position is one from which the egotistical act of autobiography may acceptably issue. Similarly, readers of such a narrative already know, or else they would not be reading, why the autobiographer has a claim on their attention. Autobiographers write, and their readers read, not in search of the already known ending but in search of the beginning and the middle. *How* did the figure whose life commands our attention achieve his or her eminence?

The autobiography of success, then, like the story of conversion, works by emphasizing the distance between the struggling protagonist—Franklin with his "puffy rolls" under his arms, wandering the streets of Philadelphia—and the secure autobiographer, writing from a vantage point of assured success. By the time Franklin began writing America's most famous autobiography of success, he knew exactly where he stood. He was the man whose face in Paris was "as well known as that of the moon"; he was the man who had audiences and dinner with kings; he was a man who had reached a "State of Affluence & some Degree of Reputation in the World" (qtd. in Silverman vii; Franklin 3). "Even when he began the book," Kenneth Silverman writes, "knowledge of his accomplishments was so widespread that he could take it for granted. He therefore wrote from the point of view of his own legend. He would show his readers how he became what he knew he had in their minds become" (ix).

The "commendable curiosity" that licensed *My Bondage and My Freedom* also authorized Douglass's other two autobiographies, as well as the autobiographies of other African American writers such as Booker T. Washington and Richard Allen. Douglass's *Narrative* (1845) and Washington's *Up from Slavery*, indeed, make two of the best examples, along with Franklin's, of the autobiography of success. This fact invites a consideration of the role of race in the construction of the successful selves at the heart of such narratives. For in the nineteenth century, success was a narrative of white men. To be sure, Douglass, Washington, and Allen look back over their lives and find particularly dramatic trajectories of progress upward from poverty, illiteracy, and enslavement. But black men had to lay claim to this narrative form and its languages, just as lower-class and African American women had to borrow, and often transform, the language of domesticity. And when they did so, they engaged in what Sacvan Bercovitch calls a "process of Americanization," a ritual designed to prove to their American readers that they belonged (*American Jeremiad* 18).[17] Race, then, is clearly relevant in the making of autobiography. But what I am discussing here—the complete alienation of women from the narrative of success, a narrative about how to become a man, not a human being—is mainly an issue of gender.

Booker T. Washington could justify the black male self by borrowing from the most prominent cultural myth of American manhood and the narrative form that went with it. As the successful founder and leader of Tuskegee University, as spokesperson for a race, as an authority who visited and dined with America's "kings" of government and business, Washington knew how to compose a confident narrative of success. Knowing his "ultimate achievements," he could measure the distance he had traveled from his humble beginnings in Virginia to the platform of the Atlanta Exposition (Sturrock 55). Or, to cite another example of the African American "success narrative," consider this from Frederick Douglass's *Narrative*: "I look upon my departure from Colonel Lloyd's plantation as one of the most interesting events of my life. It is possible, and even quite probable, that but for the mere circumstance of being removed from that plantation to Baltimore, I should have to-day, instead of being here seated by my own table, in the enjoyment of freedom and the happiness of home, writing this Narrative, been confined in the galling chains of slavery" (273). A clear sense of the distance between "then" and "now" affords this autobiographer a distinct advantage in plotting his life, in discovering the crises and turning points that have led him to his present position, and in appropriating—by demonstrating how he became a "man"—the form of the success narrative.

Composing a retrospective, "well-made" autobiography replete with closure requires, in other words, that the autobiographer have knowledge of the ending or at least some *sense* of one—provisional though it must be given that all autobiography necessarily represents the "incomplete" life.[18] To quote James Cox, "The convention of autobiography . . . presupposes a complete life or the completing of a life. It involves the writer in some form of ending or envisioning an end to a narrative that he helplessly wants to be equal to his life" (128). Narrating the story of his conversion in *Surprised by Joy*, C. S. Lewis rigorously selects only those experiences that upon reflection seem to have been beckoning him on toward conversion. Knowing the end of the story, he is able, according to the subtitle, to perceive "The Shape of [His] Early Life." The ending he has in mind becomes the criterion for editing his many memories of his early life: "As the plot quickens and thickens toward its end," Lewis tells us, "I leave out more and more of such matters as would go into a full autobiography" (215). Even the millennially minded Peter Cartwright had little difficulty imagining an end to his potentially endless affairs. As the "oldest presiding elder in all the Western country," he proudly concludes his autobiography with the following statistics: he had attended fifty-three conferences, delivered approximately 14,600 sermons, and, perhaps most important, outlived his father's entire family, most members of the Western Conference of 1804, most of the early bishops, "every presiding elder" for whom he worked on circuits, and "hundreds and thousands of my contemporary ministers and members, as well as juniors" (338-40). "Insofar as the narrative is equal to the life," Cox reminds us, "it cannot be finished without death, either actual or metaphorical" (128). Having lived a long and profitable life, Cartwright is ready to "conclude" his life story.[19]

Itinerant Autobiographies: Narrating the Unsettled Life

Now we have already noticed that the female autobiographers under study here had particular trouble with endings. Sexton, faced with a publisher's demand for cuts, could achieve them by simply subtracting the last ten years of her life, without fear that any sense of narrative closure would be lost in the transaction: there was evidently none to lose. Others could not resist adding on to the narratives they had considered finished—again, evidently, without feeling that narrative closure was at risk. They did so, I would posit, because they lacked the two invaluable assets that had made Cartwright's and Finney's task so easy: the authority to write in the first place, and the means to turn a life into a story. Both of these assets, it will have been noticed, are essentially based on the same fact: their institutionally certified eminence, securely in place by the time they began to write. What they had, in other words, was an *ending*: they knew how the story turned out and—secure in that ending—could confidently scan the long chronicle that preceded it in search of a narrative line. Which is precisely what Nancy Towle, Jarena Lee, and their sister autobiographers—and even some of their male contemporaries—were unable to do.

They could define and delineate the subject of their conversion. They were converted and sanctified under a "faire and easie" theological system that had made it possible for them to take their conversion and sanctification for granted.[20] Unlike Puritans who related the narratives of their conversions to a community of saints who would pass judgment on the validity of their accounts, each of these women could be confident that hers was a legitimate conversion, that she would not be judged on *its* form. More important, knowing how that particular story turned out, these women could easily perceive or imagine the significant signposts that got them there. And, given their familiarity with the archetype of conversion, they could readily adopt their private story of awakening to sin and conversion into a narrative familiar to their readers. The archetype of conversion was as congenial to their experiences as to those of Brown, Cartwright, and Finney.

The classic American success story remained an elusive one for these American women, despite the fact that as these preachers tell it—and as I discussed in chapter 2—they had one "success" after another in the marketplace of salvation, each of which they meticulously "add" to their tales of productivity. For while the story of conversion was historically a gender-neutral paradigm—Christiana's pilgrimage being much like Christian's—the Franklinesque story of success was not. It was, as we have seen, a story told from a confident position of "authority"; it was a story of evolution, of a man's linear progress from lowly itinerant to presiding elder or college president or even, in Cartwright's words, famous "eccentric minister"; it was a story that called for a writer who had "arrived" at a state of self-knowledge sufficient to make easy the task of envisioning or, in the case of black men, appropriating, the pattern—the beginning, middle, and even the end of the story (12).

Whether compiling her narrative in 1832 or 1893, none of the women in this study had achieved the sort of "fixed" authoritative "end" within the public world of institutional religion that characterized the lives of George Brown, Charles Finney, or Richard Allen: they remained forever on the outside, charismatic preachers, yes, purveyors of history, never. The stress placed by evangelical religious movements upon the inner witness of the Spirit—as opposed to education—in the formation of their ministry did open many doors for women like Nancy Towle and Zilpha Elaw, if they could claim just such extraordinary inspiration. Even then, however, these women were limited to positions variously labeled exhorter, local preacher, and approved preacher. By the 1860s, renewal sects such as the Methodists and the United Brethren had begun to move from the periphery to the center of American religion; and with their new status came institutionalization, respectability, and an unwillingness to credit the spiritual gifts of women. Though women in the nineteenth century made enormous progress in their struggle for leadership positions within the hierarchy of the church, no woman had really "arrived" at an identifiable—though provisional—"end" in the way that George Brown had. Though a woman like Towle could truthfully claim to feel periodically "in delivering [her] message to the people, like one, possessed of great authority," the equality of spiritual gifts among God's prophets did not effectively diminish the hierarchy of the church and the sexism of evangelical religion in general (24).[21] As Elder J. Chadwick argued in the *Christian Palladium* in 1841, women could "'tell the story of Calvary, and invite sinners to Christ,'" but not as preachers: "'The ministerial and pastoral office implies *authority*, and, as such, is given exclusively to men'" (qtd. in Brekus 289). These women's lives, in other words, could not easily be made to fit the shape—the upward trajectory—of the "male" version of the American success story.

"Breaking up housekeeping," these seven women began what was no doubt an enabling journey to Dennis Creek and Philadelphia and Newcastle, a journey that offered them adventurous lives remarkably free from the physical and social constraints with which most women of the nineteenth century lived (Lee 18). Leaving home and familial and (for all except Sexton) conjugal ties meant, however, losing the primary source of security—physical, institutional, psychological, and narrative—available to white, middle-class women and adopted by many black women of the century, with little hope of realizing it, as Brown, Cartwright, and Finney did, in the wide world through which they began to travel. It meant, in other words, alienating themselves from that other prominent narrative of success, this one gendered female. The marriage plot was the only story of success—the only "end"—available to them as writers of women's lives. There were no familiar stories that chronicled a woman's development or evolution, that would comprehend—the way men's stories did—the whole of their lives: birth, conversion, education, marriage, vocation, independent achievement and success. In fact, as Nina Baym's research indicates, unorthodox nineteenth-century women looking for a narrative model would uncover few stories in the fiction of the day that would treat the lives of adult women at all, either within or without marriage.[22] Certainly there were none that would delineate the stories (of success and failure) of poor, Northern, or enslaved black women. Their situation, not unlike that of the fugitive slave Harriet Jacobs who wrote *Incidents in the Life of a Slave Girl* in the 1850s, was the reverse of that of a man like P. T. Barnum, who knew *too many* stories by which to order his life.[23] Where he had an embarrassment of riches, they were impoverished, having cultural ideologies and biblical precedents from which they could weave an identity but no readily available *story*. In part, then, the endless travels that these autobiographers so scrupulously document serve as a figure for their ongoing quest for a plot, for a different kind of story for and about women. Carolyn Heilbrun finds this need for stories a common phenomenon among women autobiographers. "Many moving lives of women" have been written, lives that do not revolve around the marriage plot, but, according to Heilbrun, these lives "are painful, the price is high, the anxiety is intense, because there is no script to follow, no story portraying how one is to act, let alone any alternative stories" (39).

Despite their active pursuit of a vocation of their own—or God's—choosing, these preachers were in many ways like their domestic counterparts who remained unmarried. "Unmarried women," Nancy Cott reminds us, "were 'unsettled,' in the language of the day, and had stronger motives for self-scrutiny—for the examination of their prospects—than did married women who had made their most significant life-choice" (*Bonds* 15). Though these preachers had made a significant life choice, as long as doors remained—literally at times—closed to them, as long as the pulpit was a contested site, they would remain forever "unsettled," literally as itinerants, but institutionally and, more important, psychologically as well. Having either rejected marriage altogether or "settled" in it for only a brief period, most of these women would have recognized the irony in Fanny Fern's harangue on marriage in "The Tear of a Wife": "'What have you to cry for? A-i-n-t y-o-u m-a-r-r-i-e-d? Isn't that the *summum bonum*,—the height of feminine ambition? You can't get beyond that! It is the jumping-off place! You've arriv! [*sic*]—got to the end of your journey!'" (324–25).

Having voluntarily abandoned a socially and psychologically "settled" existence within the home and having been denied access to more "settled," authoritative positions within institutional religion, these evangelical women wrote from a precarious, ill-defined position: marginalized from both the male and female paradigms of development (and their requisite endings), they construct stories full of questions and departures, not answers and endings. No clear paradigms existed in their culture to tell them where or who they were. Their journey as God's messengers had not led them any closer to a godlike knowledge of self that makes easy the "mastery" of narrative form, the transformation of the formless life into a "purposeful," patterned autobiography.[24]

When I claim that these formless texts reveal an insecurity, a felt lack of authority or even selfhood, in their authors, I run a significant risk: that of undervaluing the sincere faith these women all possessed. I have no reason to believe that any of them was dissembling when she claimed that God had called her to her work, that he was her constant companion in moments of loneliness or opposition, and that the feeling of his presence and approval more than made up for the many discomforts the itinerant life involved. How, then, could they have felt anything but secure and confident? But just as we need to avoid undervaluing the faith of these autobiographers, we need also to avoid oversimplifying it. Religious faith, after all, is as often the companion of doubt as its antidote; even the great figures of the Bible, who believed they had seen God and heard his voice, are said to have experienced many moments of doubt about the validity of their prophetic enterprises. In a well-known scriptural passage, the father of a child possessed by a "dumb spirit" begged Jesus, "Lord, I believe; help thou mine unbelief" (Mark 9:17, 24). Agnosticism, says Frederick Buechner, describes "some people all of the time and all people some of the time" (*Wishful Thinking* 1). There is no reason to suppose that these women were any more immune to periodic doubt than other religious believers have been. But the real issue here is not the character of these women's belief but the shape of the narratives in which they tried to testify to that belief. A secure believer—even one who can locate herself most securely in the Bible—might still be an insecure author, uncertain how the experience of transcendence and its aftermath could be rendered as history.

The more secure the belief, in fact, the more acutely the problem might have arisen. Inheritors of the Christian tradition, theoretically at least, plotted their spiritual course on a theological, rather than temporal, grid. These women's narratives, like all spiritual autobiographies, reflect "eschatological coordinates, in relation to which it is possible for each individual to pinpoint his own position between a beginning and an end predestined by the Creator of the world" (Gusdorf, "Scripture" 120-21). Focusing, however, on one's position in the larger scheme of Christian revelation could make difficult the task of pinpointing the beginning, middle, and end of the autobiographical *Life*: for the Christian evangelist, to quote Georges Gusdorf, "Birth and death do not define the true beginning and end of the human journey; there does indeed exist a biological logic of growth and decline, a historical logic of events, but these are sequences that do not carry their own internal and final justification" ("Scripture" 121). Or, in the words of C. S. Lewis, "The horror of the Christian universe was that it had no door marked *Exit*" (171). The Christian's pilgrimage, in other words, was no easy thing to plot.

A Charles Finney could, nonetheless, easily select a purpose for his autobiography, as his editor informs us, and compose a unified "narrative which gives him chiefly in one line of his work, and one view of his character": knowing where he stood, he could select material with which to fashion a story out of a fragmented existence (636). His female counterparts, however, though they had a clear sense of the literal miles they had traveled as itinerant preachers, had no sense of the shape of the journey they had made from their own humble beginnings as sinful girls to successful, even, in limited circles, well-known preachers of the gospel. While George Brown and most of his male associates traveled, as we know, along assigned "circuits," these female evangelists seem to have traveled in circles.[25] A "circuit," one might say, is a kind of organized circle, one designed, paradoxically, to lead somewhere; and, indeed, the circular travels of some male itinerants did, in the end, resolve themselves into linear careers—success stories—leading to prestigious and responsible positions within the hierarchy of their ecclesiastical establishments. But where Peter Cartwright could imagine his journey as a climbing spiral—always moving around, but always moving up—Lydia Sexton and Zilpha Elaw could draw only a random game of connect the dots, heading everywhere but leading to no particular "place" in their culture. Their daring ambitions had not brought them any closer to the "jumping-off place!" Thus, these women end up writing in circles, like scouts lost in the woods, searching for the narrative trail. Their circular journeys—literally and psychologically speaking—end in formless, serial narratives that beg to know when, when will we reach the end of our journey? When will we be "settled"?[26]

The answer seems to be never. Like the many nineteenth-century women who also challenged cultural norms by pursuing public, and quite political, work as reformers, journalists, and speakers, these preachers led lives characterized by an extraordinary degree of "geographic mobility and physical freedom" (C. Peterson 16). And by writing their *Lives* so that "preaching events give way to the transitions between them," as Katherine Bassard observes, they clearly call our attention to the itinerant's "agency," to her "ownership of her body," in a period "in which it was dangerous and transgressive for either African Americans or women to travel freely unaccompanied" (91-92). In her analysis of Lee's autobiographies, Bassard rightly reminds us of Emerson's famous assessment of the meaning of "transitions" in "Self-Reliance": "Power ceases in the instant of repose; it resides in the movement of transition from a past to a new state, in the shooting of the gulf, in the darting to an aim" (89). By writing *Lives* full of transitions, these women lay claim not only to cultural and physical freedom but also to a certain power. In doing so, they anticipate contemporary feminism that "has always had a very keen awareness of the intersection of space and power" (Rose 142).

And yet by emphasizing the movement of the body, its transitions from point A to point B, these *itinerant autobiographies* suggest that these evangelists were also insecure, as narrators, as preachers, and as nineteenth-century America women. They knew they were being judged by the gaze of curious onlookers and critics of women's "exceptional" status, who watched them as they traveled about on horseback and in carriages, ferries, and ships. These autobiographers, as I noted in chapter 3, testify to a degree of discomfort with their place—and that of their bodies—in the spaces in which they moved as preachers of the gospel. In a book significantly subtitled *The Limits of Geographical Knowledge*, Gillian Rose helps us understand the origins of such discomfort:

> Unlike men who believe they can transcend the specificities of their body and see themselves and their intentions as the originating co-ordinate for organizing everyday space, women see their bodies as objects placed in space among other objects. Because our bodies are an object to us, we see ourselves as positioned in a space not our own. And that space can feel like an alien territory. Women's sense of embodiment can make space feel like a thousand piercing eyes. . . . This produces a sense of space as something tricky, something to be negotiated, a hazardous arena. (146)

Theoretically these female itinerants were *free* to be *moved* solely by the Spirit. But their autobiographies make clear that this very freedom made them ever vulnerable in the world of evangelical religion and in their culture at large. While Nancy Towle would forcefully declare her independence—"I am . . . accountable to no mortal, for my procedure—nor hath any human being, any control over me"—her autobiography tells another story (232). Though some of these women were granted the privilege of preaching by powerful male officials such as Bishop Richard Allen, they were not assigned particular circuits, nor did they find much in the way of support from institutions like the African Methodist Episcopal Church.

Thus one of the subjects of these narratives—the autobiographers' emphasis on "feverish" productivity analyzed in chapter 2—and their form highlight the authors' dependence on an evaluative system that measured and remeasured their worth according to the amount of work "added" to the record of their lives. There could be no rest for the weary worker who plied her trade outside the official network of support: "seals" to her ministry must be forever forthcoming for those whose authority was derived from God rather than a quarterly conference. Having entered the competitive marketplace of evangelical religion, and having done so by laying claim to an inner witness of the Spirit, these women perceived that theirs must be a story of exceptional success if they wished to maintain what little authority God's official servants had granted them. Hence they compiled their *Lives* as they no doubt lived them, anxious to appear busier and more successful than their male counterparts. Indeed, busyness was a paramount consideration for all Christians living in a millennial age of energy and usefulness, and, more particularly, for female evangelists competing in the marketplace of salvation. There is no end, each of these women implies, to what I can add to this text; there is, moreover, no easy way to "edit" my activities: they might all be important in this evangelical count-inghouse of success and in my quest for distinction. As these autobiographers make clear, if you are not traveling toward any particular destination, then to stop is simply to quit, not to arrive. Stopping is failure. With no end in sight for the journey, there could be no end—at least no easily identifiable one—to the autobiography. And while it is certainly true that all evangelicals, male and female, believed their work would end only with the conversion and reformation of the democratic nation and the world, female itinerant evangelists were burdened by another, seemingly endless, quest for recogni-tion and authority. Though they could always hope for a rewarding end, theirs remained an unfinished business. Their additive method of composition—like their adoption of the century's quantitative ethic as a measure of power and success—is thus an index of their anxiety as "unsettled" preachers, as "unsettled" women in nineteenth-century American culture.[27]

On Gender and Genre

These autobiographies, then, call our attention to the relationship between social and literary authority and thus to the "gender of genre." But the issue is not a simple one. It is important here to note that the paratactic, additive, and seemingly formless quality that characterizes all these autobiographies by female evangelists also characterizes the personal narratives of several male itinerants. Many male itinerants, to be sure, wrote narratives like those of Cartwright and Finney. But many others did not, using instead the additive, serial method we have seen at work in the autobiographies of some of these women. It is difficult to generalize about those who did and those who did not. Some of the formless personal narratives by men—Francis Asbury's and Heman Bangs's, for example—were simply published journals that made no claim of being finished au-tobiographies; some of them—like that of Abraham Snethen and, again, Heman Bangs—were posthumous gatherings of material selected and pieced together by surviving friends, again making no claim to literary unity; and some are apparently genuine efforts, like those of our seven women, to make stories out of vast, shapeless, and repetitive records of experience. What, then, is the relationship between this genre and the gender of the authors? A glance at some of these male autobiographies may help clarify this issue. The *Life, Experience, and Travels of John Colby, Preacher of the Gospel* (as an itinerant for the Church of Christ) is a case in point. This autobiography, printed in 1815, reads much like that of his contemporary Nancy Towle:

> The next day, I went on through Lake Common, (which is the name of a river or creek,) which I forded forty-four times, in going thirty miles. I tarried Tuesday night, in Newbury, at one Smith's. The next day I went down to Jaysburgh, a little village near Susquehannah West Branch. Here I attended a meeting among a set of lukewarm baptists, and had not a very good time. The following evening I went about a mile, and attended a meeting at Loyal Sock. Next day went through Jersey shore, crossed Pine Creek, and went up the Susquehannah river, about twenty miles into Dunstable. (54)

Or consider this fragment from *The Life of David Marks*, the self-styled, Freewill Baptist "boy preacher":

Saturday, May 5, I went to Jerusalem, and gave out appointments for the next day. Sabbath morning, at the hour of nine, we met for worship on the west hill of Jerusalem. The assembly was large, and it was a time of Emmanuel's power: several wept, and kneeled for prayers. At one o'clock, P.M., the Lord assisted me in speaking to a crowded and solemn assembly on the east hill of Jerusalem: two manifested a resolution to seek the Lord. At three o'clock, P.M., I met another congregation in the north part of the town, and enjoyed the presence of my Master. (42)

Certainly, like their sister itinerants, both Marks and Colby were preachers who had no secure place within an ecclesiastical structure (at least when they printed their narratives in their midtwenties) and who belonged to "anti-denominational denominations," institutions that, minding the example of the primitive church described in the Book of Acts, tried to resist being institutionalized. Whether or not they chose the travelogue as a form for their autobiographies—an impossible question to answer in their cases as in those of our seven women—Colby and Marks did choose the marginalized and somewhat formless careers that gave rise to them. Marks, to put it another way, did not have to be the "boy preacher" in the same way that Zilpha Elaw had to be the "colored female preacher."

The form of these autobiographies by male itinerants carries something of the same meaning as does that of these women's autobiographies: it signifies, to put the best face on it, agency—freedom from institutional structure being, in these cases, symbolized by freedom from plot. Or to view it in a different, and perhaps darker, light, the lack of narrative structure symbolizes a lack of both literary and institutional authority, a marginalized status. Now as I showed in chapter 3, this lack was, for men and women, a kind of blessing as well as a curse, for the outsider's status conferred its own kind of authority. Who, after all, were the Hebrew prophets, who were John the Baptist and Christ himself, but outsiders, opposed, resisted, and menaced by the insiders? As Elaw remembers, a prophet too readily honored in her home and homeland might turn out to be no prophet at all (Elaw 83; Matthew 13:57). But, and obviously, this marginalized status also involved many discomforts and practical disadvantages, to which none of these evangelists could have been entirely indifferent. Among those disadvantages, I have argued, is the literary one of being cut off from most of the familiar, ordered narratives by which a life can easily be transformed into a *Life*. The "boy preacher" and his kin, when they chose a posture of alienation from established ecclesiastical structure, may well have been choosing, whether they knew it or not, to labor under this literary disadvantage when the time came to write the autobiography. Only a few of them overcame this disadvantage any better than our women did.

So what is the relationship between gender and genre, between the sex of the author and the form of the autobiography? Not the simple one: it is not the case that only a woman could write this way. It does seem to be the case, though, that in the evangelical world of the American nineteenth century, it would have been very difficult for women to have written any other way. It is not hard to find men who lapsed, for whatever reasons, into serial and shapeless autobiographical form; but it is difficult to find itinerant women who wrote in any other form. If I am right about the relationship between institutional and literary authority, between the trajectory of the career and the trajectory of the autobiographical plot, this should not be surprising. It was possible, of course, for a male preacher like Abraham Snethen to be a "barefoot preacher," to *choose*—for good reasons—to take off his shoes and accept the outsider's status whose literary symbol is the formless autobiography. It was not easy for a female preacher in the nineteenth century to choose anything else.

These itinerant autobiographies serve, then, as powerful reminders of how issues of literary authority are related to those of political and institutional authority. Marginalized from the nineteenth century's stories, and their endings, of both women and men, these women had not attained an authoritative "end," a state of "complete" self-knowledge that had empowered men like Brown and Cartwright to give structure and closure to their stories. Nor had they, it would seem, the postmodern wherewithal to reassure themselves that such totalizing self-knowledge was ultimately false to experience, to interrogate the sexual and textual politics of closure, to appreciate, in other words, that closure— (signifying woman's imprisonment in patriarchal plots and ways of knowing)— was "bad" and its absence— (signifying her freedom from such plots and attitudes)— was "good."[28] Rather, these additive, inconclusive narratives forcefully demonstrate the anxiety that comes from the inability to resolve conflicts, to make sense of one's life, to give form to one's fragmented existence, contrived though that form may be. These stories poignantly reveal the pain to which contemporary theorists are blind when they criticize male autobiographers like Henry Adams for closing over gaps in their experience, for choosing only one aspect of their identity to stand for the whole, for looking back over the life and perceiving or imposing there a pattern and a meaning. Indeed, the ability to unify one's personal experience into a meaningful whole is, in the words of James Olney, "the only way man has of making the universe stop pounding and washing away at his little light of consciousness" (*Metaphors* 16). Living in a century that made difficult this task of finishing the life stories of unorthodox women, these autobiographers can only look to a future age when equality of faith would become equality of sex, when stories about adventurous women would be the rule, not the "exception," when they, too, would have a godlike, psychologically empowering perspective from which to write their lives.

The Call of the Preachers, the Cry of the Faithful

Evangelical Women Writers and the Search
for an Interpretive Community

How long, O Lord, how long, ere woman shall be clothed with the Sun,
walk upon the moon, and be crowned with Apostolick glory?
  Harriet Livermore, A *Narration of Religious Experience in Twelve Letters*

These fragments I have shored against my ruins.
  T. S. Eliot, *The Waste Land*

If this year your story is one of loss, and you are as an exile in a strange
land, remember that even in such a place the Lord's song will yet be sung.
In God's good time, even exiles at last come home.
  Dan Wakefield, *Returning*

All potential autobiographers have facts, and dates, and memories—reliable or not—with
which to work as they construct a narrative of their lives; some of them even have diaries and journals upon which to draw. "But to organize events into stories," Patricia
Spacks argues, "not merely sequences of happenings but sequences of meaning, requires
'making up,' of patterns if not of events. To understand one's life as a story demands
that one perceive that life as making sense" ("Selves" 131). When the preachers in this
study began the process of exploring their lives by keeping journals and, later, by writing autobiographies, they wrestled with the issue of identity, an issue made acute by
their awareness that they preached to and wrote for an audience that might well "judge"
them (Towle 254). The problem of identity and audience could not easily be resolved,
even under the aegis of a genre that critics have long understood as an educational,
introspective tool, designed to help the struggling writer "impose order, form, and
meaning on the facts of an existence" (Maynes 105). "The autobiography is, or can be,"
Robert Sayre maintains, "that second house into which we are reborn, carried by our
own creative power. We make it ourselves, then remake it—make it new" ("Autobiography" 148). These women "wandering through our land," to quote Judge —— once again,
with their "wild visions" had indeed left their first homes, literally and psychologically.
They wandered through their culture and then through their self-writings in search of a
language that could adequately represent that "second house into which they were reborn." And, in part, they were successful. Their autobiographies tell stories of women
who did make it themselves and then make it new. In appropriating the prominent

languages of their day—domesticity, competitive individualism, evangelicalism—as well as a powerful tradition of biblical typology, they were able to deconstruct old forms of womanhood and reconstruct new ones. Working with the only materials at hand, they created wonderfully complex female characters. Reading the *Vicissitudes* of Nancy Towle, Judge —— could begin to answer his own question: "Say, *female stranger*, who art thou?" (Towle 254).

At times, however, these autobiographies read like one long struggle to find meaning in and give order to lives for which there were few precedents, an almost overwhelming task of cutting and pasting textual identities with words and images that could only partially describe "strangers" to their culture. Speaking the language of their culture, these autobiographers find themselves, perhaps inevitably, constructing their lives on paradoxical or competing terms. They are self-reliant, competitive individualists, successful entrepreneurs in the marketplace. But they are also selfless prophets, chosen to be God's representatives on earth. They are tenacious, courageous women asserting self in history but also spiritual autobiographers effacing self into a timeless pattern. They are singular in their own time and representative in sacred history.[1] Many of them renounced their status as wives, mothers, daughters, domestics, mammies, and Jezebels. And all of them embraced that normally masculine prerogative that David Potter calls "the principle of mobility," seeking advancement in the marketplace of evangelicalism; and yet they also invoke a principle of status, slipping comfortably into the familiar and prestigious station of prophet and martyr (105). They are authorities and victims—though never defenseless—challenging their culture and at the same time situating themselves in its most treasured myths. They advance their cause by embracing seemingly paradoxical definitions of self, constantly choosing among the many paradigms available to them as women, as Americans, as Christians. Constructing the self out of paradox, they were able to create and maintain a female identity that gave them both the risk of challenging hegemonic values and the security of appealing to them. The latter stance, it is important to recognize, is not particularly a retreat from the former; in these autobiographies self-effacement and self-assertion always coexist, side by side. Hence, no doubt, the sense of insecurity that all these autobiographies express: as if at any moment the careful equilibrium established between conflicting fictions of selfhood may collapse.

But in an equilibrium, after all, change is inevitably destructive. Engaged in a tug-of-war with herself and her readers, any of these autobiographers could gain ground only by simultaneously losing it. Accordingly, they must resist simple categorization, undertaking necessarily endless negotiations with the many patterns of selfhood to which their culture gave them access. It would therefore be a mistake, I believe, to conceive of these women as the passive objects of cultural power. All of them seem to have recognized the futility of seeking some Archimedean fulcrum, entirely outside their particular culture, from which to exert their influence. But they all learned the trick of moving very freely within the space that culture afforded them. Like their tireless peregrinations across the American landscape, their ceaseless wandering among cultural paradigms was both the symbol and the means of their remarkable freedom.

And yet, though it is currently fashionable to valorize the "fluid," as opposed to the "fixed," identity, to praise texts in which "the fixed identity of woman" is replaced with "the *improvised mobility* of a modernist subjectivity," these autobiographies force us to consider what it might have been like to write such an easily changed or readily changing identity in nineteenth-century America, an identity, moreover, that tends, as fluids do, to take on the shape of its container (Miller, *Subject* 258). Though it may well be true, as Teresa De Lauretis argues, that "subjectivity is an ongoing construction, not a fixed point of departure or arrival from which one then interacts with the world," that these women had no choice but to engage in an endless process of identity negotiations, it is also true, as these stories attest, that the process of trying on identities, like so many hats in a millinery of culture, can be a daunting, enormously stressful task (159). Restlessly trying to create a textual identity that would be acceptable to the audiences who watched and judged them, these itinerant preachers invite us to consider whether all their *identities*, drawn from the dominant culture, ever equal *an identity*. Do they "add up," or do they simply remain in flux, each one "added on" to, but never integrated with, the others, just as each journalistic fragment is carefully added to their narratives? Do these women, in other words, ever realize a "self" in their autobiographies? Like their quest for a plot, their quest for an identity remains, it seems to me, incomplete at the "end" of their textual self-representations.

These autobiographies demonstrate, then, what postmodern theorists have long contended: the autobiographical self is far from an essential, inviolable being: it is, rather, a fragmented, decentered construction of language, dependent on its readers either to fill in the gaps and paste over the holes or to deconstruct the fragile creation before them. These preachers, of course, would not—indeed could not—speak in these twentieth-century terms; if their autobiographies are any indication, however, I strongly suspect that they did *feel* theirs was an almost impossible project, that no manner of shoring up the self with journalistic fragments would build them a "new house."

That would have to come, they realized, from their readers. Indeed, all the texts in this subtradition of women's evangelical autobiography are clearly audience-centered, much in the same way that their sermons no doubt were. None of these women left behind collections of their sermons; they claim to have been inspired by God and to have spoken extemporaneously.[2] But what we know about the evangelical climate in which they worked justifies an assumption that these women were fully as concerned as their male counterparts with what Nathan Hatch calls "The Sovereign Audience" (*Democratization* 125). As Hatch convincingly argues, "Each [new sect] was wedded to the transforming power of the word, spoken, written, and sung; . . . each was supremely confident that the vernacular and the colloquial were the most fitting channels for religious expression; and each was content to measure the success of individuals and movements by their ability to persuade" (*Democratization* 127). Certainly, each of these women impresses us with her intense desire to "persuade," to convert her lay readers, by "testify[ing]," in the words of Julia Foote, "more extensively to the sufficiency of the blood of Jesus Christ to save from all sin," in this case, in a small volume designed primarily for African Americans who might not be able to afford "expensive works on this important Bible theme" (163). Foote earnestly believes that the story of her conversion and evangelical labors can "promote the cause of holiness in the Church": "why not," she asks her readers, "yield, believe, and be sanctified now—now while reading?" (234).

But these works are obviously audience-centered in another way. Like black autobiographers in the nineteenth century, these women realized that "theirs was a rhetorical situation" (Andrews, *To Tell* 17). As women often challenged for their participation in a field dominated by men, these autobiographers were not simply motivated by an unselfish desire to spread the good news of the gospel. Evangelicalism, then as now, called them to testify as part of their spiritual journey, but their own need for validation called them to undertake another discursive pilgrimage as well, to open a discourse with a wide and critical world. What William Andrews has written about African American autobiographers applies equally to these women, white and black: they "could not think of their task simply as the objective reconstruction of an individual's past or a public demonstration of the qualities of selfhood or a private meditation on the meaning of a life of struggle," or, I would add, simply an instructive guide to conversion (17). Estranged from popular nineteenth-century women's scripts and unable to understand fully the *quality* of their "strange" lives in the "strange" masculine world of evangelical religion, these women invite the reader to become more than another convert in their ledgers: indirectly at least, these complex, additive narratives look to the reader for some sort of final arbitration about a woman's right to leave her father's or husband's home, to roam the country "immodestly" unescorted, to enter the pulpit with or without official sanction—indeed, to have "authority" as a preacher and as an autobiographer. Historically, spiritual narratives have often been books about community and judgment, about election and damnation, at least that is how it was for the Puritans— even secular ones like Franklin—who constructed their stories within and for a community of believers.[3] The authority of itinerant preachers, moreover, was always tied to a community of listeners: "Only the response *from* the congregation reveals the presence of authority" (Mathews, "Evangelical America" 29). Will you, these narrators seem to ask their dear readers, lend validation and closure to our unfinished *Lives*, these unfinished selves? Will you respond to our call and thereby lend us the authority we desire and deserve?

The "self," of course, has always been a problematic construct. It is, James Olney warns, "infinitely difficult to get at, to encompass, to know how to deal with: it bears no definition . . . it is not known except privately and intuitively; it is, for each of us, only itself, unlike anything else experienced or experienceable" (*Metaphors* 23). Indeed, as we have seen, the self that bears little relation to the characters that abound in an autobiographer's culture cannot easily be known even "privately," let alone publicly by a reader. As I have argued, to be recognizable as a story, the plot must be in some way standard: a private story is in some sense a contradiction in terms. That is why these women borrow terms most familiar to their culture when constructing their identities. That is also why these storyless women settle for "opening" a discourse—a conversation, if you will—that might ultimately lead to some consensus about where, amid the facts of their existence, the narrative line in fact runs, to some consensus about "who art thou"— about, in other words, plot and character (Towle 254). What these women are writing is, thus (to borrow a feminist buzzword), "relational," not in the sense that they don't "oppose [themselves] to all others," or that they don't "feel [themselves] to exist outside of others, and still less against others," but in the sense that they invite a community of readers to "collaborate" in their efforts to rebuild their social, cultural, and psychological homes, in Sayre's terms to "make them new" (Friedman 56).[4]

Making it new, I believe, is what these texts may ultimately be about. When these women decided to record their experiences for posterity, they necessarily engaged a tradition among nineteenth-century evangelical Protestant denominations of marketing one's life as a "model" of conversion and righteous living, a model even more effective than those provided by scriptural characters. As Bishop C. D. Foss put it his introduction to *Forty Witnesses: Covering the Whole Range of Christian Experience* (1888), a collection of brief spiritual relations: "Man is the great revelation of God. All honor to 'God's word written'; but the practically decisive revelation to God to the individual sinner is not usually through the Bible, but through some 'living epistle'" (11). The tradition did not originate in the Second Great Awakening. In his "Faithful Narrative of the Surprising Work of God," Jonathan Edwards observed, "There is no one thing that I know of, that God has made such a means of promoting his work amongst us, as the news of others' conversion" (176). This habit of preferring contemporary accounts of spiritual living to those of the Bible did, however, become extremely popular in the nineteenth century: "Christian biography," the Reverend John Holmes Acornley wrote in 1892 in *The Colored Lady Evangelist*,

> has often been blessed of God in the reclaimation [sic] and salvation of those who have been living at variance with his will, and in violation of his law. Blasphemers and perse-cutors have been led, by the quiet perusal of the record of the inner lives of God's chil-dren, to change their sentiments and conduct, to open their hearts to the influence of the Divine Spirit, and to realize and experience that change we call conversion. (7)

Though spiritual writers and autobiographers were anxious to assure their readers that they were "Bible Christians," that the Bible was the best guide for Christian living, they nonetheless produced and reproduced the nineteenth century's evangelical version of the self-help book.[5] Collections of "Pious Lives," such as Samuel Burder's *Memoirs of Eminently Pious Women*, found their way into many religious homes in nineteenth-century America, readers believing, like writers and reviewers, in the remarkable power of the word to convert and to socialize. In *Forty Witnesses*, temperance advocate Frances Willard remembers being "deeply impressed" by the "*Life of Hester Ann Rogers; Life of Carvosso; Life of Mrs. Fletcher;* Wesley's *Sermons on Christian Perfection,* and Mrs. Palmer's *Guide to Holiness*"; her "reading of these books" led her to "pray for holiness of heart" (73). Amanda Berry Smith recalls meeting a woman who received the "blessed experience of full salvation" while "reading Mrs. Phebe Palmer's book, 'The Way of Faith'" (213). Laura Haviland claims to have been "encouraged to return" to the Lord by reading a book about "the Christian experience of one whose exercises of mind traced through my own experience, even to my present despairing state" (31). And Methodist Elbert Osborn's autobiography is full of references to the many books—the *Letters of Mrs. Hester Ann Rogers,* the *Life of Benjamin Abbott,* the *Portraiture of Methodism*—that his father purchased from circuit riders: "I have reason to thank God," Osborn reflects, "for the deep and lasting impressions made on my mind through their instrumentality; and I have no doubt much good has been done through the books which the Methodist itin-erants have scattered through the land," particularly "religious biography" (23, 48). Even evangelical novels were considered powerful tools in the dissemination of "good." As one reviewer of Susan Warner's best-selling *The Wide, Wide World* argued, this book is "capable of doing more good than any other work, other than the Bible" (qtd. in Dob-son 12). The reverse could also be true: "The nineteenth century knew," Barbara Wel-ter writes, "that girls *could* be ruined by a book" (*Dimity* 34). As Zilpha Elaw remarks in her *Memoirs*, "Take heed what you read" (52).

And in an evangelical age when language—as opposed to the sacraments—was felt to be of tremendous importance and converts were the objects of fierce competition, spiritual narratives, no less than evangelical novels and essays, assumed a large part in what Hatch aptly calls "an explosion of popular printed material" in the early nineteenth century (*Democratization* 125). Given the degree to which women were considered "naturally" more religious than men, it should also come as no surprise that Timothy Merritt, editor of *The Guide to Christian Perfection*, should specifically direct his attention to women in the journal's first issue, published in 1839: "A Word to the Female Members of the Church.—Many of you have experienced the grace of sanctification. Should you not then, as a thank-offering to God, give an account of this gracious dealing with your souls, that others may be partakers of this grace also? *Sisters in Christ*, may we not expect that you will assist us both with your prayers and pens?" (qtd. in Hardesty, Dayton, and Dayton 232).

And assist they did, though not always limiting their accounts to God's "gracious dealing" with their souls. For, as I have indicated in previous chapters, these particular women's autobiographies are as much about the "dealings" of these courageous authors as about the work of God's grace. One could argue, in fact, that these women wrote autobiographies that anticipate the narrative strategies of twentieth-century women writers who "write beyond the ending": they look beyond both the conventional understanding of the spiritual narrative as an aid in conversion and the "formerly conventional structures of fiction and consciousness about women" (DuPlessis x). Once their lives moved beyond the conventional ending—beyond their awakening to sin and salvation, beyond the social conventions or "patterns of learned behavior" prescribed for women—these evangelical women lacked the "script," which would have "suggest[ed] sequences of action and response, the meaning we give these, and ways of organizing experience by choices, emphases, priorities" (DuPlessis 2). But they kept on writing nonetheless, disrupting formal and thematic patterns of women's stories and, no doubt, disturbing many readers.

Indeed, when Jarena Lee decided to expand the first edition of her autobiography, she initially sought permission from the A.M.E. Church's Book Concern, knowing that traveling preachers were required to seek approval before proceeding with publication. The Book Concern, which found the *Religious Experience and Journal* "written in such a manner that it is impossible to decipher much of the meaning contained in it," denied her request, though given their financial troubles, they might well have profited from a second edition that promised to be as popular as her first (Payne, *History* 190). "We shall have to apply to Sister Lee," the Book Concern further noted, "to favor us with an explanation of such portions of the manuscript as are not understood by us" (Payne, *History* 190). With Frances Foster I find little in Jarena Lee's second autobiography that cannot easily be understood—at least from the distance of 150 years. It is likely that the Book Concern "had been tested for their ability to accept the testimony of an African American woman and been found wanting" (Foster, *Written by Herself* 75). Or perhaps the men of the Book Concern genuinely could not "decipher the meaning" of Lee's autobiography because it was, by the standards of 1845, an unorthodox, though not unprecedented, story. Lee's was a private narrative: it did not assume a culturally familiar, certainly not a culturally validated, shape that would have made sense to the A.M.E. Book Concern.

It is also possible, as Catherine Brekus suggests, that they rejected Lee's book because they understood it all too clearly. By 1845 "few African Methodist clergymen wanted to memorialize a woman who so perfectly symbolized the uneducated, visionary enthusiasm of their early history" (296). Given that the Concern had been established to "publish religious tracts and pamphlets as was deemed best for the interests of the Connection," we can only assume these men made the right decision: the second edition of Jarena Lee's *Life* clearly was not in the best interest of the "Connection," at least in the terms by which that, or any other, patriarchal religious institution understood and defined itself (qtd. in Foster, *Written by Herself* 74). Though Jarena Lee's second autobiography, like those of her sister itinerants, did follow the "established literary tradition for spiritual autobiography," it also deviated from that tradition in subtle yet subversive ways, which the Book Concern probably recognized (Foster, *Written by Herself* 75). The traditional form was established to guide the narrator to an understanding of her spiritual condition and the community of readers to Christian conversion; and certainly these women wrote their books hoping that their readers would unite "with God while time and opportunity is given, and be one of that number who shall take part in the first resurrection" (Lee 31). But the form established by these female evangelists also, and essentially, guides the reader to a different sort of awakening, the sort with which Kate Chopin's Edna Pontellier might well have identified. They align themselves with "male" myths of competitive individualism, "female" stories of domesticity, and biblical stories of prophecy and persecution. They even undertake a bit of biblical criticism to prove a woman's right to preach. In doing so these women autobiographers have "sensational," even radical, "designs" on their readers.[6] With some "fancy rhetorical footwork," they work explicitly and implicitly to convert opponents of women's assumption of public roles such as "preacher"—opponents who are directly addressed and indirectly apparent on every page, with every defensive self-construction (LaPrade 26). These autobiographers want their readers to recognize women's potential for success in the pulpit, and, in some cases, following Wollstonecraft, to vindicate more generally "'the rights of woman'" (Towle 241).

These women write to awaken their female readership to the possibilities of a new story with a new ending: theirs is, after all, primarily a story of a woman's career as an evangelist, not of her conversion and spiritual introspection. Nancy Towle tells us that she writes "especially, for the encouragement of my *own sex*, that may succeed me in the *Lord's Vineyard*," for there are few women who have "courage sufficient" to chart the unknown waters of female evangelism; in her writing, as in her life, she sought to empower other women, just as she had been "strengthened" by the women preachers of her day (7, 21). A full sixty years later, in 1893, Amanda Smith concludes her autobiography in the hope not only that her "own people will be led to a more full consecration" but also "that the Spirit of the Lord may come upon some of the younger women who have talent, and who have had better opportunities than I have ever had . . . so that when I have fallen in battle, and can do no more, they may take up the standard and bear it on" (505-6). Directed toward their "dear sisters," these autobiographies testify to their authors' "awareness of the meaning of the cultural category *woman* for the patterns of women's individual destiny" (Foote 227; Friedman 40-41).

There is no way to assess the effect these texts actually had on their evangelically oriented audience, no way to know how many women heard Towle or Foote or Smith calling them out of their homes, calling them to lose their domestic lives in the name of Christ. We can speculate about the ways in which these autobiographies could alter a woman's "horizon of expectations," about the ways in which "reading provided space— physical, temporal, and psychological—that permitted women to exempt themselves from traditional gender expectations, whether imposed by formal society or by family obliga- tion" (Jauss 18; Sicherman 202). In her study of the reading habits of nineteenth-century women, Susan Harris found that women "shared an interest in, and admiration for, outstanding women, that they desired an education that would give them what they conceived of as power in the world of ideas, and that they were intensely attracted to fictional heroines who determined to develop themselves professionally" (30). Women and young girls were, not surprisingly, interested in biographies of and autobiographies by missionary women (Welter, *Dimity* 91; Cott, *Bonds* 140–41).

Stories of such derring-do, as reader-response theorists have discovered, provided women with much more than a means of escape, more than a means of satisfying, even pacifying, desire. As Janice Radway's research on the reading of romance novels reminds us, "People do not ingest mass culture whole but often remake it into something they can use" (26). Susan Harris believes that nineteenth-century women brought a "multi- leveled approach to their readings," that they were fully capable of "decoding" what she calls an "exploratory text," a book, in other words, that ended with the standard, cultur- ally valorized romance plot but that covertly explored the possibilities of a woman's fulfillment outside that plot (18, 78). Women easily recognized and enjoyed the more subversive—or "private"—plot, and they were fully able to imagine an alternative ending. Reading offered women "a world in which to formulate aspirations and try out different identities," as Barbara Sicherman's research reveals (208). Reading "encouraged new self-definitions and, ultimately, the innovative behavior associated with the Progressive generation" (Sicherman 202). Indeed, the editors of *Our Famous Women*, a collection of biographical essays on famous American women published in 1886, were responding "to a perceived need on the part of many women for a sense of their peers' reactions to changes in their society" (Kelley 133). The collection was, they argued, "the simple story of what a few women have done," a story that could provide "inspiration and incentive to the many women who long to do" and thus "kindle new hopes and ambitions in unknown hearts" (Phelps et al., v–vi). In altering a woman's "horizon of expectations," therefore, reading might well bring about a "horizon change" (Jauss 18).

We read, some have said, to know we are not alone. So, too, do we write. By braving the opposition of all those male book concerns in order to present a unique woman's life, uniquely told, to the public, these autobiographers serve as models for change. As Frances Foster has written of the century's black women writers, these autobiographers "used the Word as both a tool and a weapon to correct, to create, and to confirm their visions of life as it was and as it could become" (*Written by Herself* 2). Or, in the words of bell hooks, "One confronts and accepts dispersal and fragmentation as part of the construction of a new world order that reveals more fully where we are, who we can become" (148). "When cultural definitions of the female life course are in dispute," as they were in nineteenth-century America, "activism is a critical mode women use to resolve felt dissonance between cultural codes and subjective experience. Narratives about individual transformations, cast as conversions in life stories, serve as models for en- visioned change in the social and cultural order that accommodate female activists' self-understandings" (Ginsburg 60). By focusing almost exclusively on their "conversions" to lives of itinerancy, Nancy Towle, Jarena Lee, and the rest begin the arduous process by which the "old plots" for women are delegitimized and new roles for women become attractive to female "converts," acceptable to their families and friends, and, ultimately, authorized in the culture at large.

Though they spent their days preaching the gospel, these autobiographers were more than passive vessels bearing God's Word. They inevitably borrowed a language and a genre that were, as we have seen, "half someone else's" (Bakhtin 294). But they insisted on writing their own stories—knowing well how their lives (as represented in their many letters and journals) could easily be misconstrued, in the words of Nancy Towle, should God "cut [them] off in the completion of it": "I had," Towle professes, "valuable writings by me, which I had believed, I should publish to the world. . . . and none other, than myself, was capable of doing this" (109). An independent itinerant, Towle found that "there was no *publisher*, to advocate the cause of one, not immediately with *their pales,*—and especially that travelled with the testimony of Jesus:—(unless it were the 'Christian Connexion;' and their work, was so circumscribed, that I preferred, rather, setting my letters on foot, in my own hand writing.)" (5). As Christine Krueger discovered when researching the lives of England's first generation of women preachers, the work of many publishers was "circumscribed" when it came to telling a woman's story: "Any manuscripts a woman preacher left behind were at the mercy of friends and relatives, of editors, biographers, and publishers. If any among this group were hostile to women's preaching, that aspect of her life simply disappeared" (75).[7] And, indeed, in America one need only look to the *Life* of Methodist Hannah Reeves to grasp the literary and historical importance of a female evangelist's taking charge of her own story. The posthumous biography of Reeves, written by George Brown in 1870, is significantly titled *The Lady Preacher: or, the Life and Labors of Mrs. Hannah Reeves, Late the Wife of the Rev. WM. Reeves, D.D., of the Methodist Church.* She is, in this configuration, a mere appendage of her husband and the church. Once Brown begins reporting events that occurred after Reeves's marriage, he found it "impossible," he confesses, "to separate her life entirely from that of her husband" (100). Most of Brown's information, moreover, comes from her husband's memories and journal, not her own. Thus, rather than present her opinions or feelings about a particular event or about her life in general, her biography gives us Mr. Reeves's conclusions. This is a book, in other words, about the subjectivity of Mr., not Mrs., Reeves.[8]

The women in this study rarely speak directly about this issue of control, or about their fears of losing it. We can speculate, however, that they were familiar with the problem, given the extent to which the *Lives* of pious women, written and published by their friends, relatives, or editors, dominated the vast evangelical publishing industry.[9] Their autobiographies bear witness to their desire to emphasize their preaching careers, even to write a "revenge on history," a history that until recently had denied them voice (Gusdorf, "Conditions" 36). They bear witness as well to a willingness to write the genre to make room for new "forms" of womanhood, for the female reader seeking to explore such new forms of being, and, ultimately, for the creation of new opportunities for women. Though these women had difficulty describing (and perhaps even understanding) their own stories, they could summon a readership that would help create a world—help constitute an interpretive community, a community of believers (saints?)—in which their story would someday make sense. Just as they had sometimes appropriated the lives of eighteenth-century Methodist women preachers as models in their own quest for a new place in American culture, so, too, might their stories of resistance to the dominant culture's gender norms strengthen other young women in their efforts to reenvision womanhood.[10] These are, then, stories with "moral consequences" (Jauss 38). Someday, these dialogic narratives dream, ours might be exemplary—rather than experimental—*Lives*; someday we might achieve a state of self-understanding and authority necessary to write "complete" *Lives*; someday women autobiographers, like P. T. Barnum, might have too many stories to tell; someday the wide world might regard us as friends, not "strangers"; perhaps someday "unorthodox" women readers and women writers might know they are not alone. Someday, in other words, even exiled women, with their wild visions, might come home.

Notes

Introduction

The phrase used in the title is that of Thomas K. Doty, from his introduction to Julia Foote's spiritual autobiography, *A Brand Plucked from the Fire* (165).

1. It seems likely that "Miss M——" was Elice Miller Smith, a well-known itinerant preacher whom Towle describes in her autobiography as a "preacher . . . more universally admired, than any other *female* of America" (184). Elice Miller is also mentioned in the autobiography of the Methodist Protestant George Brown, D.D., published in 1866. Brown observes the popularity of Miller when she visited his circuit but acknowledges that Bishop Soule, who was also passing through his circuit at the time, opposed her ministry and derisively called her "that strolling girl" (183).

2. Recent historians suggest that evangelical revivalism was a continuous feature of the American landscape from the 1730s—with the awakenings in Jonathan Edwards's Northampton and the arrival of George Whitefield—through the 1840s. See, for example, James Bratt.

3. For a discussion of this urban revival of 1858, see Kathryn Long.

4. On the empowerment of religion for women and blacks, see Catherine Brekus, Joanna Bowen Gillespie, Susan Juster, Nellie McKay, and Albert Raboteau.

5. Though they were familiar with the ideology of domesticity that permeated the literature of the Northeast, Southern ladies were influenced primarily by the plantation household, which they shared with white men and black slaves. See Elizabeth Fox-Genovese, *Within the Plantation Household*.

6. On the ways in which bourgeois individualism "offered even the excluded a hegemonic discourse that they would gradually claim for themselves," see Fox-Genovese, *Within the Plantation Household* (60).

7. See, for example, Catherine Brekus; Karen Hansen, Nancy Hewitt, and Suzanne Lebsock; Dorothy O. Helly and Susan M. Reverby; Susan Juster; Linda Kerber, "Separate Spheres, Female Worlds, Woman's Place: The Rhetoric of Women's History"; Linda Kerber et al.; Martin Marty, "Religion: A Private Affair, in Public Affairs"; and Mary Ryan, *Women in Public*.

8. According to historians of American religion, reform efforts began to ebb in the decades after the Civil War, when postmillennialism gave way to a more pessimistic premillennialism and many turned away from social issues to Fundamentalism and questions of theology. The "postmillennial" Social Gospel movement was an important exception after the war, just as the

Millerite movement, which numbered at least fifty thousand, serves as evidence that premillennialism was a feature of the religious landscape before the Civil War.

9. Though that situation is rapidly changing with the appearance of a comprehensive study of late-eighteenth- and early nineteenth-century female preaching by Catherine Brekus and books on the writings of nineteenth-century black women by Katherine Bassard, Frances Foster, Joycelyn Moody, and Carla Peterson.

10. According to Brekus, the Christian Connection and the Freewill Baptists were much more likely to encourage women to preach in the early nineteenth century than the Methodists, who "were less tolerant of female preaching than Wesley had been" (133).

11. Throughout these chapters I have chosen to cite the Bible, even when the autobiographers do not, to emphasize the extraordinary degree to which these women make use of what they would have said was their most important (and sometimes only) book.

12. The phrase is that of Rebecca Cox Jackson, a Methodist turned Shaker Eldress, whose journal has recently been published for the first time under the title *Gifts of Power: The Writings of Rebecca Jackson, Black Visionary, Shaker Eldress.*

13. According to Brekus, there were at least ten other nineteenth-century women, whose preaching careers began by the 1840s, who wrote autobiographies.

14. We know the names of a few other women who worked as traveling preachers in the eighteenth- century. Sarah Townsend was a leader of New Light meetings at Oyster Bay on Long Island in the 1770s; throughout the 1760s and 1770s, Martha Marshall accompanied her husband in Virginia, where they exhorted crowds and established Separate Baptist congregations. In his *Memoirs of the Life of Mrs. Sarah Osborn* (1799), the New Divinity minister Samuel Hopkins recognized the active role Osborn played in the Newport, Rhode Island, revival of 1766-67. Margaret Meuse Clay was tried in Chesterfield County, Virginia, for unlicensed preaching in the 1770s. And in the 1790s Mary (Molly) Savage (later Card) and Sally Parsons preached in New Hampshire under the aegis of the Northern Freewill Baptists. For more information, see Billington, Brekus, Dennett, Larson, and Lynch.

15. There were prominent exceptions, particularly later in the century among the Universalists, the first denomination to ordain women and permit them to be settled within a particular congregation. In 1863 Olympia Brown became the first woman to be ordained by the Universalists; shortly thereafter, the Universalists also ordained Phebe Ann Coffin Hanaford, Augusta Chapin, Mariana Thompson-Folsom, Prudy Le Clerc, Lorenza Haynes, and Ada Bowles. In 1853 Antoinette Brown Blackwell became the first woman to be ordained by the Congregationalists, a denomination that ordains ministers within a congregation; the ordination took place at a Baptist church in South Butler, New York, because that was the largest building in town. Years later she became a Unitarian and served its congregations as an ordained minister. Helanor M. Davidson was the first woman ordained by the Methodist Protestant Church; Anna Howard Shaw, whose petition for ordination in 1880 was denied by the Methodist Episcopal Church, was ordained that same year by the Methodist Protestants.

See the collective biography *Daughters of America; or, Women of the Century* (1883) by Phebe Hanaford for brief sketches of the lives of many nineteenth-century women preachers, many of whom, like Hanaford herself, worked among the Universalists. See also Anna Howard Shaw's *The Story of a Pioneer* for an account of her quest for ordination. On the presence of several unordained women preachers who were nonetheless associated with a particular Freewill Baptist church, see James Lynch, "Baptist Women in Ministry through 1920."

16. Historians have recovered the names of—and in a few cases some biographical information about—many of these nineteenth-century itinerant women. What follows is a sampling of the findings of Billington, Brekus, Calvo, Dennett, Dodson, Lynch, William Noll, and Spencer.

Harriet Livermore—or, as she called herself, "The Pilgrim Stranger"—was a prominent evangelist loosely associated with both the Congregationalists and the Church of the Brethren (Dunkers) in the first half of the century. Sarah Righter Major, one of Livermore's converts, followed in her footsteps, becoming an evangelist at age twenty. Preaching among the Freewill Baptists in the first half of the century were Almira Bullock (who frequently traveled with her husband, Jeremiah), Hannah Fogg, Judith Prescott, Dolly Quinby, Betsey Stuart, Sarah Thornton, Susan Humes, Martha Spaulding, and Clarissa Danforth. Sarah Hodges and Abigail Roberts worked among Christians in western New York in the early nineteenth century. Speaking out against slavery and racism, Maria W. Stewart was a preacher associated with the African Baptists of Boston. Chastity Opheral, like Lydia Sexton, was an evangelist associated with the United Brethren. Preaching under the Methodists or one of the various Methodist splinter groups (Primitive Methodists, Protestant Methodists, Reformed Methodists, Wesleyan Methodists, etc.) were Fanny Newell, Eliza Barnes, Ruth Watkins, Anne Wearing, Salome Lincoln (who also worked among Freewill Baptist and Congregational churches), Hannah Reeves, Phoebe Palmer, Hannah Whitall Smith (a prominent figure in the Methodist Holiness and Higher Christian Life movements), Amanda M. Way, Maggie Newton Van Cott (the first woman licensed to preach in the Methodist Episcopal Church in 1869 and the preacher shown on the cover of *Some Wild Visions*), and Jennie Fowler Willing (licensed as a local preacher in 1873). Women were similarly active as preachers in the African Methodist Episcopal Church and the African Methodist Episcopal Church Zion: in addition to Jarena Lee, Zilpha Elaw, and Julia Foote, Sophie Murray, Elizabeth Cole, Rachel Evans, Harriet Felson Taylor, and Sojourner Truth were African Methodist evangelists in antebellum America. In the latter half of the century, Margaret Wilson, Lena Doolin-Mason, Emily Calkins Stevens, Harriet Baker, Mary Palmer, Melinda M. Cotton, Emma Johnson, and Mary L. Harris, to name only a few, were active A.M.E. preachers. Noted evangelists among the Universalists were Maria Cook, Lydia Jenkins, Sally Barnes Dunn, and Mary Livermore. And, of course, the Society of Friends continued to support women preachers like Sybil Jones, Sarah Hunt, Hannah Field, Elizabeth Collins, Elizabeth Newport, Priscilla Cadwallader, Rachel Barker, Esther Frame, Drusilla Wilson, and Rhoda Coffin, many of whom were influenced by the Holiness Revival of the 1860s and 1870s that inspired Julia Foote, Lydia Sexton, and Amanda Smith.

On Harriet Livermore, see John Greenleaf Whittier, *Snowbound: A Winter Idyl*, where she is ridiculed as a "not unfeared, half-welcome guest." In 1826 she published *A Narration of Religious Experience in Twelve Letters*. Following her death in 1868, a distant cousin, the Reverend S. T. Livermore, wrote a biography of this pioneering evangelist entitled *The Pilgrim Stranger*. See Brekus and Jürisson for more information about her life. Though Clarissa Danforth left no autobiographical accounts of her ministry, her work is discussed in the autobiographies of several of her contemporaries, such as John Colby's *Life, Experiences, and Travels of John Colby, Preacher of the Gospel*. On Maria Stewart, see *Meditations from the Pen of Mrs. Maria W. Stewart* (1879), and *Productions of Mrs. Maria W. Stewart* (1835); and Marilyn Richardson, ed., *Maria W. Stewart, America's First Black Woman Political Writer: Essays and Speeches*. For other biographies of and autobiographies by famous preaching women, see John Holmes Acornley, *The Colored Lady Evangelist, Being the Life, Labors and Experiences of Mrs. Harriet A. Baker*; Margaret Van Cott; John O. Foster, *Life and Labors of Mrs. Maggie Newton Van Cott, the First Lady Licensed to Preach in the Methodist Episcopal Church in the United States*; Sarah Hunt, *Journal of the Life and Religious Labors of Sarah Hunt*; Rufus Jones, *Eli and Sybil Jones: Their Life and Work*; Almond H. Davis, *The Female Preacher, or Memoir of Salome Lincoln, afterwards the wife of Elder Junia S. Mowry*; Fanny Newell; Ann Townsend, *Memoir of Elizabeth Newport*; Phoebe Palmer; Richard Wheatley, *The Life and Letters of Mrs. Phoebe Palmer*; George Brown, *The Lady Preacher: or the Life and Labors of Mrs. Hannah Reeves*; Hannah Whitall Smith, *The Unselfishness of God and How I Discovered It: A Spiritual Autobiography*.

17. Sanctification, also called holiness or perfection, is a second experience of grace—salvation or justification being the first—in which the believer is empowered to meet the requirements of the new law. The belief in holiness stemmed from the teachings of Jesus as outlined

in the Gospels, where evidence can be found to prove that the early church believed an ideal life could be lived in this world (Matthew 5:48; Luke 6:36). While the belief implied some moral cleansing, most advocates of holiness considered that perfection in this life was relative—it was a freedom from "intentional sin" only: final perfection came only after death. And just as the Gospels and Pauline letters differ in their depiction of the experience—it appears alternately an instantaneous emotional experience and a gradual process—so, too, have perfectionists differed in their description of how one obtains and maintains sanctification. The belief in sanctification gained prominence in the nineteenth century, particularly among the Methodists, who were anxious to revive Wesley's understanding of the experience he called "perfect love": according to Wesley, who seemed to believe both in an instantaneous experience of grace and in a growth toward holiness, the sanctified face the same temptations as the rest of humankind, but their souls were now turned toward God's will rather than away from it.

For our purposes, sanctification is important because it was the Holiness movement that maintained lay leadership by women once marginal sects such as the Methodists gained respectability and abandoned their more radical innovations. Given the degree to which "holiness" overcame "nature," many historians have found in the marginal movement a feminist impulse, and indeed the sanctified women in this study all believed that an experience of sanctification was a gift of inner peace, as well as a gift of power that could lead to the dissolution of gender and race hierarchies. An experience of perfection was particularly important psychologically and socially for women who might need the self-confidence freedom from sin could bring and who could use the experience to justify an unorthodox life. As Jean Humez has pointed out, the Holiness movement "was from the outset a predominantly female affair, growing even more disproportionately attractive to women as the century advanced," with a "particularly strong appeal for black women" (Introduction 5). Indeed, all four black women in this study were promoters of holiness. Supporters of holiness insisted that it could only be maintained by public professions; the literature is full of accounts of women who lost the experience by being too shy to speak publicly of it. To maintain the gift, women had to transcend their culture's prescriptions against women's public speaking. Holiness and Higher Life movements continued throughout the century (indeed, they continue today), reaching a peak from 1867 through the 1870s, when the interdenominational National Camp Meeting Association for the Promotion of Holiness was founded in Vineland, New Jersey.

On sanctification, see Dorothy Bass; William Boardman; Melvin Dieter; Charles Ferguson; R. Newton Flew; Jean Humez, Introduction, *Gifts of Power*; Charles Edwin Jones; John Leland Peters, David Peterson; J. C. Pollock; Jean Miller Schmidt; Hannah Whitall Smith; Robert Pearsall Smith; and Timothy Smith, *Revivalism and Social Reform*.

18. *Religious Experience and Journal of Mrs. Jarena Lee, Spiritual Narratives*, ed. Susan Houchins (1849; New York: Oxford UP, 1988). All subsequent parenthetical references are to this edition unless otherwise noted.

19. In 1794 Richard Allen, then a licensed preacher of the Methodist Episcopal Church, organized an independent black congregation in Philadelphia after being discriminated against at Saint George's. In 1816, along with disgruntled blacks from Baltimore and other places, Allen formed the African Methodist Episcopal Church. At about the same time, in 1821, the African Methodist Episcopal Zion Church was founded in New York City. See Richard Allen; Daniel Payne.

20. For a discussion of the limited educational opportunities for black children in Northern schools, see Leonard Curry.

21. See also Genesis 49:1, Isaiah 2:2, Micah 4:1, Acts 2:17, 2 Timothy 3:1, James 5:3, and 2 Peter 3:3.

22. Sexton refers here to one of several sects called "Christians" that sprang up in the nineteenth century. Shortly after mentioning her attendance at this "New Light" meeting, Sexton

writes that she traveled from Liberty, Ohio, to Dayton, from "the First Christian (New Light) Church, to attend the Second Christian (Campbellite) Church" (192). This second reference lets us assume that the "Christians" to whom she was first attracted were the "Stonites," or former New Light Presbyterians who, led by Barton Stone of Cane Ridge revival fame, spread throughout Kentucky and, according to Sydney Ahlstrom, "swept every Presbyterian church but two into their movement" in southeastern Ohio (446). They no doubt found their way to Liberty, Ohio, as well, a town in the southwestern portion of the state. Stone and other leaders of the Cane Ridge revival realized in 1803 that they no longer believed in the Reformed doctrine and Presbyterian polity. In June 1804 "they published the 'Last Will and Testament of the Presbytery of Springfield,' abandoned the 'traditions of men,' took the Bible as their only creed and law, and adopted for themselves the name 'Christians'" (Ahlstrom 446).

23. According to Ahlstrom, a Holiness Revival occurred in almost every denomination, including the Methodist Episcopal Church, during the Gilded Age. Though Charles Wesley himself had countenanced a belief in sanctification or holiness, Methodists in general were skeptical of the Pentecostal blessing, finding it "disruptive and unseemly" (817). Not finding it so, the Wesleyan Methodist Church seceded from the Methodist Episcopal Church in 1843; the Free Methodist Church would follow suit in 1859–60, after the great revival of 1858.

24. As the century wore on, even evangelical sects such as the Methodists and Christians retreated from their radical support of a prophetic ministry. In his *Recollections of Itinerant Life* (1866), for example, the Reverend George Brown of the Methodist Protestant Church concluded that the church stands in need of a more educated ministry now that we live in a more "cultivated age," which meant that even this more radical denomination, which was one of the first to ordain women, would frown upon most women, who could claim only spiritual, rather than learned, gifts (436).

25. Nina Baym would also include in this grouping tourists such as Anne Royall, who traveled around the country in the 1820s researching the guidebook *Sketches of History, Life, and Manners, in the United States*, which she published in 1826. See Baym's *American Women Writers and the Work of History, 1790–1860*. For an account of nineteenth-century female activists who found themselves walking the halls of the legislature on behalf of various benevolent causes, see Lori Ginzberg. For a discussion of the relation between marginality, geographic mobility, and empowerment among African American women in the nineteenth century, see Carla Peterson. On women in public more generally, see Glenna Matthews, *The Rise of Public Woman*; Dorothy O. Helly and Susan M. Reverby; Nancy A. Hewitt and Suzanne Lebsock; and Mary Ryan, *Women in Public: Between Banners and Ballots, 1825–1880*.

26. See Ernest Lee Tuveson, *Redeemer Nation: The Idea of America's Millennial Role*.

27. Saint Augustine long ago recognized that excessive travel is a metaphor for human ambition. In Books I through IV of the *Confessions*, travel and home stand for the opposites of secular ambition and "spiritual resignation to the eternal will of God" (Spengemann, *Forms of Autobiography* 20). Interestingly, in these nineteenth-century women's spiritual autobiographies, travel stands for both secular ambitions and resignation to the will of God; home, on the other hand, signals a resignation to the will of husbands, fathers, and clergymen, a sort of repose that these women thoroughly reject.

28. Appropriating images of space to represent woman's powerlessness as well as her desires, these autobiographers anticipate the work of twentieth-century feminists whose theoretical explorations of the politics of gender and the politics of location involve the figurative use of space. In *Feminism and Geography*, Gillian Rose notes how often spatial images appear in the titles of critical and theoretical works by feminist scholars: see, for example, *Feminist Theory: From Margin to Center*, by bell hooks; *Charting the Journey*, ed. by S. Grewal et al.; *In Other Worlds*, by G. Spivak; *Epistemology of the Closet*, by E. Sedgwick; and, of course, *A Room of One's Own*, by V. Woolf (140). As books about women and itinerancy, these autobiographies are

particularly relevant for feminist theorists today; for in their frequent peregrinations and preaching engagements, these women literalized the quest for a place, voice, and change.

29. On the relationship between the margin and the center in American religion, see R. Laurence Moore's *Religious Outsiders and the Making of Americans* and note 24 in chapter 3.

Chapter 1

The phrase used in the title is that of Jarena Lee (18).

1. See also Julie Roy Jeffrey, as well as Herrick Eaton's manual for wives of itinerants published in 1851.

2. Focusing as they so often do on their difficult marriages, these spiritual autobiographies, particularly those by black women, are reminiscent of the "scandalous" subtradition of eighteenth-century women's autobiography about the bad marriages of women. See Estelle Jelinek, *The Tradition of Women's Autobiography*, 33-37. These evangelical autobiographies can also be situated within the subtradition of American literature—of which Chopin's *The Awakening* is a seminal work—that critiques the constraints of marriage.

3. This is an approximation based on the autobiography, which omits the exact date of her marriage.

4. See Linda K. Kerber, *Women of the Republic: Intellect and Ideology in Revolutionary America*. This politicization of motherhood continued throughout most of the nineteenth century as republican motherhood gave way to an ideology of true womanhood, in which, as Barbara Welter argues, white women were not only the promoters of republican principles but also the source of moral virtue in the home. See also Sheila Rothman, who contends that during the Progressive Era at the turn of the century an ideology of "educated motherhood" superseded notions of motherhood based on women's natural religiosity. For my purposes, however, it is important to recognize that regardless of the ideological base, the nation's reverence for motherhood and domesticity continued throughout the century.

5. For a complete analysis of this phenomenon, see Ann Douglas; William McLoughlin, Introduction, *The American Evangelicals, 1800-1900: An Anthology*; and Barbara Welter, *Dimity Convictions*. Both Welter and Douglas use the term "feminization" to refer to the growing female audience for religion and the softening of Calvinist theology. Douglas, however, severely critiques the phenomenon, which she regards (wrongly, I believe) as the spark that led to the flame of mass consumption in modern culture. On the debate regarding Douglas's thesis, see David Schuyler; David S. Reynolds, "The Feminization Controversy: Sexual Stereotypes and the Paradoxes of Piety in Nineteenth-Century America."

6. Julia Foote's situation with the Primes, though initially marked by tenderness and concern, becomes physically and psychologically oppressive for Foote after she is falsely accused of stealing pound cakes from the family's cellar. Despite Foote's vehement protestations of innocence, she is whipped by Mrs. Prime, who "insist[s] that [Julia] should confess that [she] took the cakes" (175). Threatened with another whipping should she continue refusing to confess, Foote reports that "[she] carried the rawhide out to the wood pile, took the axe, and cut it up into small pieces, which [she] threw away, determined not to be whipped with that thing again" (175-76). Foote's strength and determination in this situation prepare the reader for her later power struggles with the men of her church. For an interesting parallel, see Harriet Wilson's autobiographical novel *Our Nig*.

7. On the role of domestic servitude in the lives of nineteenth-century black women, see Dorothy Sterling.

8. Patricia Collins also argues that African Americans often considered "private" space to be that which was out of reach of whites; private space was not, therefore, necessarily domestic

space, nor was it necessarily oppressive. Carla Peterson similarly contends that black women and men participated in a "community sphere," "an intermediate sphere" that was both public (because it lay outside the home) and private (because the "values" of the home were practiced there and because it lay outside the "gaze of the dominant culture") (16). The autobiographies of Lee, Elaw, Foote, and Smith, however, go to great lengths to distinguish between a private, domestic situation and the informal public world to which they were called to care for the family of God.

9. On the creation, prominence, and purpose of these images, in both the nineteenth and twentieth centuries, see Deborah Gray White.

10. For an informative discussion of the ways in which the political desires of nineteenth-century black women are encoded in works of fiction, see Claudia Tate. Though she focuses primarily on the many sentimental novels published by black women at the end of the century, she situates these texts in the prominent domestic discourses of such antebellum protest fiction as *Uncle Tom's Cabin*, *Incidents in the Life of a Slave Girl*, and *Our Nig*.

11. As historians have noted, another strategy employed by blacks in the war against racial injustice in both the nineteenth and the twentieth century was to emphasize difference, to construct a "self-representation essentially antithetical to that of whites" (Higginbotham, "African-American Women's History" 269).

12. This was true during the mid–nineteenth century and certainly in the 1890s, when black women began to form national organizations, such as the National Federation of Afro-American Women, the National League of Colored Women, and the National Association of Colored Women.

13. See George Fredrickson's *The Black Image in the White Mind: The Debate on Afro-American Character and Destiny, 1817–1914*. Historians continue to debate the degree to which the households of slaves and free blacks in the nineteenth century were marked by a sexual equality not found in white households. Deborah Gray White, for example, argues that slave women "learned that black women had to be the maidservants of whites, but not necessarily of men" (118). "The disenfranchisement and oppression of all blacks," in the words of Linda Perkins, "left little room for male chauvinism" ("Black Women" 321). But, as Susan A. Mann reminds us, "the greater relative equality" experienced in the households of slaves and sharecroppers "should neither be exaggerated nor romanticized given the fact that it was premised on the poverty and deprivation of both sexes" (796).

14. For a discussion of these destinies, see the recent work of Cindy Aron; Dorothy Helly and Susan Reverby; Lori Ginzberg; Karen Hansen; Susan Juster; Linda Kerber; Glenna Matthews; and Mary Ryan.

15. Carroll Smith-Rosenberg argues that "the revolutionary thrust of religion ebbed" at midcentury: "Deemphasizing the intense piety of revivalistic conversions, clergyman now argued that salvation blossomed within the Christian nursery as a result of loving, maternal discipline. Reinstating the time-honored boundaries encircling women's sphere, evangelical ministers shepherded their female adherents back towards the contained family and traditional femininity" ("Women and Religious Revivals" 202–3). While it is certainly true that theologians like Horace Bushnell had turned to what William McLoughlin calls "Romantic Evangelicalism," which emphasized the importance of Christian nurture in the home, the autobiographies considered here reveal a thriving remnant who continued to step outside the "contained family and traditional femininity" long after midcentury.

16. The significance of lay–and female–leadership in the early nineteenth century, as I pointed out in the introduction, was hardly unprecedented. One need only remember the seventeenth-century Quakers, or the prominence of lay leaders during and after the Great Awakening. As Timothy Hall and others have argued, the appearance of itinerant preachers, George Whitefield being the most famous, on the religious landscape of eighteenth-century America was the cause of great debate and despair among the established clergy, who feared that an emphasis on a prophetic, rather than educated, ministry disrupted spatial and social boundaries, as lay preach-

ers challenged parish boundaries and encouraged blacks, women, Indians, and children to ex-hort their "betters." In the nineteenth century, lay leadership was particularly (though not exclu-sively) important among Methodists. On the history of Methodism in nineteenth-century America, see Sidney Ahlstrom; Emory Bucke; Charles Ferguson; Nancy Hardesty, *Women Called to Wit-ness*; Donald Mathews, "Evangelical America—The Methodist Ideology" and *Religion in the Old South*; Albert Raboteau, *Slave Religion* and "The Black Experience in American Evangelicalism"; Russell E. Richey, Kenneth E. Rowe, and Jean Miller Schmidt; Rosemary Ruether and Rose-mary Keller; Rosemary Ruether and Eleanor McLaughlin; A. Gregory Schneider; Hilah E. Thomas and Rosemary Skinner Keller; and William Warren Sweet.

17. Carla Peterson, in her study of the lives and writings of nineteenth-century black female social activists, finds that many black women discussed being sick or debilitated *during* their ca-reers. She speculates that such illnesses may have been the result of "the bodily degradation to which these women were subjected or as a psychosomatic strategy for negotiating such degrada-tion" (21). Female preachers do write about the inevitable hardships and bodily pain they experi-enced *when* they traveled; but to an even greater degree they emphasize what they suffered *before* they began traveling, when they ignored a God who called them to the active life of an evangelist.

See also Joycelyn Moody for a discussion of the "sentimental trope of the sick black woman's body" in the autobiographies of African American preachers Jarena Lee and Zilpha Elaw (67). It is important to recognize, however, that the "trope" of the sick body, juxtaposed to a refusal to accept God's call, was also a prominent feature of autobiographies by white women and their male contemporaries. See the work of Nancy Towle, Harriet Livermore, Laura Haviland, Ben-jamin Putnam, and Lorenzo Dow, for example, or that of Heman Bangs, whose children died and business burned before he heeded a call he had heard seven years earlier.

18. Listening to the spiritual life stories of Pentecostal women preachers in the 1980s, Elaine Lawless discovered that these women, though subservient to men in all aspects of their lives, often disrupted worship services by testifying at great length, thereby limiting the time the male preacher could spend in the pulpit and, in effect, usurping his authority. Like their nineteenth-century sisters, however, none of the women Lawless interviewed claimed to have been testifying with that purpose in mind.

19. In "'My Spirit Eye'"Humez writes about the works of Jarena Lee, Julia Foote, and Amanda Smith.

20. In this respect, Towle differs from the "literary domestics" who dominated the literary marketplace in the nineteenth century and who assured their readers that were it not for ex-treme financial hardship—the need to be "useful" to their families—they would never have taken up the pen.

21. One is reminded of Mother Ann Lee, who was once stripped of her clothing by oppo-nents who believed she was a British spy, and of Sojourner Truth, who bared her chest in re-sponse to an opponent who questioned her right to speak publicly and challenged her sexual identity.

22. See Carla Peterson for a discussion of the tension experienced by "black women cultural workers"—writers, preachers, reformers—who exposed themselves in public despite opposition from the black male elite who sought to challenge the dominant culture's perception of the "black female body as unruly, grotesque, carnivalesque" (20–21).

23. On women's work in the Civil Service, see Cindy Aron.

24. It might be tempting to explain away Elaw's lifelong acceptance of women's subordina-tion, to argue that her stance ironically stems from her own unhappy marriage, which she blamed on the absence of a father figure to guide her choice of a mate: in a weak moment, lacking paternal supervision, she yoked herself to an unbeliever and consequently suffered tremendously in her marriage. The text would clearly support such speculation, but that would take us beyond the scope of the autobiography itself into the realm of psychoanalysis.

25. Donald Mathews argues that "the revolutionary quality of the early Evangelical movement was not its assault upon power, for it made none, but its weakening of the cultural, religious, and psychological constraints upon people of relatively low estate by elevating them in their own esteem and giving them the personal discipline to use their lives as best they could in Christian service" (*Religion in the Old South* 78–79).

26. In the past few decades feminist literary historians have begun the task of recuperating and reinterpreting the lost voices of nineteenth-century women writers who borrowed and revised the dominant culture's admonitions. It is now a critical commonplace to acknowledge the ways in which "women's fiction" (Nina Baym's term) or "exploratory fiction" (Susan Harris's) pays homage to and subverts the tenets of domesticity. Gillian Brown and others have urged contemporary readers to consider the "politicization of domesticity" in such sentimental novels as *Uncle Tom's Cabin*, in which the reader is forced to reckon with the power of women and their orderly households to reform a disorderly nation. For detailed readings of the fiction of nineteenth-century women writers, see Elizabeth Ammons, "Stowe's Dream of the Mother-Savior: *Uncle Tom's Cabin* and American Women Writers before the 1920s"; Nina Baym, *Women's Fiction*; Gillian Brown; Susan K. Harris; Mary Kelley; Claudia Tate; and Jane Tompkins, *Sensational Designs*.

27. This stance is, of course, nothing new. Women in the nineteenth century have much in common with their medieval sister Margery Kempe, whose "silence about physical motherhood prepares the way for her story of spiritual motherhood" (Smith, *Poetics* 74). And Quaker women preachers, Janis Calvo has discovered, were similarly unwilling to discuss child-care practices. "Those instances in which child care is explicitly mentioned," Calvo argues, "reveal an improvisational approach to the problem, trusting God to keep them safe in their parent's absence, and ready in any case to resign oneself to his will" (83–84).

28. Patricia Hill argues that women in the nineteenth century were assured that joining the foreign missions movement did not make them participants in the women's rights movement, the former being the duty of a mother and a Christian. Missionary work, they were told, would in fact make them better mothers. These female itinerants—who worked in both home and foreign missions—reveal a different attitude toward motherhood in their autobiographies. Their unwillingness to discuss their roles as mothers points to their recognition—and perhaps their fear—that motherhood and missionary work did not walk comfortably hand in hand. For more information on women and missionary work, see R. Pierce Beaver; Dana Robert.

29. Recently, feminist theorists have begun to examine the potential of the margin as a space from which women can better examine the "center" of the dominant culture, resist domination, and remain open to radical possibilities of change. These critics, in the words of bell hooks, also make a "definite distinction between that marginality which is imposed by oppressive structures and that marginality one chooses as site of resistance—as location of radical openness and possibility" (153). The women in this study discovered the usefulness of the margin as a textual space that enabled them simultaneously to explain themselves and to critique the culture that excluded them from its center.

30. By midcentury, Brekus argues, this term would lose its more radical meaning as the ideology of domesticity encouraged sects like the Freewill Baptists, Christians, and Methodists to "define women in more narrow terms" (294).

31. For a good summary of the relationship between the individual and the community in nineteenth-century evangelical religion, see Leonard I. Sweet, "Nineteenth-Century Evangelicalism." According to Sweet, "one of the most appealing features of evangelicalism was its offer of community, especially to persons who lived on the ground floor of a multistoried, hierarchical society" (887). Donald Mathews makes a similar argument in the first chapter of *Religion of the Old South*. For more on the balance between individualism and community values within evangelicalism, see chapters 2 and 3.

32. For a discussion of the significance of Methodist classes and societies in the lives of African Americans, see Donald Mathews, "Evangelical America—The Methodist Ideology." Mathews contends that the Methodist society was a private, liminal place where blacks were encouraged to define themselves according to the divine rather than to the dictates of white America.

33. On the difficulties black men faced in the workforce, see Leonard Curry; James Horton.

34. Carla Peterson argues that black women who dared to lecture publicly during the century experienced profound economic uncertainty as a result. And Nancy Hewitt contends that only white women who *lacked* economic security continued to pursue "increasingly radical social critiques and wider roles for women" at midcentury (235). Interestingly, these itinerant women seem to have embraced economic insecurity, confident in God's ability to provide the minimal support they needed. Their humiliation before God gave them both a wider social role *and* financial means.

35. Cartwright, for example, describes in lurid detail his dispersal of a crowd of "rabble and rowdies" at a camp meeting: "About the time I was half through my discourse, two very fine-dressed young men marched into the congregation with loaded whips, and hats on, and rose up and stood in the midst of the ladies, and began to laugh and talk. . . . I requested them to desist and get off the seats; but they cursed me. . . . I stopped trying to preach, and called for a magistrate. There were two at hand, but I saw they were both afraid. . . . They ordered me to stand off, but I advanced. One of them made a pass at my head with his whip, but I closed in with him, and jerked him off the seat. A regular scuffle ensued. . . . In the scuffle I threw my prisoner down, and held him fast; he tried his best to get loose; I told him to be quiet, or I would pound his chest well. . . . An old and drunken magistrate came up to me, and ordered me to let my prisoner go. I told him I should not. . . . Then one of my friends, at my request, took hold of my prisoner, and the drunken justice made a pass at me; but I parried the stroke, and seized him by the collar and the hair of the head, and fetching him a sudden jerk forward, brought him to the ground, and jumped on him. . . . Just at this moment the ringleader of the mob and I met. . . . It seemed at that moment I had not power to resist temptation, and I struck a sudden blow in the burr of the ear and dropped him to the earth. . . . Seeing we had fallen on evil times, my spirit was stirred within me. I said to the elder, 'I feel a clear conscience, for under the necessity of the circumstances we have done right, and now I ask to let me preach'" (71).

Some male itinerants, seeking to prove that God was on their side, resort to the strategy employed by female evangelists, reminding readers what lay in store for the hecklers who opposed their ministries. In his 1831 autobiography, for example, David Marks writes of a man who promised to bring whips and whiskey to the "next meeting." "Sickness," however, "immediately confined him, so that at my next meeting he was unable to attend. One of his children was taken ill about the same time, and died in a few days" (63).

36. See Matthew 24:35; Mark 13:31; Luke 21:33.

37. See, for example, Elisabeth Schussler Fiorenza, Carol Meyers, Elaine Pagels, and Phyllis Trible.

38. Clarke's work, in eight volumes, was originally published between 1810 and 1825 under the title *The Holy Bible . . . with a commentary and critical notes*. It was reprinted in a standard six-volume edition in 1851.

39. Note that Lee's point about Mary, quoted earlier, might well have come from Fletcher, who makes a similar argument: "No, I do not apprehend Mary could in the least be accused of immodesty when she carried the joyful news of her Lord's resurrection, and in that sense taught the teachers of mankind" (qtd. in Hardesty, Dayton, and Dayton, "Women in the Holiness Movement: Feminism in the Evangelical Tradition" 228).

40. See Wollstonecraft, *A Vindication of the Rights of Woman*.

41. See the work of contemporary feminist theologian Letty Russell.

42. The phrase is that of Patricia Hill. Feminist critics have often noted how, in the words of Barbara Epstein, "domesticity promised women seclusion from the harsh and uncertain economic world and relative comfort. But it also involved exclusion from the exploration and adventures that were open to at least some men" (75). These autobiographies are important in part because they remind us that opportunity for adventure was open to some women in the nineteenth century, and indeed, for many of them, this adventure led to fame throughout America, Canada, and England.

Chapter 2

The phrase used in the title is that of Zilpha Elaw (51–52).

1. Interestingly for our purposes, Sarah Ingraham assures her readers that Prior never "neglect[ed] the duties of *home*" (18). Her usefulness as a minister did not negate her usefulness as a domestic, true woman: "She was remarkably devoted to her husband . . . and few know or practise better 'the art of making *home* happy' . . . than did this humble, self-denying Christian" (18). For a brief discussion of how posthumous memoirs like Prior's—even when compiled from documents left by the deceased—often de-emphasize their public labors, see Brekus (261–62).

2. And as James Bratt argues, the hostility between Protestants and Catholics would heighten in 1845, with the potato blight that brought about a wave of immigration of Germans and Irish Catholics.

3. Historians of British literature tend to define the period from 1832 (with the First Reform Bill) until 1901 (with the death of Queen Victoria, who came to the throne in 1837). Americanists define the period similarly as beginning sometime in the 1830s, with the rise of an evangelical middle class, and declining, though not terminating, at the end of the century, with the demise of that class, the death of Queen Victoria, and the rise of modernism. For my purposes, though Jarena Lee, Zilpha Elaw, and Nancy Towle began preaching in 1819, 1825, and 1821, respectively, all but Towle wrote and printed their autobiographies much later, Lee in 1849 and Elaw in 1845, clearly in the Victorian Age. The careers and narratives of Lydia Sexton, Laura Haviland, and Julia Foote, all of whom began preaching in the 1840s and published their stories around 1880, situate them squarely in the age Tuveson describes, as do the later career and autobiography of Amanda Berry Smith, who began preaching in 1870 and compiling her autobiography in the early 1890s.

4. Historians of American religion have well documented these evangelical impulses toward voluntarism and reform in the first half of the century. See, for example, Nancy Hardesty, *Women Called to Witness*; Patricia Hill; William McLoughlin, Introduction, *The American Evangelicals 1800–1900*; Timothy Smith, *Revivalism and Social Reform*; and Ernest Lee Tuveson.

5. For a discussion of the rise and popularity of the notion of "no creed but the Bible," see Nathan Hatch, "Sola Scriptura and Novus Ordo Seclorum."

6. This was, as Harry Stout discovered, a prominent feature of the letters and journal of George Whitefield, who "described no moments of idleness, boredom, self-censure, or passivity, though surely such occurred" (53).

7. Katherine Bassard calls it "an Anglo-Protestant interpretation of Psalm 51 and the Fall in Genesis" (96).

8. Perhaps this is the place to point out that my reading of Lee's autobiography, and particularly of her description of her conversion, differs significantly from that of Katherine Bassard. She draws our attention to the fact that Lee's first experience of God occurs "outside any formal religious structure[s] . . . like Bibles, hymnbooks, preachers, churches, or missionaries" (95). While this was certainly a significant aspect of Lee's religious life and autobiography, it was not, as Bassard implies, particularly African American or African Methodist, or even particularly unusual. Experiencing God without "mediating structures" was a central tenet of Protestantism,

and countless Protestants, white and black, male and female, have had similar experiences. As Perry Miller wrote long ago, "What is persistent, from the covenant theology . . . to Edwards and to Emerson is the Puritan's effort to confront, face to face, the image of a blinding divinity in the physical universe, and to look upon that universe without the intermediacy of ritual, of ceremony, of the Mass and the confessional" (Errand 185). Bassard also argues that Lee's conversion, at a moment in the service when the "text was barely announced" and the sermon proper had not yet begun, involves a "rewriting of the conversion narrative as an implicit critique of mainline Christian styles of worship. . . . Lee's conversion at the very start of the sermon is possible because in African American religious ritual, the sermon is simply the climax in a series of spiritual events" (98–99). I find nothing particularly unusual or subversive about the timing of her conversion given that sermons occur as part of a series of spiritual events in most Christian worship services. Bassard's emphasis on Bakhtin and other contemporary theorists leads her away from Lee's religious world and provides her less with a means to understand this complex autobiography than an opportunity to ignore it. Under Bassard's theoretical lens much gets lost, particularly the sincerity of her faith, the role of the Evangelical (Protestant) tradition in Lee's religious experiences, and even, curiously, her extensive use of the Bible in her writing—this despite Bassard's call for "greater biblical literacy" among literary critics (141).

9. Virginia Lieson Brereton, in her study of women's conversion narratives, argues that "most nineteenth-century women writers expended fewer words and images in describing their actual conversions than upon the experience of conviction" (21). She speculates that conversion received little emphasis because as "good Victorians" women could not make use of sexual metaphors and sensuous imagery that writers traditionally employed in describing the conversion experience. Although the white women preachers I have studied may well have felt some Victorian restraints, the African American women make much use of sensuous imagery. I would argue that it was an obsession with their work, rather than a lack of metaphors, that influenced their decisions to devote little space to either conviction or conversion.

10. For more information on the "morphology of conversion" and preparationist theology, see Edmund S. Morgan, Visible Saints: The History of a Puritan Idea. Revisionist historians are beginning now to deconstruct this monolithic model of Puritan preaching and conversions. See, for example, Janice Knight.

11. The phrase is that of Thomas Weld, the London agent of the Massachusetts Bay Colony, in his 1644 preface to John Winthrop's analysis ("Short Story") of the Antinomian Controversy. For a detailed discussion of the controversy, see William K. B. Stoever. For Finney's account of the controversy surrounding his use of new measures in the promotion of religious revivals, see The Memoirs of Charles G. Finney. For Lyman Beecher's and Asahel Nettleton's accounts, see Letters of the Rev. Dr. Beecher and Rev. Mr. Nettleton on the "New Measures" in Conducting Revivals of Religion.

12. The notion of perfectionism, sanctification, or holiness can be found throughout the Old and New Testaments; see, for example, Matthew 6:48. It is important to note that for some holiness advocates sanctification was an emotional experience, for others an act of will, for some an instantaneous experience that was sufficient unto itself, for others an instantaneous experience followed by a gradual process of growth throughout one's life. The Holiness movement (or Wesleyan Holiness) continues today, as does the Higher Life movement (or Keswick Holiness), which arose out of Wesleyan Holiness and was introduced to a largely upper-class audience and to the British by W. E. Boardman, and by Robert Pearsall Smith and Hannah Whitall Smith, both of whom experienced holiness or sanctification through the work of the Methodists in the 1860s. Through their testimonies and publications, the Smiths, Boardman, and Anglican clergyman Rev. H. W. Webb-Peploe emphasized an experience of sanctification that "stressed the 'suppression' of sin rather than its eradication, and spoke in terms of 'yielding' (consecration) and the counteracting grace of being filled with the Holy Spirit" (Schmidt, "Holiness" 821).

Their terminology tended to appeal more to Quakers, Congregationalists, Baptists, and Presbyterians. The seminal texts of the Higher Life movement continue to be the ever-popular *The Christian's Secret of a Happy Life* (1875), by Hannah Whitall Smith; *Holiness through Faith* (1870), by Robert Pearsall Smith; and *The Higher Christian Life* (1858), by William Boardman. Important texts of Wesleyan Holiness are the journal *The Guide to Holiness* (1845–1901), initially edited by Phoebe Palmer, as well as her *Pioneer Experiences* (1868), *The Way of Holiness* (1843), *Faith and Its Effects* (1852), and *The Promise of the Father* (1859). For more information on these movements, see the work of Melvin Dieter, Newton Flew, Charles Edwin Jones, David Peterson, J. C. Pollock, Harold Raser, Vinson Synan, and Charles Edward White.

13. See *Christian Nurture* (1847, 1861). Here Bushnell proposes that conversion was a gradual process to be effected over the course of one's life by means of Christian education and growing awareness.

14. The Methodist weekly *Zion's Herald* once lauded Phoebe Palmer's books for their ability to "make working Christians" (qtd. in Sweet, "Nineteenth-Century Evangelicalism" 877).

15. On the Evangelical United Front, see Charles Foster.

16. Conversely, continues Finney, "Want of success in a minister (*other things being equal*) proves, (1.) either that he was never called to preach, and has taken it up out of his own head; or (2.) that he was badly educated, and was never taught the very things he wants most to know; or (3.) if he was called to preach, and knows how to do his duty, he is too indolent and too wicked to do it" (*Lectures* 186). Authority, Donald Mathews reminds us, "was not resident in the office of itinerant but in the action that he made possible. If the words he spoke or chanted did not elicit communal response and regeneration, his authority was diminished for the moment" ("Evangelical America" 20).

17. On support for female itinerants by male itinerants, see the autobiographies of George Brown, Lorenzo Dow, Zilpha Elaw, Jarena Lee, Lydia Sexton, and Amanda Smith.

18. Collins argues that black women who serve as domestic workers often occupy this paradoxical territory. On intimate terms with some members of the family, particularly the children, black women domestics also know that they are not part of that family. For Collins, the "outsider-within stance" can be a useful tool in undermining the credibility of ideologies of race, class, and gender. Indeed, as I will argue in chapter 3, though their paradoxical position both within and without evangelical religion caused them anxiety, these preachers used their position to critique their male colleagues and to claim the honors they had been denied.

19. For a more detailed discussion of this trend, see Brekus (284–98). For an account of this process in the African Methodist Episcopal Church, see Jualynne Dodson.

20. Stephen Railton notes that a similar emphasis on volume can be found in the literary marketplace of nineteenth-century America, where it was believed that "the people could be counted on to determine literary achievement. Literally *counted* on, as numbers came to play an increasing role in assigning status and rank in the republic of letters" (17).

21. Carroll Smith-Rosenberg agrees, noting that though Charles Finney openly opposed "the unrestrained drive for material advancement . . . the two pillars of his revivalistic message would become the pillars of a new commercial order: optimism and self-help" (*Disorderly Conduct* 153).

22. This would have been particularly true, Jacqueline Jones has demonstrated, for African American women who were valued by the dominant culture as members of the workforce, not as mothers and homemakers.

23. For a discussion of how new Darwinian rhetoric drew upon old village values, see Robert Wiebe, 136.

24. One is reminded here of advertising executive Bruce Barton's best-seller *The Man Nobody Knows* (1925), which depicts Jesus Christ as one of the world's most remarkable businessmen.

25. As Ursula King and other sociologists of religion have noted, "The more institutionalized a religion becomes, the more it generally excludes women from positions of authority and

power. Typically women hold higher positions in archaic, ancient, tribal and relatively non-institutionalized forms of religion (such as shamanism, possession rites, spiritualism or in non-hierarchical groups such as the Society of Friends) than they do in the highly differentiated religious traditions with their complex structures" (38).

26. Reading these and other autobiographies by nineteenth-century women preachers, I have found that it was not an uncommon gesture for female itinerants to encourage other young women who wanted to take up the cross. The ordained Methodist Protestant minister Anna Howard Shaw is a case in point. In her autobiography, *The Story of a Pioneer*, she writes of an encounter with the evangelist Mary Livermore: "Mary A. Livermore came to Big Rapids, and as she was then at the height of her career, the entire countryside poured in to hear her. . . . When she had finished speaking I joined the throng that surged forward from the body of the hall, and as I reached her and felt the grasp of her friendly hand I had a sudden conviction that the meeting was an epoch in my life. I was right. Some one in the circle around us told her that I wanted to preach, and that I was meeting tremendous opposition. She was interested at once. . . . 'My dear,' she said, quietly, 'if you want to preach, go on and preach. Don't let anybody stop you'. . . . These were almost my first encouraging words. . . . I have always felt since then that without the inspiration of Mrs. Livermore's encouragement I might not have continued my fight. Her sanction was a shield, however, from which the criticisms of the world fell back" (65–66).

27. Autobiography is what Georges Gusdorf calls "a second reading of experience" that "appeases the more or less anguished uneasiness of an aging man who wonders if his life has not been lived in vain, frittered away haphazardly, ending now in simple failure" ("Conditions" 38–39).

28. Sidonie Smith's reading of the *Book* of Margery Kempe reminds us that these female evangelists were not the first women to enter the public sphere with a handicap, nor were they the first to justify that entrance. "The *Book*," Smith argues, "simultaneously reveals the fragility and the marginality of her public position as it chronicles the increasing vulnerability of her apparently ubiquitous voice: The more she emerges as a public figure, the more she invites censure, even charges of heresy: and the more she invites censure, the more she must justify her words and her behavior. . . . In fact, the rather stable story of spiritual conversion is syncopated by the constant mobility, the unending quest to gain exoneration, blessing, and support and to avert condemnation and burning" (*Poetics* 76–79).

29. See David Levin, "In the Court of Historical Criticism: Alger Hiss's Narrative."

30. See Elizabeth Bruss; H. Porter Abbott. Looking for a theory of autobiography that does not limit the nature of the genre with prescriptive definitions, Bruss contends that autobiography is not a form but an act that involves both author and reader in a shared understanding of the meaning of the genre. Abbott, drawing on the work of Bruss, argues for an understanding of autobiography as personal action. He suggests that many readers of autobiography have always thought of it in this way: "The student who cannot STAND Benjamin Franklin or Carobeth Laird or Jean-Jacques Rousseau is usually reading their autobiographies as acts—acts of self-aggrandisement, acts of vindictiveness, acts of self-protection—carried out by the authorial subject. They are aware, in other words, of the author present in the text, pushing and shoving, in short, doing something for himself" (601). Abbott calls for a theory of autobiographical reading—an appropriate "autobiographical response"—which is based on an "analytic awareness of the author in action" (601).

Chapter 3

1. On the ways in which Evangelical Christianity provided a framework for female homosocial bonding, see Nancy Cott, *The Bonds of Womanhood*; Nancy Hardesty, *Women Called to Witness*; Evelyn Brooks Higginbotham, *Righteous Discontent*; Patricia Hill; Donald Mathews, *Religion in*

the Old South; Anne Firor Scott, *The Southern Lady;* Timothy Smith, *Revivalism and Social Reform;* and Hilah Thomas and Rosemary Skinner Keller, *Women in New Worlds.*

2. On the phenomenal success of these sects, see John B. Boles; Nathan Hatch, *The Democratization of American Christianity;* Martin Marty, *Righteous Empire;* Donald G. Mathews, *Religion in the Old South* and "The Second Great Awakening as an Organizing Process, 1780–1830: An Hypothesis."

3. The dilemma these women faced is in some ways analogous to the one faced by capitalists such as Andrew Carnegie. Capitalistic success—which in the age of mass production could only be mass success—tended to undermine the individualism that industrialists claimed as their cardinal virtue. Andrew Carnegie, who rose from bobbin boy to telegraph operator to steel magnate by ceaselessly distinguishing himself from his colleagues, ended up ushering in an age of mass consumption (the necessary twin of mass production) in which each widget running off the assembly line was like every other widget, and each customer was seemingly indistinguishable from his or her fellows. So, too, do these evangelists, whose customers are a faceless mass, strive mightily to present themselves as individuals, speckled birds and gazing stocks, set apart by God's favor and their own remarkable energy.

4. To a certain degree all autobiography, even spiritual autobiography, insists on the uniqueness of the autobiographer. The dilemma faced by these women was only an extreme version of the problem faced by any spiritual autobiographer (or biographer), particularly of the Reformed variety: how to make a life story both singular (an accurate portrayal of individual experience) and representative of universal experience. In his *Confessions,* for example, Saint Augustine clearly believes that his story is a typical one and yet in its exclusive focus on the self, the *Confessions* necessarily stresses his uniqueness. Margery Kempe negotiates her singularity and representativeness by conveying her unique experience in conventional language, "so as to express a unique personality in the formulas of typical experience" (Fleishman 71). For more detailed accounts of this spiritual and autobiographical dilemma, see Sacvan Bercovitch, *The Puritan Origins of the American Self;* Avrom Fleishman, *Figures of Autobiography;* David Levin, *Cotton Mather: The Young Life of the Lord's Remembrancer, 1663–1703;* and G. A. Starr.

5. Sexton's allusion to Medusa, a mythological figure often associated in literature with images of sexuality, reminds us once again of the ways in which preaching involved these women in a crisis of gender. In Sexton's interpretation of the dream, the snakes are associated with the enemies who find her public (masculine) performances threatening (castrating?); we might also speculate that the Medusa is a projection of Sexton herself, for as I noted in chapter 1, she was often troubled by the question of sexual definition once she began to think about "breaking up housekeeping." Here Sexton simultaneously asserts herself and denies her role in the victory by describing her conquest of the snakes in both active and passive terms. For a brief discussion of the mythological figure and the castration complex, see Freud's "Medusa's Head" in Elisabeth Young-Bruehl, *Freud on Women: A Reader.*

6. See, for example, the autobiographies of Lorenzo Dow, James Horton, David Marks, and Abraham Snethen.

7. The figurative use of warfare is a common feature of the Bible and spiritual autobiographies. For the evangelical women in this study, however, the language of war often refers to their actual experiences as pioneering women challenging the dominance of men in religious structures.

8. Hannah Whitall Smith, a lay evangelist who, along with her husband, founded the Higher Life movement in England, and whose spiritual volumes continue to be published and read by evangelical Christians, makes a similar claim in her spiritual autobiography, *The Unselfishness of God and How I Discovered It: A Spiritual Autobiography:* "I have felt that to be endorsed was to be bound, and that it was better, for me at least, to be a free lance, with no hindrances to my absolute mental and spiritual freedom" (220–21). Towle even anticipates that famous "Lady"

portrayed by Henry James, who had "a certain instinct, not imperious, but persuasive, [that] told her to resist—murmured to her that virtually she had a system and an orbit of her own" (*The Portrait of a Lady* 156).

Max Weber long ago noted in *The Sociology of Religion* the sociological and political marginalization that makes Towle's "critical distance from dominant values" possible: "Groups which are at the lower end or altogether outside of the social hierarchy stand to a certain extent on the point of Archimedes in relation to social conventions, both in respect to the external order and in respect to common opinions. Since these groups are not bound by social conventions they are capable of an original attitude towards the meaning of the cosmos" (qtd. in Scott, *Domination and the Arts of Resistance* 124). Carroll Smith-Rosenberg similarly concludes that some women in Jacksonian America "remain[ed] marginal to the established structure" of revivalism, which enabled them to "escape the impact of rituals of mediation and consensus" and to "maintain their assault on all structure" (*Disorderly Conduct* 158).

9. There are important exceptions to this generalization. Consider, for example, the eighteenth-century spiritual autobiography of the Quaker Elizabeth Ashbridge, which is currently receiving long-overdue recognition in the canon of American literature. As the story of a reluctant itinerant—from England to Ireland to America—who eventually finds the Inner Light, accepts the Quaker faith, endures much opposition from her husband, and eventually becomes a "she preacher," *Some Account of the Fore Part of the Life of Elizabeth Ashbridge* indicates that the individualistic, oppositional quests of nineteenth-century evangelical women preachers were not unprecedented. For more information on the history of women's preaching, see Catherine Brekus, Rebecca Larson, and Deborah Valenze.

10. Sidonie Smith argues that when women write autobiography they necessarily embark on a journey into masculine territory: "Responding to the generic expectations of significance in life stories, [the female autobiographer] looks toward a narrative that will resonate with privileged cultural fictions of male selfhood. . . . She embraces, that is, the ideology of individualism" (*Poetics* 52).

It is important to note how the works of the black women autobiographers considered here differ from those of other black women writers of the century, who often focus, according to Patricia Hill Collins, on the "connectedness among individuals"; rather, the story these particular African American spiritual autobiographies tell *is* a story in which self is defined "as the increased autonomy gained by separating oneself from others" (105). While my literary research has not uncovered the extent to which defining the "self in opposition to others" is a literary posture rather than a lived reality, it is important to recognize the ways in which these autobiographies differ from efforts by other black women writers to conceptualize black womanhood.

11. Perhaps here is the place to state that by reading these autobiographies as expressions of nineteenth-century—and Protestant—individualism, I am at odds with recent criticism by Katherine Bassard and Joycelyn Moody, and to a certain degree with that of Catherine Brekus. Brekus rightly calls attention to the emphasis female preachers placed on their deep connection with God. She argues that "in striking contrast to literary figures such as Emerson and Thoreau, they contributed little to the American celebration of individualism and self-reliance. A woman who spoke as a mouthpiece was not an individual with a voice of her own, but a powerless object" (192). I believe, however, that otherworldly experiences of the divine—even the assertion that one is a mouthpiece—do not necessarily exempt one from more worldly encounters, in this case with the ideologies made prominent by Protestant Evangelicalism and Revivalism and by American culture in general. Pens in God's hands, these autobiographers nonetheless construct narratives in which they are also assertive, self-reliant individualists.

In her work on Lee and Elaw, Moody argues that "each narrator resists distinguishing themselves [sic] from other members of the religious community, the African American community, and the women's community to which she belongs, to assert instead a collective identity" (54).

Bassard professes, in a somewhat obfuscatory manner, that in her first exhortation Lee "seeks to create a heterophonous base for community, one that, ultimately, will do away with the need for hegemonic practices within the boundaries of collective subjectivity" (107). Jarena Lee, Bassard argues, "*performs* community" (93). Certainly, as I have noted earlier, these women remember in their stories the women with whom they traveled, they remember the praying bands that gave them comfort before they became itinerant preachers, and, as in the case of Julia Foote, they speak quite directly and forcefully to their "Christian Sisters." But such acts of remembrance should not obscure for us the drama of individualism that is also at work in these narratives. And though the autobiographies by nineteenth-century female itinerants, like all spiritual autobiographies, reveal an "evangelizing impulse that makes a communal responsibility of autobiography"—though they write their books in the sincere hope of converting others and enlarging the body of Christ—this is an abstract sort of collectivity that cannot easily be equated with the type of fellowship a Jarena Lee experienced before moving to Snow Hill (Shea, *Spiritual* 249).

12. These dialogues and confrontations with Satan can be readily compared to other forms of veiled dissent, such as spirit possession and "hysterical" illness, "in which personal responsibility may be disavowed" (Scott, *Domination* 141). See also I. M. Lewis, *Ecstatic Religion: A Study of Shamanism and Spirit Possession*, upon which Scott's analysis is based.

13. Rev. Allen and the African Methodists were adhering, of course, to Saint Paul's scriptural prohibition of women's speaking in the churches. See 1 Corinthians 14:34.

14. Interestingly, the early-nineteenth-century itinerant John Colby (Church of Christ) cites this biblical text as well. He uses it, however, not to describe a depression brought about by opposition to his person or his preaching but to describe his feelings when working among a rather hard-hearted people who seemed to care little for the state of their souls (47).

15. Looking at women in the black Baptist church from 1880 to 1920, Evelyn Brooks Higginbotham also found that black women "expressed a dual gender consciousness—defining themselves as both homemakers and soldiers. Their multiple consciousness represented a shifting dialogic exchange in which both race and gender were ultimately destabilized and blurred in meaning" (142).

16. Julia Foote's (1823–1900) case bears a remarkable resemblance to that of Elizabeth Packard (1816–c.1890), who was imprisoned in a psychiatric facility in 1860 by her husband, forbidden to receive visits from her children, deprived of inherited income, and prohibited from reading or writing. All of this was a result of her unwillingness to keep silent about her own theological opinions.

On gender and psychiatric incarceration, see Phyllis Chesler; Michel Foucault, *Madness and Civilization: A History of Insanity in the Age of Reason*; Sandra M. Gilbert and Susan Gubar; and Barbara Hill Rigney.

17. On the objectification of blacks in the white field of vision, see Frantz Fanon. Interestingly, he describes the experience of objectification in much the same terms Amanda Smith employs in her autobiography: "And then the occasion arose when I had to meet the white man's eyes. An unfamiliar weight burdened me. . . . In the white world the man of color encounters difficulties in the development of his bodily schema. . . . The body is surrounded by an atmosphere of certain uncertainty. . . . 'Look, a Negro!' It was an external stimulus that flicked over me as I passed by. I made a tight smile. 'Look, a Negro!' It was true. It amused me. 'Look, a Negro!' The circle was drawing a bit tighter. . . . On that day, completely dislocated, unable to be abroad with the other, the white man, who unmercifully imprisoned me, I took myself far off from my own presence, far indeed, and made myself an object" (110–12).

18. Higginbotham reports that the black Baptist women (1880–1920) also "spoke as if ever-cognizant of the gaze of white America." That gaze, in rendering them objects rather than subjects, had the negative effect of increasing their anxiety—the pressure to measure up by Victorian

America's standards—for "in panoptic fashion [it] focused upon each and every black person and recorded his or her transgressions in an overall accounting of black inferiority" (*Righteous Discontent* 196).

19. On the ways in which women are made to feel out of place in public spaces, see Gillian Rose.

20. See, for example, Jarena Lee's epigraph from Joel 2:28 and Nancy Towle's from Micah 6:4 and Judges 4:9.

21. David Marks, the itinerant who would promote himself as the "boy preacher," prefaces his 1831 autobiography with the same passage from Jeremiah and also describes his call by borrowing Jeremiah's words (32). So, too, does Lorenzo Dow (17–18). Both men claim to have resisted their calls because, like Jeremiah himself, they thought of themselves as children (Jeremiah 1:6). Certainly reluctance to accept a call from God was often a feature of autobiographies by male itinerants, who desired to appear humble before God and their readers, but, as Brekus discovered, "few waited more than a few weeks or months to begin their careers in the pulpit" (190).

22. Nineteenth-century readers would have assumed that Daniel lived under an earlier ruler than Antiochus.

23. In her journal the Methodist Phoebe Palmer also aligns herself with the prophet Daniel. Immediately before being attacked in the *Advocate* for her views on complete sanctification, Palmer dreams of being in a lion's den: "Seizing hold of the mouth of this huge lion, I," writes Palmer, "with a strength which I knew could only have been supernatural, kept his mouth closed." Indeed, she succeeds in doing the same thing to her more human opponent: "Thank the Lord, I think I kept his mouth shut, through the power of Daniel's God" (Wheatley, *The Life and Letters of Mrs. Phoebe Palmer* 93–94). Battling lions serves here as a figure for her resistance to conservative religious forces that were appalled by her promotion of holiness.

24. Finding value in marginalization is by no means peculiar to nineteenth-century evangelical women. As David Levin observes in his reading of Cotton Mather, Jonathan Edwards, and Benjamin Franklin, it is a general problem in Christian piety, which calls one "to be at once proud and humble, distinct from counterfeit Christians and yet self-effacing" ("Edwards" 44). American Puritans, Andrew Delbanco argues, faced a particularly troublesome problem. Emigrating "out of"—rather than "into"—the spiritual wilderness of England, the migrating Puritans were acutely aware that many would accuse them of deserting their English brethren, abandoning the heroic struggle for a life of spiritual ease. Not surprisingly, then, the Puritans felt an intense need for justification. Hence, they began to make much use of "the language of heroic struggle" in their literature; they began as well to "seek opposition in America," to invent enemies—"Indians, 'Antinomians,' eventually Quakers and 'witches'"—who assured these anxious pilgrims that their decision to immigrate (flee?) to America had indeed been the right one (Delbanco 103, 14). Ultimately, the Puritans, "caught in a contradiction of their own making," could not, in the manner of John Knox, "savor" such persecution (Delbanco 113–14). As religious fervor dwindled, they had to mourn, in the words of Thomas Shepard, the lack of "enemies to hunt you to heaven" (qtd. in Delbanco 114).

I would also like to acknowledge here the important work of R. Laurence Moore, who argues that the "history of religion is so filled with martyrs that one must wonder whether religion could exist without them" (*Religious Outsiders* 33). Moore's study of the Mormons, Catholics, Jews, Christian Scientists, and Protestants of various Premillennial and Fundamentalist denominations leads him to conclude that these groups "followed a lesson, already by their time well established in American experience, that one way of becoming American was to invent oneself out of a sense of opposition. . . . In defining themselves as being apart from the mainstream, Mormons [for example] were in fact laying their claim to it. By declaring themselves outsiders, they were moving to the center" (*Religious Outsiders* 45–46). Such "strategies of differentiation" can even be found in the spiritual autobiographies by some nineteenth-century male itinerant preachers. In his narrative of 1831, for example, the Freewill Baptist David Marks stifles an urge to complain about "exposing himself to a premature death for the welfare of [his] fellow mortals" (114). As he understood it, "*Thou hast received thy pension, a hundred fold in this life, with persecution, which is a part of thy salary; therefore thou art blessed*" (114). Similarly, the "barefoot preacher" Abraham Snethen remembers deliberately going where he was not wanted, as if to receive that pension: "Wherever I heard of a place where they refused to have preaching, there I sent an appointment, and there I turned up ready for meeting, when the time arrived and the more they threatened me, the more I was sure to go" (136). But, of course, Snethen could have worn shoes had he wanted and could have avoided most opposition, while female itinerants could not. Snethen's sister itinerants simply had to embrace and make use of what was thrown their way.

It seems evident, then, that though many religious groups and individuals from George Whitefield to Jim Jones have employed "strategies of differentiation," those people did not *feel* themselves to be at the *center* of the dominant culture, to be part of what Moore has identified as a tradition of sorts. Whether or not "nothing was more 'normal' or 'typical' of American life than the process of carving out a separate self-identification," these seven autobiographies by female itinerants attest both to their feelings of marginalization, in America and in the evangelical and Holiness circles in which they moved, and to their desire to make use of it (209). They do not attest to any sense of being part of the center of American religious culture.

25. Showalter argues that women writers, like literary subcultures, go through three phases, which she labels "feminine," "feminist," and "female." The feminine phase is "a prolonged phase of *imitation* of the prevailing modes of the dominant tradition, and *internalization* of its standards of art and its views on social roles." The feminist phase is marked by "*protest* against these standards and values, and *advocacy* of minority rights and values." The female phase "is a phase of *self-discovery*, a turning inward freed from some of the dependency on opposition, a search for identity" (13). As Showalter points out, these are not absolute categories, and the phases often overlap in the same writer. My reading of these seven spiritual autobiographies reveals a world in which imitation, internalization, protest, and self-discovery coexist, as they must have coexisted in the lives themselves. Struggling against a powerful consensus, these seven women are at times unable to break out of internalized patterns of behavior even as they move onward in their quest for autonomy and identity.

26. According to Brekus, "it was this theme of 'feminine' weakness transformed into strength that made female preachers' conversion stories sound distinctive from men's" in the first half of the nineteenth century (181).

27. Higginbotham has discovered in the writings of black Baptist women, particularly that of Virginia Broughton, similar accounts of opposition—often followed by divine intervention. In her autobiography (1907), Broughton tells the story of a man who threatened his wife with death if she dared attend a Bible Band meeting. He "was not permitted to live long enough to prohibit that good woman a second time from going when her missionary sisters called a meeting" (*Twenty Year's* 39). "His death," as Higginbotham observes, "served to reinforce perceptions of the divine sanction of their work and helped diminish further persecution in the area. As rumors of male hostility spread," moreover, "the women acquired the image of martyrs for their cause and began to gain a greater following among both men and women" (*Righteous Discontent* 72).

28. For more information on the popularity of particular spiritual narratives in nineteenth-century American evangelical circles, see Virginia Lieson Brereton (10–13).

29. I am indebted in my discussion of the "uses of marginality" to William Andrews's readings of African American autobiography from 1850 to 1865, specifically Frederick Douglass's *My Bondage and My Freedom* and Harriet Jacobs's *Incidents in the Life of a Slave Girl*. See *To Tell a Free Story*.

30. Lydia Sexton, having preached for seven years with a quarterly-conference license from the United Brethren, sought a permanent license in 1852; the quarterly license, having to be renewed on an annual basis, was "very inconvenient," for at times she "had to travel a hundred miles or more for that purpose" (400). "I felt," remembers Sexton, "that I would be glad to get a permit from the annual conference to travel at large and preach where I could seemingly do the most good, as it would save me the trouble of traveling to quarterly conference every year" (400). It would also save her the obeisance and forced humility necessarily involved in having to "request" a license year after year despite her obvious qualifications. Sexton's requests were, however, rebuffed by Bishop David Edwards, who, though he did not object to women preaching, did oppose "licensing them" (401). He preferred to control her by forcing her appearance at each conference. She would have to wait another seven years before being granted a permanent license from the annual conference of the United Brethren.

The Methodist Phoebe Palmer believed that all ordinations were unscriptural and counterfeit; hence her own unwillingness to seek ordination.

31. Elaine Lawless reports that in rescripting their life stories contemporary Pentecostal women preachers similarly accord a privileged position to the opposition they had encountered and thereby call attention to the authenticity of their call: "As one woman so aptly put it: 'I've been told folks don't believe in women preachers. I've told them they didn't hire me and they sure couldn't fire me. *God* called me and I'll be here!'" ("Rescripting" 70).

32. See Penn, *No Cross, No Crown.*

33. Carla Peterson discovered a similar strategy among African American women who sought to compete in the public world of civic debate: these nineteenth-century women "consciously adopt[ed] a self-marginalization that became superimposed upon the already ascribed oppressions of race and gender and that paradoxically allowed empowerment" (17).

Chapter 4

1. See, for example, Jerome Buckley; Roy Pascal; and Karl Weintraub. It should be remembered that Adams himself excised twenty years (from age thirty-three to age fifty-four) of his life from his autobiography, no doubt to lend it the narrative shape critics have so admired. "This is a story of education, not of adventure!" he argues at the beginning of chapter 21. "It is meant to help young men . . . but it is not meant to amuse them. What one did—or did not do—with one's education, after getting it, need trouble the inquirer in no way; it is a personal matter only which would confuse him" (314).

2. Many writers have been "alienated" from their stories to some degree. Think of William Bradford's *Of Plymouth Plantation* or Harriet Wilson's *Our Nig.* But the habit of writing one's story in the third person obviously differs from the manner in which these evangelical women write their first-person narratives.

3. Karl Joachim Weintraub uses the term "additive autobiography" to refer to the works of medieval writers who, rather than write one definitive, distinct autobiography, chose to include autobiographical material in numerous "writings devoted to wider objectives . . . thus producing a characteristic cumulative genre" (49).

4. Zilpha Elaw similarly informs her readers that the length of her autobiography was dictated by her material circumstances: "I am compelled to omit much interesting and important matter relative to my religious experience and life, and pass to the more strikingly eventful points, lest I should swell these pages beyond my present limited means for the press" (64).

5. According to Couser, "No scholar seems prepared to state exactly how many different editions of his autobiography Barnum published . . . because Barnum so frequently updated the 1869 edition with supplementary chapters" (61). Joseph Fichtelberg maintains that this tendency to revise and reissue one's life story is a peculiarly American phenomenon, related to American

autobiographers' irrepressible desire to claim "the millennial identity"—to forge a unity between the individual and the community—along with their Puritan ancestors who argued "that New England was New Jerusalem, the site of the Millennium" (50). And, as Fichtelberg points out, the obsessive revising of texts indicates that such faith in the identity between the self and the nation was necessarily a dream: used by Franklin, hopefully and desperately asserted by Whitman.

6. Though I agree with William Andrews's assertion that "contemporary readers . . . are likely to find the added pages of the 1849 edition often tedious reading," as I have argued in chapter 2 and will argue here, these pages do have much to tell us about "the inner character of the woman who wrote them" and her life as a female evangelist (Introduction, *Sisters* 23). Studying the career of George Whitefield, for example, Harry Stout came to believe that "the very lack of information on his inner and private life supplied important clues to the man. In fact, [he] became convinced that Whitefield lived his life almost exclusively for public performance" (xv).

7. See Georges May, *L'autobiographie*.

8. Interestingly, Methodist Peter Cartwright tells his readers that had he not given up "journalizing" after several years as an itinerant, he would have found it easier to fill his narrative with "facts, dates, names, and circumstances" (12, 13).

9. It should also be noted that this "hybrid" form of the spiritual autobiography and travelogue was not, as Joanne Braxton implies, unique to black women; it was a common feature of evangelical autobiographies in both the eighteenth and nineteenth centuries. While Jarena Lee made good use of the "hybrid" form in question and also, in the words of Katherine Bassard, of the "strategy . . . of multiply inscribing events," she did not "invent" either (Braxton 10; Bassard 93).

10. He has not apparently, encountered the autobiographies of nineteenth-century evangelical women. Indeed, given their status as "outsiders within" the male evangelical landscape, one might consider rigorously editing one's spiritual experience and evangelical labors in the manner of a C. S. Lewis a more perverse method of composition.

11. I am not the first critic to take to task genre theorists whose inordinately prescriptive definitions of "good" or "ideal" autobiography have excluded women's life-writing. See, for example, Estelle Jelinek, *The Tradition of Women's Autobiography* and Introduction, *Women's Autobiography: Essays in Criticism*; Felicity Nussbaum, *The Autobiographical Subject: Gender and Ideology in Eighteenth-Century England*; Sidonie Smith, *A Poetics of Women's Autobiography*; and Norine Voss.

12. Elder Benjamin Putnam's autobiography, written in 1821 after he joined the Baptist Church, is another book that avoids the paratactic method. He devotes little of his *Sketch* to his itinerary because his *primary purpose* in writing in the first place is to convince a large audience that the doctrines he once preached as an evangelist for the Freewill Baptists and Christians are in fact delusions. Feeling responsible for the souls to whom he preached such "error," and knowing that he cannot possibly find them on his travels again, he pens his narrative to "preach" and propagate the truths that his study of Scripture has now made clear to him (6).

13. Indeed, it seems likely that even the prior act of examining and understanding one's life is essentially literary; that the process of deletion, enhancement, and plotting engages us even before we set pen to paper, and even if we never do. As Barbara Hardy contends, "In order really to live, we make up stories about ourselves and others, about the personal as well as the social past and future" (qtd. in Spacks, "Selves" 131).

14. Jean Starobinski contends that *all* autobiography is a form of conversion narrative given that "it is the internal transformation of the individual . . . that furnishes a subject for a narrative discourse in which 'I' is both subject and object" (78).

15. For more information on Puritan and evangelical spiritual autobiography, see Elizabeth Kaspar Aldrich; Virginia Lieson Brereton; William Haller; Christine L. Krueger; Edmund S. Morgan, *Visible Saints*; Roger Sharrock; Daniel Shea, *Spiritual Autobiography in Early America*; and G. A. Starr.

16. This point applies equally well to biography.

17. On the ways in which nineteenth-century African Americans developed literary strategies to prove that they were of "the people," see William Andrews, *To Tell a Free Story*.

18. The history of autobiography would suggest, moreover, that imagining an end to an ongoing story need not be the creative property of legendary figures alone. The writer Willie Morris, for example, reminds us that almost anything in the life can be presented as the "subject's ultimate achievement": *North toward Home* moves teleologically toward the ending in which the Mississippi-born author simply finds himself more at home in the North than the South (Sturrock 55).

19. As good, onward Christian soldiers, both Cartwright and Finney do pay a kind of lip service to the future, but they are not paralyzed by their consciousness of futurity.

20. The phrase, again, is that of Thomas Weld from his 1644 preface to John Winthrop's analysis ("Short Story") of the Antinomian Controversy. For a detailed discussion of the controversy, see William K. B. Stoever.

21. At their 1880 General Conference, the Methodist Episcopal Church approved women for the subordinate positions of Sunday school superintendents and teachers but ceased licensing women as local preachers. They denied Anna Howard Shaw's request for ordination in the 1880s (she was later ordained by the Protestant Methodists); not until 1974 were women ordained in the M.E. Church. A similar reaction against women occurred in the African Methodist Episcopal Church. The A.M.E. General Conference defeated a petition to provide for women's preaching in 1844, 1848, and 1852. In 1868 they sanctioned the positions of stewardess, exhorter, missionary, and evangelist, all of which were subordinate to the ordained positions held by men. When in 1884 the A.M.E. finally licensed women as local preachers (evangelistic laborers), the gesture was (so Jualynne Dodson speculates) not so much a recognition of women's rights as a measure of control. Similarly, after the Civil War single women were finally granted permission to work as missionaries, a move, according to Barbara Welter, that signaled "less a victory than a strategic retreat by the opposition," who feared woman's agitation in the women's movement more than her Christian work in a remote corner of the world ("She Hath Done" 111).

22. Nina Baym, *Women's Fiction: A Guide to Novels by and about Women in America, 1820–1870*. Joanne Dobson has uncovered only two novels of the period that deal extensively and candidly with the life of a married woman: A. D. T. Whitney's *Hitherto* (1869) and Elizabeth Stuart Phelps's *The Story of Avis* (1877).

23. When writing her narrative, Jacobs found herself alienated from all available narrative forms. Slave narratives, 88 percent of which were written by men, were largely gendered male and depicted women primarily in positions of victimization rather than positions—like the one in which Jacobs saw herself—of creative resistance. Nor would the sentimental, seduction, and domestic novels of the century prove congenial to her legitimate story of "illegitimate" romance and children, escape, domestic servitude, and poverty in the North. Jacobs was clearly constrained by the laws of genre. Nonetheless, like the evangelical preachers in this study, she sought to make use of and at times subvert such laws in the writing of her now-classic autobiography. On the relationship between issues of gender and the form of the slave narrative, and particularly on the ways in which Douglass's *Narrative* came to be considered "representative" of the genre, see Deborah McDowell, "In the First Place: Making Frederick Douglass and the Afro-American Tradition."

24. This is the case with much women's autobiography. As Norine Voss argues, critics who valorize the artistic, finely wrought autobiography, assume "a state of full self-knowledge free from conflict, a condition that women's status in a patriarchal culture often prevents them from attaining (or that, if attained, their vulnerability to attack makes them hesitant to reveal)" (219).

25. Their experience thus resembles that of the transient Americans Daniel Boorstin describes in *The Americans: The National Experience*: "These were not men moving ever *toward* the west, but men ever moving *in* the west. The churning, casual, vagrant, circular motion around

and around was as characteristic of the American experience as the movement in a single direction. . . . More than anything else, they valued the freedom to move. . . . Americans thus valued opportunity, or the chance to seek it, more than purpose" (95). And as I have argued elsewhere, these women did relish the freedom to move and the opportunities available to them within evangelicalism and revivalism; at the same time, however, their autobiographies testify to their longing for the sort of "purpose" that characterizes the lives of their male counterparts.

26. There are autobiographies written by unconventional women, even unconventional itinerant women, that are not characterized by the sort of narrative uncertainty I have been describing here. As noted earlier, Susan Waugh found that most women in her 1980s workshops wrote structured, "finished" autobiographical narratives, not additive, fragmented ones. The eighteenth-century Quaker Elizabeth Ashbridge was able to compose a short autobiographical narrative with a clear beginning, middle, and end. Though her life and her textual self-representation were marked by her many travels in the Old and New World and by her sincere quest for self-definition in the face of opposition from her spouse and from hostile Puritans, she had no difficulty turning her itinerant life into a well-made narrative. But Ashbridge was telling a relatively simple story, and one for which she had ample precedent: though her *Account* describes a life that was wildly disordered in many respects, its main narrative line throughout is Ashbridge's own quest for the Inner Light and her parallel struggle to convert her dissolute husband. The resolution of these plots forms the ending of the *Account*; though Ashbridge later had a career as a kind of Quaker itinerant, this career barely comes into her autobiography. This is to say that Ashbridge was able to avoid the severest narrative frustrations of her nineteenth-century successors, all of whom felt compelled to devote most of their autobiographies to their careers, which tended to resist being plotted in conventional terms.

27. For Estelle Jelinek, the tradition of women's autobiography is marked by such anxiety: "In contrast to the self-confident, one-dimensional self-image that men usually project, women often depict a multidimensional, fragmented self-image colored by a sense of inadequacy and alienation, of being out-siders or 'other'; they feel the need for authentication, to prove their self-worth" (*Tradition* xiii).

28. For a discussion of narrative line and closure in women's fiction, see Nancy Miller, *Subject to Change: Reading Feminist Writing*.

Afterword

For the title of this chapter I borrow the terms of Charles Cohen, whose book *God's Caress: The Psychology of Puritan Religious Experience* is subdivided into sections entitled "The Call of the Preachers" and "The Cry of the Faithful."

1. Here we might recall the terms that Sacvan Bercovitch borrowed from Melville's Plotinus Plinlimmon: these preachers were "horologically" unique but "chronometrically" typical (*American Jeremiad* 28–29). On the paradoxical relationship between uniqueness and representativeness in Puritan spiritual biography, see Bercovitch, *The Puritan Origins of the American Self*; G. A. Starr.

2. Though both Julia Foote and Lydia Sexton include brief sermons in their autobiographies.

3. As Daniel Shea reminds us in his *Spiritual Autobiography in Early America*, Quaker journals and Puritan spiritual autobiographies "share a staple subject matter in the experience of conversion, recall providential events gratefully, and together obey the didactic, evangelizing impulse that makes a communal responsibility of autobiography" (249).

4. Jane Marcus argues in "Invincible Mediocrity: The Private Selves of Public Women" that the "common thread running through women's autobiographies" is just this: "collaboration" of the writer and her reader (137).

5. Nancy Towle, for example, introduces her autobiography with the proud claim that the "[Bible], and sometimes a Bible Dictionary, [had] been for the most part, my only *Library*" (Preface 11).

6. *Sensational Designs* is the title of Jane Tompkins's groundbreaking book on the cultural work of nineteenth-century American fiction.

7. Curiously, the same could be true for men who left behind memoirs that mention the careers of preaching women. While David Marks referred to any number of preaching women in *The Life of David Marks* (1831), his wife, editing the book in 1846 after his death, studiously "removed all the references—no matter how small—to the women her husband had once defended" (Brekus 296).

8. And, as Brekus discovered when reading Reeves's eulogy in the *Methodist Quarterly Review*, she was ultimately attacked for her "failure as a mother": her children, the review noted, "were born but to die thus prematurely; for the maternal profession—and it is such—precludes another set of duties alien to it" (298).

9. Interestingly, Nancy Towle writes that she was asked to preach in the Salem Chapel in London but was opposed by the superintendent, who sent another preacher to "occupy the pulpit in [her] stead" (69). That superintendent was none other than Henry Moore, who compiled the *Life* of the famous Methodist preacher Mary Bosanquet Fletcher, and significantly titled it to emphasize not her life as a preacher but her marriage to one: *The Life of Mrs. Mary Fletcher: Consort and relict of the Rev. John Fletcher, Vicar of Madeley, Salop.*

10. According to Hardesty, Dayton, and Dayton, the *Lives* of British women evangelists were popular among nineteenth-century women and did serve as models for American women searching for new roles in the benevolent empire. See "Women in the Holiness Movement: Feminism in the Evangelical Tradition."

Bibliography

Primary Sources

Acornley, Rev. John H. *The Colored Lady Evangelist, Being the Life, Labors and Experiences of Mrs. Harriet A. Baker.* Brooklyn: n.p., 1892. New York: Garland, 1987.

Adams, Henry. *The Education of Henry Adams: An Autobiography.* 1918. Boston: Houghton Mifflin, 1961.

Addams, Jane. *The Second Twenty Years at Hull-House.* New York: Macmillan, 1930.

——. *Twenty Years at Hull-House.* New York: Macmillan, 1910.

Allen, Rev. Richard. *The Life Experience and Gospel Labors of the Rt. Rev. Richard Allen.* 1833. Nashville: Abingdon, 1960.

Ashbridge, Elizabeth. *Some Account of the Fore Part of the Life of Elizabeth Ashbridge.* 1774. *Journeys in New Worlds.* Ed. William L. Andrews. Madison: U of Wisconsin P, 1990. 147–71.

Augustinus, Aurelius. *The Confessions.* New York: Penguin, 1961.

Bangs, Heman. *The Autobiography and Journal of Rev. Heman Bangs.* Ed. His Daughters. New York: N. Tibbals and Son, 1872.

Beecher, Lyman. *The Autobiography of Lyman Beecher.* Ed. and introd. Barbara M. Cross. 2 vols. Cambridge: Belknap-Harvard UP, 1961.

Boardman, William. *The Higher Christian Life.* Boston: Henry Hoyt, 1858.

Booth, Catherine. *Female Ministry; or, Woman's Right to Preach the Gospel.* London: Morgan and Chase, n.d. *Holiness Tracts Defending the Ministry of Women.* Ed. Donald Dayton. New York: Garland, 1985.

Boyd, Robert. *Personal Memoirs: Together with a Discussion upon the Hardships and Sufferings of Itinerant Life; and also a Discourse upon the Pastoral Relation.* Cincinnati: Methodist Book Concern, R. P. Thompson, 1868.

Broughton, Virginia. *Twenty Year's* [sic] *Experience of a Missionary.* 1907. *Spiritual Narratives.* Ed. and introd. Susan Houchins. New York: Oxford UP, 1988.

Brown, George. *The Lady Preacher: or, the Life and Labors of Mrs. Hannah Reeves, Late the Wife of the Rev. WM. Reeves, D.D., of the Methodist Church.* Philadelphia: Daughaday and Becker; Springfield, Ohio: Methodist Publishing House, 1870. New York: Garland, 1987.

——. *Recollections of Itinerant Life: Including Early Reminiscences.* 3rd ed. Springfield: Methodist Protestant Publishing House; Cincinnati: R. W. Carroll and Co., 1866.

Browning, Robert. *The Poems and Plays of Robert Browning.* New York: Modern Library, 1934.

Bunyan, John. *Grace Abounding to the Chief of Sinners.* Ed. and introd. Roger Sharrock. 1666. Oxford: Clarendon-Oxford UP, 1962.

——. *The Pilgrim's Progress, from This World, to That Which Is to Come.* 1678. New York: Penguin, 1987.

Bushnell, Horace. *Christian Nurture.* 1861. Cleveland: Pilgrim, 1994.

Carlyle, Thomas. Characteristics. *The Norton Anthology of English Literature.* Ed. M. H. Abrams et al. 4th ed. Vol. 2. New York: Norton, 1979. 964-75.

——. *Sartor Resartus. The Norton Anthology of English Literature.* Ed. M. H. Abrams et al. 4th ed. Vol. 2. New York: Norton, 1979. 975-1006.

Carnegie, Andrew. *The Autobiography of Andrew Carnegie.* Boston: Houghton Mifflin, 1920.

Cartwright, Peter. *Autobiography of Peter Cartwright.* 1856. Introd. Charles Wallis. New York: Abingdon, 1956.

Child, Lydia Maria. "Speaking in the Church." *A Lydia Maria Child Reader.* Ed. Carolyn L. Karcher. Durham: Duke UP, 1997. 354-57.

Clarke, Adam. *The Holy Bible containing the Old and New Testaments . . . with a commentary and critical notes designed as a help to a better understanding of the sacred writings.* 6 vols. New York: N. Bangs and J. Emory, 1825-26.

Colby, John. *Life, Experience, and Travels of John Colby, Preacher of the Gospel.* Portland: A. and J. Shirley, 1815.

Conant, William C. *Narratives of Remarkable Conversions and Revival Incidents.* New York: Derby and Jackson, 1858.

Cooper, Anna Julia. *A Voice from the South.* 1892. Introd. Mary Helen Washington. New York: Oxford UP, 1988.

Davis, Almond. *The Female Preacher, or Memoir of Salome Lincoln, afterwards the Wife of Elder Junia S. Mowry.* 1843. New York: Arno, 1972.

Dayton, Donald, ed. *Holiness Tracts Defending the Ministry of Women.* New York: Garland, 1985.

Delany, Martin. *The Condition, Elevation, Emigration, and Destiny of the Colored People of the United States.* 1852. New York: Arno, 1968.

Douglass, Frederick. *My Bondage and My Freedom.* 1855. Ed. and introd. Philip Foner. New York: Dover, 1969.

——. *Narrative of the Life of Frederick Douglass.* 1845. *The Classic Slave Narratives.* Ed. and introd. Henry Louis Gates Jr. New York: Mentor, 1987.

Dow, Lorenzo. *The Dealings of God, Man, and the Devil, as Exemplified in the Life, Experience, and Travels of Lorenzo Dow.* 4th ed. Norwich: William Faulkner, 1833.

Eaton, Herrick M. *The Itinerant's Wife: Her Qualifications, Duties, Trials, and Rewards.* New York: Lane and Scott, 1851. *The Nineteenth-Century American Methodist Itinerant Preacher's Wife.* Ed. and introd. Carolyn De Swarte Gifford. New York: Garland, 1987.

Edwards, Jonathan. "A Faithful Narrative of the Surprising Work of God." *The Great Awakening.* Ed. C. C. Goen. New Haven: Yale UP, 1972. Vol. 4 of *The Works of Jonathan Edwards.* Ed. John Smith. 12 vols. 1957-94.

Elaw, Zilpha. *Memoirs of the Life, Religious Experience, Ministerial Travels and Labors of Mrs. Zilpha Elaw, an American Female of Colour.* 1846. *Sisters of the Spirit.* Ed. and introd. William L. Andrews. Bloomington: Indiana UP, 1986. 49-160.

Ellison, Ralph. *Invisible Man.* 1947. New York: Vintage, 1990.

Emerson, Ralph Waldo. *Selections from Ralph Waldo Emerson.* Ed. Stephen Whicher. Boston: Houghton Mifflin, 1957.

Fern, Fanny. *Fern Leaves from Fanny's Portfolio.* Auburn: Derby and Miller, 1853.

Finley, James B. *Sketches of Western Methodism.* 1854. New York: Arno, 1969.

Finney, Charles G. *Lectures on Revivals of Religion.* 1835. Cambridge: Belknap-Harvard UP, 1960.

——. *The Memoirs of Charles G. Finney*. 1876. Ed. and introd. Garth M. Rosell and Richard A. G. Dupuis. Grand Rapids: Academie, 1989.

Fletcher, Miriam. *The Methodist; or, Incidents and Characters from Life in the Baltimore Conference*. 2 vols. New York: Derby and Jackson, 1859.

Foote, Julia. *A Brand Plucked from the Fire: An Autobiographical Sketch by Mrs. Julia A. J. Foote*. 1879. *Sisters of the Spirit*. Ed. and introd. William L. Andrews. Bloomington: Indiana UP, 1986. 161-234.

Foss, C. D. Introduction. *Forty Witnesses: Covering the Whole Range of Christian Experience*. Ed. Olin Garrison. 1888. Freeport, PA: Fountain, 1955.

Foster, John O. *Life and Labors of Mrs. Maggie Newton Van Cott, the First Lady Licensed to Preach in the Methodist Episcopal Church in the United States*. 1872. New York: Garland, 1987.

Franklin, Benjamin. *The Autobiography of Benjamin Franklin. Autobiography and Other Writings*. Ed. and introd. Kenneth Silverman. New York: Penguin, 1986.

Fuller, Margaret. *Woman in the Nineteenth Century*. 1855. New York: Norton, 1971.

Garrison, Olin, ed. *Forty Witnesses: Covering the Whole Range of Christian Experience*. 1888. Freeport, PA: Fountain, 1955.

Gilbert, Olive. *Narrative of Sojourner Truth*. 1850. Ed. Margaret Washington. New York: Vintage, 1993.

Grimké, Sarah M. *Letters on the Equality of the Sexes and Other Essays*. 1838. Ed. and introd. Elizabeth Ann Bartlett. New Haven: Yale UP, 1988.

Guyon, Madame. *Autobiography of Madame Guyon*. 1708. Trans. Thomas Taylor Allen. 2 vols. London: Kegan Paul, Trench, Trubner & Co., 1898.

Hanaford, Phebe. *Daughters of America; or, Women of the Century*. Boston: B. B. Russell, 1883.

Haviland, Laura Smith. *A Woman's Life-Work: Labors and Experiences of Laura S. Haviland*. 1881. Salem, NH: AYER, 1984.

Hawthorne, Nathaniel. *Tales and Sketches*. Ed. Roy Harvey Pearce. New York: Library of America, 1982.

Henry, Rev. Thomas W. *From Slavery to Salvation: The Autobiography of Rev. Thomas W. Henry of the A.M.E. Church*. 1872. Ed. Jean Libby. Jackson: UP of Mississippi, 1994.

Horton, James. *A Narrative of the Early Life, Remarkable Conversion, and Spiritual Labours of James P. Horton*. N.p.: n.p., 1839.

Hughes, Thomas. *The Manliness of Christ*. Boston: Houghton, Osgood and Co., 1880.

Hunt, Sarah. *Journal of the Life and Religious Labors of Sarah Hunt*. Philadelphia: Friends Book Association, 1892.

Hunter, Fannie McDowell. *Women Preachers*. Dallas: Berachah Printing Co., 1905. *Holiness Tracts Defending the Ministry of Women*. Ed. Donald Dayton. New York: Garland, 1985.

Ingraham, Sarah R., comp. *Walks of Usefulness or, Reminiscences of Mrs. Margaret Prior*. New York: American Female Moral Reform Society, 1843. New York: Garland, 1987.

Jackson, Rebecca. *Gifts of Power: The Writings of Rebecca Jackson, Black Visionary, Shaker Eldress*. Ed. and introd. Jean McMahon Humez. N.p.: U of Massachusetts P, 1981.

Jacobs, Harriet. *Incidents in the Life of a Slave Girl*. 1861. Ed. Jean Fagan Yellin. Cambridge: Harvard UP, 1987.

James, Henry. *The Portrait of a Lady*. 1882. New York: Penguin, 1984.

Jones, Rufus. *Eli and Sybil Jones: Their Life and Work*. Philadelphia: Porter and Coates, 1889.

Lee, Jarena. *The Life and Religious Experience of Mrs. Jarena Lee, a Coloured Lady*. 1836. *Sisters of the Spirit*. Ed. and introd. William L. Andrews. Bloomington: Indiana UP, 1986. 25-48.

——. *Religious Experience and Journal of Mrs. Jarena Lee*. 1849. *Spiritual Narratives*. Ed. and introd. Susan Houchins. New York: Oxford UP, 1988.

Lee, Luther. *Woman's Right to Preach the Gospel. A Sermon, Preached at the Ordination of the Rev. Miss Antoinette L. Brown.* Syracuse: by the author, 1853. *Holiness Tracts Defending the Ministry of Women.* Ed. Donald Dayton. New York: Garland, 1985.

Letters of the Rev. Dr. Beecher and Rev. Mr. Nettleton on the "New Measures" in Conducting Revivals of Religion. New York: n.p., 1828.

Lewis, C. S. *Surprised by Joy: The Shape of My Early Life.* New York: Harcourt, 1955.

Livermore, Harriet. *A Narration of Religious Experience in Twelve Letters.* Concord: Jacob Moore, 1826.

Livermore, Mary A. *The Story of My Life.* Hartford: A. D. Worthington, 1897.

Livermore, Rev. S. T. *The Pilgrim Stranger.* Hartford: n.p., 1884.

Marks, David. *The Life of David Marks: To the 26h Year of His Age. Including the Particulars of His Conversion, Call to the Ministry, and Labours in Itinerant Preaching.* Limerick: Morning Star, 1831.

Mather, Cotton. *Ornaments for the Daughters of Zion.* Boston: S. G[reen] and B. G[reen], 1692.

Mossell, Mrs. N. F. *The Work of the Afro-American Woman.* 1894. New York: Oxford UP, 1988.

Newell, Rev. E. F. *Life and Observations of Rev. E. F. Newell, who has been more than forty years an Itinerant Minister in the Methodist Episcopal Church.* Compiled by C. W. Ainsworth. Worcester: C. W. Ainsworth, 1847.

Newell, Fanny. *Memoirs of Fanny Newell; Written by Herself, and Published by the Desire and Request of Numerous Friends.* 3rd ed. Springfield and New York: n.p., 1833.

North, Elizabeth Mason. *Consecrated Talents: or, the Life of Mrs. Mary W. Mason.* New York: Carlton and Lanahan, 1870. New York: Garland, 1987.

Osborn, Elbert. *Passages in the Life and Ministry of Elbert Osborn, an Itinerant Minister of the Methodist Episcopal Church, Illustrating the Providence and Grace of God.* New York: Joseph Long King, 1847.

Osborne, Lucy Drake. *Heavenly Pearls Set in a Life: A Record of Experiences and Labors in America, India, and Australia.* New York: Fleming H. Revell, 1893.

Packard, Elizabeth. *The Liabilities of the Married Woman.* New York: Pelletreau and Raynor, 1873.

——. *Modern Persecution or Insane Asylums Unveiled.* New York: Pelletreau and Raynor, 1873.

Palmer, Phoebe. *Faith and Its Effects.* 1867. *The Devotional Writings of Phoebe Palmer.* Ed. Donald W. Dayton. New York: Garland, 1985.

——. *The Promise of the Father.* 1859. Ed. Donald W. Dayton. New York: Garland, 1985.

——. *The Way of Holiness.* 1867. *The Devotional Writings of Phoebe Palmer.* Ed. Donald W. Dayton. New York: Garland, 1985.

——, ed. *Pioneer Experiences; or, The Gift of Power Received by Faith.* 1868. Ed. Donald W. Dayton. New York: Garland, 1984.

Payne, Daniel Alexander. *History of the African Methodist Episcopal Church.* 1891. New York: Arno, 1969.

——. *Recollections of Seventy Years.* 1888. New York: Arno, 1968.

Penn, William. *No Cross, No Crown.* 1668. London: Edward Marsh, 1849.

Phelps, Elizabeth Stuart, et al. *Our Famous Women: An Authorized Record of the Lives and Deeds of Distinguished American Women of Our Times.* Hartford: A. D. Worthington, 1884.

Prentiss, George L. *The Life and Letters of Elizabeth Prentiss.* New York: Anson D. F. Randolph, 1882. New York: Garland, 1987.

Prior, Margaret. *Walks of Usefulness or, Reminiscences of Mrs. Margaret Prior.* Compiled by Sarah R. Ingraham. New York: American Female Moral Reform Society, 1843. New York: Garland, 1987.

Putnam, Benjamin. *A Sketch of the Life of Elder Benj. Putnam, Embracing His Christian Experience, Call to the Ministry, Together with an Account of the Religious Changes Through which he* has passed, Especially those of Recent Date; with Some of the Most Prominent Reasons for His Present Views of Divine Truth. Woodstock: David Watson, 1821.

Richardson, Marilyn, ed. Maria W. Stewart, America's First Black Woman Political Writer: Essays and Speeches. Bloomington: Indiana UP, 1987.

Robinson, Mary Stevens. "Mrs. Hannah Pearce Reeves, Preacher of the Gospel." Methodist Quarterly Review 59 (1877): 430-47.

Rowlandson, Mary. The Sovereignty and Goodness of God, Together with the Faithfulness of His Promises Displayed, Being a Narrative of the Captivity and Restoration of Mrs. Mary Rowlandson. 1682. Ed. Neal Salisbury. Boston: Bedford, 1997.

Sexton, Lydia. Autobiography of Lydia Sexton. The Story of Her Life through a Period of over Seventy-two Years, from 1799 to 1872. 1882. New York: Garland, 1987.

Shaw, Anna Howard. The Story of a Pioneer. New York: Harper, 1915.

Sheldon, Charles M. In His Steps: What Jesus Would Do. 1896. Philadelphia: Henry Altemus, 1899.

Shilling, Henry. Preface to 1955 reprint. Forty Witnesses: Covering the Whole Range of Christian Experience. Ed. Rev. S. Olin Garrison. 1888. Freeport: Fountain, 1955.

Shorter, Susan. The Heroines of African Methodism. Jacksonville: Chew, 1891.

Smith, Amanda Berry. An Autobiography: The Story of the Lord's Dealings with Mrs. Amanda Smith, the Colored Evangelist. 1893. New York: Oxford UP, 1988.

Smith, Hannah Whitall. The Christian's Secret of a Happy Life. 1885. The Devotional Writings of Robert Pearsall Smith and Hannah Whitall Smith. Ed. Donald W. Dayton. New York: Garland, 1984.

——. The Unselfishness of God and How I Discovered It: A Spiritual Autobiography. New York: Fleming H. Revell, 1903.

Smith, Logan Pearsall. Philadelphia Quaker: The Letters of Hannah Whitall Smith. New York: Harcourt, 1950.

Smith, Robert Pearsall. Holiness through Faith; light on the way of holiness. 1870. The Devotional Writings of Robert Pearsall Smith and Hannah Whitall Smith. Ed. Donald W. Dayton. New York: Garland, 1984.

Snethen, Abraham. Autobiography of Abraham Snethen, the Barefoot Preacher. Collected and compiled by Mrs. N. E. Lamb. Corrected and revised by J. F. Burnett. Dayton: Christian Publishing Association, 1909.

Stanton, Elizabeth Cady. Eighty Years and More. London: T. Fisher Unwin, 1898.

Stanton, Elizabeth Cady, et al. The Woman's Bible. 2 vols. New York: European Publishing, 1895-98.

Stevens, Abel. The Women of Methodism: Its Three Foundresses, Susanna Wesley, the Countess of Huntingdon, and Barbara Heck; with sketches of their female associates and successors in the early history of the denomination. New York: Carlton and Lanahan, 1869. New York: Garland, 1987.

Stewart, Maria. Meditations from the Pen of Mrs. Maria W. Stewart. Washington: W. Lloyd Garrison and Knap, 1879.

——. Productions of Mrs. Maria W. Stewart. Boston: Published by Friends of Freedom and Virtue, 1835.

Strong, Josiah. Our Country. 1886. Ed. Jurgen Herbst. Cambridge: Belknap-Harvard UP, 1963.

Taylor, Marshall W. Life, Travels, Labors, and Helpers of Mrs. Amanda Smith, the Famous Negro Missionary Evangelist. Cincinnati: Cranston and Stowe, 1887.

Tennyson, Alfred Lord. The Poems and Plays of Alfred Lord Tennyson. New York: Modern Library, 1938.

Teresa, Saint. *The Life of St. Teresa of Jesus.* 1568. Trans. David Lewis. 1870. London: Thomas Baker, 1916.

Thoreau, Henry David. *Walden.* New York: Signet, 1960.

Towle, Nancy. *Vicissitudes Illustrated in the Experience of Nancy Towle, in Europe and America.* Charleston: James Burges, 1832.

Townsend, Ann. *Memoir of Elizabeth Newport.* Philadelphia: John Comly, 1874.

Tucker, Mary Orne. *Itinerant Preaching in the Early Days of Methodism, by a Pioneer Preacher's Wife.* Ed. Thomas W. Tucker. Boston: B. B Russell, 1872. *The Nineteenth-Century American Methodist Itinerant Preacher's Wife.* Ed. and introd. Carolyn De Swarte Gifford. New York: Garland, 1987.

Twain, Mark. *Adventures of Huckleberry Finn.* Ed. Walter Blair and Victor Fischer. 1885. Berkeley: U of California P, 1985.

Van Cott, Margaret. *The Harvest and the Reaper, Reminiscences of Revival Work of Mrs. Maggie N. Van Cott.* New York: N. Tibbals and Sons, 1876.

Wakefield, Dan. *Returning: A Spiritual Journey.* New York: Doubleday, 1988.

Washington, Booker T. *Up from Slavery.* 1901. New York: Penguin, 1986.

Wheatley, Richard. *The Life and Letters of Mrs. Phoebe Palmer.* 1881. New York: Garland, 1984.

Willard, Frances E. *Do Everything: A Handbook for the World's White Ribboners.* Chicago: Woman's Temperance Publishing Association, n.d. *The Ideal of "The New Woman" According to the Women's Christian Temperance Union.* Ed. and introd. Carolyn De Swarte Gifford. New York: Garland, 1987.

——. *Glimpses of Fifty Years.* Chicago: H. J. Smith, 1889.

——. *Home Protection Manual: Containing an Argument for the Temperance Ballot for Woman and How to Obtain It as a Means of Home Protection.* 1817. *The Ideal of "The New Woman" According to the Woman's Christian Temperance Union.* Ed. and introd. Carolyn De Swarte Gifford. New York: Garland, 1987.

——. *How to Win: A Book for Girls.* New York: Funk and Wagnalis, 1886. *The Ideal of "The New Woman" According to the Woman's Christian Temperance Union.* Ed. and introd. Carolyn De Swarte Gifford. New York: Garland, 1987.

——. *Women in the Pulpit.* Chicago: Woman's Temperance Publication Association, 1889. *The Defense of Women's Rights to Ordination in the Methodist Episcopal Church.* Ed. and introd. Carolyn De Swarte Gifford. New York: Garland, 1987.

Wilson, Harriet. *Our Nig: or Sketches from the Life of a Free Black.* 1859. New York: Vintage, 1983.

Winthrop, John. "A Model of Christian Charity." *The Puritans in America: A Narrative Anthology.* Ed. Alan Heimert and Andrew Delbanco. Cambridge: Harvard UP. 1985. 81-92.

Wise, Daniel. *Bridal Greetings: A Marriage Gift in Which the Mutual Duties of Husband and Wife Are Familiarly Illustrated and Enforced.* New York: Carlton and Phillips, 1854. *The American Ideal of the "True Woman" as Reflected in Advice Books to Young Women.* Ed. and introd. Carolyn De Swarte Gifford. New York: Garland, 1987.

——. *The Young Lady's Counsellor: or, Outlines and Illustrations of the Sphere, the Duties, and the Dangers of Young Women.* New York: Carlton and Porter, 1851. *The American Ideal of the "True Woman" as Reflected in Advice Books to Young Women.* Ed. and introd. Carolyn De Swarte Gifford. New York: Garland, 1987.

Wittenmyer, Annie. *Women's Work for Jesus.* 1871. New York: Garland, 1987.

Woolman, John. *The Journal of John Woolman.* 1774. New York: Carol Publishing Group, 1961.

Secondary Sources

Abbott, H. Porter. "Autobiography, Autography, Fiction: Groundwork for a Taxonomy of Textual Categories." *New Literary History* 19 (1988): 597-615.

Ahlstrom, Sidney. *A Religious History of the American People.* New Haven: Yale UP, 1972.

Aldrich, Elizabeth Kaspar. "'The Children of These Fathers': The Origins of an Autobiographical Tradition in America." *First Person Singular: Studies in American Autobiography.* Ed. A. Robert Lee. New York: St. Martin's, 1988. 15-36.

Alexander, Jon, ed. *American Personal Religious Accounts 1600-1980.* Studies in American Religion. Vol. 8. New York: Edwin Mellen, 1983.

Alter, Robert. *The Art of Biblical Narrative.* New York: Basic, 1981.

Ammons, Elizabeth. *Conflicting Stories.* Oxford: Oxford UP, 1991.

——. "Stowe's Dream of the Mother-Savior: *Uncle Tom's Cabin* and American Women Writers before the 1920s." *New Essays on Uncle Tom's Cabin.* Ed. Eric Sundquist. Cambridge: Cambridge UP, 1986. 155-95.

Anderson, Olive. "Women Preachers in Mid-Victorian Britain: Some Reflexions on Feminism, Popular Religion and Social Change." *Historical Journal* 12 (1969): 467-84.

Andrews, Doris. "The African Methodists of Philadelphia, 1794-1802." *Perspectives on American Methodism.* Ed. Russell E. Richey, Kenneth E. Rowe, and Jean Miller Schmidt. Nashville: Kingswood-Abingdon, 1993. 145-55.

Andrews, William. "Dialogue in Antebellum Afro-American Autobiography." *Studies in Autobiography.* Ed. James Olney. New York: Oxford UP, 1988. 89-98.

——. Introduction. *Sisters of the Spirit.* Bloomington: Indiana UP, 1986. 1-22.

——. *To Tell a Free Story.* Chicago: U of Illinois P, 1986.

Aptheker, Bettina. *Woman's Legacy: Essays on Race, Sex, and Class in American History.* Amherst: U of Massachusetts P, 1982.

Ardener, Shirley. Introduction. *Women and Space: Ground Rules and Social Maps.* Oxford: Berg, 1993.

Armstrong, Nancy. *Desire and Domestic Fiction: A Political History of the Novel.* New York: Oxford UP, 1987.

Aron, Cindy. *Ladies and Gentlemen of the Civil Service.* New York: Oxford UP, 1987.

Asher, Lyell. "Petrarch at the Peak of Fame." *PMLA* 108 (1993): 1050-63.

Atkinson, Clarissa W., Constance H. Buchanan, and Margaret R. Miles, eds. *Immaculate and Powerful: The Female in Sacred Image and Social Reality.* Boston: Beacon, 1985.

Bakhtin, M. M. *The Dialogic Imagination.* Ed. Michael Holquist. Trans. Caryl Emerson and Michael Holquist. Austin: U of Texas P, 1981.

Barkun, Michael. *Crucible of the Millennium: The Burned-Over District of New York in the 1840s.* Syracuse: Syracuse UP, 1986.

Bass, Dorothy C. "'In Christian Firmness and Christian Meekness': Feminism and Pacifism in Antebellum America." *Immaculate and Powerful.* Eds. Clarissa Atkinson, Constance Buchanan, and Margaret Miles. Boston: Beacon, 1985. 201-25.

Bassard, Katherine Clay. *Spiritual Interrogations: Culture, Gender, and Community in Early African American Women's Writing.* Princeton: Princeton UP, 1999.

Baym, Nina. *American Women Writers and the Work of History, 1790-1860.* New Brunswick: Rutgers UP, 1995.

——. "Melodramas of Beset Manhood: How Theories of American Fiction Exclude Women Authors." *American Quarterly* 33 (1981): 123-39.

——. *Novels, Readers, and Reviewers: Responses to Fiction in Antebellum America.* Ithaca: Cornell UP, 1984.

——. *Women's Fiction: A Guide to Novels by and about Women in America, 1820-1870.* Ithaca: Cornell UP, 1978.

Beaver, R. Pierce. *American Protestant Women in World Mission: History of the First Feminist Movement in North America.* Grand Rapids: Eerdmans, 1980.

Behnke, Donna. *Religious Issues in Nineteenth-Century Feminism.* Troy, NY: Whitson, 1982.

Bell, Susan Groag, and Marilyn Yalom, eds. *Revealing Lives: Autobiography, Biography, and Gender.* Albany: State U of New York P, 1990.

Bellah, Robert N. *The Broken Covenant: American Civil Religion in Time of Trial.* New York: Seabury, 1975.

Benes, Peter, ed. *Itinerancy in New England and New York.* Boston: Boston University, 1986.

Benstock, Shari, ed. *Feminist Issues in Literary Scholarship.* Bloomington: Indiana UP, 1987.

——, ed. *The Private Self: Theory and Practice of Women's Autobiographical Writings.* Chapel Hill: U of North Carolina P, 1988.

Bercovitch, Sacvan. *The American Jeremiad.* Madison: U of Wisconsin P, 1978.

——. *The Puritan Origins of the American Self.* New Haven: Yale UP, 1975.

Billington, Louis. "'Female Laborers in the Church': Women Preachers in the Northeastern United States, 1790-1840." *Journal of American Studies* 19 (1985): 369-94.

Blauvelt, Martha Tomhave. "Women and Revivalism." *Women and Religion in America.* Vol. 1. Ed. Rosemary Ruether and Rosemary Keller. San Francisco: Harper, 1981. 1-9.

Bloom, Harold. *A Map of Misreading.* New York: Oxford UP, 1975.

Boles, John B. *The Great Revival, 1787-1805.* Lexington: U of Kentucky P, 1972.

Boorstin, Daniel J. *The Americans: The National Experience.* New York: Vintage, 1965.

Boydston, Jeanne, Mary Kelley, and Anne Margolis. *The Limits of Sisterhood: The Beecher Sisters on Women's Rights and Woman's Sphere.* Chapel Hill: U of North Carolina P, 1988.

Bratt, James D. "The Reorientation of American Protestantism, 1835-1845." *Church History* 67 (1998): 52-82.

Brauer, Jerald C. "Conversion: From Puritanism to Revivalism." *Journal of Religion* 58 (1978): 227-43.

——. *Protestantism in America.* Philadelphia: Westminster, 1965.

Braxton, Joanne M. *Black Women Writing Autobiography.* Philadelphia: Temple UP, 1989.

Bree, Germaine. "Autogynography." *Studies in Autobiography.* Ed. James Olney. New York: Oxford UP, 1988. 171-79.

Brehm, Sharon S., and Jack W. Brehm. *Psychological Reactance: A Theory of Freedom and Control.* New York: Academic, 1981.

Brekus, Catherine A. *Strangers and Pilgrims: Female Preaching in America, 1740-1845.* Chapel Hill: U of North Carolina P, 1998.

Brereton, Virginia Lieson. *From Sin to Salvation: Stories of Women's Conversions, 1800 to the Present.* Bloomington: Indiana UP, 1991.

Brereton, Virginia Lieson, and Christa Ressmeyer Klein. "American Women in Ministry: A History of Protestant Beginning Points." *Women of Spirit.* Ed. Rosemary Ruether and Eleanor McLaughlin. New York: Simon, 1979. 301-32.

Britton, James. *Language and Learning.* Coral Gables: U of Miami P, 1970.

Brodzki, Bella, and Celeste Schenck, eds. *Life/Lines: Theorizing Women's Autobiography.* Ithaca: Cornell UP, 1988.

Brown, Earl Kent. "Women of the Word: Selected Leadership Roles of Women in Mr. Wesley's Methodism." *Women in New Worlds.* Ed. Hilah Thomas and Rosemary Keller. Nashville: Abingdon, 1981. 69-87.

Brown, Gillian. *Domestic Individualism: Imagining the Self in Nineteenth-Century America.* Berkeley: U of California P, 1990.

Brown, Herbert Ross. *The Sentimental Novel in America, 1789-1860.* Durham: Duke UP, 1940.

Brumberg, Joan Jacobs. "Zenanas and Girless Villages: The Ethnology of American Evangelical Women, 1870-1910." *Journal of American History* 69 (1982): 347-71.

Bruss, Elizabeth W. *Autobiographical Acts.* Baltimore: Johns Hopkins UP, 1976.

Bucke, Emory, ed. *The History of American Methodism.* 3 vols. Nashville: Abingdon, 1964.

Buckley, Jerome Hamilton. *The Turning Key: Autobiography and the Subjective Impulse since 1800.* Cambridge: Harvard UP, 1984.

Buechner, Frederick. *The Clown in the Belfry.* New York: Harper,1992.

——. *Wishful Thinking: A Seeker's ABC.* 1973. New York: Harper, 1993.

Butler, Jon. *Awash in a Sea of Faith: Christianizing the American People.* Cambridge: Harvard UP, 1990.

——. "Enlarging the Body of Christ: Slavery, Evangelism, and the Christianization of the White South, 1690-1790." *The Evangelical Tradition in America.* Ed. Leonard Sweet. Macon: Mercer UP, 1984. 87-112.

Butler, Judith. *Gender Trouble: Feminism and the Subversion of Identity.* New York: Routledge, 1990.

Butterfield, Stephen. *Black Autobiography in America.* Amherst: U of Massachusetts P, 1974.

Bynum, Caroline. *Jesus as Mother: Studies in the Spirituality of the High Middle Ages.* Berkeley: U of California P, 1982.

Calvo, Janis. "Quaker Women Ministers in Nineteenth Century America." *Quaker History* 63 (1974): 75-93.

Campbell, Joseph. *Hero with a Thousand Faces.* 1949. New York: World, 1971.

Carby, Hazel. *Reconstructing Womanhood: The Emergence of the Afro-American Woman Novelist.* New York: Oxford UP, 1987.

Carwardine, Richard. *Trans-Atlantic Revivalism: Popular Evangelicalism in Britain and America, 1790-1865.* Westport, CT: Greenwood, 1978.

Chandler, Alfred D. *The Visible Hand: The Managerial Revolution in American Business.* Cambridge: Belknap-Harvard UP, 1977.

Chatman, Seymour. *Story and Discourse: Narrative Structure in Fiction and Film.* Ithaca: Cornell UP, 1978.

Chesler, Phyllis. *Women and Madness.* New York: Doubleday, 1972.

Christ, Carol P. *Diving Deep and Surfacing.* Boston: Beacon, 1980.

——. "Spiritual Quest and Women's Experience." *Womanspirit Rising.* Ed. Carol Christ and Judith Plaskow. San Francisco: Harper, 1979. 228-45.

Christ, Carol P., and Judith Plaskow. Introduction. *Womanspirit Rising: A Feminist Reader in Religion.* Ed. Carol Christ and Judith Plaskow. San Francisco: Harper, 1979.

Christ, Carol P., and Charlene Spretnak. "Images of Spiritual Power in Women's Fiction." *The Politics of Women's Spirituality.* Ed. Charlene Spretnak. New York: Anchor-Doubleday, 1982. 327-43.

Clark, Elizabeth A., ed. *Women and Religion: A Feminist Sourcebook of Christian Thought.* New York: Harper, 1977.

Clebsch, William A. *From Sacred to Profane America: The Role of Religion in American History.* New York: Harper, 1958.

Cmiel, Kenneth. *Democratic Eloquence: The Fight over Popular Speech in Nineteenth-Century America.* New York: Morrow, 1990.

Cohen, Charles. *God's Caress: The Psychology of Puritan Religious Experience.* Oxford: Oxford UP, 1986.

Cohen, Ralph, ed. *New Directions in Literary History.* Baltimore: Johns Hopkins UP, 1974.

Collins, Patricia Hill. *Black Feminist Thought: Knowledge, Consciousness, and the Politics of Empowerment.* Boston: Unwin Hyman, 1990.

Coon, Lynda L., Katherine J. Haldane, and Elisabeth W. Sommer. Introduction. *That Gentle Strength: Historical Perspectives on Women in Christianity.* Charlottesville: UP of Virginia, 1990.

Cott, Nancy F. *The Bonds of Womanhood.* New Haven: Yale UP, 1977.

——. "Young Women in the Second Great Awakening in New England." *Feminist Studies* 3 (1975): 16-22.

——, ed. *Root of Bitterness: Documents of the Social History of American Women.* New York: Dutton, 1972.

Coultrap-McQuin, Susan. *Doing Literary Business: American Women Writers in the Nineteenth Century.* Chapel Hill: U of North Carolina P, 1990.

Couser, G. Thomas. *Altered Egos: Authority in American Autobiography.* New York: Oxford UP, 1989.

Cox, James. *Recovering Literature's Lost Ground.* Baton Rouge: Louisiana State UP, 1989.

Cross, Whitney R. *The Burned-Over District: The Social and Intellectual History of Enthusiastic Religion in Western New York, 1800–1850.* Ithaca: Cornell UP, 1950.

Culley, Margo. "What a Piece of Works Is 'Woman'!: An Introduction." *American Women's Autobiography.* Ed. Margo Culley. Madison: U of Wisconsin P, 1992. 3–31.

——, ed. *American Women's Autobiography: Fea(s)ts of Memory.* Madison: U of Wisconsin P, 1992.

Curry, Leonard P. *The Free Black in Urban America 1800–1850.* Chicago: U of Chicago P, 1981.

Daly, Mary. *Beyond God the Father: Toward a Philosophy of Women's Liberation.* Boston: Beacon, 1973.

Danforth, Mildred E. *A Quaker Pioneer: Laura Haviland Superintendent of the Underground.* New York: Exposition, 1961.

Davidson, Cathy N. *Revolution and the Word: The Rise of the Novel in America.* New York: Oxford UP, 1986.

——, ed. *Reading in America: Literature and Social History.* Baltimore: Johns Hopkins UP, 1989.

Davis, Charles, and Henry Louis Gates Jr., eds. *The Slave's Narrative.* New York: Oxford UP, 1985.

Davis, Judy, and Juanita Weaver. "Dimensions of Spirituality." *The Politics of Women's Spirituality.* Ed. Charlene Spretnak. New York: Anchor-Doubleday, 1982. 368–72.

Dayton, Donald W. "Evangelical Roots of Feminism." *Covenant Quarterly* 34 (1976): 41–56.

Dayton, Donald W., and Lucille Sider Dayton. "Evangelical Feminism: Some Aspects of Its Biblical Interpretation." *Explor* (1976): 17–22.

Dayton, Lucille Sider, and Donald W. Dayton. "'Your Daughters Shall Prophesy': Feminism in the Holiness Movement." *Methodist History* 14 (1976): 67–92.

Dearborn, Mary V. *Pocahontas's Daughters: Gender and Ethnicity in American Culture.* New York: Oxford UP, 1986.

DeBerg, Betty A. *Ungodly Women: Gender and the First Wave of American Fundamentalism.* Minneapolis: Fortress, 1990.

De Lauretis, Teresa. *Alice Doesn't: Feminism, Semiotics, Cinema.* Bloomington: Indiana UP, 1984.

Delbanco, Andrew. *The Puritan Ordeal.* Cambridge: Harvard UP, 1989.

Dennett, Lena Fenner. "Freewill Baptist Women." *American Baptist Quarterly* 13 (1994): 391–94.

Dickerson, Vanessa D. "A Spirit of Her Own: Nineteenth-Century Feminine Explorations of Spirituality." *That Gentle Strength.* Ed. Lynda Coon et al. Charlottesville: UP of Virginia, 1990. 243–58.

Dieter, Melvin E. *The Holiness Revival of the Nineteenth Century.* Metuchen, NJ: Scarecrow, 1980.

Dieter, Melvin, Anthony Hoekema, Stanley Horton, J. Robertson McQuilkin, and John Walvoord. *Five Views on Sanctification.* Grand Rapids:Academie, 1987.

Diprose, Rosalyn, and Robyn Ferrell, eds. *Cartographies, Poststructuralism and the Mapping of Bodies and Spaces.* St. Leonards, Austral.: Allen and Unwin, 1991.

Dobson, Joanne. *Dickinson and the Strategies of Reticence: The Woman Writer in Nineteenth-Century America.* Bloomington: Indiana UP, 1989.

Dodson, Jualynne. "Nineteenth-Century A.M.E. Preaching Women: Cutting Edge of Women's Inclusion in Church Polity." *Women in New Worlds.* Ed. Hilah Thomas and Rosemary Keller. Nashville: Abingdon, 1981. 276–92.

Donovan, Josephine. "Toward a Women's Poetics." *Feminist Issues in Literary Scholarship.* Ed. Shari Benstock. Bloomington: Indiana UP, 1987. 98-109.

Douglas, Ann. *The Feminization of American Culture.* New York: Knopf, 1977.

DuPlessis, Rachel Blau. *Writing beyond the Ending.* Bloomington: Indiana UP, 1985.

Eakin, Paul John. "The Referential Aesthetic of Autobiography." *Studies in the Literary Imagination.* 23 (Fall 1990): 129-44.

Eliade, Mircea. *The Sacred and the Profane: The Nature of Religion.* Trans. Willard R. Trask. 1957. New York: Harper, 1959.

Epstein, Barbara Leslie. *The Politics of Domesticity: Women, Evangelism, and Temperance in Nineteenth-Century America.* Middletown: Wesleyan UP, 1981.

Fanon, Frantz. *Black Skin, White Masks.* 1952. Trans. Charles Lam Markmann. New York: Grove Weidenfeld, 1967.

Ferguson, Charles W. *Methodists and the Making of America.* Austin: Eakin, 1983.

Fetterly, Judith. *The Resisting Reader.* Bloomington: Indiana UP, 1978.

Fichtelberg, Joseph. *The Complex Image: Faith and Method in American Autobiography.* Philadelphia: U of Pennsylvania P, 1989.

Fiorenza, Elisabeth Schussler. *In Memory of Her: A Feminist Theological Reconstruction of Christian Origins.* New York: Crossroad, 1983.

——. "Word, Spirit and Power: Women in Early Christian Communities." *Women of Spirit.* Ed. Rosemary Ruether and Eleanor McLaughlin. New York: Simon, 1979. 15-28.

Fleishman, Avrom. *Figures of Autobiography: The Language of Self-Writing in Victorian and Modern England.* Berkeley: U of California P, 1983.

Flew, R. Newton. *The Idea of Perfection in Christian Theology.* New York: Humanities, 1968.

Flynn, Elizabeth, and Patrocinio Schweickart, eds. *Gender and Reading: Essays on Readers, Texts, and Contexts.* Baltimore: Johns Hopkins UP, 1986.

Folkenflik, Robert, ed. *The Culture of Autobiography and Constructions of Self-Representation.* Stanford: Stanford UP, 1993.

Foster, Charles I. *An Errand of Mercy: The Evangelical United Front, 1790-1837.* Chapel Hill: U of North Carolina P, 1960.

Foster, Frances Smith. "Between the Sides: Afro-American Women Writers as Mediators." *Nineteenth-Century Studies* 3 (1989): 53-64.

——. "Neither Auction Block nor Pedestal: 'The Life and Religious Experience of Jarena Lee, A Coloured Lady.'" *The Female Autograph.* Ed. Domna Stanton. Chicago: U of Chicago P, 1984. 126-30.

——. *Witnessing Slavery: The Development of Ante-bellum Slave Narratives.* Westport: Greenwood, 1979.

——. *Written by Herself: Literary Production by African American Women, 1746-1892.* Bloomington: Indiana UP, 1993.

Foucault, Michel. *Discipline and Punish: The Birth of the Prison.* Trans. Alan Sheridan. New York: Vintage, 1979.

——. *Madness and Civilization: A History of Insanity in the Age of Reason.* Trans. Richard Howard. New York: Pantheon, 1965.

Fox-Genovese, Elizabeth. "Between Individualism and Fragmentation: American Culture and the New Literary Studies of Race and Gender." *American Quarterly* 42 (1990): 7-34.

——. "Culture and Consciousness in the Intellectual History of European Women." *Signs* 12 (1987): 529-47.

——. *Feminism without Illusions: A Critique of Individualism.* Chapel Hill: U of North Carolina P, 1991.

——, and Eugene Genovese. *Fruits of Merchant Capital: Slavery and Bourgeois Property in the Rise and Expansion of Capitalism.* Oxford: Oxford UP, 1983.

——. "My Statue, My Self: Autobiographical Writings of Afro-American Women." *The Private Self*. Ed. Shari Benstock. Chapel Hill: U of North Carolina P, 1988. 63–89.

——. "Religion in the Lives of Slaveholding Women of the Antebellum South." *That Gentle Strength*. Ed. Lynda Coon et al. Charlottesville: UP of Virginia, 1990. 206-29.

——. "To Write My Self: The Autobiographies of Afro-American Women." *Feminist Issues in Literary Scholarship*. Ed. Shari Benstock. Bloomington: Indiana UP, 1987. 161-80.

——. *Within the Plantation Household: Black and White Women of the Old South*. Chapel Hill: U of North Carolina P, 1988.

Fredrickson, George. *The Black Image in the White Mind: The Debate on Afro-American Character and Destiny, 1817-1914*. New York: Harper, 1971.

Frerichs, Ernest S., ed. *The Bible and Bibles in America*. The Bible in American Culture 1. Atlanta: Scholars, 1988.

Frieden, Sandra. "Transformative Subjectivity in the Writings of Christa Wolf." *Interpreting Women's Lives*. Ed. Personal Narratives Group. Bloomington: Indiana UP, 1989. 172-88.

Friedman, Susan Stanford. "Women's Autobiographical Selves: Theory and Practice." *The Private Self*. Ed. Shari Benstock. Chapel Hill: U of North Carolina P, 1988. 34-62.

Frye, Marilyn. *The Politics of Reality: Essays in Feminist Theory*. Freedom, CA: Crossing, 1983.

Frye, Northrop. *The Secular Scripture*. Cambridge: Harvard UP, 1976.

Gaustad, Edwin Scott. *The Great Awakening in New England*. New York: Harper, 1957. Gloucester: Peter Smith, 1965.

——. *A Religious History of America*. New York: Harper, 1966.

——. *Religious Issues in American History*. New York: Harper, 1968.

Geertz, Clifford. *The Interpretation of Cultures*. New York: Basic, 1973.

George, Carol V. R. *Segregated Sabbaths: Richard Allen and the Emergence of Independent Black Churches, 1760-1840*. New York: Oxford UP, 1973.

Gerlach, Luther P., and Virginia H. Hine. *People, Power, Change: Movements of Social Transformation*. New York: Bobbs-Merrill, 1970.

Gilbert, Sandra M., and Susan Gubar. *The Madwoman in the Attic: The Woman Writer and the Nineteenth-Century Literary Imagination*. New Haven: Yale UP, 1979.

Giles, Mary E. *The Feminist Mystic and Other Essays on Women and Spirituality*. New York: Crossroad, 1982.

Gillespie, Joanna Bowen. "'The Clear Leadings of Providence': Pious Memoirs and the Problems of Self-Realization for Women in the Early Nineteenth Century." *Journal of the Early Republic* 5 (1985): 197-221.

Gilmore, Leigh. *Autobiographics: A Feminist Theory of Women's Self-Representation*. Ithaca: Cornell UP, 1994.

Ginsburg, Faye. "Dissonance and Harmony: The Symbolic Function of Abortion in Activists' Life Stories." *Interpreting Women's Lives*. Ed. Personal Narratives Group. Bloomington: Indiana UP, 1989. 59-84.

Ginzberg, Lori D. *Women and the Work of Benevolence: Morality, Politics, and Class in the Nineteenth-Century United States*. New Haven: Yale UP, 1990.

Goode, Gloria Davis. "Preachers of the Word and Singers of the Gospel: The Ministry of Women among Nineteenth Century African-Americans." Diss. U of Pennsylvania, 1990.

Grant, Jacquelyn. "Black Women and the Church." *All the Women Are White, All the Blacks Are Men, But Some of Us Are Brave*. Ed. Gloria T. Hull, Patricia Bell Scott, and Barbara Smith. New York: Feminist, 1982. 141-52.

Gravely, Will B. "African Methodism and the Rise of Black Denominationalism." *Perspectives on American Methodism*. Ed. Russell E. Richey, Kenneth E. Rowe, and Jean Miller Schmidt. Nashville: Kingswood-Abingdon, 1993. 108-26.

Greaves, Richard L., ed. *Triumph over Silence: Women in Protestant History*. Westport: Greenwood, 1985.

Gunn, Giles, ed. *The Bible and American Arts and Letters*. The Bible in American Culture 3. Philadelphia: Fortress; Chico: Scholars, 1983.

Gusdorf, Georges. "Conditions and Limits of Autobiography." *Autobiography: Essays Theoretical and Critical*. Ed. James Olney. Princeton: Princeton UP, 1980. 28-48.

——. "Scripture of the Self: 'Prologue in Heaven.'" Trans. Betsy Wing. *Studies in Autobiography*. Ed. James Olney. New York: Oxford UP, 1988. 112-27.

Hall, Timothy D. *Contested Boundaries: Itinerancy and the Reshaping of the Colonial American Religious World*. Durham: Duke UP, 1994.

Haller, William. *The Rise of Puritanism*. 1938. Philadelphia: U of Pennsylvania P, 1984.

Hambrick-Stowe, Charles E. *The Practice of Piety: Puritan Devotional Disciplines in Seventeenth-Century New England*. Chapel Hill: U of North Carolina P, 1982.

Hampsten, Elizabeth. "Considering More Than a Single Reader." *Interpreting Women's Lives*. Ed. Personal Narratives Group. Bloomington: Indiana UP, 1989. 129-38.

Hansen, Karen V. *A Very Social Time: Crafting Community in Antebellum New England*. Berkeley: U of California P, 1994.

Hardesty, Nancy. "Minister as Prophet? or as Mother? Two Nineteenth-Century Models." *Women in New Worlds*. Ed. Hilah Thomas and Rosemary Keller. Nashville: Abingdon, 1981. 88-101.

——. *Women Called to Witness: Evangelical Feminism in the 19th Century*. 1984. Knoxville: U of Tennnessee P, 1999.

——. *Your Daughters Shall Prophesy: Revivalism and Feminism in the Age of Finney*. Brooklyn: Carlson, 1991.

Hardesty, Nancy, Lucille Sider Dayton, and Donald W. Dayton. "Women in the Holiness Movement: Feminism in the Evangelical Tradition." *Women of Spirit*. Ed. Rosemary Ruether and Eleanor McLaughlin. New York: Simon, 1979. 225-54.

Harpham, Geoffrey Galt. "Conversion and the Language of Autobiography." *Studies in Autobiography*. Ed. James Olney. New York: Oxford UP, 1988. 42-50.

Harris, Barbara J., and JoAnn K. McNamara, eds. *Women and the Structure of Society: Selected Research from the Fifth Berkshire Conference on the History of Women*. Durham: Duke UP, 1984.

Harris, Sharon M. Introduction. *American Women Writers to 1800*. New York: Oxford UP, 1996.

Harris, Susan K. *19th-Century American Women's Novels: Interpretive Strategies*. Cambridge: Cambridge UP, 1990.

Hart, Francis R. "Notes for an Anatomy of Modern Autobiography." *New Directions in Literary History*. Ed. Ralph Cohen. Baltimore: Johns Hopkins UP, 1974. 221-47.

Hartman, Mary S., and Lois Banner, eds. *Clio's Consciousness Raised: New Perspectives on the History of Women*. New York: Harper, 1974.

Hatch, Nathan O. *The Democratization of American Christianity*. New Haven: Yale UP, 1989.

——. "Millennialism and Popular Religion in the Early Republic." *The Evangelical Tradition in America*. Ed. Leonard Sweet. Macon: Mercer UP, 1984. 113-30.

——. "Sola Scriptura and Novus Ordo Seclorum." *The Bible in America: Essays in Cultural History*. Ed. Nathan O. Hatch and Mark A. Noll. New York: Oxford UP, 1982. 59-78.

Haytor, Mary. *The New Eve in Christ: The Use and Abuse of the Bible in the Debate about Women in the Church*. London: SPCK, 1987.

Heidt, Edward R. *Vision Voiced: Narrative Viewpoint in Autobiographical Writing*. New York: Peter Lang, 1991.

Heilbrun, Carolyn G. *Writing a Woman's Life*. New York: Norton, 1988.

Helly, Dorothy O., and Susan M. Reverby. Introduction. *Gendered Domains: Rethinking Public and Private in Women's History.* Ed. Dorothy Helly and Susan Reverby. Ithaca: Cornell UP, 1992.

Hewitt, Nancy A. "The Perimeters of Women's Power in American Religion." *The Evangelical Tradition in America.* Ed. Leonard I. Sweet. Macon: Mercer UP, 1984. 233-56.

Hewitt, Nancy A., and Suzanne Lebsock, eds. *Visible Women: New Essays in American Activism.* Chicago: U of Illinois P, 1993.

Higginbotham, Evelyn Brooks. "African-American Women's History and the Metalanguage of Race." *Signs* 17 (1992): 251-74.

——. "The Problem of Race in Women's History." *Coming to Terms: Feminism, Theory, Politics.* Ed. Elizabeth Weed. New York: Routledge, 1989. 122-33.

——. *Righteous Discontent: The Women's Movement in the Black Baptist Church 1880-1920.* Cambridge: Harvard UP, 1993.

Hill, Patricia. *The World Their Household: The American Woman's Foreign Mission Movement and Cultural Transformation 1879-1920.* Ann Arbor: U of Michigan P, 1985.

Hoffmann, Leonore, and Margo Culley, eds. *Women's Personal Narratives: Essays in Criticism and Pedagogy.* New York: MLA, 1985.

Hogeland, Ronald W. "'The Female Appendage': Feminine Life-Styles in America, 1820-1860." *Civil War History* 17 (1971): 101-14.

Holden, Pat, ed. *Women's Religious Experience.* Totowa, NJ: Barnes, 1983.

Homans, Margaret. *Bearing the Word: Language and Female Experience in Nineteenth-Century Women's Writing.* Chicago: U of Chicago P, 1986.

hooks, bell. *Yearning: Race, Gender and Cultural Politics.* Boston: South End, 1990.

Horton, James Oliver. *Free People of Color: Inside the African American Community.* Washington: Smithsonian, 1993.

Houchins, Susan E. Introduction. *Spiritual Narratives.* New York: Oxford UP, 1988.

Hovet, Theodore. "Phoebe Palmer's 'Altar Phraseology' and the Spiritual Dimension of Woman's Sphere." *Journal of Religion* 63 (1983): 264-80.

Howarth, William L. "Some Principles of Autobiography." *Autobiography: Essays Theoretical and Critical.* Ed. James Olney. Princeton: Princeton UP, 1980. 84-114.

Huggins, Nathan. *Harlem Renaissance.* New York: Oxford UP, 1971.

Hull, Gloria, Patricia Bell Scott, and Barbara Smith, eds. *All the Women Are White, All the Blacks Are Men, But Some of Us Are Brave.* Old Westbury: Feminist, 1982.

Humez, Jean McMahon. Introduction. *Gifts of Power: The Writings of Rebecca Jackson, Black Visionary, Shaker Eldress.* N.p.: U of Massachusetts P, 1981.

——. "'My Spirit Eye': Some Functions of Spiritual and Visionary Experience in the Lives of Five Black Women Preachers, 1810-1880." *Women and the Structure of Society.* Ed. Barbara J. Harris and JoAnn K. McNamara. Durham: Duke UP, 1984. 129-43.

——. "Visionary Experience and Power: The Career of Rebecca Cox Jackson." *Black Apostles at Home and Abroad.* Ed. David W. Wills and Richard Newman. Boston: Hall, 1982. 105-32.

Iglehart, Hallie. "The Unnatural Divorce of Spirituality and Politics." *The Politics of Women's Spirituality.* Ed. Charlene Spretnak. New York: Anchor-Doubleday, 1982. 404-14.

Israel, Adrienne M. *Amanda Berry Smith: From Washerwoman to Evangelist.* Lanham: Scarecrow, 1998.

James, Edward, Janet Wilson James, and Paul S. Boyer, eds. *Notable American Women, 1607-1950.* 3 vols. Cambridge: Belknap-Harvard UP, 1971.

James, Janet, ed. *Women in American Religion.* Philadelphia: U of Pennsylvania P, 1980.

Jauss, Hans Robert. "Literary History as a Challenge to Literary Theory." *New Directions in Literary History.* Ed. Ralph Cohen. Baltimore: Johns Hopkins UP, 1974. 11-42.

Jay, Paul. *Being in the Text: Self-Representation from Wordsworth to Roland Barthes.* Ithaca: Cornell UP, 1984.

Jeffrey, Julie Roy. "Ministry through Marriage: Methodist Clergy Wives on the Trans-Mississippi Frontier." *Women in New Worlds.* Ed. Hilah Thomas and Rosemary Skinner Keller. Nashville: Abingdon, 1981. 143–60.

Jelinek, Estelle C. "The Paradox and Success of Elizabeth Cady Stanton." *Women's Autobiography: Essays in Criticism.* Ed. Estelle C. Jelinek. Bloomington: Indiana UP, 1980. 71–92.

——. *The Tradition of Women's Autobiography: From Antiquity to the Present.* Boston: Twayne, 1986.

——, ed. *Women's Autobiography: Essays in Criticism.* Bloomington: Indiana UP, 1980.

Jones, Charles Edwin. *A Guide to the Study of the Holiness Movement.* Metuchen, NJ: Scarecrow, 1974.

——. *Perfectionist Persuasion: The Holiness Movement and American Methodism, 1867–1936.* Metuchen, NJ: Scarecrow, 1974.

Jones, Howard Mumford. *The Age of Energy: Varieties of American Experience.* New York: Viking, 1971.

Jones, Jacqueline. *Labor of Love, Labor of Sorrow: Black Women, Work, and the Family from Slavery to the Present.* New York: Basic, 1985.

Jürisson, Cynthia. "Federalist, Feminist, Revivalist: Harriet Livermore (1788–1868) and the Limits of Democratization in the Early Republic." Diss. Princeton Theological Seminary, 1994.

Juster, Susan. *Disorderly Women: Sexual Politics and Evangelicalism in Revolutionary New England.* Ithaca: Cornell UP, 1994.

Kaplan, E. Ann. "Is the Gaze Male?" *Powers of Desire: The Politics of Sexuality.* Ed. Ann Snitow, Christine Stansell, and Sharon Thompson. New York: Monthly Review, 1983. 309–27.

Keller, John. *The Second Great Awakening in Connecticut.* Lexington: U of Kentucky P, 1942.

Kelley, Mary. *Private Woman, Public Stage: Literary Domesticity in Nineteenth-Century America.* Oxford: Oxford UP, 1984.

Kerber, Linda. "Separate Spheres, Female Worlds, Woman's Place: The Rhetoric of Women's History." *Journal of American History* 75 (1998): 9–39.

——. *Women of the Republic: Intellect and Ideology in Revolutionary America.* 1980. New York: Norton, 1986.

Kerber, Linda, Nancy Cott, Robert Gross, Lynn Hunt, Carroll Smith-Rosenberg, and Christine Stansell. "Beyond Roles, Beyond Spheres: Thinking about Gender in the Early Republic." *William and Mary Quarterly* 46 (1989): 565–81.

Kimball, Gayle. *The Religious Ideas of Harriet Beecher Stowe.* Studies in Women and Religion 8. New York: Edwin Mellen, 1982.

King, Ursula. *Women and Spirituality.* London: Macmillan Education, 1989.

Kissel, Susan S. "Writer Anxiety versus the Need for Community in the Botts Family Letters." *Women's Personal Narratives.* Ed. Leonore Hoffman and Margo Culley. New York: MLA, 1985. 48–56.

Knight, Janice. *Orthodoxies in Massachusetts.* Cambridge: Harvard UP, 1994.

Krueger, Christine. *The Reader's Repentance: Women Preachers, Women Writers, and Nineteenth-Century Social Discourse.* Chicago: U of Chicago P, 1992.

Kuykendall, John W. *Southern Enterprize: The Work of National Evangelical Societies in the Antebellum South.* Westport: Greenwood, 1982.

Lambert, Frank. *"Pedlar in Divinity": George Whitefield and the Transatlantic Revivals, 1737–1770.* Princeton: Princeton UP, 1994.

Lang, Amy Schrager. *Prophetic Woman: Anne Hutchinson and the Problem of Dissent in the Literature of New England.* Berkeley: U of California P, 1987.

LaPrade, Candis A. *Pens in the Hand of God: The Spiritual Autobiographies of Jarena Lee, Zilpha Elaw, and Rebecca Cox Jackson.* Diss. U of North Carolina at Chapel Hill, 1994.

Larson, Rebecca. *Daughters of Light: Quaker Women Preaching and Prophesying in the Colonies and Abroad, 1700–1775*. New York: Knopf, 1999.

Lawless, Elaine. *Handmaidens of the Lord: Pentecostal Women Preachers and Traditional Religion.* Philadelphia: U of Pennsylvania P, 1988.

——. "Rescripting Their Lives and Narratives: Spiritual Life Stories of Pentecostal Women Preachers." *Journal of Feminist Studies in Religion* 7.1 (Spring 1991): 53–71.

Lee, Susan Dye. "Evangelical Domesticity: The Woman's Temperance Crusade of 1873–1874." *Women in New Worlds.* Ed. Hilah Thomas and Rosemary Keller. Nashville: Abingdon, 1981. 293–309.

Leibowitz, Herbert. *Fabricating Lives: Explorations in American Autobiography.* New York: Knopf, 1989.

Lejeune, Philippe. *On Autobiography.* Trans. Katherine Leary. Ed. Paul John Eakin. Minneapolis: U of Minnesota P, 1989.

Levin, David. *Cotton Mather: The Young Life of the Lord's Remembrancer, 1663–1703.* Cambridge: Harvard UP, 1978.

——. "Edwards, Franklin, and Cotton Mather: A Meditation on Character and Reputation." *Jonathan Edwards and the American Experience.* Ed. Nathan O. Hatch and Harry S. Stout. New York: Oxford UP, 1988. 34–49.

——. "In the Court of Historical Criticism: Alger Hiss's Narrative." *Virginia Quarterly Review* 52 (1976): 41–78. Rpt. in *Forms of Uncertainty.* Charlottesville: UP of Virginia, 1992. 110–53.

Lewis, I. M. *Ecstatic Religion: A Study of Shamanism and Spirit Possession.* 1971. New York: Routledge, 1989.

Lindley, Susan Hill. *"You Have Stept Out of Your Place": A History of Women and Religion in America.* Louisville, KY: Westminster John Knox P, 1996.

Lionnet, Francoise. *Autobiographical Voices: Race, Gender, Self-Portraiture.* Ithaca: Cornell UP, 1989.

Lobody, Diane H. "'That Language Might Be Given Me': Women's Experience in Early Methodism." *Perspectives on American Methodism.* Ed. Russell E. Richey, Kenneth E. Rowe, and Jean Miller Schmidt. Nashville: Kingswood-Abingdon, 1993. 127–44.

Loewenberg, Bert James, and Ruth Bogin, eds. *Black Women in Nineteenth-Century American Life.* University Park: Pennsylvania State UP, 1976.

Logan, Rayford. *The Betrayal of the Negro from Rutherford B. Hayes to Woodrow Wilson.* 1965. New York: Da Capo, 1997.

Long, Elizabeth. "Women, Reading, and Cultural Authority: Some Implications of the Audience Perspective in Cultural Studies." *American Quarterly* 38 (1986): 591–612.

Long, Kathryn. *The Revival of 1857–58: Interpreting an American Religious Awakening.* New York: Oxford UP, 1998

Luker, Ralph E. "Religion and Social Control in the Nineteenth-Century American City." *Journal of Urban History* 2 (1976): 363–68.

Lynch, James R. "Baptist Women in Ministry through 1920." *American Baptist Quarterly* 13 (December 1994): 304–18.

——. "A Preliminary Check List of Baptist Women in Ministry through 1920." *American Baptist Quarterly* 13 (December 1994): 319–71.

Mann, Susan A. "Slavery, Sharecropping, and Sexual Inequality." *Signs* 14 (1989): 774–98.

Marcus, Jane. "Invincible Mediocrity: The Private Selves of Public Women." *The Private Self.* Ed. Shari Benstock. Chapel Hill: U of North Carolina P, 1988. 114–46.

Marsden, George M. "Everyone One's Own Interpreter? The Bible, Science, and Authority in Mid-Nineteenth-Century America." *The Bible in America: Essays in Cultural History.* Ed. Nathan O. Hatch and Mark A. Noll. New York: Oxford UP, 1982. 79–100.

Marty, Martin E. *Pilgrims in Their Own Land: 500 Years of Religion in America*. Boston: Little, 1984.

——. "Religion: A Private Affair, in Public Affairs." *Religion and American Culture* 3 (1993): 115-27.

——. *Religion and Republic*. Boston: Beacon, 1987.

——. *Righteous Empire: Protestantism in the United States*. New York: Scribner's, 1970.

Mason, Mary G. "The Other Voice: Autobiographies of Women Writers." *Life/Lines*. Ed. Bella Brodzki and Celeste Schenck. Ithaca: Cornell UP, 1988. 19-44.

Mason, Mary Grimley, and Carol Hurd Green, eds. *Journeys: Autobiographical Writings by Women*. Boston: Hall, 1979.

Mathews, Donald G. "Evangelical America—The Methodist Ideology." *Perspectives on Methodism*. Ed. Russell Richey, Kenneth Rowe, and Jean Miller Schmidt. Nashville: Kingswood-Abingdon, 1993. 17-30.

——. *Religion in the Old South*. Chicago: U of Chicago P, 1977.

——. "The Second Great Awakening as an Organizing Process, 1780-1830: An Hypothesis." *American Quarterly* 21 (1969): 23-43.

Matthaei, Julie. *An Economic History of Women in America: Women's Work, the Sexual Division of Labor, and the Development of Capitalism*. New York: Schocken, 1982.

Matthews, Glenna. *"Just a Housewife": The Rise and Fall of Domesticity in America*. New York: Oxford UP, 1987.

——. *The Rise of Public Woman: Woman's Power and Woman's Place in the United States, 1630-1970*. New York: Oxford UP, 1992.

May, Georges. *L'autobiographie*. Paris: PUF, 1979.

Maynes, Mary Jo. "Gender and Narrative Form in French and German Working-Class Autobiographies." *Interpreting Women's Lives*. Ed. Personal Narratives Group. Bloomington: Indiana UP, 1989. 103-18.

McDowell, Deborah. "In the First Place: Making Frederick Douglass and the Afro-American Narrative Tradition." *African American Autobiography: A Collection of Critical Essays*. Ed. William L. Andrews. Englewood Cliffs: Prentice Hall, 1993. 36-58.

McKay, Nellie Y. "Nineteenth-Century Black Women's Spiritual Autobiographies: Religious Faith and Self-Empowerment." *Interpreting Women's Lives*. Ed. Personal Narratives Group. Bloomington: Indiana UP, 1989. 139-54.

McLoughlin, William G. Introduction. *The America Evangelicals, 1800-1900: An Anthology*. New York: Harper, 1968. Gloucester: Peter Smith, 1976.

——. *Revivals, Awakenings, and Reform*. Chicago: U of Chicago P, 1978.

——, ed. *The American Evangelicals, 1800-1900: An Anthology*. New York: Harper, 1968. Gloucester: Peter Smith, 1976.

Mehlman, Jeffrey. *A Structural Study of Autobiography*. 1971. Ithaca: Cornell UP, 1974.

Meyers, Carol. *Discovering Eve: Ancient Israelite Women in Context*. New York: Oxford UP, 1988.

Miller, Nancy. "Emphasis Added: Plots and Plausibilities in Women's Fiction." *The New Feminist Criticism*. Ed. Elaine Showalter. New York: Pantheon, 1985. 339-60.

——. *The Heroine's Text*. New York: Columbia UP, 1980.

——. *Subject to Change: Reading Feminist Writing*. New York: Columbia UP, 1988.

——, ed. *The Poetics of Gender*. New York: Columbia UP, 1986.

Miller, Page Putnam. *A Claim to New Roles*. Metuchen, NJ: American Theological Library Association and Scarecrow, 1985.

Miller, Perry. *Errand into the Wilderness*. 1956. Cambridge: Harvard UP, 1981.

——. *The Life of the Mind in America: From the Revolution to the Civil War*. New York: Harcourt, 1965.

Moody, Joycelyn. *Sentimental Confessions: Spiritual Narratives of Nineteenth-Century African American Women*. Athens: U of Georgia P, 2001.

Moore, R. Laurence. *Religious Outsiders and the Making of Americans*. New York: Oxford UP, 1986.

——. *Selling God: American Religion in the Marketplace of Culture*. New York: Oxford UP, 1994.

Morgan, Edmund S. Introduction. *Puritan Political Ideas, 1558–1794*. Ed. Edmund S. Morgan. New York: Bobbs-Merrill, 1965.

——. *Visible Saints: The History of a Puritan Idea*. Ithaca: Cornell UP, 1963.

Morton, Nelle. *The Journey Is Home*. Boston: Beacon, 1985.

Muir, Elizabeth Gillan. *Petticoats in the Pulpit: The Story of Early Nineteenth-Century Methodist Women Preachers in Upper Canada*. Toronto: United Church Publishing House, 1991.

Neuman, Shirley, ed. *Autobiography and Questions of Gender*. London: Frank Cass, 1991.

Nisbet, Robert. *The Quest for Community: A Study in the Ethics of Order and Freedom*. 1953. San Francisco: ICS, 1990.

Noll, Mark A. "The Image of the United States as a Biblical Nation, 1776–1865." *The Bible in America: Essays in Cultural History*. Ed. Nathan Hatch and Mark Noll. New York: Oxford UP, 1982. 39–58.

Noll, William T. "Women as Clergy and Laity in the 19th Century Methodist Protestant Church." *Methodist History* 15 (January 1977): 107–21.

Norton, Mary Beth. *Founding Mothers and Fathers: Gendered Power and the Forming of American Society*. New York: Knopf, 1996.

——. *Liberty's Daughters: The Revolutionary Experience of American Women, 1750–1800*. Boston: Little, 1980.

Nussbaum, Felicity. *The Autobiographical Subject: Gender and Ideology in Eighteenth-Century England*. Baltimore: Johns Hopkins UP, 1989.

——. "Eighteenth-Century Women's Autobiographical Commonplaces." *The Private Self*. Ed. Shari Benstock. Chapel Hill: U of North Carolina P, 1988. 147–72.

——. "Toward Conceptualizing Diary." *Studies in Autobiography*. Ed. James Olney. New York: Oxford UP, 1988. 128–40.

Olney, James. "'I Was Born': Slave Narratives, Their Status as Autobiography and as Literature." *The Slave's Narrative*. Ed. Charles Davis and Henry Louis Gates Jr. New York: Oxford UP, 1985. 148–75.

——. *Metaphors of Self*. Princeton: Princeton UP, 1972.

——, ed. *Autobiography: Essays Theoretical and Critical*. Princeton: Princeton UP, 1980.

——. *Studies in Autobiography*. New York: Oxford UP, 1988.

Pagels, Elaine. *Adam, Eve, and the Serpent*. New York: Random, 1988.

——. *The Gnostic Gospels*. New York: Random, 1979.

Papashvily, Helen W. *All the Happy Endings: A Study of the Domestic Novel in America, the Women Who Wrote It, the Women Who Read It, in the Nineteenth Century*. New York: Harper, 1956.

Pascal, Roy. *Design and Truth in Autobiography*. London: Routledge and Kegan Paul, 1960.

Perkins, Linda. "Black Women and Racial 'Uplift' Prior to Emancipation." *The Black Woman Cross-Culturally*. Ed. Filomina Chioma Steady. Cambridge: Schenkman, 1981. 317–34.

——. "The Impact of the 'Cult of True Womanhood' on the Education of Black Women." *Journal of Social Issues* 39.3 (1983): 17–28.

Personal Narratives Group, eds. *Interpreting Women's Lives: Feminist Theory and Personal Narratives*. Bloomington: Indiana UP, 1989.

Peters, John Leland. *Christian Perfection and American Methodism*. New York: Abingdon, 1956.

Peterson, Carla L. *"Doers of the Word": African-American Women Speakers and Writers in the North (1830–1880)*. New York: Oxford UP, 1995.

Peterson, David. *Possessed by God: A New Testament Theology of Sanctification and Holiness.* Grand Rapids: Eerdmans, 1995.

Peterson, Linda. "Female Autobiographer, Narrative Duplicity." *Studies in the Literary Imagination* 23 (Fall 1990): 165-76.

——. "Gender and Autobiographical Form: The Case of the Spiritual Autobiography." *Studies in Autobiography.* Ed. James Olney. New York: Oxford UP, 1988. 211-22.

——. *Victorian Autobiography: The Tradition of Self-Interpretation.* New Haven: Yale UP, 1986.

Phy, Allene Stuart, ed. *The Bible and Popular Culture in America.* The Bible in American Culture 2. Philadelphia: Fortress; Chico: Scholars, 1985.

Pierard, Richard V. *The Unequal Yoke: Evangelical Christianity and Political Conservatism.* New York: Lippincott, 1970.

Pollock, J. C. *The Keswick Story: The Authorized History of the Keswick Story.* London: Hodder and Stoughton, 1964.

Poovey, Mary. "*Persuasion* and the Promises of Love." *The Representation of Women in Fiction.* Ed. Carolyn Heilbrun and Margaret Higonnet. Baltimore: Johns Hopkins UP, 1983. 152-79.

Porterfield, Amanda. *Female Piety in Puritan New England: The Emergence of Religious Humanism.* New York: Oxford UP, 1992.

——. *Feminine Spirituality in America: From Sarah Edwards to Martha Graham.* Philadelphia: Temple UP, 1980.

Potter, David. *People of Plenty: Economic Abundance and the American Character.* Chicago: U of Chicago P, 1945.

Pullin, Faith. "Enclosure/Disclosure: A Tradition of American Autobiography by Women." *First Person Singular: Studies in American Autobiography.* Ed. A. Robert Lee. New York: St. Martin's, 1988. 125-50.

Rabinowitz, Richard. *The Spiritual Self in Everyday Life: The Transformation of Personal Religious Experience in Nineteenth-Century New England.* Boston: Northeastern UP, 1989.

Raboteau, Albert. "Black Christianity in North America." *Encyclopedia of American Religious Experience.* Ed. Charles H. Lippy and Peter W. Williams. Vol. 1. New York: Scribner's, 1988. 635-48.

——. "The Black Experience in American Evangelicalism." *The Evangelical Tradition in America.* Ed. Leonard Sweet. Macon: Mercer UP, 1984. 181-98.

——. *Slave Religion.* Oxford: Oxford UP, 1978.

Radway, Janice. "Reading Is Not Eating: Mass-Produced Literature and the Theoretical, Methodological, and Political Consequences of a Metaphor." *Book Research Quarterly* 2 (1986): 7-29.

Railton, Stephen. *Authorship and Audience: Literary Performance in the American Renaissance.* Princeton: Princeton UP, 1991.

Raser, Harold E. *Phoebe Palmer: Her Life and Thought.* Lewiston, NY: Edwin Mellen, 1987.

Reimer, Gail Twersky. "Revisions of Labor in Margaret Oliphant's Autobiography." *Life/Lines.* Ed. Bella Brodzki and Celeste Schenck. Ithaca: Cornell UP, 1988. 203-20.

Relph, E. *Place and Placelessness.* London: Pion, 1976.

Renza, Louis. "The Veto of the Imagination: A Theory of Autobiography." *New Literary History* 9 (1977): 1-26.

Reynolds, David S. *Beneath the American Renaissance: The Subversive Imagination in the Age of Emerson and Melville.* Cambridge: Harvard UP, 1989.

——. "The Feminization Controversy: Sexual Stereotypes and the Paradoxes of Piety in Nineteenth-Century America." *New England Quarterly* 53 (1980): 96-106.

——. "From Doctrine to Narrative: The Rise of Pulpit Storytelling in America." *American Quarterly* 32 (1980): 479-98.

Richey, Russell E. *Early American Methodism*. Bloomington: Indiana UP, 1991.

Richey, Russell, Kenneth E. Rowe, and Jean Miller Schmidt, eds. *Perspectives on American Methodism*. Nashville: Kingswood-Abingdon, 1993.

Rigney, Barbara Hill. *Madness and Sexual Politics in the Feminist Novel*. Madison: U of Wisconsin P, 1978.

Robert, Dana L. *American Women in Mission: A Social History of Their Thought and Practice*. Macon: Mercer UP, 1997.

Romero, Lora. *Home Fronts: Domesticity and Its Critics in the Antebellum United States*. Durham: Duke UP, 1997.

Romines, Ann. *The Home Plot: Women, Writing and Domestic Ritual*. Amherst: U of Massachusetts P, 1992.

Rose, Gillian. *Feminism and Geography: The Limits of Geographical Knowledge*. Minneapolis: U of Minnesota P, 1993.

Rosell, Garth M. "Charles G. Finney: His Place in the Stream." *The Evangelical Tradition in America*. Ed. Leonard Sweet. Macon: Mercer UP, 1984. 131-48.

Rosenblatt, Roger. "Black Autobiography: Life as the Death Weapon." *Autobiography: Essays Theoretical and Critical*. Ed. James Olney. Princeton: Princeton UP, 1980. 169-80.

Rothman, Sheila M. *Woman's Proper Place: A History of Changing Ideals and Practices, 1870 to the Present*. New York: Basic, 1978.

Rourke, Constance. *American Humor: A Study of the National Character*. New York: Harcourt, 1931.

Ruether, Rosemary, ed. *Religion and Sexism: Images of Woman in the Jewish and Christian Traditions*. New York: Simon, 1974.

Ruether, Rosemary, and Rosemary Keller, eds. *Women and Religion in America*. Vol. 1. New York: Harper, 1981.

Ruether, Rosemary, and Eleanor McLaughlin, eds. *Women of Spirit*. New York: Simon, 1979.

Russell, Letty. *Household of Freedom: Authority in Feminist Theology*. Philadelphia: Westminster, 1987.

——, ed. *Feminist Interpretation of the Bible*. Philadelphia: Westminster, 1985.

Ryan, Mary. "A Women's Awakening: Evangelical Religion and the Families of Utica, New York, 1800-1840." *Women in American Religion*. Ed. Janet James. Philadelphia: U of Pennsylvania P, 1980.

——. *Women in Public: Between Banners and Ballots, 1825-1880*. Baltimore: Johns Hopkins UP, 1990.

Salem, Dorothy. *To Better Our World: Black Women in Organized Reform, 1890-1920*. Black Women in United States History. Ed. Darlene Clark Hine. Vol. 14. Brooklyn: Carlson, 1990.

Sanchez-Eppler, Karen. "Bodily Bonds: The Intersecting Rhetorics of Feminism and Abolition." *Representations* 24 (1988): 28-59.

Sandeen, Ernest R. *The Bible and Social Reform*. The Bible in American Culture 6. Philadelphia: Fortress; Chico: Scholars, 1982.

Sasson, Diane. *The Shaker Spiritual Narrative*. Knoxville: U of Tennessee P, 1983.

Sayre, Robert. "Autobiography and the Making of America." *Autobiography: Essays Theoretical and Critical*. Ed. James Olney. Princeton: Princeton UP, 1980. 146-68.

——. *The Examined Self: Benjamin Franklin, Henry Adams, Henry James*. Princeton: Princeton UP, 1964.

Schenck, Celeste. "All of a Piece: Women's Poetry and Autobiography." *Life/Lines*. Ed. Bella Brodzki and Celeste Schenck. Ithaca: Cornell UP, 1988. 281-305.

Schmidt, Jean Miller. "Holiness and Perfection." *Encyclopedia of American Religious Experience*. Ed. Charles H. Lippy and Peter W. Williams. Vol. 2. New York: Scribner's, 1988. 815-29.

——. "Reexamining the Public/Private Split: Reforming the Continent and Spreading Scriptural Holiness." *Perspectives on American Methodism*. Ed. Russell E. Richey, Kenneth E. Rowe, and Jean Miller Schmidt. Nashville: Kingswood-Abingdon, 1993. 228–47.

Schneider, A. Gregory. *The Way of the Cross Leads Home: The Domestication of American Methodism*. Bloomington: Indiana UP, 1993.

Schor, Naomi. *Reading in Detail: Aesthetics and the Feminine*. New York: Methuen, 1987.

Schuyler, David. "Inventing a Feminine Past." *New England Quarterly* 51 (1978): 291–308.

Scott, Anne Firor. *The Southern Lady from Pedestal to Politics, 1830–1930*. Chicago: U of Chicago P, 1970.

——. "Women, Religion and Social Change in the South 1830–1930." *Religion and the Solid South*. Ed. Samuel S. Hill, Jr. Nashville: Abingdon, 1972. 92–121.

Scott, James C. *Domination and the Arts of Resistance*. New Haven: Yale UP, 1990.

——. *Weapons of the Weak: Everyday Forms of Peasant Resistance*. New Haven: Yale UP, 1985.

Selby, Gary. "'Your Daughters Shall Prophesy': Rhetorical Strategy in the 19th Century Debate over Women's Right to Preach." *Restoration Quarterly* 34 (1992): 151–67.

Shapiro, Ann R. *Unlikely Heroines: Nineteenth-Century American Women Writers and the Woman Question*. New York: Greenwood, 1987.

Sharrock, Roger. Introduction. *Grace Abounding to the Chief of Sinners*. Ed. Roger Sharrock. Oxford: Clarendon-Oxford UP, 1962.

Shea, Daniel B., Jr. "Elizabeth Ashbridge and the Voice Within." *Journeys in New Worlds*. Ed. William Andrews. Madison: U of Wisconsin P, 1990. 119–46.

——. *Spiritual Autobiography in Early America*. Princeton: Princeton UP, 1968.

Showalter, Elaine. *A Literature of Their Own: British Novelists from Bronte to Lessing*. Princeton: Princeton UP, 1977.

Sicherman, Barbara. "Sense and Sensibility: A Case Study of Women's Reading in Late-Victorian America." *Reading in America*. Ed. Cathy Davidson. Baltimore: Johns Hopkins UP, 1989. 201–25.

Silverman, Kenneth. Introduction. *Benjamin Franklin: The Autobiography and Other Writings*. New York: Penguin, 1986.

Simson, Rennie. "The Afro-American Female: The Historical Context of the Construction of Sexual Identity." *Powers of Desire: The Politics of Sexuality*. Ed. Ann Snitow, Christine Stansell, and Sharon Thompson. New York: Monthly Review, 1983. 229–35.

Sizer, Sandra S. *Gospel Hymns and Social Religion: The Rhetoric of Nineteenth-Century Revivalism*. Philadelphia: Temple UP, 1978.

Sklar, Kathryn Kish. *Catharine Beecher: A Study in American Domesticity*. 1973. New York: Norton, 1976.

——. "The Last Fifteen Years: Historians' Changing Views of American Women in Religion and Society." *Women in New Worlds*. Ed. Hilah Thomas and Rosemary Keller. Nashville: Abingdon, 1981. 48–68.

Smith, Sidonie. "Construing Truths in Lying Mouths: Truthtelling in Women's Autobiography." *Studies in the Literary Imagination* 23 (Fall 1990): 145–64.

——. *A Poetics of Women's Autobiography: Marginality and the Fictions of Self-Representation*. Bloomington: U of Indiana P, 1987.

——. "Resisting the Gaze of Embodiment: Women's Autobiography in the Nineteenth Century." *American Women's Autobiography*. Ed. Margo Culley. Madison: U of Wisconsin P, 1992. 75–110.

——. *Subjectivity, Identity, and the Body: Women's Autobiographical Practices in the Twentieth Century*. Bloomington: Indiana UP, 1993.

Smith, Sidonie, and Julia Watson. Introduction. *De/Colonizing the Subject: The Politics of Gender in Women's Autobiography*. Minneapolis: U of Minnesota P, 1992.

——, eds. *Women, Autobiography, Theory: A Reader*. Madison: U of Wisconsin P, 1998.

Smith, Timothy. *Revivalism and Social Reform: American Protestantism on the Eve of the Civil War*. New York: Abingdon, 1957. Baltimore: Johns Hopkins UP, 1980.

——. "Righteousness and Hope: Christian Holiness and The Millennial Vision in America, 1800-1900." *American Quarterly* 31 (1979): 21-45.

Smith-Rosenberg, Carroll. *Disorderly Conduct: Visions of Gender in Victorian America*. New York: Knopf, 1985.

——. "The Female World of Love and Ritual: Relations between Women in Nineteenth-Century America." *Signs* 1.1-2 (1975): 1-29.

——. *Religion and the Rise of the City*. Ithaca: Cornell UP, 1971.

——. "Women and Religious Revivals: Anti-ritualism, Liminality, and the Emergence of the American Bourgeoisie." *The Evangelical Tradition in America*. Ed. Leonard I. Sweet. Macon: Mercer UP, 1984. 199-232.

Snitow, Ann, Christine Stansell, and Sharon Thompson, eds. *Powers of Desire: The Politics of Sexuality*. New York: Monthly Review, 1983.

Sommer, Doris. "'Not Just a Personal Story': Women's *Testimonios* and the Plural Self." *Life/Lines*. Ed. Bella Brodzki and Celeste Schenck. Ithaca: Cornell UP, 1988. 107-30.

Spacks, Patricia Meyer. "Female Rhetoric." *The Private Self*. Ed. Shari Benstock. Chapel Hill: U of North Carolina P, 1988. 177-91.

——. *Imagining a Self: Autobiography and Novel in Eighteenth-Century England*. Cambridge: Harvard UP, 1976.

——. "Selves in Hiding." *Women's Autobiography: Essays in Criticism*. Ed. Estelle Jelinek. Bloomington: Indiana UP, 1980. 112-32.

Spector, Judith, ed. *Gender Studies: New Directions in Feminist Critcism*. Bowling Green: Bowling Green State University Popular P, 1986.

Spencer, Carole D. "Evangelism, Feminism and Social Reform: The Quaker Woman Minister and the Holiness Revival." *Quaker History* 80 (1991): 24-48.

Spengemann, William C. *The Adventurous Muse: The Poetics of American Fiction, 1789-1900*. New Haven: Yale UP, 1977.

——. *The Forms of Autobiography: Episodes in the History of Literary Genre*. New Haven: Yale UP, 1980.

Spretnek, Charlene, ed. *The Politics of Women's Spirituality*. Garden City, NY: Anchor, 1982.

Stallybrass, Peter, and Allon White. *The Politics and Poetics of Transgression*. Ithaca: Cornell UP, 1986.

Stanton, Domna C., ed. *The Female Autograph*. Chicago: U of Chicago P, 1984.

Starobinski, Jean. "The Style of Autobiography." *Autobiography: Essays Theoretical and Critical*. Ed. James Olney. Princeton: Princeton UP, 1980. 73-83.

Starr, G. A. *Defoe and Spiritual Autobiography*. New York: Gordian, 1971.

Sterling, Dorothy. *We Are Your Sisters: Black Women in the Nineteenth Century*. New York: Norton, 1984.

Stoever, Wm. K. B. *"A Faire and Easie Way to Heaven": Covenant Theology and Antinomianism in Early Massachusetts*. Middletown: Wesleyan UP, 1978.

Stout, Harry S. *The Divine Dramatist: George Whitefield and the Rise of Modern Evangelicalism*. Grand Rapids: Eerdmans, 1991.

Strasser, Susan. *Satisfaction Guaranteed: The Making of the American Mass Market*. New York: Pantheon-Random, 1989.

Sturrock, John. "The New Model Autobiographer." *New Literary History* 9 (1977): 51-63.

Suleiman, Susan R., and Inge Crosman, eds. *The Reader in the Text: Essays on Audience and Interpretation*. Princeton: Princeton UP, 1980.

Sweet, Leonard I. *Black Images of America, 1784-1870*. New York: Norton, 1976.

——. *The Minister's Wife: Her Role in Nineteenth-Century American Evangelicalism.* Philadelphia: Temple UP, 1983.

——. "Nineteenth-Century Evangelicalism." *Encyclopedia of American Religious Experience.* Ed. Charles H. Lippy and Peter W. Williams. Vol. 2. New York: Scribner's, 1988. 875-99.

——, ed. *Communication and Change in American Religious History.* Grand Rapids: Eerdmans, 1993.

——. *The Evangelical Tradition in America.* Macon: Mercer UP, 1984.

Sweet, William Warren. *Methodism in American History.* Nashville: Abingdon, 1961.

Synan, Vinson. *The Holiness-Pentecostal Movement in the United States.* Grand Rapids: Eerdmans, 1971.

Tate, Claudia. *Domestic Allegories of Political Desire: The Black Heroine's Text at the Turn of the Century.* New York: Oxford UP, 1992.

Thomas, George M. *Revivalism and Cultural Change: Christianity, Nation Building, and the Market in the Nineteenth-Century United States.* Chicago: U of Chicago P, 1989.

Thomas, Hilah E., and Rosemary Skinner Keller, eds. *Women in New Worlds: Historical Perspectives on the Wesleyan Tradition.* Nashville: Abingdon, 1981.

Tompkins, Jane. *Sensational Designs: The Cultural Work of American Fiction 1790-1860.* New York: Oxford UP, 1985.

——, ed. *Reader-Response Criticism.* Baltimore: Johns Hopkins UP, 1980.

Trible, Phyllis. *Texts of Terror: Literary-Feminist Readings of Biblical Narratives.* Philadelphia: Fortress, 1984.

Tucker, Cynthia Grant. *Prophetic Sisterhood: Liberal Women Ministers of the Frontier, 1880-1930.* Boston: Beacon, 1990.

Tuveson, Ernest Lee. *Redeemer Nation: The Idea of America's Millennial Role.* Chicago: U of Chicago P, 1968.

Valenze, Deborah. *Prophetic Sons and Daughters: Female Preaching and Popular Religion in Industrial England.* Princeton: Princeton UP, 1985.

Voss, Norine. "'Saying the Unsayable': An Introduction to Women's Autobiography." *Gender Studies.* Ed. Judith Spector. Bowling Green: Bowling Green State University Popular P, 1987. 218-33.

Wach, Joachim. *Sociology of Religion.* Chicago: U of Chicago P, 1944.

Wallis, Charles. Introduction. *Autobiography of Peter Cartwright.* New York: Abingdon, 1956.

Walters, Ronald G. *American Reformers, 1815-1860.* New York: Hill and Wang, 1978.

Warren, Joyce W. *The American Narcissus: Individualism and Women in Nineteenth-Century American Fiction.* New Brunswick: Rutgers UP, 1984.

Washington, Joseph R. *Race and Religion in Early Nineteenth Century America, 1800-1850: Constitution, Conscience, and Calvinist Compromise.* Lewiston, NY: Edwin Mellen, 1988.

Watkins, Owen C. *The Puritan Experience.* London: Routledge and Kegan Paul, 1972.

Watt, Ian. *The Rise of the Novel.* Berkeley: U of California P, 1957.

Waugh, Susan. "Women's Shorter Autobiographical Writings: Expression, Identity, and Form." *Women's Personal Narratives.* Ed. Leonore Hoffmann and Margo Culley. New York: MLA, 1985. 144-52.

Weber, Max. *The Protestant Ethic and the Spirit of Capitalism.* Trans. Talcott Parsons. New York: Scribner's, 1930.

Weintraub, Karl Joachim. *The Value of the Individual: Self and Circumstance in Autobiography.* Chicago: U of Chicago P, 1978.

Welter, Barbara. *Dimity Convictions: The American Woman in the Nineteenth Century.* Athens: Ohio UP, 1976.

——. "She Hath Done What She Could: Protestant Women's Missionary Careers in Nineteenth-Century America." *American Quarterly* 30 (1978): 624-38. Rpt. in *Women in American Religion.* Ed. Janet James. Philadelphia: U of Pennsylvania P, 1980. 111-25.

Wesley, Charles. *Richard Allen: Apostle of Freedom.* Washington: Associated, 1935.

Wessinger, Catherine. "Going Beyond and Retaining Charisma: Women's Leadership in Marginal Religions." *Women's Leadership in Marginal Religions.* Ed. Catherine Wessinger. Chicago: U of Illinois P, 1993. 1-23.

White, Charles Edward. *The Beauty of Holiness: Phoebe Palmer as Theologian, Revivalist, Feminist, and Humanitarian.* Grand Rapids: Francis Asbury, 1986.

White, Deborah Gray. *Ar'n't I a Woman?* New York: Norton, 1985.

Wiebe, Robert H. *The Search for Order 1877-1920.* New York: Hill and Wang, 1967.

Williams, Delores S. "Black Women's Literature and the Task of Feminist Theology." *Immaculate and Powerful.* Ed. Clarissa Atkinson, Constance Buchanan, and Margaret Miles. Boston: Beacon, 1985. 88-110.

Williams, Sherley Anne. "The Blues Roots of Contemporary Afro-American Poetry." *Afro-American Literature: The Reconstruction of Instruction.* Ed. Dexter Fisher and Robert B. Stepto. New York: MLA, 1979. 72-87.

Wills, David W. "Womanhood and Domesticity in the A.M.E. Tradition: The Influence of Daniel Alexander Payne." *Black Apostles at Home and Abroad.* Ed. David W. Wills and Richard Newman. Boston: Hall, 1982. 133-46.

Wolch, Jennifer, and Michael Dear, eds. *The Power of Geography: How Territory Shapes Social Life.* Boston: Unwin Hyman, 1989.

Wolff, Cynthia Griffin. *Emily Dickinson.* New York: Knopf, 1986.

Wollstonecraft, Mary. *A Vindication of the Rights of Woman.* 1792. New York: Knopf, 1992.

Wood, Forrest G. *The Arrogance of Faith: Christianity and Race in America from the Colonial Era to the Twentieth Century.* New York: Knopf, 1990.

Woolf, Virginia. *The Death of the Moth and Other Essays.* New York: Harcourt, 1942.

Yee, Shirley. *Black Women Abolitionists: A Study in Activism, 1828-1860.* Knoxville: U of Tennessee P, 1992.

Yellin, Jean Fagan. *Women and Sisters: The Antislavery Feminists in American Culture.* New Haven: Yale UP, 1989.

Young-Bruehl, Elisabeth. *Freud on Women: A Reader.* New York: Norton, 1990.

Index

Abbott, Benjamin, 141
Abbott, Porter, 19, 81, 160n.30
abuse, during domestic service, 31, 152n.6
Acornley, Rev. John Holmes, 141, 149n.16
action, in salvation, passivity vs., 57, 63-64,
   85-86
activists
   black women as, 38, 151n.25, 154n.17
   itinerant evangelists as, 13-19, 144-46
Adams, Henry, 76, 112, 125, 136, 166n.1
additive autobiographies, 113-17, 134, 136,
   140, 166n.3
adversaries, of female itinerants, 89-100
   destruction of, 39, 49-50, 156n.35
   inventing them, as common strategy of
      differentiation, 164n.24
   racist and sexist, 90-92, 97-100,
      163nn.14-16
   Satan as, 93-97, 163n.12
   slavery, as metaphor of, 95-97
   See also female itinerant evangelists; male
      itinerant evangelists; marginalization;
      entries for particular autobiographers
African Americans
   autobiographical forms used by, 93-95,
      127-28, 139-40, 144, 162nn.10-11,
      168n.17, 168n.23
   biblical metaphors of slavery and freedom,
      use of, 95-97
   and the black Methodist class, 84,
      156n.32
   community sphere of, vs. "private" sphere,
      152-53n.8
   competitive individualism, adopting the
      philosophy of, 76, 93, 162nn.10-11

educational opportunities in North, 150n.20
gender conventions among, 17, 31-33,
   153n.13
ideologies of domesticity and true
   womanhood, relation to, 31-33, 43, 68,
   76, 153nn.10-12, 159n.22
men, oppression of, 28, 31-33, 49,
   156n.33
self-marginalization of, 110, 166n.33
See also black female itinerant preachers;
   female itinerant evangelists; slave
   narratives; entries for particular
   autobiographers
African Methodist Episcopal (A.M.E.)
   Church
   Book Concern of, 142-43
   classes, appeal of, 84, 156n.32
   female preachers and, 7, 9, 12, 27, 41,
      70, 98-99, 103, 133, 142, 148n.10,
      149n.16, 168n.21
   gender hierarchy in, 9, 12-13, 17,
      163n.13, 168n.21
   ordination and licensing of women
      preachers, 7-8, 73-74, 130, 168n.21
   origin of, 9, 150n.19
   See also Allen, Richard; Bethel A. M. E.
      Church; Payne, Daniel
African Methodist Episcopal Zion Church,
   12, 40, 55, 99, 149n.16, 150n.19
age of reform. See reform movements
age of revivalism. See evangelicalism and
   revivalism
agnosticism, 131
agricultural economy, and domestic ideology,
   29

opposition to, 49–50, 72, 89–90, 166n.30

productivity of, in marketplace of
salvation, 61–62, 70, 72

quantification, as literary strategy and
measure of success, 61–62, 70, 72, 74

racism and slavery, response to, 14, 49–50

traveling companions of, 84

Sharrock, Roger, 167n.15

Shaw, Anna Howard, 148n.15, 160n.26,
168n.21

Shea, Daniel, 163n.11, 167n.15, 169n.3

Shepard, Thomas, 164n.24

Shilling, Henry, 83

Shorter, Susan, 10

Showalter, Elaine, 107, 165n.25

sin, suppression of, 64–65, 150–51n.16,
158n.12. *See also* sanctification

Sisters in Christ, 66, 143

slave narratives, 95, 128, 139, 168n.23

slavery, as Christian metaphor, 95–97, 102

Smith, Amanda Berry
attitude toward money, 78
autobiographical form used by, 113, 141,
143
biblical criticism and defense of women's
preaching, 51–52
call to preach, 13, 27–28
conversion of, 13
and domestic ideology: defining herself by
using language of, 43, 49, 156n.34;
influence on, at end of career, 66;
internalization of, 68, 94–95; rejecting
plot of, 27–28, 39, 41, 49, 82
as domestic servant, 13, 31–32, 49
dress of, 78, 103
life summary of, 12–13
marginalization and the gaze, 101–4, 109–
10
marriages of, 27–28, 49
as mentor, 143
as mother, 13, 27, 31–32, 94–95
opposition to, 68, 71, 94–97
ordained by God, 109–10
productivity of, in marketplace of
salvation, 59, 66–67, 70–71
quantification, as literary strategy and
measure of success, 66, 70–71, 74
racism and slavery, response to, 16–17,
94–97
sanctification of, 13, 17, 96–97, 101,
103
visionary experiences of, 27

Smith, Elice Miller, 3, 35, 37, 147n.1

Smith, Hannah Whitall, 103, 149n.16,
150n.17, 158–59n.12, 161n.8

Smith, James, 13, 27–28, 31, 49

Smith, Laura. *See* Haviland, Laura

Smith, Robert Pearsall, 103, 150n.17, 158–
59n.12

Smith, Sidonie, 23, 81, 94, 108, 120,
155n.27, 160n.28, 162n.10, 167n.11

Smith, Timothy, 4, 59, 150n.17, 157n.4,
161n.1

Smith-Rosenberg, Carroll, 6, 84, 159n.21,
162n.8

Snethen, Abraham, 18, 50, 70, 134–36,
161n.6, 165n.24

social class, domestic ideology and, 31–33

Social Gospel movement, 147n.8

socialization, of religion, 79. *See also*
institutionalization

social work, by nineteenth-century American
women, 6, 43, 144

Society of Friends. *See* Quakers

Sojourner Truth, 21, 149n.16, 154n.21

Somer, Doris, 107

Soule, Bishop Joshua, 147n.1

Southern women, domestic ideology and, 6,
147n.5

space, imagery of, and gender politics, 24,
151n.28, 164n.19

Spacks, Patricia M., 137

Spaulding, Martha, 34, 84, 113, 149n.16

Spengemann, William, 92, 116

spirit possession, 94–95, 163n.12

spiritual authority, of female itinerants. *See*
authority

spiritual autobiography(ies). *See*
autobiography

spiritual individualism, 6, 85–86, 91,
162n.11
and competition among sects and
preachers, 70–76

stammering, biblical metaphor of, 106

Stanton, Elizabeth Cady, 5, 53

Starobinski, Jean, 167n.14

Starr, G. A., 65, 120, 124, 161n.4, 167n.15,
169n.1

Sterling, Dorothy, 152n.7

Stewart, Maria W., 21, 149n.16

Stoever, William K. B., 158n.11, 168n.20

Stone, Barton, 151n.22

Stout, Harry, 75, 157n.6, 167n.6

Stowe, Harriet Beecher, 65, 153n.10, 155n.26

Strasser, Susan, 77

Stuart, Betsey, 84, 149n.16

Sturrock, John, 120, 122, 128, 168n.18

submissiveness
as stereotype of black women, 32
and women, 5, 30, 54

Printed in the United States
66412LVS00004B/13-24